ELITES FOR PEACE

D1608184

Elites for Peace

The Senate and the Vietnam War, 1964–1968

GARY STONE

The University of
Tennessee Press /
Knoxville

Stone, Gary, 1957–
    Elites for peace : the Senate and the Vietnam War, 1964–1968 /
Gary Stone.—1st ed.
    p.   cm.
Includes bibliographical references and index.
ISBN-13: 978-1-57233-579-0 (hardcover : alk. paper)
ISBN-10: 1-57233-579-3 (hardcover : alk. paper)
  1. Vietnam War, 1961–1975—United States.
  2. United States. Congress. Senate—History—20th century.
  3. Vietnam War, 1961–1975—Protest movements—United States.
  4. United States—Politics and government—1963–1969.
  I. Title.
DS558.S77 2007
959.704'31—dc22   2006035374

To the memory of my mother
Sonia Zita Stone
(1933–1989)

FROM ARTICLE 1, SECTION 8,
OF THE U.S. CONSTITUTION:

Congress shall have the Power . . .

To declare War, grant Letters of Marque and Reprisal, and make Rules concerning Captures on Land and Water;

To raise and support Armies, but no Appropriation of Money to that Use shall be for a longer Term than two Years;

To provide and maintain a Navy;

To make Rules for the Government and Regulation of the land and naval Forces;

To provide for calling forth the Militia to execute the Laws of the Union, suppress Insurrections and repel Invasions;

To provide for organizing, arming, and disciplining the Militia, and for governing such Part of them as may be employed in the Service of the United States, reserving to the States respectively, the Appointment of the Officers, and the Authority of training the Militia according to the discipline prescribed by Congress. . . .

CONTENTS

ILLUSTRATIONS

FOREWORD
Ross Baker

The Vietnam War is not ancient history. It has not receded into the mists of time like the French and Indian War or even World War I. And today, almost any military action involving American forces invites, at least in some minds, comparison to Vietnam. It has become the reigning analogy to be invoked by dissenters from our nation's military engagements overseas. The frequency by which the term "quagmire" is used to characterize military stalemates underscores the durability of the Vietnam-era lexicon. Certainly, it has made its appearance in debates over the wisdom and necessity of the role of the United States in Iraq. And while the desert wastes of Anbar province and the hills of the I Corps area near the seventeenth parallel bear little physical resemblance to each other, they inspire the same sense of dread and military frustration. The Vietnam-Iraq continuum, moreover, is tangibly sustained by the senior leaders of the contemporary American military having been junior officers in Vietnam. They carry with them not only the lessons of that war but, more problematically, an attachment to its doctrines and tactics. The Vietnam War, however, was not fought exclusively in Indochina. It was also fought in the legislative chambers in Washington and on the campuses and streets of the United States. It is the latter two venues, the campuses and the streets, that have survived as the most vivid domestic battlegrounds, yet they did not serve as the nurseries of discord. The genesis of dissent and its earliest, and certainly most influential, manifestations were on Capitol Hill. It is this point that Gary Stone makes so eloquently in *Elites for Peace: The Senate and the Vietnam War, 1964–1968*.

Through meticulous scrutiny of proceedings on the Senate floor and in its committee rooms, and of related published and archival documents, Stone presents a novel and convincing yet controversial argument that the protest movement had its inspiration, in substantial measure, from above. No group of Americans has better claim on the title of "elite" than members of the U.S. Senate, especially the Senate of 1964–68, which resembled the "club" described by William S. White in his 1956 book, *Citadel*. Still in the chamber during that period were such deeply conservative southern Democratic senators—the very core of the club—as James O. Eastland of Mississippi and Richard B. Russell of Georgia. The very age of the senators seemed to underline their conservatism and distance from their country-men. In 1965, the year of the first antiwar protest by Students for a Democratic Society, only twelve of one hundred senators had been born since 1920, in contrast to 71 percent of the general population. Indeed, more than a third of the Senate had been born before the onset of the twentieth century. That a youth-based protest movement might have been nurtured in such an environment of power, privilege, and age seems, to put it mildly, counterintuitive. And Stone's thesis is not only counterintuitive; it challenges the received wisdom of even the most respected historians of the period that an out-of-touch national leadership left the heavy lifting of dissent to alienated students and the leaders of the New Left. Typical of this view is the assertion by Doris Kearns Goodwin in *Lyndon Johnson and the American Dream* that, "in the absence of response from either party, the peace movement developed essentially outside of the established political system." But, as Stone calls on us to recognize, it was the very prestige and eminence of these senators that invested their doubts about the wis-dom of the Vietnam War with so much influence and, more importantly, respectability.

Stone rejects the notion that, throughout the Cold War, Republican and Democratic senators alike were enthusiastic and unified in their sup-port of the foreign policy forged by the executive branch. He concedes that senators of both parties, acquiescing to the demands of both Democratic and Republican presidents, gave their votes to various Cold War measures. But, calling attention to the speeches that senators delivered prior to their votes, Stone observes that the votes were rarely unanimous and that the Republicans who voted "yay" often did so grudgingly, and with a sense of foreboding about where these measures might lead. It was one thing for Senate Republicans to rally around their Wisconsinite colleague Joseph McCarthy in his crusade against alleged Communists in the United States; it was another thing for them to give unequivocal support to the president (especially when the president was a Democrat) when, under the banner of anti-Communism, he deployed American solders and money from the

American taxpayer to Asia and Europe, some of the money finding its way into the coffers of "socialist" governments like that of Great Britain. As Stone suggests, "Lyndon Johnson's war" was particularly unattractive to Senate Republicans, "as it combined a misallocation of resources to an overseas adventure (to the neglect of subversion closer to home), an expensive and ineffective military strategy emphasizing ground infantry, ambitious public works schemes, oppressive taxation, and inflationary spending" and "even stoked the old Republican suspicion of Democratic deference to Whitehall since Johnson insisted on fighting the war while at the same time permitting British flagships to trade with the enemy." Meanwhile, Stone finds that in the years after Eisenhower was inaugurated Democratic internationalists increasingly spoke of the necessity of reaching an accommodation on nuclear weaponry with the Soviet Union, a goal the internationalists viewed as essential if a third world war was to be avoided. The escalation of the war in Vietnam inevitably heightened this fear not only because it inhibited American efforts to reach arms agreements with the Soviet Union but because the war, especially when it involved actions near the Chinese border, had the potential to provoke a general war with one or both of the great Communist powers.

It is therefore not surprising to learn that, although in August 1964 the Senate gave nearly unanimous approval to the Gulf of Tonkin Resolution, senators of both parties preceded their votes with expressions of apprehension about the dangers of a widening conflict in the region. Significantly, the same senators failed to make even a single profession of support to the South Vietnamese government, whose defense was the resolution's supposed raison d'être. By the middle of 1965, Johnson's decision to escalate the war was opposed in the Senate by, among others, the Democratic majority leader and four powerful southern committee chairmen, as well as several high-ranking Republicans. In public, however, these dissenting views were disclosed, if at all, only equivocally or in muted tones and received full expression only in private communications to the president.

One fact that may have served to inhibit, for a time, the formation of the group of senators willing to express their skepticism against the war publicly, was the greater collegiality that prevailed in the Senate in those days. It was a Senate in which colleagues actually dined and played tennis

and poker with one another. The effect of ideological polarization, a fea-
ture of the contemporary Senate, probably militates, to a degree, against
social interaction among senators but probably is less influential than the
preoccupation of senators with fund-raising, the activity that senators like
least but which is required for those who desire re-election. Even in the
1964–68 period, however, the old institutional camaraderie of the Senate
was beginning to wane.

Another factor that inhibited the growth of dissent—and this is
pointed out in some detail by the author—was deference to the executive. While the Republican Congress of 2001–6 was certainly deferential
to President George W. Bush on matters relating to Iraq, the acquiescence
of the Vietnam-era senators was of a different order. These Democrats
were, to one degree or other, all products of the New Deal and venerated Franklin D. Roosevelt, whose plans often ran afoul of congressional
obstructionism. These were, in effect, anti-legislative legislators, particularly those who had suffered through Senate filibusters of civil rights bills
that had been endorsed by the White House. The Senate, moreover, was
the preeminent symbol of federalism at a time in which virtue, in the eyes
of American intellectuals, was situated in Washington and defiance and
obstruction were lodged in the states, especially those south of the Mason-
Dixon Line. Added to these retardants of dissent was the post–World War
II tradition of bipartisan foreign policy—a principle sometimes honored
more in the breach as it was during the McCarthy period. Some senators, at
least, believed devoutly that an enlightened foreign policy came out of the
professional diplomats of the State Department rather than the Congress
that had delivered up such monstrosities as the Bricker Amendment, which
would have sharply circumscribed the president's treaty-making powers.

While the Eastlands and the Russells were not the first to express their
misgivings, it was a group of Democrats (and some Republicans) even
more privileged socially than the southerners who fired the first shots. A
partial listing of the early dissenters brings to mind the Social Register.
Joseph S. Clark, a blueblood from Philadelphia; Claiborne Pell, a pillar of
Newport, Rhode Island, society; Alaska's Ernest Gruening, born into a
wealthy German Jewish family in New York, and a graduate of Hotchkiss,
Harvard College, and Harvard Medical School; William Proxmire, from a
socially prominent Wisconsin family; and Philip Hart of Michigan, married

to an heiress of the Briggs fortune, were all in a vanguard led by J. William Fulbright of Arkansas, an atypical southerner of that era with his Oxford (England, not Ole Miss) education. This is not to mention such relatively early doves as John Sherman Cooper, a fabulously wealthy Kentuckian; New Jersey's Clifford Case, formerly a partner at a major Wall Street law firm; Robert Kennedy (and less vocally his bother Edward); the Maryland patrician Joseph Tydings; Charles Percy, the billionaire president of Bell & Howell; and, by late 1967, signaling the disenchantment of big business with the war, the industrialists Stuart Symington, Democrat of Missouri, and Thruston Morton, Republican of Kentucky. Of course, not all of the early dissenters came from such privileged backgrounds, but even these men tended to have backgrounds and connections extending beyond their home states. Among these were Frank Church, a Stanford-educated Idahoan, an expert on foreign policy, who once confessed that, despite their prominence in his state's agriculture, he had never seen a sugar beet; the genteel Tennessean Albert Gore Sr., who had been a protégé of FDR's Secretary of State Cordell Hull; Ohio's Stephen Young, who had been a protégé of Woodrow Wilson's Secretary of War Newton Baker; George McGovern and Abe Ribicoff, both of whom had served in the Kennedy administration; Mike Mansfield of Montana and Wayne Morse of Oregon, both of whom had been directed by Roosevelt to carry out sensitive assignments during World War II; and Eugene McCarthy, who had served in the State Department's military intelligence division.

While the only votes cast against the 1964 Tonkin Gulf Resolution were from the brilliant but mercurial Wayne Morse of Oregon and the contrarian Ernest Gruening, it was not until such steady and respected voices as Idaho's Frank Church and solid Republicans, such as New Jersey's Clifford Case and Vermont's George Aiken, began to question the wisdom of the war that Lyndon Johnson's White House and the top-shelf media practitioners with whom these senators interacted came to take the dissent seriously.

Although Stone sees the early Senate dissenters as encouraging and giving respectability to the nascent protest movement, he argues that the senators themselves were encouraged and given respectability by such sources of elite opinion as articles, editorials, and columns in prestigious newspapers. With respect to the last of these sources, a notable revelation to those without personal memory of the era must certainly be the outsized influence of Walter Lippmann, who both influenced and was influenced by the Senate dissenters. The clout of such contemporary pundits as George Will or David Brooks, or even Rush Limbaugh, hardly measures up to the political muzzle velocity of a Lippmann piece, and probably cannot move a single senator, to say nothing of the many that were influenced by Lippmann, his column, and his salon.

The argument for the Congress's stake in the genesis of the anti–Vietnam War movement is, for Gary Stone, an audacious move but one that has already been joined by other unorthodox notions that cast skeptical eyes on the beloved "revolution from below" theories of some social historians. Some examples of these refreshing new appraisals are those which have challenged the longstanding orthodoxy surrounding partisan realignment. Long held to have been the result of mass movements, the periodic rise and fall of partisan majorities in the electorate may well have been kicked off by the actions of party caucuses within Congress.

Stone does not overstate his case. He does not deny the coexistence of Senate dissension and a militant antiwar movement outside the halls of government. He insists only that the movement did not become a truly mass movement (in numbers and in composition) until several years after the emergence of significant dissension in the Senate. Nor does he suggest that the Senate was the principal force behind the decisions made by Johnson after the 1968 Tet offensive. The author also refrains from attributing to senators moral and intellectual qualities that they did not have; the subject of his book is politicians, not saints, and not philosophers. As the book reveals, the senators often articulated interesting ideas, but, as they themselves readily acknowledged, these were usually borrowed from others. And Stone never suggests that, having given impetus to the larger antiwar movement, the senators should necessarily be viewed as superior in courage or moral worth to the men and women who were part of that movement. His is a work of elite history, not a work of elitist history.

Even if Stone's thesis is unpersuasive to those readers who cling tenaciously to the conventional view of anti–Vietnam War activity, this book can be read—and enjoyed—purely as an astute and intimate portrait of the U.S. Senate in a period that many people today consider its Homeric age.

Those senators who are looked upon by legislative historians as larger-than-life figures but whose stature has been diminished by the passage of time spring vividly to life in *Elites for Peace*. The book is the product of considerable inspiration and impeccable research and is presented to the reader in an accessible and engaging fashion. It also adds significantly not only to the literature of the U.S. Senate but also to our understanding of a period that has been the great imperfectly healed wound of recent American history.

ACKNOWLEDGMENTS

No debt exceeds that owed to Michael and Nancy Frydland (Nancy Lee Meade when this project began). In a time, prior to the completion of this project, when my family needed a home, they let us into their own. Despite great difficulty in their own lives, they acted with graciousness, generosity, and gallantry. After she and her husband sheltered us, fed us, clothed us, charmed our children, and showered us with gifts, Nan took on the arduous, tedious, time-consuming task of typing the manuscript that ultimately metamorphosed into this book. And she did this not only voluntarily but without even a request for help.

A special acknowledgment must also be extended to several individuals employed by the University of Tennessee Press, in particular, Scot Danforth, acquisitions editor, Stan Ivester, managing editor, and Bob Land, freelance copyeditor. The fact that their labors took place outside my range of vision in no way lessens my duty to thank them for all they have done. Cf. "The Cobbler and the Elves." Of course, a very privileged position on the list of my creditors must be given to my wife Rachel Feldman, who, among many other contributions, read the entire manuscript and offered many useful suggestions on how to make it better.

Emphatic thanks must also be extended to Alan Brinkley, the provost of Columbia University, who sponsored the doctoral dissertation that is a lineal, though rather different looking, ancestor of this book. I am also grateful to Betsy Blackmar, who headed the dissertation committee and later actively helped transform the dissertation into a book; to Anders Stephanson, the second reader, who must take responsibility for any errors or deficiencies of the present work; and to the visiting readers Robert David "KC" Johnson and Ross Baker. A substantial early debt must be acknowledged to Sean Wilentz, whose persuasive comments played a crucial role in delineating my subject. Special mention should be made of the assistance provided by G. William Domhoff, whose work on the American upper class, which I first encountered as a high school student, has influenced me ever since. Special mention should also be made of the late Richard Neustadt, who sent me a very helpful letter setting forth his observations about Lyndon Johnson and his critics on the left and right.

Other significant debts incurred at various stages of this project are owed to Edward (Ned) Schneier, Anna K. Nelson, Nigel Bowles, Allen Matusow, William C. Gibbons, Barbara Kellerman, Marvin Small, and June Bingham. Also providing important advice at various stages in preparing this work were George McKenna, George Reedy, Richard Herring, Arthur Schlesinger Jr., Walt Whitman Rostow, Joan McKinney, Richard L. Bushman, Jack Garraty, David Cannadine, Sylvana Patriarca, Stephen West, Jeff Sklansky, Aaron Brenner, Bernard Norwitch, Harry Schwartz, Herbert Jolovitz, Joseph R. L. Sterne, Franscesca Morgan, Sven Beckert, and Lisa McGirr.

I should also give thanks for the help I received from the many archivists and librarians, along with the other individuals who help make archives and libraries function. Regretfully, I can list only a few by name: Richard McCully, historian in the legislative division of the National Archives; Betty Austin, archivist at the Fulbright Library; Heather Moore, photo historian at the Senate Historical Office (who is largely responsible for the pictures that appear in this book); also of that office, Donald Ritchie, associate historian, Betty K. Coed, assistant historian, and Liz Stranegen; and Harry Middleton and Linda Seelke at the Lyndon Baines Johnson Library. I am also grateful for grants that supported my research from the Everett M. Dirksen Congressional Center and the Lyndon Baines Johnson Library.

Finally, I would like to acknowledge the hospitality extended to me during my research by David Reynolds of the Texas Bar, by Stephen Pershing of the Virginia Bar, by the medievalist Mary Blockley of the University of Texas, by Daniel Osher, and by several other University of Texas students whose names I cannot recall but whose kindness I will always remember.

INTRODUCTION

"Every senator in this chamber is partly responsible for sending 50,000 young Americans to an early grave. This chamber reeks of blood. Every senator here is responsible for the human wreckage at Walter Reed and Bethesda Naval and all across our land—young men without legs or arms, or genitals, or faces or hopes."[1] The words, spoken by George McGovern, although unappreciated by some of his colleagues,[2] pointed to an indisputable fact: that the massive and protracted carnage in Vietnam could not have taken place without the complicity of the United States Senate, the congressional chamber endowed by the Constitution and by historical precedent with the greatest capacity to help or hinder a president who wants to wage war.

I

The Senate's decisive, if not exclusive, power in matters of war and peace is inscribed in the Constitution. The Senate shares with the House of Representatives the power to raise and support armies, to fund military operations, and to declare war.[3] In addition, through the exercise of its treaty power, an opposition exceeding a third of the Senate can prevent any foreign military commitment from becoming the law of the land.[4] The Senate is further given the exclusive power, if supplied a bill of impeachment, to try officials (including the president) for high crimes or misdemeanors, a phrase that presumably includes such grave offenses as usurpations of Congress's war powers and the prosecution of armed hostilities in violation of international law. If the Senate finds the allegations to be true, it is then fully empowered to impose sanctions, including removal of the official from office.[5]

Beyond these formal powers, senators carry the prestige inherited from their institutional ancestors in the ancient Roman Senate, in the privy council of English kings, and in the eighteenth-century House of Lords. U.S. senators are considered to be (and consider themselves to be) leaders of the nation, entitled to significant deference in the making of decisions affecting peace and war. Even when they refrain from exercising their constitutional powers, senators expect their words to be listened to attentively by the executive branch's highest officers, by the news media, and by the country as a whole. If often unable to influence the president directly, their status is such that senators can expect to change the political environment in which he operates by voicing their opinions and thereby encouraging the growth of similar opinions throughout the society.

Notwithstanding the general truth of McGovern's accusation, it would be wrong to conclude that all those who sat in the Senate during the Vietnam War share the same level of culpability for its carnage, or to conclude that the chamber as a whole, even if it did "reek of blood," deserves the same historical verdict as that rendered upon the responsible officers of the executive branch. Although only a tiny minority of senators sought to use their constitutional powers to stop the bloodshed, at least from the time President Lyndon Johnson escalated the war in early 1965, a remarkable number of senators—including the majority leader and four powerful committee chairmen—did take actions calculated to persuade the president to change his course. Many communicated their criticisms to the president privately, some voiced their dissent openly, and several Senate committees conducted investigations into various aspects of the war. The most notable of these were Foreign Relations Committee hearings that were televised in early 1966 and in March 1968. These public manifestations of senatorial doubt fueled public debate about the war and lent the prestige of the Senate to protests well beyond the halls of government. By early 1968 these cumulative efforts, along with the course and costs of the war itself, began to change the way major figures in the executive branch thought about Vietnam. And by March the president himself changed his mind, a transformation made dramatically visible to the American people at the end of the month when he announced that he would seek disengagement from Vietnam and would not seek reelection. The story of the Senate and Vietnam is therefore not merely one of inaction and the abdication of power, but also one of action and the exercise of influence. And, as shall be seen, the action and influence were exercised not only by liberals and Democrats but by senators who were conservative and Republican.

II

The two decades immediately preceding the Vietnam controversy are commonly considered years in which a "bipartisan Cold War consensus" prevailed between the two major parties. The existence of this consensus is thought to be proven by, among other things, the votes that Senate majorities of both parties gave to the measures that were the foundation of Cold War foreign policy: Greek-Turkish aid, the Marshall Plan, and the North Atlantic Pact. This widely accepted thesis, however, fails to take account of the doubts and forebodings that Republican senators expressed even as they gave Truman their votes. In fact, as would be readily apparent to any person who has read the debates that preceded the roll calls, many Republicans were deeply disturbed by the far-flung military and economic commitments that characterized postwar American foreign policy. The absence of an authentic bipartisan consensus was revealed perhaps most clearly during the Korean War when Republican senators first rallied to General MacArthur and his defiantly daring plans for expanding the war, and then coalesced around Ohio's Robert Taft as he attacked the war as imprudent and illegal and argued for a radical repudiation of the global reach of American policy.[6]

The notion of bipartisan consensus also fails to acknowledge the pressure that was placed on Republican senators to gain their cooperation. As Taft recalled:

> the programs were broached in the most general terms, then substantially advanced by the State Department through secret briefing conferences and through indoctrination of friendly editors, columnists, and commentators before they were submitted to the public or Congress. After that if anyone dared to suggest criticisms or even a thorough debate, he was at once branded an isolationist and a saboteur of unity and the bipartisan foreign policy.[7]

Moreover, once the measures were before Congress, the administration and its supporters made full use of external events to create an atmosphere of crisis that required rapid congressional compliance to avert disaster. The appropriation of funds to aid Greece and Turkey was made as the administration urged that the failure to do so would risk not only the fall of those countries but, ultimately, the Middle East and all of Europe to Communism.[8] The Senate's approval of $17 billion of aid to Western Europe was voted in the aftermath of the Communist coup in Czechoslovakia and upon the urging of former isolationist Arthur Vandenberg (R-Mich.), who told his colleagues that the appropriation was necessary "to stop World War III before it starts."[9] Likewise, the subsequent creation of the Military Defense Assistance Program and approval of over $1 billion in arms mostly to NATO members were decisively aided by the dramatic announcement that the Soviets had exploded an atomic bomb.[10]

Aside from expressing the predictable opportunism of an opposition party, Republican criticism of the Cold War jibed nicely with several of the party's traditional concerns: its emphasis on defense of American interests in the New World; its vigilance against European and especially British efforts to influence American foreign policy for their own objectives; the party's preference for a military strategy based on sea and air power; its fear of the budgetary and inflationary effects of spendthrift internationalist policies; and its hostility to the manner in which these policies, even while employed ostensibly to fight Communism, seemed to promote socialistic economic schemes abroad reminiscent of those that Democratic administrations sought to impose at home.[11] The war in Vietnam aroused many of these traditional Republican concerns as it combined a misallocation of resources to an overseas adventure (to the neglect of subversion closer to home), an expensive and ineffective military strategy emphasizing ground infantry, and ambitious public works schemes—all made possible by oppressive taxation and inflationary spending at home. The war even stoked the old Republican suspicion of Democratic deference to Whitehall since Johnson insisted on fighting the war while at the same time permitting British flagships to trade with the enemy. This passivity was made all the more outrageous by the president's cooperation with the British embargo against the white government of Rhodesia, which—like the Americans of 1776—had declared its independence from the Crown. And this suspicion may well have been reinforced by the fact that many of the Vietnam War's official and unofficial promoters were men from the same Anglophilic eastern-based foreign policy establishment that had done so much to advance other unfortunate policies of the Cold War era.

III

The inauguration of Dwight Eisenhower in 1953 ended twenty continuous years of Democratic control of the White House. For isolationist
Republicans, pleasure in the defeat of Adlai Stevenson was tempered by
disappointment that the victor was a man who had won the party's nomination by beating Robert Taft, who was one of their own. Their defeat at
the Republican convention in 1952, moreover, was an addition to a losing
streak that had begun with the nomination of Wendell Willkie in 1940 and
had continued with the nomination of Thomas Dewey in 1944 and 1948,
both internationalists with stronger ties to Wall Street than to the less-
cosmopolitan elites of the American heartland. Needless to say, the isolationist Republicans persisted in their hostility to Cold War policies, albeit
often in muted tones. Meanwhile, Senate internationalists, most of whom
were Democrats, began their own deviation from Cold War orthodoxy,
juxtaposing their own version of internationalism to that of the administration. The content of their dissent developed in dialectical opposition to
the policies of the Eisenhower administration, above all, those identified
with Secretary of State John Foster Dulles.

It was the fate of Dulles, as it had been for Truman's Secretary of State
Dean Acheson, to become, in the eyes of his opponents, the personifica-
tion of all that was wrong with American foreign policy and thereby to
become the favorite object of their attacks. Thus, just as Acheson had
been an irresistible target for discontented conservatives, Dulles became
a lightning rod for dissent from the left. Each secretary, however, stood in
a different relationship to his opponents. The Republicans who had hated
Acheson had hated him not only for what he did but for what he was; they
had hated him as a creature whose very appearance ("elegant moustache,
well-cut clothes, black homburg"), manner of speech, education, family,
and affiliations, marked him as a man from an alien and hostile race.[12] By
contrast, the cosmopolitan senators found in Dulles an adversary who by
birth and background was one of their own: a descendant of two secretaries of state, legal counsel to the American delegation at Versailles, a
pillar of the Wall Street bar, a prominent member of the internationalist
wing of the Republican Party and of the Council on Foreign Relations,
and even, for a time, an internationalist New York senator. However, as

became increasingly clear in his service as secretary of state, his Cold War internationalism was of a different stripe than their own.

Early signs of difference were suggested during his nomination hearing when he testified that the Soviet leadership "believes that human beings are somewhat superior animals—and as long as it does I do not see how there can be any permanent reconciliation."[13] Later signs included his announcement that the United States would oppose Communism through the "instant" use of nuclear weapons in "massive retaliation" and his boast that he had defended American interests through a strategy of "brinksmanship."[14] Consistent with these remarks, his entire tenure was characterized by an approach to foreign relations that eschewed subtle diplomacy and instead embraced a bellicose moralism by which all nations and movements that were not unambiguously anti-Communist and pro-American were deemed to be pro-Communist and anti-American.

This approach—and the policies that reflected its official sanction—were profoundly disturbing to a whole generation of moderate and liberal internationalists whose opposition to Communism was tempered by a profound fear of a nuclear conflagration. Especially after the 1955 Geneva Summit, which raised their hopes for détente with the Communist world, Dulles came to represent to them an increasingly intolerable obstacle to reaching this most pressing goal and, indeed, a potential cause of a general war between the superpowers.

In this context of disappointment, fear, and frustration, Senate internationalists developed a program and vision of foreign affairs that might be called "anti-Dullesism." Opposed to Dulles's Manichaean vision of world affairs, his opponents asserted that the world was complex and characterized more by shades of gray than by simple distinctions of black and white. Instead of Dulles's policies, which could only work to increase Communist unity and push neutralists toward the Communist camp, his opponents argued for a nuanced approach calculated to encourage neutralism and division within the Communist camp. Likewise, they called upon the administration to abandon its practice of invariably supporting anti-Communist dictatorships against their revolutionary challengers.

With respect to national defense, they opposed Dulles's emphasis on nuclear weaponry, insisting instead on a varied repertoire of policies that took the avoidance of a third world war as the highest strategic priority.

And more fundamentally, in juxtaposition to the reduction of American foreign policy to anti-Communism, his opponents offered a program that subordinated anti-Communism to a broader vision that emphasized disarmament and the strengthening of the United Nations and other institutions of international law, indeed, a return to the pacifist goals to which all the great powers had pledged their allegiance at the close of the Second World War. Needless to say these anti-Dulles senators found relief in his death and replacement by Christian Herter, and soon thereafter in the election of John Kennedy, who had himself been an internationalist senator and a critic of Dulles.[15]

Under Kennedy, a foreign policy oriented by pragmatism was substituted for the rigid ideological compass that guided Dulles. Kennedy's pragmatism, however, carried with it an indifferent, if not contemptuous, attitude toward the barriers imposed by international law. Lacking any inhibitions save those based on power, Kennedy was capable of pursuing his foreign policy goals with a ruthlessness equaling that of any of his predecessors, and during the Cuban missile crisis, showed a willingness to pursue his goals by making a gamble whose stakes surpassed any placed at risk by the brinksmanship of Dulles.

It would be wrong, however, to see Kennedy's foreign policy as merely that of Dulles dressed in a different costume, the cloak of a Renaissance politician rather than the armor of a Puritan warrior. Acting as his own de facto Secretary of State, Kennedy in several respects was—or at least seemed—the very antithesis of Dulles: in his capacity to curry the acclaim of people in the postcolonial world by, at least rhetorically, identifying the United States with their revolutionary aspirations; in his readiness to settle the crisis in Laos by supporting the creation of a coalition government that included Communists; and, above all, in his reaching the Limited Test Ban Treaty with the Soviet Union, a pact that aroused hopes of a continuing improvement in relations between the superpowers and even an eventual end to the Cold War.

A sense of the public readiness for a continuation and extension of these policies was also seen in the overwhelming vote for Lyndon Johnson. The results of the 1964 elections confirmed the belief of these senators in not only the desirability but the political viability of foreign policy that gave greater emphasis to the pursuit of peace than the struggle against

Communism. With the election of Johnson the anti-Dulles forces in the Senate had, in fact, reason to believe that the new regime was their own and that the trajectory of American foreign policy would be one through which, by successive steps, their own goals would be attained.

Their expectations were disappointed. The turning point was 1965, the year Johnson massively escalated American involvement in Vietnam and sent the Marines to the Dominican Republic. Both of these actions seemed to represent a regression to the very policies that they thought the United States was finally abandoning: the support of repressive dictatorships, an indiscriminate hostility to popular insurgencies, an eschewing of possibilities for compromise with neutralist governments and movements that included Communists, an emphasis on unilateral action at the expense of collaboration with other nations and institutions such as the Organization of American States and the United Nations, and an apparent indifference to the negative image such actions created in the eyes of even America's closest allies.

The escalation of military involvement in Vietnam caused particular anxiety in that it threatened to provoke Chinese and even Soviet intervention with the attendant risk of a third world war. In any case, the intervention interrupted progress in improving relations with the Soviet Union, threatened to reverse the trend toward greater autonomy among the states within the Soviet bloc, and had the potential to push the Russians and Chinese into a united front against the Americans.

IV

The Vietnam War became an American war because Johnson chose to make it one. There is little evidence that he made this choice out of concern for the welfare of the Vietnamese people, or that it was dictated by a consensus of opinion that the victory of Communism in Vietnam would be followed by its spread to other countries of the region. Nor is there credible evidence that Johnson was motivated by a belief that such a victory would be seriously detrimental to the interests of other countries of the so-called Free World, or to American credibility among them. The historical record suggests instead that he was motivated in part by a personal desire not to be *identified with* a South Vietnamese defeat, and the record also suggests that his decision was significantly motivated by domestic political concerns.

One political scientist has offered the hypothesis that Johnson's decision was a contrivance specifically calculated to placate conservative congressional forces that would otherwise interfere with his legislative program. The proponent of this view however concedes—as I think he must—that his theory is speculative.[16] More difficult to refute is the more general perception of historians and contemporaries alike that the president's policies were forged in the fear that the collapse of Saigon would be followed in the United States by the onslaught of powerful rightist forces against his party and against his administration.

In this regard, the travails of Truman undoubtedly loomed large in Johnson's memory.[17] As a senator he had had a front-row seat to the predations of Joseph McCarthy and other Republicans in the wake of the triumph of Communism in Eastern Europe and its spread through China and down the Korean peninsula. Indeed, it is inconceivable that any Democrat who had served in the Senate in the final years of the Truman presidency could have forgotten how the political atmosphere in Washington had been electrified by Republican charges of treachery at the highest levels of government, or have forgotten the frustration and anger that had spread among the electorate as the carnage in Korea continued, or have forgotten the vast throngs that had gathered in the streets to hail General MacArthur after his brazen defiance of civilian authority.

Johnson had also been witness to more recent developments that could have only served to increase the effect on him of these McCarthy-era traumas. The waning of the Eisenhower presidency and the return of the Democrats to the White House at the beginning of the 1960s corresponded to a right-wing revival. Among the more dramatic manifestations of this were the mass meetings at which leaders of the officer corps attacked the Democratic administration for acquiescing to Communism, and the subsequent congressional investigations of Fulbright and the Kennedy administration for "muzzling the military," when the latter had the temerity to order the soldiers to cease. Another manifestation, even more reminiscent of the early 1950s, was the shrill Republican attacks on the administration after the Bay of Pigs fiasco. Even Johnson's defeat of Goldwater could not have obscured from the president the fact the Republicans were willing to nominate a man from their far right wing, nor the fact that nearly twenty-seven million Americans were willing to give such a man their vote.[18]

Behind these phenomena stood vast armies of the discontented, millions of men and women with a profound sense of alienation from those in power. Swelling the ranks of patriotic and veterans' organizations, and holding some significant posts in the officers' corps and a few seats in Congress, they represented the nucleus of a potential threat to reigning elites.[19] If their exclusion from power rendered them relatively harmless in the short run, it also gave them an amorphous quality that, like the monstrous shapes that haunt the nursery at night, made them all the more frightening inasmuch as their exact size and potential strength could not be accurately discerned.

Always remembering Truman's fate, Johnson feared these forces; he feared what they were and he feared what they could become. And, in particular, he feared what they might do to him if he allowed Saigon to fall. He therefore committed himself to the defense of its regime, and having adopted this policy, he pursued it rigidly and cold-bloodedly, rejecting alternatives.

There were alternatives. Although counterfactual scenarios are by their nature speculative, the notion that Johnson could have made different choices is not a mere matter of imposing the proverbial perfect vision of hindsight. Nor is it the ex post facto imposition on Johnson of an ethical standard that, if followed, would have necessarily led to a political disaster for his administration and his party. It is, in fact, a matter of historical record that as early as 1965 Johnson had had the benefit of the advice of several highly sophisticated men on how he might reasonably expect to extricate himself from Vietnam without incurring a domestic political disaster. And there were facts of contemporary political life that strongly suggested these alternatives could have been implemented successfully. If, like Truman, Johnson faced an ascendant right, in certain respects his situation was considerably safer than that faced by Truman fifteen years before.

By 1965 Cold War tensions had lessened, and along with them public opposition to the reaching of accommodations with the Communists. Unlike Truman, Johnson held his office by virtue of a "peace candidacy" that had resulted in a landslide electoral victory and the popular repudiation of his opponent's program of intransigent anti-Communism. Also, in contrast to Truman, Johnson enjoyed an immense Democratic majority in both houses of Congress. Nor did he have to contend with McCarthy and the movement identified with his name; "McCarthyism" had by then become a pejorative label, and McCarthy himself had gone to his grave eight years before, but not before being censured and abandoned by majorities of both parties. Nor did Johnson have to contend with an American movement advocating the interests of the Saigon government of even roughly comparable strength to the China lobby or to the ethnic constituencies that had concerned themselves with the travails of Eastern Europe during the Truman presidency. Moreover, as already noted, Johnson was favored by the presence in the Senate of several influential conservative opponents of escalation, senators who could be expected to act as a shield against any rightist attacks that might have followed the collapse of South Vietnam in the aftermath of an American withdrawal. The likelihood that Johnson could have executed such a political strategy would have been enhanced by his talents as a master politician and manipulator of men, above all, as a manipulator of those holding seats in the Senate, an institution he himself had once led with almost legendary success.

This, of course, was the road not taken, and the historical record demonstrates that Johnson rejected alternative proposals, just as it demonstrates that he greeted with apprehension rather than hope developments and institutions that might have facilitated a withdrawal from Vietnam. He, for example, never made serious use of the United Nations. Nor did he avail himself of the mechanisms created by the Geneva Accords, or of any of the other structures of international law that might have provided a face-saving means for the United States to extricate itself from the war. Likewise, he rebuffed the offers of the United Kingdom, France, and other countries to effect a compromise settlement. He similarly refused to pursue various North Vietnamese "peace feelers." Nor did he consider making American public opinion more amenable to disengagement by pointing to the absence of support for the intervention from other countries in and beyond Southeast Asia, the so-called dominoes for whose protection the war was ostensibly being fought, or by pointing to the incapacity of the South Vietnamese government to purge itself of corruption, to conduct necessary reforms, or even to inspire its own people to defend it against the ostensible invader from the north. Nor did he do anything to encourage (and in fact, did everything to discourage) the emergence of a regime in South Vietnam that would provide the most honorable basis for United States withdrawal: a regime that would seek on its own a peace accord with the enemy or a regime that would itself ask the Americans to leave.[20]

It is beyond the bounds of this work to assess all of the ramifications of the choice that Johnson made. The war he chose to fight is a matter of historical record along with the fact that the terms upon which the Americans finally withdrew seven years later were no better than those Johnson could have obtained in 1964. In the end, the war was responsible for the deaths of some fifty-eight thousand Americans and between three and four million Vietnamese. Needless to say the general consequences of Johnson's decision to fight rather than withdraw were foreseeable to his contemporary critics, and the specific number of casualties was, if anything, smaller than that feared in 1965, when many predicted that Vietnam would lead to a general war among the superpowers. And there is little reason to believe that Johnson, even as he made his choice, was significantly more optimistic than his critics.[21]

By the standards of most who have considered the matter, the president's Vietnam policies were imprudent, illegal, or immoral (or some combination of these). But judged by the standard of the president's own political goals, his policies cannot be deemed a complete failure. They may well have prevented his worst fears from materializing: the fall of Saigon during his administration and the emergence of a rightist opposition on a scale faced by Truman fifteen years before. They also may have sustained, at least during 1964 and 1965, a conservative quiescence that permitted the enactment of significant parts of his domestic legislative program. To this limited extent, Johnson's appeasement of the right "worked." By the same token, it must be conceded that his policies prevented Robert Kennedy from emerging, as Johnson with reason feared he might, as the leader of a powerful hawk movement capitalizing on an alleged betrayal of his brother's legacy by failing to stay the course in Vietnam.

Of course, by using such crude methods to pursue his goals, Johnson created new problems that would ultimately undermine his presidency. While preventing a rightist reaction comparable to that faced by Truman, Johnson's policies aroused what ultimately became a massive public opposition to the war. Parallel to the ascent of public opposition, the foreign policy establishment, divided by the war in 1965, in the wake of the Tet offensive became almost unanimously united in the conviction that the United States had to find a way out of Vietnam.

His appeasement of the Republicans, moreover, was only successful to the extent it prevented the type of partisan attacks faced by Truman in the final three years of his presidency. Instead of such a frontal assault, Johnson faced a more subdued response from the Republicans, typically a nominal support for the war combined with a persistent criticism of its consequences and the means used to pursue it. Although in themselves less damaging than the attacks launched against Truman, these criticisms caused real harm to Johnson because he needed Republican support to compensate for the opposition he increasingly faced within his own party. Johnson also faced criticism from southern Democrats, who vacillated between calls for escalation and an announced readiness to let the South Vietnamese government fend for itself. Particularly after the 1967 Congo intervention, senators from the former Confederacy showed an increased tendency to oppose interventionism anywhere in the world, a tendency that coincided with a secular trend of declining southern internationalism. Finally, Johnson faced the challenge of Robert Kennedy, although not, as he had feared, for failing to prosecute the war. Instead he faced the unsettling spectacle of opponents of the war coalescing around Kennedy as the most prominent advocate of their cause.

V

For those readers interested in such things, I shall briefly comment here on how some of the choices and opinions in this book relate to those of other writers. My most emphatic challenge has been to the belief that Senate dissension on Vietnam emerged suddenly in the final years of the Johnson presidency and that its appearance represented a radical rupture in what had been some two decades of Cold War consensus. I have therefore rejected David Kaiser's claim that "the decision to fight in Vietnam reflected contemporary wisdom" and, as a corollary, I have rejected James T. Patterson's claim that passage of the Gulf of Tonkin Resolution "indicated the power of Cold War consensus in the United States."[22] I have rejected these claims for the simple reason that they are inconsistent with the credible evidence that I have found in a great variety of sources. What I found instead is that,

by 1965, the "contemporary wisdom" among both liberals and conservatives was (though not for entirely the same reasons) more apprehensive
than supportive of the president's decision to escalate the war. For the same
reason I have had to reject Terry Dietz's thesis that the Senate Republicans
were largely supportive of Johnson's policies.

On the other hand, my conclusions extend, rather than contradict,
those reached by Gary Riechard with respect to Democratic senators during the Eisenhower years, the period that was the starting point for a transformation of so-called Cold War liberalism to the left. My conclusions are
also consistent with Carl Solberg's opinion that the Vietnam War was less
an expression of Cold War hostilities than the "strange sequel" to the Cold
War, which, at least as that concept was understood at its outset, ended in
1962 with the normalization of Soviet-American relations signified by the
Khrushchev-Kennedy agreement to limit nuclear testing.[23] In the same
vein, as already suggested, this study shares Fredrik Logevall's emphasis on
the elements in the American political environment of the mid-1960s that
would have been conducive to decreasing rather than increasing American
involvement in the war.

Consistent with this paradigm, I have not portrayed antiwar senators as
"lonely dissenters." The notion of lonely dissent, which so easily attaches
itself to accounts of legislators resisting the pressure of their peers,[24] can
be misleading to the extent it obscures the positive reinforcement that
Vietnam dissenters received from powerful forces both inside and outside
the Senate chamber. Conversely, it can obscure the real loneliness of a
senator such as Paul Douglas who, by supporting the war, found himself
emotionally battered by the anger of the liberal constituents for whom he
was once an object of affection.[25]

For similar reasons I have suggested that had Johnson decided not to
escalate the war in 1965, he would have enjoyed the support of virtually
the entire Senate Democratic leadership as well as an array of influential
men outside of government. I therefore, like Kaiser and Logevall, believe
that such a decision would not have necessarily amounted to the signing of
his own political death warrant.[26] This is not to say that the avoidance of
political death would have been a certainty, or to imply that avoidance of

that fate would have not required Johnson to make use of all of his political talent.[27]

In this I follow the majority of writers who acknowledge the existence of powerful forces on Johnson's right; unlike Doris Kearns, I believe that Johnson's fear of these forces was based on reality. I also reject Kaiser's view that there was no real threat to Johnson from the right, as well as Kaiser's view that Johnson himself did not believe that such a threat existed.[28] Just as I have emphasized that the political culture in the time of Eisenhower was not uniformly conservative, I have found that the right remained a powerful and even ascending force during the presidencies of his two Democratic successors.[29] Kaiser's belief in the absence of a potential threat from the right is apparently a consequence of his failure to look beyond Congress to the growing grassroots movements that under volatile conditions, such as the "loss of Vietnam," could provide the impetus for a rapid shift of congressional Republicans to postures reminiscent of those assumed during the Truman years. Moreover, I do not share Kaiser's belief that transcripts of Johnson's telephone calls prove "beyond any doubt" [!] that Johnson escalated the war "simply because it had to be done and had confidence in the nation's ability to do it," a belief apparently based on the premise that Johnson was unfailingly honest, or at least unfailingly honest when speaking with his leading Vietnam advisors.[30] Needless to say, the premise requires a very long leap of faith.

Because of the wide focus of this work, I have given, at best, abbreviated attention to the particular biographical facts that affected the way individual senators responded to the war. By contrast, I have given emphasis to the evolution of the larger political environment during the war itself, which provided the direct impetus for their responses. It is almost axiomatic, of course, that the manner in which senators responded to these influences was dependent on their backgrounds and on the personal experiences that forged their characters and deeper beliefs. My study is therefore intended to supplement rather than supplant the still small, but growing literature on the lives of particular senators.[31]

Finally, I should note this book's place in the expanding historiography of 1960s, particularly its affinity with relatively recent works that counterbalance the common images of the protest movements of the decade as a Peter Pan Neverland populated by oddly behaved children in strange costumes, a world devoid of adults, except when, in the manner of Captain Hook, they appear as villains. In the same vein, it is an implicit counterbalance to accounts such as Tom Powers's *Vietnam: The War at Home* that tend to reduce the antiwar movement to the New Left, and the New Left to Students for a Democratic Society (SDS).[32] On the other hand, the present volume is complementary to Charles DeBenedetti's posthumously published *American Ordeal*.[33] Although that work is largely a survey of the extragovernmental protest movement against the war, it may be favorably distinguished from the usual accounts of the period by its refusal to fixate on SDS[34] and by its insistence on giving due attention to clergy, religious and liberal pacifists, and other parts of the protest movement that were not rooted on the college campus. Thus, DeBenedetti brings into the story people who are neither young nor radical, a project which, in a work of vastly more modest scope, I have carried in a different direction.

CHAPTER 1

1953–1964: Discussion Opens

I

On June 30, 1953, Barry Goldwater rose in the Senate chamber and recited the opening lines of the Declaration of Independence. After quoting their famous enumeration of inalienable rights secured by governments "instituted among men deriving their just powers from the consent of the governed," Goldwater told his colleagues that the Vietnamese were now seeking the same liberty that the American colonists had sought 177 years ago. If the Senate now voted to support the French it would be "saying to the great men who penned that document and whose ghosts must haunt these halls that we do not believe that entirely in the Declaration of Independence, that perhaps all men are not created equal, that they are perhaps not endowed by their creator with certain unalienable rights, and that perhaps we have a right to support countries who wish to enslave other people."[1] The occasion of the Arizona Republican's recital was a debate on a provision of the proposed Mutual Security Act authorizing the earmarking of $400 million for France's war against the Vietnamese patriots, organized in the Communist-led Vietminh. The French goal was not only to defeat the Vietminh but to restore their colonial authority. Goldwater's principal ally in this debate was Democratic Senator John Kennedy of Massachusetts.

The French war in Indochina was a perverse sequel to the Second World War. During World War II, the Vietminh had led the pro-Allied resistance in opposition to the French colonial authorities. The Vietminh had been aligned with the Allies; the French administration, with the Axis. With the surrender of Japan and fall of its collaborators at the end of the war, the Vietminh had formed the Democratic Republic of Vietnam with a Declaration of Independence whose opening lines tracked those of its

American counterpart, including an enumeration of inalienable rights secured by governments "instituted among men deriving their just powers from the consent of the governed."

The birth of the new republic was formally announced by Vietminh leader Ho Chi Minh, who read the Declaration before a massive audience in Hanoi's Ba Dinh Square on September 2, 1945. Among those on the reviewing stand were several representatives of the United States, whose intelligence agents had assisted Ho during the war, fully aware that he was a Communist.

Between the time of Ho's reading at Ba Dinh Square in 1945 and Goldwater's recital in the Senate eight years later, U.S. foreign policy had undergone a radical transformation. Immediately after the war, the Americans had pursued a policy of continued alliance with the other victors. The United States and Soviet Union, along with France, China, and the United Kingdom, had been expected to guarantee world peace by presiding over the newly created United Nations, whose charter had been carefully crafted so as to have the effect of forbidding war in the absence of their unanimous agreement.

Largely forgotten is the optimism that had been felt among people throughout the world at the time the United Nations was created. It had seemed to many that, after two world wars and some seventy-five million deaths, the countries of the world had finally come to their senses and found a way to settle their differences peacefully. To many it also seemed likely that the United States, the host of the United Nations, would play a major role in ensuring the strength of the United Nations and in helping it prevent new wars.

They were wrong. In less than three years, the United States embarked on a foreign policy conducted largely in implicit defiance of the U.N. Charter. For the Americans this meant forging new coalitions—independent of the United Nations—that were directed against the Soviet Union and against all other countries and movements deemed to operate in support of its interests. The decision to support the French effort in Indochina was but one of the many consequences of that transformation.[2] But it was a consequence that raised difficulties for many senators, including Goldwater and Kennedy. They were in favor of fighting Communism, but they were troubled by a policy of fighting Communism by supporting French imperialism. Forming an alliance, the two newly elected senators had proposed amendments conditioning the authorization on France taking steps to end its colonial domination of the area.[3]

A rhetorical launching pad for this opposition was found in the U.S. Declaration of Independence and the country's origins in a struggle against a European imperialist power. Following Goldwater's lead, other senators offered their own variations on this theme. Dennis Chavez (D-N.Mex.) gave a speech in which he emphasized the kinship between the Indochinese situation and that of "the American colonies at the time they engaged in the struggle with England";[4] A. Willis Robertson (D-Va.) made his point by quoting Patrick Henry;[5] Guy Gillette (D-Iowa) asked whether Dulles intended that the United States should help France "perpetuate some remnant of her colonial empire;"[6] and William Langer (R-N.Dak.) asserted that had Americans listened to the "theories" of the foreign aid advocates, "America would still be a colony subject to England."[7]

According to Langer, the proposal to aid the French was a consequence of a more general problem that now beset American foreign policy. The United States, in Langer's view, had become through its foreign aid program an accomplice of European imperialism. By supporting colonial regimes "whose business is conducted at the point of a gun held in the hand of European exploiters," the United States helped the Europeans

> to deindustrialize these lands rather than to industrialize them, to use them, in short as sources of raw materials and as exclusively held markets for printed cottons and the usual low-grade exports which may be sold to underprivileged people. Special care at all times is taken to ensure the native keeping his place and to prevent his developing ambitious ideas by which he aspires to become master of his own affairs or to conduct as his own business the colonial possessions. . . . Why should we spend $600 million to keep the poor natives of Indochina subservient to France? . . . Are all of these natives wrong? Whether we go to Africa, Malaya, or Indochina, are all these natives wrong when they fight England, France and other countries which force their will upon them at the point of a gun? Why should the United States make enemies of all these natives? Why should the 450 million people of India regard the United States as their enemy and Russia as their friend?[8]

Although not adopting Langer's theory of imperialism, other senators conceded that in Indochina the Communists had more support than
the regime the United States was funding. Thus Ralph Flanders (R-Vt.)
lamented that the Indochinese "seem to be more interested in independence than they are in freedom from communism," and Kennedy observed
that "the majority of the population appears to be in sympathy with the
communist movement of Ho Chi Minh."[9]

Everett Dirksen (R-Ill.) who, with Warren Magnuson (D-Wash), had
recently visited Indochina, emphasized the weak military situation of the
colonial regime. Vast areas, nominally controlled by the French, became
the territory of the Viet Minh each night. The cause of this crisis could not
be attributed to the balance of military forces; these, in fact, overwhelmingly favored the French. Instead it was attributable to the fact that the
Communists "preach nationalism and freedom." "If they can do that,"
Dirksen asked, "does anyone believe that sending additional planes, or sending $400 million worth of military equipment there is likely to do the job,
when there are still so many official fence sitters who believe that Ho Chi
Minh will win, and who are waiting for that day?"[10]

Absent from the record of the 1953 debate is any statement by a senator
actually favoring the intervention of American forces in Indochina. Even the
sending of military aid to Indochina in the past—to the extent such aid made
future military intervention more likely—seemed to be viewed by senators
in retrospect as unfortunate. Thus when Guy Gillette (D-Iowa) attacked
the Eisenhower administration for supporting the French in Indochina,[11]
Francis Case (R-S.Dak.), rather than defending the substantive policies of
the president, merely argued that involvement in Indochina was a legacy
of the Truman administration.[12] To the extent senators pondered the possibility of direct American military intervention in the future, they indicated
that such an eventuality would be but the undesirable consequence of a
commitment they wished had never been made.

Goldwater was the most pessimistic about the possibilities of avoiding
intervention, asserting that "as day follows night our boys will follow this
$400 million." Dirksen, who believed that the volume of military equip-
ment already supplied by the Americans "committed" the United States in
Indochina, was more equivocal but hardly cheerful. While warning that the
conflict in Indochina could "go on endlessly" and could "become another

Korea—God forbid," he found some solace in the fact that "[f]ortunately, none of our troops are in the area." However, if the conflict continued "look out. Then we shall indeed have a . . . problem which can harass and embarrass this country as nothing else could do." In another speech, Dirksen once again invoked the prospect of "an interminable thing" with "a potential which is not unlike Korea" and asked: "Will the situation not ultimately call for an invasion of American troops? That will be disaster; that will be tragedy."[13]

Although the record fails to disclose a senatorial endorsement of American military intervention, it is also bereft of any explicit senatorial statement to the effect that a Communist victory in Indochina would be tolerable. Although few senators addressed the question of the importance of the region to American interests, the few who did emphasized the dire economic and strategic effect of such a victory. In the same speech in which he recounted in scathing detail the history of French colonialism in Indochina and condemned the failure of the French to make credible moves toward independence, Kennedy also described Vietnam as "the state which is of greatest importance in the area" and explained that "the French are now fighting because they know that if they retreat, all of Southeast Asia will go to the Communists—that their position in North Africa will be endangered—and that the security of Metropolitan France itself will be threatened." Alexander Smith (R-N.J.) similarly asserted that "we cannot withdraw from Indochina" because to do so "would open up all southeast Asia to Communist domination," and would jeopardize the security of India, Pakistan, the Philippines, Australia, and New Zealand. Withdrawal would also "have drastic economic repercussions on Japan" and "would deprive us of the resources of tin and rubber which are found in southeast Asia in such abundance." Warren Magnuson (D-Wash.), for his part, emphasized the "importance of not allowing Communists to take over because of the effect such a thing would have on the rice bowl of southeastern Asia." And even Gillette, who expressed his intention of voting against the aid authorization, conceded, "I know, as everyone else knows the danger that would threaten if an attack should be launched through Indochina."[14]

Despite fear of Communist victory, no senator offered any advice about what America should do if the military situation in Indochina continued to deteriorate. Instead, senators preferred to make speeches lambasting

France for its Old World–style imperialism and condemning, more generally, America's ostensible European allies for, as in Korea, leaving the United States with the burden of fighting international Communism (all the while ungratefully benefiting from the largess of the American taxpayer).[15] When less than a year later, on April 3, 1954, Dulles directly asked congressional leaders for a resolution supporting American intervention to lift the siege at Dien Bien Phu, it was this issue—the lack of assurance that America's European allies, especially Britain, would join the United States—that led Senators Lyndon Johnson (D-Tex.), Earle Clements (D-Ky.), Richard Russell (D-Ga.), Eugene Millikin (R-Colo.), and (ultimately) William Knowland (R-Calif.) to deny the request. At the meeting, which took place at Dulles's office, it was Johnson and Clements who posed the questions that exposed the lack of allied support for intervention—as well as opposition to intervention by all the Joint Chiefs, except for Admiral Radford—and it was Johnson who expressed the vehemence of his opposition by actually pounding on Dulles's desk.[16]

In the subsequent weeks, as the French military situation became ever more precarious, discussion on Indochina once again erupted on the Senate floor. These deliberations differed from those of the previous year only in their greater intensity, undoubtedly a consequence of Eisenhower's recent decision to dispatch two hundred "technicians" to the area[17] and the rumors of imminent American intervention. As they complained about the Senate not being consulted or even informed about executive branch policy in Asia,[18] senators renewed their assaults on French imperialism and on the lethargic response of the other European allies. They also warned again of the disastrous consequences that might follow if America unilaterally involved itself in a war on the Asian landmass, including the risk that it might ignite World War III.[19] However, as they had in the past, senators also conceded that they believed the area to be one of economic and strategic importance.[20]

II

The Senate response to Eisenhower's requests for aid to France represented a departure from the rigid and bellicose pattern of foreign policy debate that had evolved during the Truman presidency. Like those of his predecessor, Eisenhower's proposals elicited disagreements among senators; but as had not been the case in the time of Truman, the disagreements were often expressed in alliances that crossed party lines, as in the already noted Goldwater-Kennedy collaboration, and in the alliance Joseph McCarthy, in the final year of his life, would forge with Oregon Democrat Wayne Morse in opposition to the Middle East Resolution.[21] The intensity of disagreement was also less pronounced than that during the Truman presidency when Republicans had mixed their dissension from Truman's policies with charges that the spread of Communism through Eastern Europe and into China was a consequence of the treachery of his party.

The election of Eisenhower gave a new freedom to Senate Democrats as they no longer carried the burden of having to defend Truman's Cold War initiatives. On the other hand, the election represented a major setback for Ohio Republicans Robert Taft and John W. Bricker, for Joseph McCarthy, and for the other Republican senators who had been at the forefront of the assault on the Truman administration. With Eisenhower's ascent to office, Taft ceased to be the leader of the Republican Party and McCarthy ceased to be its vanguard. Republican dissension, which came so easily in the time of Truman, was now inhibited by the embarrassing fact that the new Republican president had obviously been a supporter of many of Truman's policies and had played a leading role in their implementation as the North Atlantic Treaty Organization's first Supreme Allied Commander. This is not to mention his close association with the very military leaders whom McCarthy charged with treachery at highly publicized televised hearings. To the extent the Senate Republicans attacked him from the right, the Democrats were positioned to embarrass them by ostentatiously aligning themselves with the popular president.[22]

McCarthy, who had enjoyed broad Republican support during the final Truman years, now became increasingly isolated as he extended his attacks to the leaders of the United States Army. Ultimately, attacking his own senatorial colleagues, in late 1954 he would bring on himself the rare disgrace of their censure. Almost complete isolation within the Senate followed until his death three years later.[23] Similarly, in contrast to 1952 when his proposal to amend the Constitution had been hailed by even moderate Republicans, during the Eisenhower years Bricker found it considerably more difficult to gather senatorial support.

Bricker's proposal, which, if adopted, would have limited the capacity of the president to enter into binding international agreements without Senate approval, had the potential to become a rallying point for a host of conservative and ultra-patriotic constituencies enraged by allegedly gratuitous concessions to the Soviet Union made at Yalta and Potsdam. A protracted and heated congressional debate on the proposal might have also galvanized those who feared (or could be persuaded to fear) that international agreements would lead to mandatory unionization, socialized medicine, desegregation, the usurpation of states' rights by the federal government, or the substitution of United Nations sovereignty for the sovereignty of the United States. Despite this, debate on the measure was, in the words of Bricker's biographer, "[s]urprisingly . . . free of the bitterness which characterized the McCarthy era, because Bricker continually strived to prevent embarrassment to his party or its popular new president."[24] Above all, the spectacle of Eisenhower meeting with Khrushchev in Geneva suddenly made it difficult for the Republicans to argue that compromise with the Soviet Union was equivalent to the accommodation of Hitler at Munich. Indeed, the summit gave official sanction to optimism about the future course of relations between the two superpowers.

A permissive atmosphere was further fostered by constituent opinion which, although anti-Soviet and anti-Communist, was also strongly opposed to war and evinced persistent anxiety about the possibility of either another protracted Korean-type conflict or an even more devastating combat between the two superpowers.[25] Meanwhile, through books, newspaper columns, magazine articles, transcriptions of speeches and lectures, and direct communication by such influential men as Walter Lippmann, James Reston, Chester Bowles, Hans Morgenthau, and George Kennan, senators were sent the signal that responsible elite opinion favored policies considerably more imaginative and flexible than those emanating from the State Department.

It was the particular genius of Eisenhower's Secretary of State, John Foster Dulles, to arouse the wrath simultaneously of those who criticized American foreign policy for its lack of realism and for its lack of idealism. For both types of critics, the principal target was his insistence on a defense policy based principally on the country's capacity to use atomic weapons. This strategy, dubbed "the New Look," provoked strong criticism (and several high-level resignations in the armed forces) from those disturbed by a policy that seemed, by its logic, to leave the government, in the event of aggression, no other choices than inaction or Armageddon. At the same time elite opinion-makers, several of whom had hitherto helped build public support for the Cold War, were disturbed that its present captain was a man who had such difficulty distinguishing between neutrality and enmity, who was so oblivious to the possibilities offered by actual and potential differences among Communist countries, and so insensitive and indelicate in his dealings with the men who represented the great mass of awakening humanity that resided in the colonial world. Both makers of elite opinion and ordinary men and women, moreover, found little comfort in the thought that, in the nuclear age, America's foreign policy was guided by a man who could easily and even boastfully use phrases like "massive retaliation" and "brinksmanship."[26] If in the days of Acheson the memory of Munich had served to constrict public discussion and had pushed it to the right, now in the days of Dulles the memory of Hiroshima expanded the range of public discussion and pulled it to the left. The consequences were felt in the Senate, especially in the Foreign Relations Committee.[27]

To be sure, the new questioning of foreign policy did not include a challenge to the fundamental structure of the Cold War. During the Indochina debate senators, by emphasizing the affinities of the Vietminh with the Americans of 1776, seemed to be rediscovering the arguments used a decade before by Claude Pepper (D-Florida) and Glen Taylor (D-Idaho) in opposition to Greek aid and the Truman Doctrine. However, both Morse and Kennedy were careful to distinguish the two cases. Kennedy, in particular, asserted (not very accurately) that in Greece, unlike Indochina, the regime enjoyed the full support of the native population.[28] Nonetheless, Democratic senators did invoke the ideals and buoyant optimism that had accompanied the creation of the United Nations and strongly suggested that there could be more to an internationalist foreign policy than an obsessive and rigid anti-Sovietism. This attitude was illustrated by the response of John Kennedy, who had recently gained a seat in the Foreign Relations Committee, to a series of lectures of George Kennan that had been broadcast over the BBC, in which the former ambassador had called for the withdrawal of all foreign forces from Germany. When this heresy incurred the wrath and ridicule of such establishment figures as Dean

Acheson (whose denunciation of Kennan and dissociation of Kennan's proposals from the Democratic Party were ostentatiously reported on the front page of the *New York Times*), Kennedy, who had recently gained a seat on the Foreign Relations Committee, made a point of writing a letter of praise to Kennan, indicating his agreement with many of his views. The following year, Kennedy, already a senator of growing stature and obvious ambition, declared on the Senate floor that he rejected the view that "we should enter every military conflict as a moral crusade requiring the unconditional surrender of the enemy."[29]

That same year, J. William Fulbright, soon to become the chairman of the Foreign Relations Committee, observed that "if there is a single factor which more than any other explains the predicament in which we now find ourselves, it is our readiness to use the specter of Soviet Communism as a cloak for the failure of our own leadership." Stressing the need "to ask ourselves some very searching questions," Fulbright urged Americans to "stop thinking of these problems in terms of a stereotyped view of the world" and "abandon the clichés and reconsider all our assumptions."[30]

The left ascendancy reached new heights in the final two years of the Eisenhower administration. In the 1958 mid-term elections, the Democrats gained a total of fifteen seats in the Senate over the Republicans. The Democratic margin leaped from two in 1957 to thirty in 1959. These results disproportionately increased the strength of northern Democrats, whose ranks increased from sixteen to forty-one seats, and the strength of liberals within that group. Newly elected liberals included no fewer than nine senators: Clair Engle (Cal.), Vance Hartke (Ind.), Ed Muskie (Maine), Philip Hart (Mich.), Eugene McCarthy (Minn.), Harrison Williams (N.J.), Stephen Young (Ohio), Frank Moss (Utah), and Oren Long (Hawaii).[31] It was in the context of these Democratic and liberal gains that in 1959 Joseph Clark (D-Pa.), a cousin and admirer of Grenville Clark and a member of the United World Federalists, launched Members of Congress for World Peace Through the Rule of Law.[32] That such an organization, explicitly committed to fulfilling the most ambitious internationalist hopes of 1945—hopes long thought to have been eclipsed by the onset of the Cold War two years later—should operate openly in Congress and receive a largely sympathetic response from its members, was symptomatic of a broadening of the boundaries of legitimate political discussion, especially among liberals. Likewise, the growing boldness among senators impatient with the Cold War was expressed by the directness and vehemence of Fulbright's attacks on Eisenhower during the U-2 fiasco.[33] A sense of the distance traveled in a decade can be attained by recalling that a normal theme for a 1950 Senate Republican speech was an indictment of the president for his refusal to carry the Korean War into China; now in 1960 it was entirely acceptable for the chairman of the Foreign Relations Committee to attack the president for, in effect, missing an opportunity for conciliation with the Communists.

Two important qualifications, however, should be made to this portrait of a reformist ascendancy during the eight years of the Eisenhower presidency. The general trend was toward a growing openness in discussion of foreign policy, and an emancipation from the inhibitions of thought and speech that had characterized the final years of the Truman administration. Senators, however, typically exercised this newfound freedom, by making pronouncements pitched at so high a level of abstraction as to leave unchallenged the concrete policies that the United States was actually pursuing on the ground. While John Kennedy, in general terms, dissociated himself from the Cold War as a moral crusade against Communism, and as Fulbright made speeches calling for a radical reassessment of American foreign policy, Senate liberals typically acceded to the concrete policies actually proposed and implemented by the White House. Liberals thus became accomplices of Dulles as they helped ratify a vast network of bilateral and multilateral treaties, encompassing commitments to some forty nations—treaties which, no less than the North Atlantic Pact, were premised on a foreign policy whose principal object was opposition to Communism.[34] Likewise, liberals were complicit in the enactment of "area" resolutions granting the president broad discretion to take future military action in defense of Formosa (including the Quemoy and Matsu island chains immediately off the Chinese mainland) and the Middle East.[35] And it was typically conservative democrats, such as Langer and Stennis, and not liberals, who spoke out forcefully when the administration took such concrete actions as sending "technicians" to Indochina or undermining governments in Iran and Guatemala.[36] In this respect it is significant that while Kennedy embraced Kennan's proposals on Europe and U.S.–Soviet relations, he specifically dissociated himself from Kennan's

view that "we ought to be prepared to allow some [underdeveloped] countries to go Communist."[45] And it is also significant that while senators such
as Clark and Fulbright pursued the lofty goal of building the machinery for
an enduring universal peace and focused their attention on reducing the
possibility of a war between the superpowers, when faced with concrete
local conflicts as in Indochina or Iran they were remarkably unimaginative
and uncritical, and, in practice, acquiesced to or even promoted the policies
of the administration.[38] The liberal dissenters, no less than the administration they opposed, suffered the passivity that usually accompanies an
all-or-nothing approach.

The second qualification is related to the first. One of the ironies of the
period is that the senators who were most critical of the way the administration was fighting the Cold War were also those least inclined to favor
increased congressional participation in the making of foreign policy. Most
Senate liberals, persisting in an institutional bias with roots going at least
as far back as the days of Woodrow Wilson, did not favor an assertive
role for Congress. They saw a strong Senate, in particular, as a hindrance
rather than a help to the making of a better foreign policy. A consequence
of this viewpoint was that the Senate liberals helped the administration
erode congressional power by approving broad grants of executive power
in the Formosa and Middle East resolutions, and were among the most
consistent advocates of the claimed prerogatives of the presidency. Their
best hope for the Senate was that it might someday act as an auxiliary to a
strong and enlightened president.[39] This perspective would have significant
implications for the way Senate liberals responded to the Vietnam policies
of the Kennedy administration and the Johnson administration during its
first two years.

III

Predictably, liberal senators greeted the election of Kennedy with calls
for a strengthened executive and for giving proadministration senators
a degree of power commensurate with their numbers. Fulbright led the
attack in the spring of 1961 with a frontal assault on the Constitution itself.
In an address before legal scholars, he advocated that the Constitution
be radically changed to give the "Executive a measure of power in the

conduct of foreign affairs that we have hitherto withheld." Conceding that it was "distasteful and dangerous to vest the executive with powers unchecked and unbalanced," Fulbright asked rhetorically, "whether we have any choice but to do so."[40]

Two years later, in a series of Senate speeches, compared at the time by political scientist James McGregor Burns to Luther's nailing of his theses to the church door,[41] Joseph Clark made a detailed attack (including the naming of names) on "the oligarchical Senate Establishment, the majority of the members of which, by and large, are opposed to the program of the President." Attacking the system of seniority, the omnipotence of committee chairman, the unchecked and secret workings of the Democratic Steering Committee, and other "archaic, obsolete rules, customs, manners, procedures, and traditions" by which conservative senators had for generations effectively controlled the Senate, Clark complained that "the two-thirds majority of the Democratic senators who are Kennedy men, and therefore liberals" had hardly any real power in the Senate. To remedy the untenable situation, Clark called on his fellow "Kennedy men" to emulate the "Wilson men" who, through "the revolution of 1913," had torn down the old Senate procedures and brought the Senate under the control of the Progressives who would help enact the president's program.[42]

A similar view of the Senate as a potential conduit of enlightened presidential policy, particularly in foreign affairs, was offered by the Nobel Prize nuclear physicist Leo Szilard. In a memorandum to Fulbright, Szilard emphasized the power of the president to shape public and congressional opinion, noting "[t]he change in Congressional attitudes which followed the Eisenhower-Khrushchev meeting in Geneva." Now he looked with optimism to Kennedy's leadership of Congress, and was confident that "Senators who are friendly to the Administration" could be used to promote a foreign policy of disarmament and détente with the Russians. Such senators, in Szilard's vision, would act as agents of the executive branch. "All it would take to accomplish this would be for the Administration to let these Senators know that their help is needed and would be appreciated." He also suggested a system of formal or informal briefings to keep senators informed of the short- and long-term goals of the administration.[43]

In June 1962 Szilard had founded the Council to Abolish War (later renamed the Council for a Livable World), whose goals included the funding of congressional candidates "who want to work for an enlightened foreign policy."[44] Of eight Senate candidates receiving council funding in 1962, six won: George McGovern (D-S.Dak.), Clark, Frank Church (D-Idaho), Jacob Javits (R-N.Y.), Morse, and Fulbright.[45] In 1964, the council was even more successful, achieving victory for all nine of its funded candidates: Albert Gore (D-Tenn.), Hart, McCarthy, Gale McGee (D-Wyo.), Joseph M. Montoya (D-N.Mex.), Moss, Muskie, Winston Prouty (R-Vt.) and Joseph Tydings (D-Md.).[46] They, and other liberal senators, provided Kennedy with a loyal core of Senate supporters, and undoubtedly made it easier to win moderate support for his foreign policy. The crowning achievement of this White House–Senate alliance was the 80-19 ratification of the Limited Nuclear Test Ban Treaty on September 23, 1963.[47]

The subordination of liberal senators to the White House had helped Kennedy to pursue a treaty that substantially improved Soviet-American relations and reduced the risk of a third world war. But it also had the effect of giving such senators something of the docility they had had during the later Truman years, and the consequence of this parliamentary discipline was not always the promotion of détente with the Communists. Thus the Senate Democrats who ratified the Limited Test Ban Treaty also approved resolutions supporting White House policy toward Cuba and Berlin and did so unanimously and with an alacrity surpassing that with which they had given their votes to the Formosa and Middle East Resolutions during the Eisenhower years. With respect to Vietnam, despite signs of growing danger, there was a notable dearth of discussion, and the few senatorial statements that were made on the subject were generally supportive of the administration's policy. Morse, for example, called on his colleagues to understand that American aid to South Vietnam was required because "a good many of the soldiers of freedom have not been in a position where they could successfully combat guerilla warfare." It was therefore, in his view, necessary so that the Communist world will know that we can meet them on every front—Cuba, Berlin, southeast Asia, Africa. We must let them know that whenever they wish to attack freedom, we will stand firm and protect freedom."[48]

It is emblematic of the subordination of liberal senators to the executive branch during this period that even the Church resolution of 1963, at first blush an early challenge to U.S. policy in Vietnam, turns out on later inspection to be the exception that proves the rule. Offered in the context of Diem's crackdown on the Buddhists, this sense of the Senate resolution called, in the absence of an end to repressive policies, for a termination of funding to the Saigon regime. In fact, as is now known, the resolution was drafted in the State Department and introduced unchanged by Frank Church as part of a contrived "dissent" calculated by the Kennedy administration to pressure Diem into making needed reforms. Thus, such resolution cosponsors as Morse, Ernest Gruening (D-Alaska), Gaylord Nelson (D-Wisc.), Claiborne Pell (D-R.I.), Stephen Young, Clark, and McGovern, men who would later figure prominently in opposition to the war, were not acting as critics but as accomplices of administration policy in Southeast Asia.[49]

The return of the Democrats to the role of administration defender they had played during the Truman years coincided with the return of the Republicans to their earlier role as its attacker. Ending the diffuse, lowered-temperature politics of the Eisenhower era, senators of both parties reverted to the partisan acrimony that predated his inauguration. No more than eight months into the Kennedy presidency, Carl Marcy, chief of staff of the Foreign Relations Committee, wrote in a personal memorandum to Fulbright that he had "become increasingly concerned in recent weeks of a widening rift between Democratic and Republican members of the Committee." Marcy could "recall only one vote in the last ten years when members divided on a foreign policy issue along party lines. Yet in the last six weeks this has happened several times." In pondering the possible cause of Republican dissension, Marcy considered that it might be a result of the old anti–New Deal opposition to policies that promoted "fiscal irresponsibility" but thought the more likely explanation was that "the Republicans are reacting to what they believe are grabs for power by the Executive. Just as you and some liberal Republicans felt that Eisenhower was too subservient to Congress, the Republicans and the conservative Democrats think that Kennedy tends to ignore Congress, and they may have a point."[50]

Whatever its causes, Republican senators, in tones reminiscent of their attacks on Truman after the "loss" of China, went on the offensive against the administration after the Bay of Pigs fiasco. Wallace Bennett (R-Utah) undoubtedly spoke for many in his party when he characterized Kennedy's Cuba policy as "do-nothing," one of "vacillation and tardy reaction," "drift, timidity, improvisation, and indecision," and "almost total poverty."[51]

IV

The tendency toward partisanship in the wake of the Bay of Pigs was considerably lessened by the "near-death experience" of the Cuban missile crisis. The resolution of this crisis, the ratification of the Limited Test Ban Treaty, and the assassination of President Kennedy all acted to soften Republican partisanship, strengthen the position of the Democrats, and inhibit the formation of a broad-based rightist coalition comparable to that which had once united Taft, MacArthur, and McCarthy. Nonetheless, many moderates and liberals continued to perceive a growing danger from the right. This perception had many sources, including the growth of super-patriotic anti-Communist organizations such as the John Birch Society, the Christian Crusade, and the Minutemen; the "capture" of the Republican Party by Barry Goldwater; and the ostentatious refusal of the latter to denounce "extremism."[52] Even the assassination of Kennedy in Dallas—the town where right-wing mobs had not so long ago threatened Lyndon Johnson and Adlai Stevenson—was initially perceived by many as symptomatic of an ominous trend toward irrationality, violence, and extremism.[53]

For Fulbright and his informal advisor, John Kenneth Galbraith, the threat was not so much reaction as fear of reaction. In particular, in early 1964, they saw signs that the State Department, never fully recovered from the traumas of the Truman era, was increasingly prone, in Galbraith's words, to take "unsupportable" positions "out of concern for the right." Recent examples included conservative State Department pronouncements on Panama and China that appeared to leave little room for future maneuver. Reminding Fulbright of Kennedy's "intention to make you Secretary of State," Galbraith lamented the "present leadership" which "suffers from prenatal fright possibly by John W. Bricker."[54] In reply, Fulbright quoted approvingly Galbraith's complaints and added, as an additional example of State Department deference to the right, "the cutting off of aid to Britain, Yugoslavia, and France" in retaliation for their trade with Cuba.

The senator then asked Galbraith for "any suggestions as to what might be done to encourage the Administration to more enlightened and effective leadership."[55]

Fulbright might have partially answered his own question four weeks later when he delivered his highly publicized address on "Old Myths and New Realities." In this March 25, 1964 speech, offered as a contribution to the filibuster of the civil rights bill, the Arkansan enumerated a series of developments reflecting a significant easing in Soviet-American tensions and the potential for a substantial improvement in the relationship between the superpowers: the Austrian and Antarctic treaties, the resolution of the Cuban missile crisis, the Limited Test Ban Treaty, the increase in cultural and economic ties between the two blocs, and—of particular importance—the breakup of the Communist monolith and the development of "polycentrism." According to Fulbright, opportunities for improved East-West relations represented by these "new realities" collided with "old myths" about Communism, in particular the view that all Communist nations were part of a rigid, eternally antagonistic monolith to which America's only principled approach was one of uniform and unrelenting hostility. Instead, citing a recent article by George Kennan in *Foreign Affairs,* Fulbright argued that the United States should encourage "polycentrism" by acknowledging distinctions within the Communist bloc and—above all—by relaxing restrictions on trade with them. He also called upon Americans to acknowledge the fact that there was only one China, and to acknowledge such other "realities" as the colonial roots of American control of the Panama Canal, the likely failure of the American economic and military boycott of Cuba, and the fact that violent revolutions are not necessarily Soviet or Cuban inspired and unworthy of American support.

When he addressed the reality of the civil war in Vietnam, however, Fulbright could do no more than endorse the administration's stated policy of "continuation of the antiguerilla war within South Vietnam, along with renewed American efforts to increase the military effectiveness of the South Vietnamese Army and the South Vietnamese Government." Although opposed to escalation of American involvement, he rejected the proposal that the United States immediately seek a negotiated settlement because the weakness of the South Vietnamese military position made it unlikely that a favorable agreement could be reached. He also condemned

a recent French proposal that Vietnam be neutralized and expressed his
fear that France by its intervention might "set off an unforeseeable chain
of events" that she would be unable to control.[56]

Meanwhile, the situation in Vietnam continued to deteriorate as the
policies that Fulbright endorsed proved increasingly ineffective. Nine days
prior to Fulbright's speech, Secretary of Defense Robert McNamara,
recently returned from Vietnam, reported to the president that "the situation
has unquestionably been growing worse since September." The National
Liberation Front controlled about 40 percent of South Vietnamese territory, in twenty-two of forty-three provinces they controlled 50 percent or
more of the land area, "including [in the delta region surrounding Saigon]
80% of Phuoc Tuy; 90% of Binh Duong; 75% of Hau Nghia; 90% of Long
An; 90% of Kien Tuong; 90% of Dinh Tuong; 90% of Kien Hoa; and 85%
of An Xuyen." Significant sections of the South Vietnamese population
were "showing signs of apathy or indifference"; there were "some signs of
frustration within the U.S. contingent"; South Vietnamese Army (ARVN)
and paramilitary desertion rates were "high and increasing"; morale in
the hamlet militia and Self Defense Corps (charged with defending the
hamlets) was "poor and failing"; "[i]n the last ninety days the weakening of
the government's position had been particularly noticeable"; the "political
and control structure" had "disappeared" after the overthrow of Diem; and
the Khanh regime had only "uncertain viability."[57] The American response
to this situation included a significant increase in the amount of American
aid and the number of "advisers" in South Vietnam. Over the next nine
months the former would be increased by $50 million and the latter from
16,300 to 23,000. The response also included, as if to compensate for the
political and military failures in the south, an increasing concentration on
North Vietnam, including the support of South Vietnamese covert com-
mando raids on the North Vietnamese coast and on islands in the Gulf of
Tonkin.[58]

Predictably, the North Vietnamese did not remain passive in the
face of these raids on their territory. Thus on the morning of August 1,
1964, the U.S. destroyer *Maddox,* near the North Vietnamese coast, was
attacked by North Vietnamese torpedo boats whose commanders apparently assumed that the destroyer had supported the covert raid by South
Vietnamese vessels on nearby Hon Me island the previous evening. The

engagement that followed, which included the intervention of aircraft from the USS *Ticonderoga,* led to a retreat of the North Vietnamese boats, one of which was severely damaged. On August 4, 1964, another attack on American ships, the *Maddox* and the *Turner Joy,* was alleged to have taken place although, by the following day, the commander of the *Maddox* sent messages to Washington denying earlier reports of visual sightings of the alleged attackers and explaining that "freak weather effects" on the radar and sonar and "overeager" sonar operators created doubts as to what had actually transpired. The commander therefore asked that no retaliation be ordered until a "complete evaluation" was conducted. Nonetheless, within hours the White House authorized air raids on North Vietnamese targets and the State Department prepared a congressional resolution endorsing this action and granting the president broad powers to take additional measures against North Vietnam.[59]

V

The Senate in the months immediately preceding its consideration of the resolution had hardly shown signs of enthusiasm for further American involvement in Southeast Asia.

On the morning of May 23, 1964, Fulbright encountered a remarkable photograph in the *Washington Post* captioned with the description "Vietnamese soldiers hitch a Communist Viet Cong guerrilla prisoner to an armored truck carrier before dragging him through a stream to make him talk." Sending a copy of the picture to McNamara, Fulbright in an uncharacteristically intemperate tone stated: "I want to know if this is the kind of advice the numerous American advisers are giving the Vietnamese." If this type of torture were not being advised by the Americans, the chairman wanted to know "why we are not using our considerable influence with the Vietnamese to prevent it?" Fulbright expressed his own view "that torture is morally repugnant," which "ought to be sufficient reason in its own right not to practice it. But if there are those who think it is required as part of a 'realistic' approach to a tough and dirty war, let them ponder the fact that so far as I know, it has never really achieved its purpose, but on the contrary has frequently served to strengthen the sympathizers of those on whom it is practiced while degrading its practitioners. The experience of the Romans with the Christians, of the Spanish Inquisition with presumed heretics, and of the German Gestapo with the European underground are prominent examples chosen at random from history."

Emphasizing that "a major part of the problem in Vietnam is political," Fulbright decried torture as a counterproductive practice that he found "all the more disturbing because it follows reports of napalm bombing of innocent villagers simply because the presence of Viet Cong is suspected." Noting that he had been "gravely concerned over the situation in Vietnam even without reports of torture or indiscriminate bombing," Fulbright explained that even "in the best of circumstances" it was difficult to foresee "a satisfactory solution." Practices such as these, however, would alienate both the Vietnamese and the Americans and render a solution "impossible." Until now, explained Fulbright, "I have been restrained in my public statements and have supported the Administration's policy because, frankly, I have seen no alternative." Nonetheless, he warned that he could "not support a policy such as that pictured in the enclosure, nor do I believe the Congress or the American people will support it. It is bound to fail." To this he added the sentence: "This being the case, we should cut our losses and withdraw."[60]

An overview of congressional attitudes on Southeast Asia submitted to the president's National Security Advisor McGeorge Bundy ten days later also offered little encouragement for administration officials hoping for sustained congressional support for U.S. policies there. In a memorandum prepared by Assistant Secretary of State Frederick Dutton, a seasoned operative with wide-ranging political connections, Congress was divided into three groups: "Hard-Liners," "Get Out or Neutralize the Area," and "The great majority." The Hard-Liners included John McClellan (D-Ark.), Margaret Chase Smith (R-Maine), and Barry Goldwater.

In the second group ("Get Out or Neutralize the Area"), Dutton found Mansfield, Morse, Gruening, Church, Eugene McCarthy, Allen Ellender (D-La.), John Sherman Cooper, McGovern, E. L. Bartlett (D-Alaska), and Javits, as well as Richard Russell, who, although "usually a hard-liner," did not believe the area of "sufficient strategic value for us to get sucked in." Likewise, W. Stuart Symington (D-Mo.), "another hard-liner, on most problems, is one of those who would turn it over to the United Nations."

Most legislators, according to Dutton, were "cautious and noncommittal" and even "those supporting the administration's present course were often wary about it, as with Fulbright's position that we have no alternative, but he still doesn't like it." Their questions revealed fears that the conflict could lead to the use of nuclear weapons, Chinese intervention, a third world war, and a lengthy American involvement, as well as concern about the apparent superiority of the Communist capacity to "instill a will to fight." More fundamentally, members of Congress wanted to know why "a rich white nation can get at the heart of the problem in Southeast Asia."

The Dutton memorandum concluded with a large scrawl across its final page: "Public mail in Congressional offices concerning SE Asia is heavily critical—most want to disengage, a large part want to bomb N. Viet Nam. Almost all of it is hostile."[61]

CHAPTER 2

1964: An Anomalous Resolution

I

Shortly before he introduced the Gulf of Tonkin Resolution on August 5, 1964, J. William Fulbright delivered a short speech on a different subject: the Limited Test Ban Treaty that had been signed exactly one year before. Noting the Soviet Union's continued compliance with the treaty and new opportunities for détente between the superpowers, Fulbright expressed his view that the agreement symbolized "an evolving tendency toward peace."[1]

The contrast between Fulbright's optimistic notice of the treaty's anniversary and the rather grim tone of the discussion of Southeast Asia which followed brings into sharp relief the apparent incongruity of the escalation of American involvement in Vietnam at a time when expectations for détente with the Communist world were rising.

As Fulbright's speech suggested, the political environment had changed considerably since 1950 when Americans had begun to fight in Korea, the last major deployment of American armies against a Communist adversary. The intervention in Korea had been launched at a time of extreme tension in American-Soviet relations marked, in the United States, by the ascent of powerful mass and elite movements opposed to making any compromise with Communism. By the time the Senate was asked to approve the Gulf of Tonkin Resolution fourteen years later, however, the domestic and international political landscape had shifted considerably: relations between the superpowers were improving, most Americans favored an easing of Cold War tensions, and the mainstream of elite opinion had hopes that American foreign policy would finally redirect its attention to problems other than the combating of international Communism. Indeed, it is one of the many ironies of the war that Johnson's decision to increase United States involvement in Vietnam was made precisely at the moment when Americans were least likely to understand why considerable resources—least of all the lives of their sons—should be spent in a crusade against international Communism, a crusade that seemed increasingly anachronistic in light of such developments as the breakup of the Soviet monolith and the ratification of the Limited Test Ban Treaty.

Although the improvement in relations with the Soviets had been accompanied by a growing fear of China, this fear tended to redound more to the advantage of those counseling caution than combativeness toward the People's Republic. Particularly after the 1965 massacre of the Indonesian Maoists, the Red Chinese threat was seen less in its capacity to create and direct a new Comintern or to pull other governments into its orbit (or, for that matter, in its capacity to drop a nuclear bomb somewhere), than in the potential that an American intervention in the vicinity of China's borders would provoke, as in Korea, a massive influx of Chinese ground forces.[2]

For the Democrats who were the dominant party both at the time of the onset of the Korean War and at the time of escalation of involvement in Vietnam, the difference in general attitude toward foreign policy during the two conflicts was especially clear. The Korean intervention took place in the aftermath of a thorough reorientation of the foreign policy of the Democratic Party. The culmination of this process had been the 1948 election in which the Democrats had distinguished themselves as the party of intransigent opposition to international Communism. By contrast, the American escalation in Vietnam took place in the aftermath of a long process of reorientation of the Democrats *to the left* that had begun with an increasingly hostile attitude toward Dulles, and had culminated in the smashing electoral victory over Barry Goldwater. In this contest, the Democrats had emphasized fear of war over hatred of Communism. And on election day they had been confirmed in their belief that such an emphasis resonated sympathetically with the great majority of American voters.[3]

Although in retrospect Fulbright's sponsorship of the Gulf of Tonkin Resolution looms larger than his simultaneous optimism about international conciliation, for the senator himself the relationship was reversed. For him—and for many other senators—in August 1964, it had been the Senate's ratification of the Test Ban Treaty during the previous year that represented the real turning point in American foreign relations, a historic beginning that was likely—assuming Barry Goldwater lost the election—to serve as the foundation for further developments in American diplomacy in the coming decade. The resolution before them was, in comparison, but a relatively minor matter, representing neither the beginning of an armed crusade nor a turn away from the conciliatory perspective represented by the treaty. In fact, in contrast to the intense and excited attention the Senate had given to the Test Ban Treaty, the debate on the Tonkin Gulf Resolution was poorly attended,[4] and remarks by the few pro-resolution senators who did attend reflected anything but a desire to embark on a new adventure, least of all an adventure in the jungles of Southeast Asia.

II

Befitting the political environment in which it was drafted, the resolution was not couched in terms of Cold War rhetoric, but instead emphasized the specific actions alleged to have transpired in the Gulf in violation of international law, the status of the United States as a victim of those actions, and the claimed legality of an American military response to them. The resolution thus began with a series of "whereas" clauses citing the North Vietnamese "Communist regime" for having "deliberately and repeatedly" attacked American vessels in "international waters" in violation of the U.N. Charter and international law, and finding these actions to be "part of a deliberate and systematic campaign" of North Vietnamese aggression against "its neighbors" and other nations joined in collective defense of their freedom. These findings provided the basis, proclaimed in the "resolved" clause that followed, for the approval and support of Congress for "the determination of the President, as Commander in Chief, to take all necessary measures to repel any armed attack against the United States and to prevent further aggression."

In the resolution's second section, Congress declared that the United States regarded "as vital to its national interest and to world peace the maintenance of international peace and security in southeast Asia," and that "consonant with the Constitution of the United States and the Charter of the United Nations and in accordance with its obligations under the Southeast Asia Collective Defense Treaty, the United States is, therefore, prepared as the President determines to take all necessary steps, including the use of armed force, to assist any member or protocol state of the Southeast Asia Collective Defense Treaty requesting assistance in defense of freedom." In a third and final section, Congress provided for the expiration of the resolution by a presidential determination that "peace and security of the area is reasonably assured by international conditions created by the action of the United Nations or otherwise" or "earlier by concurrent resolution of the Congress."[5]

It is well known that, without strenuous presidential prompting and with little hesitation, Fulbright rapidly carried the resolution through a docile Senate with only two dissenting votes: Wayne Morse (D-Ore.) and Ernest Gruening (pronounced "greening") (D-Alaska). Well remembered is Morse's "statement for history that if we follow a course of action that bogs down thousands of American boys in Asia, the administration responsible for it will be repudiated."[6] Less well remembered are the main arguments upon which the dissenters based their case. Remembered even less are the statements that Senate supporters of the resolution made before casting their votes. These statements could hardly have been a comfort to a president seeking strong and sustained Senate support for a policy of continuing and increasing intervention in Southeast Asia. They certainly do not support the assertion made in one standard history of the period that the Senate passed the resolution "with patriotic fervor" and thereby "indicated the power of the Cold War consensus in the United States."[7]

In fact, following the cue of its preamble, supporters of the resolution rather than basing their vote on a general commitment to fight Communism in Southeast Asia or even to the defense of the Saigon government, emphasized the specific incidents in the Tonkin Gulf. Repeatedly the Senate supporters of the resolution spoke not of the need to defeat Communism but of the need to uphold various principles and traditions whose origin predated the Cold War.

Resolution cosponsor Richard Russell (D-Ga.), the chairman of the Armed Services Committee, set the tone by denying the desirability of debating the wisdom of the underlying policies that had led to the presence of American ships in the Gulf. Instead, according to Russell, "what is involved" in approving the resolution "is our right as an independent state to operate our vessels upon international waters that have been recognized as free to all states for many centuries." The Georgian also supported the president's retaliatory response as necessary to the defense of American "honor" and the "respect" of other nations. The resolution's Republican cosponsor, Leverett Saltonstall, "the gentlemanly gentleman from Massachusetts," who had chaired the Armed Services Committee back in the days of Eisenhower, similarly failed to cite the crusade against Communism as cause for support to the resolution, instead invoking ancient regional values. "From the beginning of our Nation," noted Saltonstall, "Massachusetts men have always gone down to the sea in ships." He then proceeded to argue not for the defense of freedom in Asia—he never mentioned Communism or Vietnam—but simply for the defense of the American navy and maritime rights.[8] Likewise, Hubert Humphrey (D-Minn.), a descendant of more humble New Englanders and a Norwegian sea captain, stressed that "it is a part of our national history and our national heritage to support the freedom of the seas—from the time of George Washington through the administration of Thomas Jefferson and the incidents with the Barbery pirates up to this very hour. As a great maritime power, we must insist upon a strict application of international law insofar as high seas and international waters are concerned."[9]

Even among the resolution supporters who focused attention on the alleged naval incidents, several openly expressed bewilderment, if not skepticism, that a small nation would, without provocation, attack the ships of the United States.[10] After the attack on the *Maddox,* three days prior to the Senate debate, no lesser Senate power than Russell had speculated that the North Vietnamese might have been confused by hostile naval operations and not realized that they had attacked an American destroyer.[11] Moreover, during the Senate debates not only did the first-term liberal Democrat George McGovern of South Dakota pose difficult questions to Fulbright on the context of the allegedly unprovoked attacks—including statements by the North Vietnamese government on the shelling of Hon Me and Hon Ngu prior to the incidents—but the fifth-term conservative Democrat Allen Ellender of Louisiana carried McGovern's line of questioning further, aggressively examining the Arkansan in a manner that implied a lack of full candor on the part of the administration.[12] Gaylord Nelson (D-Wisc.), for his part, challenged the wisdom of having American ships at all in the Tonkin Gulf in light of the highly charged atmosphere in the area. Asking his colleagues to place themselves in a position comparable to that of the

North Vietnamese, Nelson suggested that they consider how they themselves would feel if while "Cuban PT boats were firing on Florida, Soviet
armed ships or destroyers were patrolling between us and Cuba, 11 miles
out." Fulbright, perhaps flustered by his own secret ambivalence, retreated
from the hypothetical questions into unresponsive literalism: "We are not
firing on Cuba, nor they on us. I do not see how the case is analogous."[13]

A major concern—perhaps the greatest concern—expressed by resolution supporters was that its enactment not lead to the fighting of a land
war on the Asian mainland. Referring to his service as an officer in the
Marines during World War II, Daniel Brewster (D-Md.) recalled that he
had "had the opportunity to see warfare not so very far from this area, and
it was very mean," and noted that he "would look with great dismay on
a situation involving the landing of large land armies on the continent of
Asia." Across the aisle, Thruston Morton of Kentucky announced that he
shared "the apprehension" of Brewster and hoped that the resolution, by
demonstrating the determination of America, would enable it to "avoid
war, and not have to land vast land armies on the shores of Asia."[14]

Frank Church (D-Idaho), at the outset of the debate, had ostentatiously inserted into the record "a column by the distinguished columnist,
Walter Lippmann," an "article that shows such unusual perception and
displays such insight and wisdom that I commend it to my colleagues in
the Senate." The article argued that

> [t]he lasting significance of the [Tonkin Gulf incidents and the
> American response] is the demonstration that the United States can
> remain in southeast Asia without being on the ground. . . . Only
> a few years ago, it was the established military doctrine that we
> should not engage the American Army on the mainland of Asia.
> Our strength is in sea power. We have departed from the old doc-
> trine, perhaps because we had to. But the mainline of American
> policy should be a return to it. For it is based on a true understand-
> ing of our position on the globe.[15]

Fulbright, himself a protégé of Lippmann, throughout the Tonkin Gulf
debates lent his prestige as chairman of the Foreign Relations Committee
to the cause of opposing the use of ground troops in Vietnam. While refusing to reassure senators explicitly that the resolution would prevent such

a policy, he frankly stated it "is the last thing we would want to do." Like Lippmann, he stressed air and sea power as the key to American strength in the region: "I personally feel it would be very unwise under any circumstances to put a large land army on the Asian continent. It has been a sort of article of faith ever since I have been in the Senate, that we should never be bogged down."[16]

Related to their fear of U.S. involvement in a ground war on the Asian mainland, several senators expressed concern about the breadth of the resolution's language. Nelson sought clarification of the first section's apparently open-ended "to prevent further aggression" clause. Spessard Holland (D-Fla.) sought specification of the allies who might require American assistance under the second section. And John Sherman Cooper (R-Ky.) expressed his concern that enactment of the second section activated American responsibilities under the SEATO Treaty.

McGovern and Jacob Javits (R-N.Y.) asked whether enactment of the resolution would make it easier for the Saigon government, by taking provocative unilateral actions, to pull the United States further into armed conflict. With respect to this last source of anxiety, McGovern and Javits cited assurances made nine years earlier, prior to approval of the Formosa Resolution, that Chiang Kai-shek would not attack the Chinese mainland without prior consultation with the United States; the senators wanted to know if the Saigon regime had made similar assurances.[17]

While McGovern and Javits spoke of their fear that Asian allies would take actions which would force the United States to entangle itself in the conflict, conservative senators expressed fear that *inaction* of allies would disproportionately burden the United States and, in the words of Ellender, "that we shall once again be left holding the bag, alone." Russell himself, though seeking passage of the resolution, disclosed some anxiety on this issue, explaining that "no one feels more deeply . . . that when the United States intervenes, many others who have equal responsibility, have tended to say, 'Let Uncle Sam do it.'" Senate liberals expressed similar concerns. Referring to the signatory and protocol covered by the SEATO Treaty, Javits emphasized the need for collective action and noted that he was "sometimes inclined to agree with those who say we cannot be the policeman or guardian of the whole world." In the same vein, Claiborne Pell (D-R.I.) emphasized his hope that "other freedom loving Asian nations,

particularly Pakistan, the Philippines, and Japan, might help us carry some
of the burdens for keeping the peace in the Far East."[18]

Partisan and rightist attacks on the Johnson administration played only
a minor role in the Senate deliberations on the Tonkin Gulf Resolution.
On the other hand it is difficult not to suspect—by the very frequency
and emphatic nature of their cries for bipartisanship—that many senators
believed that the eruption of partisan divisions remained a real possibility.
It could have only been a partial comfort to the White House that such
senators as Bourke Hickenlooper (R-Iowa), Glen Beall (R-Md.), Kenneth
Keating (R-N.Y.), Thomas Kuchel (R-Calif.), and Everett Dirksen (R-Ill.), in
giving speeches in support of the resolution, dwelt at length on the importance of bipartisanship and unity while failing to state whether they sin-
cerely favored the administration's substantive policies in Southeast Asia.[19]
Nor could the White House feel that partisanship was deeply submerged
when Thruston Morton, a member of the Republican establishment,
combined his praise for Johnson's decisive action—which, in Morton's
view, would discourage the Communists from miscalculating American
intentions—with his observation that "the three major wars in which we
have been involved in this century have come about by miscalculation on
the part of the aggressor," an implicit reference to the failings of three past
Democratic administrations. Similarly, Hugh Scot (R-Pa.) revived memories of Republican attacks on Truman's handling of the Korean War, when
he applauded Johnson for not deeming parts of North Vietnam "sanctuar-
ies" from possible U.S. bombing.[20]

Nor could the White House, particularly in a year in which a man
like Barry Goldwater was considered respectable enough to win the
Republican nomination, dismiss as rantings from the fringe, the remarks
of Strom Thurmond of South Carolina and Millard Simpson of Wyoming.
Thurmond praised the resolution but expressed his hope that the United
States would abandon its "purely defensive posture in favor of a 'win policy'" and, reviving memories of Republican attacks on Truman during the
Korean War, urged that "victory, not stalemate, be our objective in dealing with Communist aggression in southeast Asia." And Simpson, after
declaring that in matters of national security "parties' lines cease to exist,"
went on to deliver a diatribe attacking Democratic administrations for
their capitulation to Communism in Cuba, and for hitherto not taking the

initiative in Southeast Asia. He closed his speech by expressing "the sincere and reverent hope" that the resolution and bombing raids indicated "an end of our policies of indecision, vacillation, and compromise and heralds the beginning of a measure of commitment that will forge victory from the Communist-fomented chaos of southeast Asia."[21]

Notwithstanding such bellicose outbursts, the dominant tone among resolution supporters was one of apprehension, gloom, and resignation. Speaker after speaker expressed hope for a negotiated settlement and for the constructive intervention of the United Nations, an institution described by Pell as "the reasoning place of men's minds which we have helped establish for this purpose." Several expressed their fervent wish that the president, "a man of peace," would find a solution obviating the need for American intervention.[22] Although, strictly speaking, the Senate did not include any pacifists,[23] several senators expressed a sense of the intrinsic horror of war. And it is likely that most of them dreaded the prospect of an American intervention that could provoke a confrontation with the Chinese or even the Soviets. "Like many other Senators," explained Cooper, "I have had some experience in war, an experience which I value above all others. Anyone who has had such experience knows, awesome as it is, that it does not make one less afraid or less courageous. It makes one determined to protect the security and honor of his country. But it makes one also more determined and more thoughtful about seeking out every honorable and just course to avoid the possibility of a great war, and the awful eventuality of a nuclear war with all the sorrow and disaster it would bring to our country and humanity." Cooper recalled that "during the early days of the Korean war, the threats of Communist China were not believed—but they were carried out. We must contemplate[,] hoping that it will not be true, the possibility of an expanded war [and] the possibility of a great war." Pell also noted the possibility that the conflict in Southeast Asia would expand into a confrontation between the United States and China.[24]

Javits reported to the Senate the many impassioned telephone calls he had begun to receive from constituents with respect to the resolution: "I was awakened three times between 12 o'clock and 3 in the morning—and I do not complain; I understand the feeling of the families involved—by people in New York telling me how deeply concerned they were and with what prayer and devotion I must determine to act on the joint resolution." Comparing the decision now before his colleagues with Truman's decision to drop an atomic bomb on Hiroshima, Javits described the Senate's task as "the sad duty which generals have in war, of comparing the number of casualties we are willing to endure in order to achieve an objective which will save even greater casualties."[25]

Perhaps the most remarkable aspect of the speeches delivered by the resolution supporters is the extent to which they already reveal a lack of authentic belief in the underlying mission of the United States in South east Asia. While basing their support on the narrow ground of the rights of American ships on the high seas or on the general desirability of national unity and bipartisanship, few senators were willing to say they actually agreed with the substantive policies pursued by the United States in Vietnam, particularly the defense of the Saigon government. Indeed, several of them actually made statements indicating doubt or disagreement with respect to those policies. Church, for example, after stating that he was only going to vote for the resolution "on the narrow grounds" of the rights of American ships which "from all we have been told were not engaged in any aggressive action against the shores of Vietnam," criticized a general approach to foreign policy that had led the United States to assume "responsibility for this remote part of the world."

Wondering whether the events in the Gulf of Tonkin "are not the natural consequence" of this approach, Church decried a foreign policy that was "more the product of our own addiction to an ideological view of world affairs—an affliction that affects us as well as the Communists—rather than a policy based on a pragmatic view of our real national interests."[26]

Speaking immediately after Church, Albert Gore (D-Tenn.), like the Idahoan a member of the Foreign Relations Committee, commended him for his "able, candid, courageous and eloquent address." Gore then revealed that at executive sessions of the Foreign Relations Committee he too had "raised critical questions" about Vietnam policy, and also noted that he had been "one of those who did not think it wise for the United States to undertake this burden after the fall of Dienbien Phu."[27]

A third resolution supporter from the Foreign Relations Committee also expressed his doubts. "I would be less than frank," said Frank Carlson (R-Kans.), "if I did not state as a member of the Committee on Foreign

Relations, that I had several times questioned the policy of this country in southeast Asia." Even the ordinarily hawkish John Stennis (D-Miss.), ranking Democrat on the Armed Services Committee, while not explaining his own reason for unhappiness, chose to observe that "none of us are happy about the situation in Vietnam or our position there."[28]

Other doubters, representing diverse regions and political environments included Wisconsin's Nelson, Alaska's E. L. "Bob" Bartlett (D), and Kentucky's Cooper. Nelson, the resolution supporter who came closest to defecting to the ranks of Morse and Gruening, actually proposed that it be amended by a clause providing, among other things, that "it was the sense of Congress that except when provoked to a greater response, we should continue to attempt to avoid a direct military involvement in the southeast Asian conflict." Bartlett described himself as having "deep doubts about the wisdom of our policy in Vietnam," emphasized the lack of a stable government in Saigon that could inspire its people to fight despite our "massive help." Bartlett further described the repeated assertion that Southeast Asia "is vital to our national security" as a proposition about which "there can be doubt."

More directly, Cooper stated that "I have not believed that southeast Asia is the chief area of interest of the United States" and, noting finite resources, described American interests as primarily in "the Western hemisphere and Europe." After indicating his support for the principle of defending American ships from attack, conceding that "a progression of events for 10 years has carried us to this point" and noting his fear that "perhaps the events are inevitable now," expressed his hope that there remained "the possibility of avoiding with honor a war in southeast Asia—a conflagration which I must say, could lead to war with Communist China, and perhaps to a third world war with consequences one can scarcely contemplate today." Thus he hoped "the President [would] use this power wisely with respect to our commitments in South Vietnam, and that he will use all other honorable means which may be available such as consultation with the United Nations, and even with the Geneva powers."[29]

Even more notable than the willingness of such a wide geographic range of senators of both parties to express doubts—despite the atmosphere of crisis and urgency with its natural tendency to quiet dissent— was the response to these doubts of the Deep South committee chairmen

to whom Johnson had entrusted the task of guiding the resolution through
the Senate: Russell and Fulbright. Rather than using their influence to
counter the doubters and build broad support for the administration's
policies in Southeast Asia, the chairmen left the doubters unchallenged
and made what amounted to a fatalistic argument in support of the resolution: after ten years of commitment of men and resources it was too
late to change course in Southeast Asia. Fulbright, remarked that "if any
mistake has been made—and I do not assert that it has been—the only
questionable area is whether or not we should ever have become involved.
That question goes back to the beginning of action in this area, and I do
not believe it is particularly pertinent or proper to the debate, because we
have become involved" though "as an academic matter the question might
be raised."[30] Russell went even further and candidly recounted his own
doubts. Recalling his longstanding opposition to intervention in Indochina,
he told his colleagues that "it is unnecessary for me to state that I had grave
doubts about the wisdom of that decision" to involve the United States in
that region, but asserted that "it would certainly do no good to dwell on
these doubts here today."[31] This type of support for the administration—an
expression of doubt or disagreement coupled with an assertion that it was
nonetheless too late to change course—placed the chairmen substantially
in the same camp as the aforementioned doubters who themselves had
used very similar formulations in their own speeches.

Conspicuously scarce in the speeches of resolution supporters were
words suggesting that they embraced American intervention in Asia as
an opportunity to confront a fundamentally oppressive and immoral system. Javits spoke, in general terms, of Communist China as an aggressive
and expansionist force, Stennis spoke of the "gravity" of the Communist
threat to Vietnam, and Thomas Kuchel (R-Calif.) spoke of his hope that
in response to American action Communism would recede "and the sun
will shine again."[32] But only Humphrey spoke of the South Vietnamese
people's cause as "their pursuit of freedom and . . . pursuit of independence
and human dignity." And even his speech focused not on Communism's
violation of individual freedom but the fact that—in his view—it sought
to expand the geographic scope of its power. Nor did Humphrey, or any
other senator, cite any atrocity stories or speculate (luridly or otherwise)
about what a Communist victory would mean for the vanquished South

Vietnamese. Significantly, none of the resolution supporters gave any praise to the Saigon government. Nor, except for the aforementioned single sentence of Humphrey, did any of the resolution supporters speak generally of the evils of Communism or the virtues of the so-called Free World. The resolution supporters, in short, justified their votes less in the language of zealous holy warriors embarking on a crusade against Communism than in the language of reluctant conscripts obligated to pursue a ten-year-old policy inherited from men whose wisdom they doubted. Moreover, to the extent that resolution supporters expressed moral indignation and invoked abstract principles they based themselves not on the Truman Doctrine's universal opposition to international Communist subversion but on the allegation that in a specific case North Vietnam had violated the rule of international law.

III

The rule of international law was also central to the arguments made by the dissenters, Morse and Gruening. Indeed, the dissenters emphatically insisted that their opposition to the resolution was an outgrowth of, and consistent with, what they saw as the highest aspiration of post–World War II bipartisan internationalism, in the words of Morse, "the substitution of the rule of law for the jungle law of military force as a means of settling disputes which threaten the peace of the world." Through three days of debate, Morse and Gruening strenuously argued the case that American policy in Vietnam violated international law and brought humanity further from fulfillment of the dream of a warless world where disputes among nations would be settled without resort to arms. Although the United States was acting within its rights when its ships in the Gulf of Tonkin returned fire with fire, the United States exceeded the limits of legitimate self-defense when it then conducted air raids on the North Vietnamese mainland. Such actions fell outside the protection of the United Nations Charter's article 51 (narrowly delineating the right of self-defense), article 2(4) (prohibiting the use of force or its threat), article 33 (requiring that parties to potentially violent disputes "first of all" seek peaceful resolution through judicial settlement, arbitration, mediation, regional agencies, or other peaceful means), and article 37 (requiring parties that have failed to reach a settlement under article 33 to refer their dispute to the Security Council). Emphasizing the mandatory language of these provisions in a charter that the Senate itself had ratified and to which the United States was legally bound, the dissenters castigated the government for, instead, taking unilateral action that placed the United States outside the law. Likewise, the United States had violated the Geneva Accords' article 16 (prohibiting the introduction of new troops to Vietnam), article 17 (prohibiting the sending of arms or other material to Vietnam), and article 18 (prohibiting the establishment of new military bases in Vietnam). More fundamentally, the United States had deliberately sought to undermine the Geneva Accords and prevent resolution of the Vietnamese civil war by supporting Diem in his refusal to hold national elections in 1956. Both the United Nations Charter and the Geneva Accords forbade the unilateral resort to arms and created mechanisms to report the violations of others.[33]

As alternatives, the dissenters urged the United States to seek a negotiated settlement, by taking advantage of de Gaulle's suggestion of a Fourteen Power Conference, by convening a conference of Southeast Asian nations, or by requesting the intervention of the United Nations. The dissenters gave particular emphasis to this last option, U.N. intervention, which Gruening believed had been successful in establishing peace at the Egyptian-Israeli border and in the Congo.[34]

Citing a letter from an unnamed Republican member of Congress, Morse approvingly recited the writer's view that "the average man of North or South Vietnam would not know what democracy looked like if he met it on the main street of Saigon." For to the Vietnamese "the difference between their governments is like the difference between tweedledum and tweedledee. But both are interested in the next bowl of rice." Morse explained that "the great need of the United States in the field of foreign policy is to export economic freedom" instead of its present policy which was "to export military aid, for our military aid makes Communists." "Unless the people are first economically free," he explained, "they cannot be politically free; and, what is more important, they will never understand political freedom until they are first economically free."[35]

Rather than helping the people of Vietnam, The United States had turned South Vietnam into an "American protectorate" and made itself the backer of a series of dictators no better than those who ruled the Communist North. American ships in the Tonkin Gulf had made themselves accomplices to the provocative actions of South Vietnam whose own ships had been shelling North Vietnamese islands there. Moreover—and here Morse inserted a front-page article from that morning's *New York Times*—the American raid appeared to be a veiled attempt to protect the Khanh dictatorship which had been under pressure to "go North." Having not disclosed its earlier raids on the North Vietnamese coast and on North Vietnamese islands, the United States claiming to be now acting in response to North Vietnamese aggression would be "greeted by considerable snickering abroad."[36]

In addition to challenging the legality of American actions under international law, Morse condemned the resolution for violating the U.S. Constitution. As he had done with the Formosa and Middle East resolutions, he characterized the Tonkin Gulf Resolution as undermining the constitutional separation of powers because it gave the president "the power to make war without a declaration of war." In contrast to Fulbright and other liberals who viewed the Constitution's emphasis on checks and balances and the limitation of executive power as an anachronistic encumbrance upon the need for a strong presidency under modern conditions of chronic crisis, particularly with respect to foreign policy, Morse argued that the very centralization of power and risks of nuclear war which characterized the present period made it all the more imperative that Congress jealously guard its powers from executive encroachment: "We have entered an era of civilization in which an unconstitutional act of war on the part of a President of the United States can lead to nuclear war and the end of this Republic, no matter how sincere a President may be in his intentions in respect to exercising the power to make war."[37]

At several points Morse referred directly to the long-term importance of the vote and despaired that senators were insufficiently concerned with the verdict that history would someday render on their actions. "Those who will follow us in the years to come," predicted Morse, "will cry out in anguish and despair in criticism over the mistake that was made in 1964 when the joint resolution was passed." Beyond the risk of a stalemate in Vietnam, Morse pointed to the danger that, as in Korea, the United States was underestimating the danger of Chinese intervention and the implications of the confrontation that would ensue if such an intervention took place.

Referring to Mao as a "desperado," Morse reminded the Senate that the "despicable Communist leader . . . placed no value on human life" and had in recent years announced a readiness to lose four hundred million lives in a war with Western imperialism. Mao, he noted, had predicted that China would actually be strengthened in the process. "I know of no reason that should justify anyone engaging in any wishful thinking of the head-in-the-sand attitude that if we kill enough and bomb enough North Vietnam and Red China will yield." Moreover, in intervening in Vietnam, the United States hopelessly placed itself in the direct path of a great historical movement against white colonialism in Asia. Such a policy would only earn the Americans hatred. "Mr. President," Morse addressed the presiding officer, "you and I will be gone in a few years; but I am satisfied that the end of the road that we are traveling today will be the engulfment and drowning in world history of the influence of the white man in Asia, if we will follow this course of action." "The United States," Morse emphasized, "can never dominate and control Asia, with 800 million people in China alone. That kind of war would create a hatred for the United States and for the white man generally that would persist for centuries. Dominating Asia, after destroying her cities and killing her millions by bombing—that is the danger that we are walking into—would not make the white man supreme in Asia—only hated. We know what the floods of human history will do. Eventually the white man will be engulfed in that Asiatic flood and drowned."[38]

III

The strong sense of foreboding expressed by Morse and Gruening about the Tonkin Gulf Resolution was not shared by many senators—including those generally critical of the administration's handling of the crisis in Southeast Asia. Any apprehensions about Johnson's policies were dwarfed by fear of what Barry Goldwater might do in Vietnam or elsewhere if he became president. *The New Republic* undoubtedly articulated the feelings of many liberals, including most of those in the Senate, when its editors tempered their disapproval of the reprisal air raids and the Tonkin Gulf naval patrols with the view that "Not 63 but 630 sorties would be Goldwater's probable riposte to a Communist stab at American ships, and he seems to have a real inclination to nuclear not conventional bombs." As for the argument that the resolution gave the president a "blank check" to act as he wished in Southeast Asia, the editors expressed little excitement since "it only allows the President to behave in an international crisis the way he would act anyhow, acting first and leaving the constitutional lawyers to argue afterward about whether he exceeded his powers."[39]

In a year when liberals had applauded the waning of senatorial power by the historic breaking of the filibuster of the president's civil rights bill, they were hardly ready to assert their moral indignation because the president overstepped his prerogatives with respect to American policy to Southeast Asia. Nor was 1964 a year when concern about the president's adherence to the U.N. Charter was going to eclipse the liberals' fear of Johnson's opponent, a man perceived as a menace to the survival of humanity itself.[40] In any case, as even Morse seemed to admit, the legal arguments made by the dissenters suggested remedies that were impracticable, if not unthinkable: a judicial injunction against the war or a verdict rendered by the Senate itself against the president on articles of impeachment.[41]

Whereas the remedies offered by Morse and Gruening were little more than phantoms, the price of joining them was all too real: a break with the president, a break with the leadership of both parties, and a break with the chairmen of the Foreign Relations and Armed Services committees. Moreover, in addition to the already-mentioned concern about a possible Goldwater victory, liberal and moderate senators had their own electorates to worry about. Because a disproportionate number of them had first been elected to the Senate six years before in 1958 (mostly in states with strong Republican parties), many were engaged in their own election campaigns, and looked anxiously toward November when voters would decide whether to grant them a second term. Aware that the President's claim that American ships had been the victims of unprovoked attacks would cause the electorate to rally around the flag, these senators probably did not want to spend time during the remainder of their campaigns explaining why they had voted against the resolution or answering charges of deficient patriotism. It is therefore not surprising to learn, for example, that when Stephen Young (who had displaced Ohio's John Bricker by a small margin in 1958) confided his doubts about what had actually transpired in the Gulf and pondered whether he should vote for the resolution, his administrative assistant bluntly told him that his coming bid for reelection made dissent unthinkable.[42]

Rather than pursue phantom remedies, Senate moderates and liberals in 1964—and, to varying degrees, well beyond that year—remained committed to a strategy of reforming American foreign policy in collaboration with the president and the foreign policy elite from which the president was likely to take his advice. In seeming viable and not unduly endangering their careers, the strategy comported with their own preference for moderation, a natural preference for men who, by virtue of their office and backgrounds, counted themselves among the country's leaders. This elite perspective, which in subsequent years would make internationalist senators anxious in the face of street demonstrations and other amateur protests made them hopeful in 1964 when they heard the president emphasize the cause of peace or when they heard the sound of pacific and enlightened proposals from men the president presumably respected, such as National Security Advisor McGeorge Bundy and the influential columnist Walter Lippmann.

Rather than break with the White House, the best policy was, in a manner analogous to that of the civil rights movement, to protect it (from rightist attacks) and use it as a vehicle to carry policy gently and gradually to the left. The task was not seen as formidable since the administration seemed to be already moving in that direction. The point was merely to persuade, in the words of a contemporary resolution of the Americans for Democratic Action, the administration "to do publicly, explicitly, and wholeheartedly what we are already doing halfheartedly, and almost surreptitiously."[43]

What held true for the president also held true for those members of the foreign policy establishment who seemed to have the greatest potential to persuade him. By invoking the authority of this establishment it was possible to give protective covering to views that went further than official policy even as they seemed to anticipate where official policy might logically evolve in the future. Fulbright had employed this strategy when he built his supposedly heretical "Old Myths, New Realities" speech around quotations from an article written by George Kennan for *Foreign Affairs,* the journal of the Council on Foreign Relations, and the transcript of a speech by a lesser-known member of the foreign policy establishment, George McGhee, a former undersecretary of state then serving as ambassador to Germany. Fulbright's speech, in turn, was widely reported in the establishment press, commented upon in favorable terms by elite journalists such as Walter Lippmann, and provided the basis for launching a Fulbright speaking tour (to largely elite audiences, of course), through which the senator built further support for his proposals. A few months later, another member of the foreign policy establishment, Grayson Kirk, perpetuated the cycle by authoring an article in *Foreign Affairs,* which used quotations from the Fulbright speech (which had become more readily accessible in the interim when Random House published it in expanded form as a book) so as to give added authority to his call for innovations. Predictably, the innovations were very similar to those originally advocated in *Foreign Affairs* by Kennan earlier in the same year, and undoubtedly had the indirect effect of adding further to the aura of respectability of Fulbright's proposals.[44] Unsurprisingly, some contemporary observers assumed that the proposals—although obviously not sanctioned by any official agency— represented not the views of one senator but the dominant perspective of those actually shaping America's approach to international relations. Thus, the *Times* of London characterized Fulbright's speech as nothing less than "a landmark in the evolution of American policy."[45]

This strategic alignment of senatorial reformers with the foreign policy establishment was consistent with the approach taken by Joseph Clark and the organization he founded in 1959, Members of Congress for World Peace Through the Rule of Law, whose members would ultimately become the core of Senate Vietnam dissenters. Beginning with five senators—three of whom could themselves be described as second-tier members of the internationalist establishment[46]—by 1962 the organization included some sixty senators, and held meetings addressed by such bona fide members of this establishment as Christian Herter, Dean Rusk, John J. McCloy, McGeorge Bundy, and Adlai Stevenson.[47] It was to men "on the inside" like these that Senate dissenters naturally turned during the early Johnson presidency, and the counsel of such insiders was clear: 1964 was a year for champions of enlightened foreign policy to defend rather than attack the White House.[48]

As for the president himself, there were signs that—with appropriate advice and sufficient protection from rightist pressures—he would become an effective instrument of reform, placing his considerable political talents at the service of policies favored by enlightened elites, including Senate advocates of détente. The president's campaign against Goldwater, which used words and images that might have been borrowed from the most militant Ban the Bomb activists,[49] seemed to promise a continuation of the trend toward détente presaged by Kennedy and the Test Ban Treaty.

Liberal optimism about the president, and the direction in which he was likely to move, was expressed at the time in both public and private statements of senators, many of whom would have agreed with a contemporary speech of John Kenneth Galbraith. Galbraith, after decrying the continued presence in the State Department of the "kind of man who loved the pristine simplicity of the Cold War—Them against Us," assured his audience of Arizona liberals that "[n]o policy could be further from the instincts of our new President, Lyndon Johnson, a protégé of Franklin D. Roosevelt, a staunch supporter of John F. Kennedy and a man of acute good sense and sound political judgment in his own right." The role of liberals, explained Galbraith, was to protect Johnson from rightist pressures by aggressively intervening in discussions of foreign policy and countering those regressive forces that would return it to the Manichaean rigidity of the days of John Foster Dulles.[50]

To be sure, there remained the problem of Vietnam. For all the ambitious discussion of setting American foreign policy on a new course, promoting disarmament, and effecting détente between the superpowers, members of the foreign policy establishment and the senators in their orbit had few constructive proposals about the real war then raging in Vietnam.[51] But from the vantage point of 1964 with the hazard of nuclear destruction hanging over all of humanity, all questions, including Vietnam, would have to be considered subordinate to that of disarmament and U.S.–Soviet relations. Instead of fixating on Vietnam, as Morse and Gruening seemed to have done, responsible senators looked to the president as the one who could complete the reorientation of American foreign policy begun by

Kennedy, a reorientation which, along with many other benefits, would facilitate the settlement of local disputes like that in Southeast Asia.

For most Senate reformers, the point was to keep a sense of perspective and to have some patience. The Tonkin Gulf Resolution was but a tactical retreat; the main thing was to beat Goldwater, hold one's own seat, and work to fulfill the enormous potential that the early Johnson presidency seemed to promise abroad and at home. As Fulbright would later recall, looking back on this period: "I thought we were on the verge of entering our golden age. We had the opportunity: unlimited wealth, technical know-how, intelligent, energetic people—people not yet worn out, not to be stratified by old and ancient traditions. We were doing almost everything I thought ought to be done. It was really a tremendous opportunity."[52]

CHAPTER 3

1965: Division

I

In 1965 few senators openly attacked the president's policies. Moreover, Morse and Ernest Gruening, the only two senators who did consistently speak out and vote against the war, were marginal figures, neither being the chairman of a major committee, a member of the Senate establishment, or even the representative of a populous state. This paucity of open dissension, however, by no means reflected a general satisfaction among senators with the president's policies. In fact, not only was dissatisfaction widespread, but it was to be found among many of the most central figures within the Senate. Indeed, all the senators with the greatest institutional responsibility for the war were actually opposed to it.

Mike Mansfield of Montana, the majority leader, the chairman of the Democratic Conference and Policy and Steering committees, a senior member of the Foreign Relations Committee, once an enthusiastic supporter of Diem, and perhaps the only senator considered by his colleagues to have expertise on Vietnam, had by early 1965 repeatedly sent the president long confidential memoranda opposing the introduction of ground troops in Vietnam. As we have already seen, Fulbright, even before the Tonkin Gulf Resolution, had written McNamara that the American intervention in Vietnam "was bound to fail" and that, "this being the case, we should cut our losses and get out." The significance of Fulbright's dissent cannot be underestimated as he was the chairman of the Foreign Relations Committee and a man whose views on matters concerning foreign policy carried great weight with Senate liberals and moderates, especially those on his committee,[1] which itself enjoyed the deference of senators on such matters. And Richard Russell, the chairman of the Armed Services Committee, the chairman of the Department of Defense Subcommittee of the Appropriations Committee, the leader of the Southern Caucus, and a senator commanding almost incalculable respect from his colleagues on military matters,[2] had already repeatedly—but privately—advised Johnson that the time had come to seek an exit from Vietnam.[3] Moreover, such other powerful committee chairmen as Allen Ellender of Louisiana and A. Willis Robertson of Virginia were also Vietnam doubters by this period.[4]

Had such influential senators in early 1965 stated publicly and forcefully the views they expressed privately or in muted tones, it is likely that they would have emboldened many of their more timid moderate and liberal colleagues to give voice to their own doubts. This is to say nothing of the president's natural enemies in the Senate, the Republicans and the newly elected Robert Kennedy (D-N.Y.) (and those senators closest to Kennedy), forces likely to join the attack once they saw that the president had been wounded. Indeed, it is inconceivable that an open call to rebellion issued by Mansfield, Fulbright, and Russell in early 1965 would not have been heeded by at least a substantial minority of the Senate, a minority whose open opposition to escalation would have greatly accelerated the spread of public opposition to the war and inhibited presidential action.

The structures inhibiting such a rebellion, however, were formidable. Chief among these were the power and influence of the president himself. In addition to his vast constitutional powers, his control of patronage, his authority as party leader, his capacity to use his office to arouse and shape public opinion, and his own personal talent for exerting psychological pressure on recalcitrant legislators, Johnson was the inheritor of a Cold War political culture demanding great deference to the executive branch in the conduct of foreign relations, particularly in armed confrontations with international Communism.

This deference was supplemented by an unwillingness, at least in early 1965, of several strategically placed Republicans to create an appearance of partisanship.[5] A similar concern accounts, in part, for Robert Kennedy's relative quiescence throughout the year. The very notoriety of his enmity toward Johnson and the expectation that he would become the pole toward which an opposition would gravitate[6] made Kennedy wary of dissenting, lest it make him an easy mark for the many who were only too ready to attribute his actions to opportunism. He also shared with the Republicans another motivation for equivocating in 1965: a calculated desire not to preclude options that might become attractive at a later date.

If there was any force that might have had the potential to overcome the gravitational pull of the executive branch in 1965, it would have been a massive expression of impassioned opposition to the war from the electorate. Public sentiment, however, at least as measured in opinion polls, was too equivocal and contradictory to offer a sense of safety to senators who might have considered a break with the president. In March, for example, when Gallup pollsters asked their respondents if they would be more or less inclined to vote for a congressional candidate "who said we should try harder to reach a compromise peace settlement in Vietnam," Republicans 70 to 15 percent and Democrats 69 to 14 percent were "more inclined."[7] On the other hand, poll respondents persisted throughout this period in granting the president himself substantial approval ratings. In May, for example, approval outpolled disapproval 64 to 12 percent (47 to 37 percent for Republicans, 79 to 11 percent for Democrats, 55 to 26 percent for Independents). In June the president's approval shot up even further: 70 to 18 percent.[8]

Nor did protest actions demonstrate the existence of a movement big enough and powerful enough to offer protection to a senator who decided to follow their lead. By the time Students for a Democratic Society led the first national protest action against the war on April 17, 1965, a demonstration that brought some twenty thousand to the nation's capital, the organization had already undergone a bitter break with its parent organization, the League for Industrial Democracy, and was shorn of almost all of its ties to the trade unions, mainstream civil rights groups, and other components of the Democratic coalition.[9] The second major set of actions, the International Days of Protest of October 15–16, had somewhat broader sponsorship and drew a larger number of participants, most notably the thirty thousand who marched down New York's Fifth Avenue, but hardly represented a mass movement. Significantly, neither of New York's senators, although both were liberals, attended the protest, and one of them, Republican Jacob Javits, stood on the reviewing stand of a patriotic pro-war demonstration that was staged a week later. Connecticut Democrat Tom Dodd, for his part, responded to the October actions by asserting that "we have to draw a line, and draw it soon, and draw it hard between the right to free speech and assembly and the right to perpetrate treason."[10] In fact, it was not until November 15 that a demonstration took place in Washington whose marchers even began to mirror a real cross-section of the adult liberal community. And even this march, sponsored by the Committee for a Sane Nuclear Policy, the most respectable peace organization, only drew thirty-five thousand participants, hardly the force needed to overcome the dictates of party, president, and opinion poll.[11]

II

The structures inhibiting dissent, however, were hardly omnipotent. Although the ambiguous contents of opinion polls hardly created a rush to dissent, their expression of significant unhappiness with the war (albeit an unhappiness coupled with approval for the president), probably helped embolden at least one Democratic senator, George McGovern of South Dakota, to give voice to his convictions. Likewise, the ideal of bipartisanship was unable to inhibit George Aiken of Vermont, the Senate's senior Republican, from speaking his mind about the war.[12] And although antiwar demonstrators may have represented too marginal a minority to influence potential Senate dissenters, the evidence shows that the few senators who did speak out in 1965 drew at least some encouragement from the minority of constituents who wrote to them, particularly those from business, the academy, and the professions. But the most important development permitting some senators to speak publicly against escalation in 1965 was the growth during that year of significant divisions within the foreign policy establishment and among the leaders of elite opinion.[13]

It is difficult to overestimate the degree of influence exercised over some senators by reporters for the so-called prestige press, editorial writers, elite columnists, and other well-known figures identified with the shaping of American foreign policy during the Cold War era.[14] Especially for senators with strong interests in foreign policy reform such as Fulbright, Joseph Clark (D-Pa.), Frank Church (D-Idaho), and Claiborne Pell (D-R.I.), these were the sources to whom they habitually looked for information, analysis, and direction. In particular, they (or at least their aides) were regular readers of elite columnists and commentators. Enlightened senators consulted these sources not only for help in forming their own opinions, but in determining whether it was prudent to express in public those opinions that they had hitherto harbored in private. As a rule, an opinion expressed on the editorial page of a prestigious newspaper or by a leading columnist represented a green light that implied at least a modicum of safety for senators who chose to move in its direction.[15] For the greater part of the Cold War—including the election year of 1964—the gravitational pull of this elite carried these senators (most of whom were Democrats) in the direction of the White House. Indeed, in the area of foreign policy, the boundary between those exercising private influence and those exercising governmental power was rather porous, with individuals moving in and out of official and unofficial posts, writing for the same publications, working for the same foundations and firms, and sustaining close formal and informal ties to people similar to themselves, irrespective of whether they were at any particular moment serving in government.[16]

In 1965, however, a gap began to appear between the position of those inside government and a growing number of influential men who stood on the outside. The accounts of reporters at publications such as the *New York Times* presented a view of the war at odds with that of the secretary of defense or the ambassador to South Vietnam; and columnists such as James Reston and Walter Lippmann, who once lent their prestige to the administration and quieted liberal doubters, now began to use their influence to open up debate on what policies the administration should follow,[17] as did renowned academicians such as Hans Morgenthau, who debated McGeorge Bundy on national television and, in a more intimate setting, offered his analysis at a dinner hosted by Church, whose guests included Fulbright and Javits.[18]

Such was the opening up of elite discussion about Vietnam in early 1965 that, for example, when Gruening, whose position on Vietnam placed him at the Senate's far left, delivered a speech on April 22 in opposition to administration policy, he was able to support his criticism with citations to books by *New York Times* reporters David Halberstam and Malcolm Browne, a favorable review of these books in the *New York Review of Books,* a column by Arthur Krock of the *New York Times,* an article by Church published in the traditionally Republican *Saturday Evening Post,* an article by Hans Morgenthau published in the *New York Times Magazine,* and two nationally syndicated columns by Walter Lippmann.[19] Sources such as these did more than give an imprimatur of respectability to the views of such outspoken critics as Morse and Gruening; they added to the anxiety of many other senators who, although unready to join the dissenters, were also unwilling to give the war their unequivocal support inasmuch as to do so would be to stake their reputations on an adventure that commentators of the stature of Morgenthau and Lippmann were predicting would end in disaster. In a few cases, moreover, the authority of such commentators actually persuaded senators to add their voices to those openly opposing escalation of the war.

Walter Lippmann—a former Council on Foreign Relations director—was especially important for the development of Senate dissent. "In foreign affairs," wrote William S. White in his classic work on the Senate, "no voice is more persuasive [to senators] than that of Walter Lippmann."[20] "Lippmann's voice," commented Harry Ashmore, an Arkansas journalist with close ties to Fulbright, "comes from above and not from below; it certainly could not be confused with the voice of the people, which is the politician's most immediate concern, but it commands attention nonetheless."[21] Comments of senators themselves tended to confirm these views, particularly their own deference to his opinions.

Lyndon Johnson, when majority leader, once prefaced his reading of a complete Lippmann column on the floor of the Senate by proudly announcing that he had recently "spent a delightful evening with Mr. and Mrs. Walter Lippmann," and described the former as "a man of true intellectual independence, who thinks through a problem and refuses to avoid logical conclusions merely because they are unpopular."[22] Seven years later, on the occasion of Lippmann's seventy-fifth birthday, Fulbright took the floor to describe Lippmann as "one of the most perceptive and reasonable commentators of the American and international scene," as a man with "a unique capacity for dissecting and analyzing the most complicated of subjects," and as one who "does not oversimplify" but "merely explains the true meaning of complex factors in our modern world," thereby rendering "a service which is of incalculable value in the understanding of our psyche on many of the subjects that confront us."[23] In fact, throughout the first two decades of the Cold War (a term Lippmann is credited with popularizing), senators seem to have never missed an opportunity to praise and cite Walter Lippmann when the columnist's views coincided with their own.[24] The practice persisted through the Johnson presidency as Senators invoked

Lippman's authority in opposition to Barry Goldwater,[25] in support of the president's retaliatory bombing raids after the Tonkin Gulf incidents,[26] and—by early 1964—in favor of seeking a negotiated settlement of the war in Vietnam.[27] This last issue, by early 1965, became a central focus of Lippmann's attention and he sought to exert his influence on senators, not only through his column,[28] but through direct communication.

In addition to helping Fulbright—who was part of his social circle—develop a coherent position on the war,[29] Lippmann wrote a letter of praise to Church in response to an article he had written on American foreign policy in Asia and Africa for the *New York Times Magazine*. Lippmann described the article as "splendid," and told Church, referring to the senator's boyhood idol, of how pleased he was "that we have another Borah from Idaho."[30] Lippmann also issued an invitation to Church, as well as McGovern and Wyoming Democrat Gale McGee to attend a party at his home, across from Washington Cathedral, at which it was agreed that Church would open Senate debate on Vietnam by delivering a speech based on the article and that the other senators would then follow with their own contributions.[31] Once again, revealing the close relationship of senator and columnist, Lippmann's column appearing on the morning immediately after the first day of Senate debate, titled "The Vietnam Debate," was cited by Church during the second day of Senate discussion. "I have closely reviewed the debate today," explained Church, "but, as history shall bear witness, nothing was said to compare, in accuracy of assessment, to the brilliant summation of Walter Lippmann . . . published in the morning's edition of the Washington Post," and he "could do no better than to read the Lippmann article into the Record."[32]

III

As agreed at the Lippmanns' party, the debate began on February 17 with a speech by Church. According to Church, the United States had become "overinvolved" in the formerly colonial world, having failed to appreciate the impracticality of imposing political and economic models there based on the successes of the industrialized capitalist democracies. The only goal of American policy in Vietnam should be to prevent its domination by China, not the defense of a particular economic system. "As Yugoslavia has proven in Europe vis-à-vis Russia," Church explained, "even a Communist government can play such a role." And there was no danger in immediately seeking a settlement with the Communists since the United States always retained the capacity to "strike back with relative impunity from the floating bases which are beyond Communist reach and inflict heavy punishment upon them."[33]

In the discussion that followed, McGovern and Gaylord Nelson (D-Wisc.) delivered speeches unequivocally endorsing Church[34] while Morse and Gruening staked out a position to his left. Morse, who reiterated his argument that the war violated international law, initially refrained from placing primary blame on the president. Instead, he pointed to perfidious forces under whose influence the president had fallen: his secretaries of defense and state; the ambassador to South Vietnam and his deputy; the Bundy brothers; "and others who have been bent on escalating the war in Asia well over a year." "If they succeed in that nefarious program," warned Morse, "the big show is on, and the world will be involved in a nuclear war."[35]

Gruening similarly warned his colleagues that a "full scale war in Vietnam" would trigger "a general war against the Red China hordes thousands of miles from our shores."[36] He also noted the hostility of the South Vietnamese to the Americans, and expressed his view that "the white man cannot . . . settle the problems of Asia." Gruening characterized the conflict as a civil war and denied that any controlling moral principle compelled the United States to intervene: "As Walter Lippmann pointed out in a recent column, we did not interfere in a case of manifest aggression when Tibet was invaded by the Chinese. We did not interfere in the more tragic case of Hungary where the people were ruthlessly mowed down by Russian tanks." If anything, the argument for intervening in Hungary was "more cogent" than that for now sending troops to Vietnam since the Hungarians, unlike the Vietnamese, "were willing to fight for their freedom."[37]

McGee and Thomas Dodd (D-Conn.) made the principal speeches opposing immediate negotiations. McGee defended the intervention as part of a history of American opposition to totalitarianism throughout the Cold War. The strategy was by necessity global and depended on a policy of refusing to make concessions to Communism in any part of the world that it threatened. At the present, Asia was the focus of Communist attention, and the United States had no choice but to "stand tall" and meet its challenge there. Moreover, according to McGee, "the domino theory is valid" and if "Vietnam goes, Cambodia goes, Thailand goes, Malaya goes, Indonesia goes, the Philippines go."

This global strategic perspective had guided America's actions since the end of World War II irrespective of the nature of the regime that was threatened by Communism. He reminded his colleagues that the Truman doctrine—the very foundation of the American Cold War policy—had been inaugurated with the defense of the Greek monarchy even though that regime "did not have the support of the people." Greece was "in the throes of a civil war, on a considerably higher level than the one now going on in Vietnam," and our priority was to stop the infiltration from the north of Communists over the border. To achieve our goals we supported "not the good guys but the bad guys in Greece—to put it simply in the vernacular. We did not back the people. We backed the monarchy; we backed those who happened to be in the driver's seat at the moment." The same policy was justified in Southeast Asia, a policy based "on a cold and hard look" at "what is really at stake." In Vietnam, "as much as we would like to see a different government and even a democratic government," what was crucial now was that we protect the existing government from the Communists. Finally, acknowledging that many Americans hoped to see their country disengage from Vietnam, McGee urged his colleagues to resist this "resurgent isolationism" that gave encouragement to America's enemies and "jeopardizes the prospects of our ultimate triumph in winning the chance to do something about a better world."[38]

Thomas Dodd's "marathon" three-hour address[39] reiterated and elaborated upon many of the themes set forth by McGee: the validity of the domino theory, the strategic importance of Vietnam, the futility of negotiating with the Communists, and the threat now posed by a "new isolationism" and its kinship with the old isolationism which had opposed intervention against Adolf Hitler. On this last theme, Dodd emphasized the "many resemblances" of the current crisis in Vietnam with that "just before Munich." However, in contrast to McGee's Realpolitik defense of American policy, Dodd argued the United States, in deciding to come to the aid of South Vietnam, no less than when it enacted Lend-Lease, was motivated by profoundly humanitarian values.

Unlike McGee and other administration supporters who rarely accompanied their denunciations of Hanoi with praise for the regime in Saigon, Dodd boldly asserted that the South Vietnamese government offered its people a way of life that was vastly superior to that of its northern adversary. "To equate an authoritarian regime like that in South Vietnam, or Taiwan, or Thailand with totalitarian rule," argued Dodd, "is tantamount to losing all sense of proportion." These regimes, unlike that of the Communists, were not guilty of mass slaughter or dictatorial control of personal life. Nor did they threaten the peace or security of their neighbors. In some cases these "free autocracies" combined "control of the press and political parties with remarkably progressive social programs." Indeed, "carefully examined" these regimes disclosed "a mixture of natural democracy at the bottom with political controls of varying rigidity at the top."

Rejecting Church's view that most Asians did not know the meaning of freedom—a view most of them would find "condescending and offensive" —Dodd enumerated the ways that the South Vietnamese understood this concept. While "westernized Saigonese intellectuals," who understandably "chafed over the political controls" of Diem, valued freedom of speech and the press and favored "some kind of parliamentary democracy," the great mass of Vietnamese always readily understood freedom as independence from foreign domination and as the enjoyment of a "type of natural freedom that is enjoyed by primitive peasants and tribesmen in many backward countries, even under political autocracies." In these countries, "the peasant is free to own his own land, to dispose of his produce, to worship according to his beliefs, to guide the upbringing of his children, to elect the local village officials." It was "these freedoms that touch his daily life that are the freedoms that really count, not the remote and abstract freedoms of constitutional and federal government." In addition to "granting him these natural freedoms, the government assists him by building schools and dispensaries and by providing seed and fertilizer, then, from the standpoint of the southeast Asian peasant, his life is full and he is prepared to fight to defend it from the Communists."

Contrary to the impression created by the press, the Communists in the south were unpopular and were able to discourage greater support for the government only through the practice of systematic terror, a practice that Dodd illustrated with accounts of decapitated teenage girls and massacred women and children. Likewise, the Buddhist protests, contrary to the commonly held view, did not represent mass opposition to the South Vietnamese government, but merely the vulnerability of the monasteries to Communist infiltration. In fact, according to Dodd, the great majority of South Vietnamese were strong supporters of the government and knew that a Communist victory would inaugurate "a bloodletting on a genocidal scale."

Dodd also distinguished himself from McGee by deemphasizing the use of bombing, instead proposing that priority be given to an "effective political warfare program." To this end Dodd proposed a major increase in the attention given to propaganda and counterinsurgency, and that Congress enact legislation forming a Freedom Academy through which an international cadre could be trained to conduct these efforts. Meanwhile, the United States should give the South Vietnamese government the "green light" to form a "Committee for the Liberation of North Vietnam" which could galvanize anti-Communist nationalists by offering them the prospect of a free and unified Vietnam. In the name of this committee, guerilla raids would be conducted against the Communists in the north so as "to make every Communist official fear the just retribution of an enraged humanity; to make every Communist arsenal, government building, communications center and transportation facility a target for sabotage; to provide a rallying point for the great masses of oppressed people who hate communism because they have known it. Only when we have given the Communists more trouble than they can handle at home, will they cease their aggression against the outposts of freedom."

Dodd also proposed that the United States provide air support for the seizure by Vietnamese and Laotian forces of Tchepone, at the "hub of the Ho Chi Minh trail" in Laos, while at the same time putting forward a "dramatic measure" suggested by the American Friends of Vietnam for "a massive southeast Asian development program based on the harnessing of the Mekong River—a kind of Tennessee Valley Authority for southeast Asia." This ambitious but "eminently sensible" program would "offer incredible promise" to Thailand, Laos, Cambodia, and South Vietnam as well as "the people of North Vietnam, which only the continued belligerence and noncooperation of their government could frustrate."[40]

In addition to these long speeches, several senators made shorter interventions in support of the administration's policies.[41] Two powerful members of the Senate establishment, Stuart Symington (D-Mo.) and

Allen Ellender (D-La.), however, coupled declarations of support for the administration with comments and questions evincing concern about the general direction of American foreign policy. Symington, the only senator serving on both the Foreign Relations and Armed Services committees, interrupted Church's speech to indicate his agreement with his contention that the United States was overextended, particularly with respect to troops stationed abroad, as well as what he saw as the excessively ideological nature of American foreign policy. Symington, who had himself run several large business corporations, called for an increase in trade with the Communist countries, decrying the fact that "our country was the only country that for ideological or any other reasons was not trying to improve its trade position" with them. He also, in a respectful and nonadversarial manner, posed questions of "my able friend from Idaho" on the specific measures the United States might take to disengage from Vietnam.

Symington's respectful treatment of Church was complemented by Ellender's interruption and hostile cross-examination of Dodd. Ellender, who had traveled to Vietnam several times (and whose state, incidentally, shared many of the geographic features of Vietnam, its history of French rule, and similarly contained in its south a great city noted for political corruption), wondered aloud if South Vietnam would, like South Korea, become a never-ending burden to the United States. He also expressed concern about the failure of South Vietnam to develop a stable government since Diem's death, and its failure to attract significant aid from America's allies. Finally, he seemed skeptical when Dodd asserted (in contrast to Ellender's own 90 percent estimate) that less than 30 percent of the South Vietnamese were Buddhists.[42]

The February Vietnam speeches (along with the questions and comments made in response to them by several leading senators) represented a new stage in the development of the Senate Vietnam controversy. They do not date the beginning of widespread senatorial unhappiness with the war, but they do mark the onset of a new feeling among senators that the war was not a fleeting matter but a major issue not likely to soon disappear, and that it was an issue of such urgency that its public discussion had become permissible and even desirable. From then on, it would be impossible for even a superficial observer to characterize the Senate as a supportive auxiliary to the president "in time of war," its patriotic unanimity marred only by the discontent of two men at the institution's margins. The issue was no longer the peculiar obsession of Morse and Gruening, but a major and difficult issue for the Senate as a whole.

The new stage of discussion was part of a larger process extending beyond the Senate chamber. By this time it was abundantly clear that apprehension about the administration's policies had made significant inroads into the mainstream of elite opinion, as could be readily seen by anyone perusing the contemporary editorials, columns, and articles in the most prestigious newspapers and journals. Whatever their views, it had become no longer possible for the nation's leaders to discuss the war without acknowledging that it was not merely a problem but a problem subject to serious debate.

This new general development was not lost on the president, nor was he unaware of its effect on the Senate. Needless to say, he did not plan to stand still and passively observe as senators, one by one, were carried into the orbit of Lippmann and other elite dissenters. On the contrary, as we shall see presently, he was determined to take a range of actions calculated to subject senators to his own gravitational pull. It was a force that had always shown itself to be formidable, and, with respect to members of his own party, one that had often shown itself to be irresistible.

CHAPTER 4

1965: The White House

I

Recently declassified White House tapes corroborate the reports of contemporary journalists[1] that the president closely monitored the opening of Senate debate on Vietnam. Discussing dissension within the Senate and elsewhere with McGeorge Bundy on February 18, 1965, Johnson made particular mention of criticisms and concerns expressed by Mansfield, Morse, Church, Symington, and McGovern, as well as Walter Lippmann. Johnson's response to the dissenters was unsubtle; he urged Bundy to remind them of their vote for the Gulf of Tonkin Resolution and to tell them that their dissension helped the enemy. In particular Bundy was directed to invite McGovern and Church to his office, and to report to them on the instability in Saigon that congressional dissent caused. Johnson wanted the senators to be told that nothing caused the South Vietnamese so much "to pee in their pants" than to read a speech by Morse or Mansfield saying we ought to run out. Johnson wanted Bundy to let the senators "know there is no greater disservice that they can render," and that if they insisted on speaking out they would be "on their own."[2]

Despite this warning, the effect on Johnson of this limited dissension should not be exaggerated. For Johnson the Senate was, above all, a legislative body, and, during 1965, he was far more preoccupied with winning votes for his ambitious program of domestic reforms than with the advice offered by senators on the general contours of American policy in Southeast Asia. He also undoubtedly drew some comfort from the fact that the criticism that was proffered did not come from the forces he feared the most: the Republicans and Robert Kennedy.

On the day the Lippman-instigated debate began, the Republican congressional leadership issued a statement supporting the president's air raids in Vietnam, and during the debate itself the few Republicans who intervened did so on the side of the administration. Dirksen, in an emotional address in which he invoked the memories of, among others, "the freezing Continentals at Valley Forge," went so far as to accuse the administration's critics of proposing "to run up the white flag" before the forces of advancing Communism.[3] Robert Kennedy, for his part, abstained from the Senate floor debate, and, as if to spite those who expected him to play the role of the president's antagonist, went so far as to delete from the final text of a speech delivered at the International Police Academy words that made even the most indirect reference to Vietnam.[4] The president may have drawn some further comfort from the fact that the members of the Senate establishment most critical of his policies—Mansfield, Fulbright, and Russell—muted their public criticism, offering their advice in the manner of privy councilors rather than in indignant declamations on the Senate floor.

The relative lack of dissent may account, in part, for the failure of the executive branch during 1965 to develop a comprehensive plan for sustaining and increasing Senate support for its Vietnam policies.[5] Lacking a plan, the formal congressional liaison apparatuses of the White House and of the Defense and State Departments stuck to their old routines, defining their tasks as merely the transmission of information to senators and the securing of their votes on legislation funding the war, tasks that excited little imagination or initiative since the votes on these measures were never in doubt.[6] The principals of these departments, McNamara and Rusk, similarly tended to see their role in administrative terms, dutifully testifying at hearings and supplying information (or misinformation), but making little real effort to win the hearts and minds of senators.[7] By contrast the president, acting in a manner more theatrical than methodical, sought to impress on senators the necessity of supporting the administration. These efforts typically involved the president in spirited confrontations with senators in groups as well as on a one-to-one basis.

Although memorable, the content and form of these encounters was of a type more likely to win immediate acquiescence than enduring allegiance. Perhaps more effective at disarming or at least delaying dissent was the ambiguity of Johnson's professed policies in Vietnam, an ambiguity displayed in conversations with senators and particularly in his speech at Johns Hopkins, which gave some senators hope that the president's views were similar to their own. As the year progressed, however, the hard reality of escalation tended to outweigh the ambiguity expressed in Johnson's speeches, and doubting senators were pulled toward disillusionment and dissent.

In the winter and spring, Johnson invited groups of senators to the White House to be briefed on Vietnam and to ask any questions they might have. These meetings were dominated by the president and bereft of real give-and-take as Johnson—even while proclaiming that he welcomed senator involvement—treated his listeners to extended monologues obviously calculated to close rather than open debate. A favorite theme of the president was the vote for the Gulf of Tonkin Resolution, which he reminded senators of as a prosecutor might, during cross-examination, remind a defendant of his confession.[8]

It is likely that senators who witnessed these performances—particularly those who had had doubts when they voted for the resolution—were unappreciative of the president's expansive interpretation of it and his claim that their votes had been given without duress or coercion. If nothing else, the president's aggressive use of a resolution that he had demanded from Congress in the midst of his election campaign showed his willingness to embarrass his benefactors, a practice which, however immediately effective, would in the long run render them less generous.

A similar lack of subtlety characterized the president's one-to-one confrontations with those opposed to escalation.[9] Although accounts of these rugged encounters with the tall finger-jabbing Texan may have inhibited other senators from dissenting, it is less likely that they actually persuaded many of the correctness of the administration's policies or forged the type of loyalty that could be expected to endure even when the president lost his popularity. When George McGovern, during a meeting with Johnson in the Oval Office, questioned the thesis that Ho was a mere instrument of Mao in light of the thousand-year history of animosity between Vietnam and China, the president suddenly became enraged: "Goddamn it, George, you and Fulbright and all you history teachers down there. I haven't got time to fuck around with history. I've got boys on the line out there who might die in the morning."[10] The president was particularly angry at Church. On the day after he launched the Vietnam debate, Johnson cornered him at a White House reception and—leaving virtually no space between himself and the senator—furiously berated him for an hour. At one point in the conversation Church mentioned his high respect for Walter Lippmann, and the president concurred. However, on the following day the president circulated an embellished account of the conversation in which he had retorted to Church's reference to Lippmann with the line, "The next time you want a dam in Idaho, Frank, go see Walter."[11]

In fact, contrary to the impression Johnson may have wished to create with this story, there is little evidence that the executive branch used federal largesse to attain compliance with its Vietnam policies. Although Johnson believed that the benefits he bestowed on senators—as president or in his old role of majority leader—gave him a moral claim on their loyalty, the record is remarkably bereft of examples of concrete rewards granted or denied because of their response to this issue. Even on domestic issues, the general rule was that benefits were allocated to senators as part of a general project of creating a sense of goodwill and gratitude on their part, rather than as "payment" for support on a particular roll call.[12] The story about Church and the dam, like Johnson's request that Adlai Stevenson remind Morse that as majority leader he had ensured his appointment to the Foreign Relations Committee, is therefore more significant in revealing the way the president thought politics ought to work than as a description of the way it actually was.[13]

More significant than Johnson's use of patronage were his efforts to ingratiate himself with legislators by suggesting the substantive similarity of their views with his own or by implying that he was moving in their direction. These efforts, however, could only have temporary effects as the president's words were invariably soon contradicted by his actions. In June, for example, the president approached Morse at a White House bill-signing ceremony and told him that he had been listening to his arguments and wanted him to prepare a memorandum explaining how the United Nations might be used to resolve the conflict. The president concluded his conversation with Morse by telling him "I think you know how much I respect your views."

Needless to say, the remarkable memorandum and proposed presidential speech that Morse presented to the White House in less than twenty-four hours did not lead Johnson to adopt Morse's proposals or, indeed, to make any deviation from the course already charted.[14] For Morse, and for the influential Foreign Relations Committee Chief of Staff Carl Marcy, who ghost-wrote the memorandum, suddenly raised hopes were followed by a renewed and deepened sense of alienation from the administration.

Also short-lived was the goodwill generated by Johnson's magnificently ambiguous address delivered at Johns Hopkins University on April 7.[15] The speech, combining pledges to stay the course, welcome negotiations, and possibly bring the New Deal to Southeast Asia, won the immediate acclaim of both hawkish and dovish senators.[16] Even before the speech was given Johnson began the work of co-optation by inviting several potentially troublesome senators to the White House to preview the text of the speech and (knowing from whence they took their cues) soliciting the views of Walter Lippmann. The president even controlled his temper with Church and allowed the Idahoan to get the last line in a humorous exchange. When Church (accompanied by McGovern and McGee) entered a small room adjacent to the Oval Office, Johnson asked Church, "How's that dam building going on in Idaho?" Church replied: "Well, Mr. President, it's going just fine. As a matter of fact, the next dam we build, we're going to call the Walter Lippmann dam." Church recalled that "[Special Assistant to the President] Jack Valenti and McGeorge Bundy were in the room, and their faces froze. And the President froze for a minute and then threw his head back and laughed, and then they laughed, and everybody laughed."[17] Johnson then spent a half hour conferring with Church, McGee, and McGovern. He also met for ninety minutes with Mansfield and Fulbright and took the additional step of ensuring Fulbright's support by exerting strong pressure on Eugene Black, a close friend of the Fulbrights, to direct the billion-dollar Southeast Asia development program to be proposed in the speech. Overcoming the former World Bank president's objections, Johnson hoped his appointment would, as Bundy suggested, "neutralize" Fulbright and other potential critics.[18] The era of good feeling generated through these efforts, however, was to be of exceedingly short duration.

II

Senate critics of escalation had barely begun to applaud the proposals made at Johns Hopkins when events intruded that once again shook their faith in the administration. Indeed, by temporarily easing their concerns, the speech may well have increased their sense of alienation from the White House when, in the months that followed, the war was rapidly escalated and the president increasingly seemed uninterested in pursuing a negotiated settlement. This dynamic of briefly raised hopes followed by deepening fears was repeated in May when a brief bombing halt—ironically, in the president's words, initiated "in deference to Mansfield and Fulbright"[19]—was followed by the revelation (through one of Pell's foreign service contacts) that the administration had failed to disclose a Hanoi "peace feeler" made immediately prior to the resumption of the bombing.[20] The revelation reinforced an already-growing tendency of senators to combine an unhappiness with the policies pursued by the administration with the belief that its public pronouncements showed a want of candor.

Significantly, it was during this period that the expression "credibility gap" entered general currency,[21] a phenomenon that was given impetus less than a month after the Baltimore speech by the wild claims made by the president in justifying the landing of the marines at Santo Domingo. This invasion of the Dominican Republic—the first overt incursion of American forces onto the soil of a Latin American country since 1925—not only widened the credibility gap but added fuel to the fire of anxieties about the administration's goals in Vietnam. If it was possible for Johnson in Latin America to emulate the policies of Calvin Coolidge, it seemed increasingly plausible that in Southeast Asia he would adopt those of Barry Goldwater.[22]

Vietnam doubters were hardly reassured when, less than a week after the Dominican invasion, the president forced senators to vote on a $700 million supplemental appropriation for Vietnam. Although doubts existed as to whether the funds were truly needed to meet a military emergency, as claimed by the administration, senators naturally did not wish to risk giving an appearance of depriving American soldiers in "an area of danger . . . the equipment and the materials by which they can execute their orders with maximum safety to themselves and to the interests of the United States."[23] At the same time, the president exploited this alleged emergency to force senators to take a vote on the merits of his Vietnam policy, emphasizing in his message to Congress that "this is not a routine appropriation" and that "each member of Congress who supports this request is also voting to persist in our effort to halt Communist aggression in South Vietnam."[24] Faced with the apparent choice of failing to equip American soldiers or authorizing future escalation, all but three senators (Morse, Gruening, and Nelson) chose the latter. To an even greater extent than with the Gulf of Tonkin

Resolution, Johnson had forced senators to go on record as accomplices to his policies, and further undermined any who might complain that the war lacked congressional authorization. Once again, at least in the short run, he had kept the Senate in his camp. And once again, through the use of overbearing and manipulative tactics, he had achieved the compliance at the price of his credibility and the good will of the men whose support he would need for the long haul.

Through the spring and into the summer, Johnson persisted in his peculiar form of "consultation" with senators, tending more to monologue than dialogue. Tom Wicker reported in June that senators "closely interested in foreign affairs" were "irritated by his habit of lecturing them at length in private sessions." In a typical case a meeting lasted four hours, and during another "a leading Senator attempted to slip out unseen—only to be called back from the door." Members of both Houses also expressed annoyance "at what they think are Johnsonian devices to mute or snuff out congressional criticism or debate." Johnson's request for a $700 million supplemental appropriation for Vietnam was pointed to as an example of this, "a request for a 'blank check' made under circumstances in which most members could not afford to oppose it."[25]

While the president insisted on senatorial support it was increasingly clear that he had little interest in any proposals or advice that senators might offer. The lack of consultation was felt all the more keenly as senators, excluded from the real councils of power, heard by press report or rumor of decisions with long-lasting implications being made at the other end of Pennsylvania Avenue. "We seem to be on the verge of another important decision regarding Vietnam," Carl Marcy wrote Fulbright in late July, "one on which the views of the Senate will not be sought until after the decision." The chief of staff, after noting that the prevailing view of the committee favored disengagement, suggested that the chairman call together a meeting of other senators "who probably have the same doubts that you have." The plan would be for the senators to discuss among themselves the crisis in Vietnam and then possibly make an authoritative recommendation to the president.[26] Meanwhile Walter Lippmann—who had been working with Marcy to develop the senator's position on Vietnam—made a telephone call to Fulbright and also proposed a meeting of leading senators to discuss Vietnam.[27] Fulbright was persuaded and on July 27 a remarkable assembly of leading senators took place in the majority leader's office.

III

As the president at the White House conferred with his advisors—none of whom were from the legislative branch—a half-mile away another group of leaders met, hoping to make one last effort to persuade him to take a different course of action. In attendance were Mansfield, Fulbright, Russell, John Sparkman (D-Ala., the ranking Democrat on the Foreign Relations Committee), John Sherman Cooper (R-Ky., a former ambassador to India), and George Aiken (R-Vt., the Senate's senior Republican and the second-ranking Republican on the Foreign Relations Committee). The outcome of the meeting was a list of nineteen "major points," which Mansfield recorded in a memorandum for the president. Most of the points were concerned with avenues of possible negotiations and with the need to provide the Soviets with a way to help establish peace. The United Nations was emphasized; a possible role for France was suggested; and the senators also pointed to "underground contact" that might be established with the Russians or even the Chinese.

The senators evinced a desire that Vietnam policy be subordinated to the long-range goals of promoting détente with the Soviets and encouraging the breakup of the Communist monolith. General concern about the effect of Vietnam on Soviet-American relations was emphasized, noting that the Russians feared that the Americans were now abandoning "peaceful coexistence." It was essential that "bridges to Eastern Europe" be maintained and that the United States continue the "encouragement of the evolution of these nations (Yugoslavia, in particular) towards full independence, political and economic, under their own unique forms of organization."

Vietnam itself was relatively unimportant to the United States. Even if the Americans triumphed in Vietnam "you still do not come out well. What have you achieved?" Vietnam was "by no means a 'vital' area of U.S. concern." After expressing a number of military concerns (the bombing was "ill advised" but should not have been limited once it began, the NLF had better fighters than the ARVN, Pleiku was dangerously exposed, the French never used conscripts), the senators emphasized "that the important thing in a situation like this, which is clearly detrimental to us is to concentrate on finding a way out; a possibility might exist in a combination of a coastal enclave strategy, a cessation of aerial bombardment and the use of all possible contacts to get negotiations underway." They also believed that Americans were "backing the President on Viet Nam primarily because he is President, not necessarily out of any understanding or sympathy with policies on Viet Nam," and warned that "beneath the support, there is deep concern and a great deal of confusion which could explode at any time; in addition racial factors at home could become involved."

Mansfield closed the memorandum, noting that, although not all of the points were unanimously approved by the senators, "there was a very substantial agreement on them. Moreover, there was full agreement that insofar as Viet Nam is concerned we are deeply enmeshed in a place where we ought not to be; that the situation is rapidly getting out of control; and that every effort should be made to extricate ourselves."[28]

The president did not follow the senators' advice. Instead, at noon on the following day, he announced the immediate deployment to Vietnam of the First Cavalry Division with supporting forces, raising the total American intervention from 75,000 to 125,000 men. Warning that even this increase would not be sufficient, he announced that additional forces would be "sent as requested" and that the draft of young men would be raised from 17,000 to 35,000 per month.[29] Thus, in the words of one historian, "quietly and without fanfare, he launched the United States on what would become its longest, most frustrating, and most divisive war."[30]

For Fulbright and those advising him, the problem did not only involve the war in Vietnam but a more general degeneration in American foreign policy that had taken place over the last two years. In a memorandum to Fulbright, Marcy described the president as having become captive to forces that were uninterested in pursuing the hopes of August 1963 when the Soviets and Americans had agreed to the Test Ban Treaty and the United States seemed to be turning to a truly enlightened foreign policy. In light of this unfortunate trajectory, he suggested that Fulbright give a speech advocating a return to the goals and strategy of 1963. Marcy warned that "such a speech would break you with the Administration and make Borah and Hiram Johnson and Cabot Lodge, Sr., look like pikers. But it is a line of action that you should perhaps consider. I don't know if I would do this if I were you!"[31]

IV

The suggestion was unappealing to Fulbright. He had not come to Congress to emulate the likes of William Borah or Hiram Johnson. He certainly did not want to surpass them as antagonists of presidential power and "make them look like pikers." The older Lodge—the great senatorial opponent of the Treaty of Versailles—had never been his hero; it was Lodge's nemesis, Wilson, whom he had admired. Likewise, Fulbright had defended the prerogatives of Roosevelt against Borah and against Johnson. He did not want to play the congressional combatant to the policies of the executive branch; he had even gone so far as to propose that the Constitution be changed to limit congressional interference in foreign policy.[32] For Fulbright, Congress was the problem, not the solution. In the Senate he had attempted to advance the foreign policy of the president, even while proposing friendly amendments. Despite his discomfort with the Vietnam intervention, he had, acceding to the president's request, delivered a speech in June in its defense, while also proposing a halt to the bombing to facilitate negotiations. The speech was appreciated by the White House, and commentators interpreted Fulbright's proposal to stop the bombing as a trial balloon sanctioned by Johnson, rather than as a sign of rift between the president and his old friend.[33] Even as the committee chairman's doubts on Vietnam had grown, he had refrained from public criticism, resisted pressure to hold public hearings, and even discouraged other Senate committees from addressing the issue openly.[34]

It was also easy for Fulbright to refrain from publicly voicing his criticism on Vietnam, an issue in which the decisions of previous administrations significantly limited the president's options, in which the adversary was Communist, and in which a Communist victory could indeed lead to Republican attacks comparable to those faced by Truman after the Chinese Revolution. On the other hand, the Dominican invasion, used to suppress an insurgency not led by Communists, suggested that the problem might be deeper and that the administration had assumed a rigid policy of opposing all revolutions in which there was any Communist participation. This, for Fulbright, was a prescription for the United States to align itself with the governments of these countries (no matter how oppressive they were), to oppose virtually all popular movements, and to leave the Communists without competition for their leadership. At the very least the Dominican intervention warranted executive session hearings, particularly in light of the confusion concerning official statements about the intervention. And in the aftermath of the invasion Fulbright did hold such hearings, while at the same time abstaining from public criticism of the administration.

This is where the matter might have stayed had several senators, apparently at the behest of the administration, not taken the Senate floor to attack the hearings and, by implication Fulbright, in virulent and misleading terms. This was too much for the Arkansan. He would have to answer the charges, and in doing so make some public statement of how his views differed from that of the administration. Thus, on September 15, Fulbright rose in the Senate and delivered a speech suggesting that, with respect to the invasion, the president had been misled by poor advice and inaccurate intelligence, and that generally the United States should assume the role of champion rather than opponent of social revolution throughout Latin America.[35]

Well aware of Johnson's sensitivity to criticism, Fulbright took precautions that he believed would cushion the impact of his dissent, most obviously the moderate tone of the speech, the coupling of criticism with praise, the attribution of all the president's errors to his advisors, and the assertion that if he (Fulbright) had been given the same intelligence he would have acted as the president had. He also sent the White House an advance copy of the text, with a cover letter calculated to soothe. Needless to say, none of this worked.

Nothing, in fact, could have prepared Fulbright for the magnitude of the president's rage. Superficial symptoms included the exclusion of Fulbright from all of the state dinners held at the White House that fall (include a major function for German Chancellor Ludwig Erhard), the denial of the use of a government jet for foreign travel, a series of abusive tirades about Fulbright to his advisors and other visitors to the White House (the contents of which invariably reached the Arkansan secondhand), and at least one very angry letter sent to him directly. Johnson further mobilized his Senate allies to deliver speeches against Fulbright, including Dodd, Russell, Russell Long (D-La.), Frank Lausche (D-Ohio), and George Smathers (D-Fla.). As the columnist Joseph Kraft described it, the attacks on Fulbright during this period were "not unlike the stoning reserved by the high priests of primitive communities for those who question the efficacy of blood sacrifice."[36]

In a deeper sense, the reaction to the speech represented a qualitative change in the relationship of the president to the chairman of the congressional committee most intimately concerned with the conduct of U.S. foreign policy. Through the intensity of his reaction, through his refusal of any conciliatory gestures, through his deafness to the equivocations in the speech, and by his branding the senator an enemy, Johnson pushed Fulbright into a role he had not wanted to play. By cutting Fulbright off, he emancipated him. The gravitational pull of the White House would hitherto never exert great influence on him. And as a consequence, the committee he chaired would cease to function as a conduit of White House policy. In fact, the Committee on Foreign Relations would soon become a center of challenge to the president's policies, not only in the Senate, but—with the assistance of the new medium of television—for the nation as a whole.[37]

CHAPTER 5

1966: The Hearings:
Dissenters at the Center

In February 1966 the Senate Foreign Relations Committee held its first public hearings on U.S. policy in Vietnam. Televised live[1] before an audience of some twenty-two million Americans, the hearings were described by one contemporary journalist as representing "a drama whose intensity and stakes have seldom been equaled in the nation's history,"[2] and by another as "the most searching public review of U.S. wartime policy since the 1951 hearings on Capitol Hill prompted by Harry Truman's firing of Gen. Douglas MacArthur."[3]

I

The hearings took place in a context of growing senatorial concern about the course of the war and the administration's attitude toward it.[4] Senate opponents of escalation were encouraged by a bombing pause in late December 1965, only to be disappointed when the bombing resumed thirty-seven days later. Although the White House labeled the pause a "peace offensive," suspicions abounded that the initiative was aimed less at starting negotiations with the enemy than at improving America's image among its friends.[5] On January 27 fifteen Democratic senators sent the president a letter imploring him to refrain from resuming the bombing and to continue his efforts to find a diplomatic solution.[6] Meanwhile a bipartisan group of senators, including Mike Mansfield of Montana, the majority leader, and George Aiken of Vermont, the much esteemed senior Republican of the Senate, had returned from a tour of Vietnam and issued a pessimistic report about the course of the combat. Finding that the United States could not attain its objectives at present force levels, the senators predicted an open-ended conflict with spiraling escalation and no foreseeable end to the fighting.[7]

According to Don Oberdorfer, a journalist sympathetic to the administration who interviewed several senators at the time of the hearings, the Mansfield-Aiken report "was taken very seriously by many members of the Senate, and it stirred up a lot of people." Even more alarming was a speech delivered by John Stennis (D-Miss.), ranking Democrat on the Armed Services Committee and chairman of its Preparedness Investigating Subcommittee. Speaking before the legislature of his home state on January 27—the same date as the letter of the fifteen Democrats—Stennis predicted that by the end of the year from 350,000 to 400,000 Americans would be in Vietnam and that ultimately they would number 600,000. He also said that if China entered the war, he favored the use of nuclear weapons. Senators told Oberdorfer that because Stennis's prior predictions of escalation had been borne out they were "completely convinced that Stennis had the inside word." The speech thus had "tremendous impact" and when its text was circulated "just scared the hell out of the Senators." Members of the Foreign Relations Committee, in particular, felt that "things are about to get really out of hand with the Chinese" and that the holding of public hearings would be "the last chance to avert a major war."[8]

Meanwhile, influential men were warning the chairman of the Foreign Relations Committee that if Congress did not act with respect to Vietnam, an antiwar movement might emerge led by irresponsible forces on the left. Walter Lippmann had suggested that "one of the principal reasons for the student protest movement has been the absence of significant debate on the official level, which is to say, in Congress."[9] A few weeks later the editors of the Wall Street Journal used their lead editorial to paraphrase approvingly the Mansfield-Aiken report and to call for congressional debate on the war. So far criticism of the war had largely come from the "New Left," the editors warned. In place of "hysterical outcries about American involvement," Congress could contribute "serious thinking about America's interest."[10]

The hearings that began a few weeks later answered the Wall Street Journal's prayer. All of the witnesses were either officials or advisors to the Johnson administration or dissenters closely identified with the foreign policy establishment or military—undoubtedly the kind of conduits of "serious thinking about America's interests" that the Journal's editors had in mind. Principal witnesses included: David Bell, the administrator for the Agency for International Development; General James Gavin, an outstanding soldier, military theorist, and industrialist, and a former ambassador to France, who had recently written a long letter to *Harper's* favoring disengagement from Vietnam; George Kennan, a central architect of American Cold War policy during the Truman presidency, former ambassador to the Soviet Union and Yugoslavia, and since 1965 a critic of American intervention in Vietnam; General Maxwell Taylor, a hero of World War II, former chairman of the Joint Chiefs of Staff, former ambassador to South Vietnam, and at the time of the hearings an advisor to the president on his policies there; and Dean Rusk, the secretary of state.[11]

The background and outlook of the senatorial critics of Vietnam policy on the Foreign Relations Committee harmonized with those of the establishment figures they interrogated. Fulbright, the committee's chairman, had himself been seriously considered for secretary of state before John Kennedy instead settled on Rusk; Gore was a protégé of Secretary of State Cordell Hull; Claiborne Pell of Rhode Island had served as a foreign service officer; and Eugene McCarthy of Minnesota had served as an intelligence officer at the Pentagon. At least three by privileged birth, marriage, or affiliation were members of the upper-class elite from which foreign-policy leaders had been drawn since the days of Elihu Root.

The administration's witnesses and their Democratic critics were united, however, by more than similar backgrounds and relationships. They were united by a common experience of the Cold War. They were all, of course, opponents of international Communism. But they were also opponents of the "massive retaliation" strategy for fighting Communism associated with Eisenhower, Dulles, and their congressional allies. Indeed, the two generals who testified—one for, one against the administration's Vietnam policies—had both left the service due to their shared dissatisfaction with the Eisenhower and Dulles approach. Generals Gavin and Taylor even shared a common history of skepticism toward the prospects for success in Vietnam.[12] All witnesses and senators had been partisans of the turn toward a more flexible and enlightened foreign policy identified with the Kennedy presidency. And the Democratic war critics on the committee had been among the strongest supporters of Johnson in his campaign against Goldwater and had, until recently, believed him when he claimed to be at least as committed to the attainment of peace as to the containment of communism. The dialogue that ensued at the hearings was therefore not merely a debate within an elite committed to the Cold War; it was even more narrowly a conversation on how to fight the *type* of cold war that both sides saw as the legacy of Kennedy and the promise of his successor's campaign.

If the differences between the two sides were narrow, the debate was hardly trivial. Precisely because of its avoidance (for the most part) of the militaristic anti-Communism of the Dulles era, the administration had created a favorable environment for its critics on the left. The administration's witnesses protested the charge that the administration was not pursuing settlement with sufficient vigor; they did not argue, as representatives of a Goldwater administration might have, that there could be no principled settlement with Communists. Likewise, Rusk, in particular, denied that the administration had a policy of fighting Communism everywhere, or regarded it as monolithic or always expansionist.

In general, with the administration's witnesses on the defensive, its critics were emboldened not only to oppose escalation of the war but the premise that the victory of Ho Chi Minh would necessarily be inimical to American interests. Going further, some Democratic critics, following the example of New Jersey Republican Clifford Case, even challenged the premise that the Cold War was in its essence a struggle of democracy against Communism. To be sure, the critics were limited by the perspective of their own elite position, their own fundamental loyalty to the structures that had given rise to the intervention in the first place. Nonetheless, following a pattern well known in history, the public airing of a debate within an elite created new opportunities for the growth of a mass movement with a radical leadership. Rather than co-opting the protests of the young radicals, the hearings helped to give their movement a new legitimacy and a heightened capacity to persuade other Americans of the righteousness of their cause.

II

The central concern expressed by the Democratic critics[13] was the prospect of a substantial and indefinite escalation of the war, a prospect that seemed all the more likely in the light of recent pronouncements by Senate hawks presumed to have especially close ties to the military.[14] The credibility of these ominous warnings was enhanced by disappointing reports from the battlefield. Rather than quieting Communist activity, the introduction of American forces had been met by an increase in Communist pressure. Instead of rapidly crushing the insurgency, the Americans faced a protracted struggle which, in the eyes of the Democratic critics, increasingly took on the appearance of a stalemate.[15]

To the extent that the Americans remained committed to defending the regime in Saigon and its enemies remained intransigent, these senators feared that the obvious response would be a further increase in the number of American troops. And yet past experience seemed to show that such an increase was more likely to lead to an open-ended spiral of escalation than to a decisive routing of the enemy.[16] Fulbright and Morse therefore confronted pro-administration witnesses with the excessively optimistic predictions they had made in the past and wondered aloud about how much credence should be given the administration's current projections.[17] Several senators wondered, moreover, if an escalation of U.S. involvement threatened to reduce further the role of the native South Vietnamese forces, the forces that President Kennedy in 1963 had declared were essential if the South Vietnamese government was to prevail. Indeed, Pennsylvania Democrat Joseph Clark inquired whether, in fact, the conflict had already become "an American war."[18]

In arguing for the poor prospects of military success the Democratic critics laid particular emphasis on the geography of Southeast Asia. Rhode Island Democrat Claiborne Pell stressed that Vietnam compared unfavorably with Korea, the Philippines, and Malaysia, because these other sites provided superior access from the sea and over land.[19] The particular difficulties of a strategy of sending soldiers into the jungle on offensive search-and-destroy operations was highlighted by Clark, who elicited testimony from Gavin on the general undesirability of such a strategy.[20] The same theme was pursued by Fulbright when he confronted Bell with Churchill's dictum that "going into the swampy jungles to fight the Japanese is like going into the water to fight a shark." Fulbright inquired of the witness whether he thought this simile was relevant "to our situation in the jungles of Vietnam."[21]

In more general terms, Fulbright tried to force Taylor to acknowledge a contradiction between the administration's intervention in Vietnam and the views of such "leading military men in our history" as Generals MacArthur, Eisenhower, and Bradley, all of whom "have stated at one time or another that we should never become involved in a major land war in Asia." More specifically, Fulbright and Church elicited testimony from Gavin on the report he had made to General Ridgway on the hazards of intervention in Indochina twelve years before, during the siege of Dien Bien Phu, hazards that he testified still existed. Fulbright also inserted into the record portions of Eisenhower's memoir, *Mandate for Change*, justifying his decision not to intervene in 1954 and actually read aloud (for the benefit of, among others, television viewers) extended excerpts from General Ridgway's memoir, *The Soldier*, explaining in even greater detail the disastrous military consequences that (in Ridgway's opinion) would have come of such an intervention. Fulbright further entered into the record Ridgway's endorsement of Gavin's testimony before the committee.[22]

The Democratic critics also made comments and posed questions that evinced considerable hostility toward nonmilitary aid to South Vietnam. Thus, they elicited testimony on allegations of corruption in the program, the profiteering of South Vietnamese officials and businessmen, and the questionable efficacy of funding an unpopular regime that was unwilling to conduct a meaningful land reform and implement other measures necessary to winning the allegiance of the South Vietnamese masses.[23] The critics also raised questions about the disruptive effects of the program on the South Vietnamese economy and its tendency to undermine the self-sufficiency of the country.[24]

More fundamentally, the Democratic critics suggested that the humanitarian component of the aid program was undermined by America's military policies. Whatever goodwill might be generated by assistance provided to refugees had to be evaluated in light of the degree to which the refugee problem itself was a consequence of American policy. "How many of them," demanded Morse, "became refugees as a result of Vietcong terrorism and how many of them became refugees as a result of the bombings, a scorched earth policy, napalm bombing, the poisoning of rice fields and other shocking actions of conducting the war?" A little later, when the AID administrator began to describe the achievements of the program in the South Vietnamese countryside, Clark intervened to ask, "How often after we make these improvements in agriculture do we go and bomb the rice field with napalm?" When, still later, the administrator blamed the lack of progress of the program on the terror campaign of the NLF, Pell requested the statistics on civilian casualties caused by both sides in the conflict. "It is equally unpleasant," observed Pell, "to be tortured, assassinated, or to be burned to death by napalm. But from the viewpoint of the impact on the country where . . . the democratic forces are naturally horrified at the assassination of city leaders and rural leaders and our allies, I wonder if that horror might not be more than balanced by the horror of those who are related or are friends of those who are killed by napalm or killed for military reasons."[25]

As disturbed as they were by American policy in South Vietnam, the Democratic critics' greatest fear was that escalation of the war above the seventeenth parallel would provoke a Chinese response with the potential of involving the United States and even the Soviet Union in a general war.[26] For Gore, it was precisely the dire prospect of such a conflict that justified the holding of hearings on Vietnam. Referring to "the imminent threat of nuclear war," he expressed regret that such hearings had not been held three years before.[27] At another point, Gore noted that, although "it was not within the power of Vietnam to bring about a third world war . . . we . . . may get into a position where unquestionably China could do so."[28] He even wondered whether the "unconditional surrender" of North Vietnam could by itself "break the plate glass window that would set off the alarms in the precipitation of a war with Russia or with China."[29]

Church, the member of the Foreign Relations Committee closest to Gore, was even more explicit in expressing his concerns about the danger of war with China. In response to his questions, Gavin said that war with China would require nuclear weapons and "the devastation would be beyond understanding." Church then proceeded to question the general on the size of the United States occupation force needed in the aftermath of a nuclear attack on China, eliciting his agreement that "at the most conservative guess" the campaign would require "many millions" of American soldiers on the Asian mainland.[30]

Pell pursued a similar line of questioning with Kennan, asking not only if Vietnam would lead to nuclear war with China but also whether the Soviet Union "will feel compelled to retaliate" if nuclear weapons were used. As likely sites of a nuclear exchange, Morse listed the cities of

Moscow, Stalingrad, New York, Chicago, and Washington. A week later, he dramatically referred to a private communication from the Soviet ambassador to the effect that Russia would "go to war against us" if the United States bombed Hanoi or Haiphong harbor. The ambassador had also told Morse that if America bombed China's nuclear installations, the Soviets would wage a war against the United States that "will not be fought in Asia alone."[31] To these ominous warnings, Morse himself reported that there were influential men in the U.S. armed forces who actually wanted a confrontation with China.[32]

Gore and Church, for their part, while not suggesting that any officers actually wanted a war with China, recalled MacArthur's prediction in 1950 that the Chinese would not respond if the Americans marched to the Yalu. And on the last day of the hearing, Fulbright told Rusk that he feared that the United States was seeking "victory" in Vietnam "even though that may result in bringing in the Chinese and possibly even the Russians, which would force World War III."[33]

III

The alternative to escalation with all its attendant dangers was, according to the Democratic critics, the reaching of a negotiated settlement. In theory this placed the critics in the same camp as the administration which itself had repeatedly proclaimed its interest in such a settlement and disclaimed the goal of a military solution. Indeed, during the recent suspension of the bombing, Ambassador Averell Harriman and others had toured the world all the while proclaiming their country's desire for peace and its readiness to reach a settlement with its Communist adversaries as soon as they ceased their "aggression."

The Senate critics, however, questioned the efficacy and even the sincerity of this public campaign. "To say we like peace, that we are peace-loving people, does not seem to mean much," said Fulbright. Real progress in achieving a settlement depended on "what you say privately to the people concerned, and how persuasive you are as to what you are willing to agree to." The only effective way to achieve peace was diplomacy "in the old-fashioned way" in which the opponent was approached "privately" and truly persuaded of America's readiness to abide by the result of a free election irrespective of its result.[34]

An authentic effort to achieve a compromise with the Vietnamese Communists would be "a major undertaking" and would require the Americans to show a heightened sensitivity to the skepticism of their adversary. The Communists, after all, had already been betrayed when, in violation of the Geneva Accords, Diem had refused to hold unification elections in 1956, a betrayal that along with the history of American intervention constituted "some very, very difficult historical facts" that placed a particularly high burden of persuasion on the United States in its effort to make the Communists believe it would actually adhere to a new compromise. The United States' claim to have no interest in staying in Vietnam seemed belied, moreover, by the extensive construction of bases and airfields there.[35]

At the core of the Communist disbelief in the American readiness to reach a good-faith settlement, according to the Democratic dissenters, was the United States' apparently unlimited and unconditional commitment to the regime in Saigon. The corollary of this commitment was a policy of relentlessly seeking the total capitulation of the regime's opponents, a policy which by its very nature precluded dialogue and negotiation. According to Gore, such a policy amounted to an effort "to exterminate the Communists." With only slight equivocations, pro-administration witnesses seemed to concede this point. Taylor, for example, denied even a scintilla of legitimacy to the Communist cause, likening it to that of "a criminal." According to Taylor, the United States had not set the goal for itself of "literally exterminating" the National Liberation Front but did seek "to have them so beaten that they would be glad to have an amnesty." As for Rusk, a compromise that contemplated anything other than an anti-Communist regime was nothing more than the surrender of "the freedom of 15 million Vietnamese."[36]

It was this actual policy of insisting on surrender (contrary to the claimed policy of seeking compromise) that accounted for the intransigence of the guerillas. "I think there is something wrong with our approach," Fulbright told Rusk. "Let's assume," he continued, "these people [the Vietnamese Communists] are utter idiots. There [still] must be something wrong with our diplomacy." Otherwise it was impossible to understand why these "primitive, difficult, poor people who have been fighting for 20 years" persisted in their struggle. "I am frank to say it puzzles me, why people [i.e. the enemy] are not more reasonable, more rational under these circumstances.

There must be some explanation, unless we just assume that the world has gone completely mad."[37]

Even as the hearings took place, the president was giving new evidence of an inflexibility that would reduce the chances of a negotiated settlement. Traveling to Honolulu to meet with the South Vietnamese president and premier, Johnson issued a ringing declaration of support to their regime and the cause of vanquishing its enemies. After reading press coverage, including a critical Walter Lippmann column, Fulbright and Morse, in turn, despaired that yet higher barriers were being erected now that would prevent any resolution of the conflict short of a crushing military defeat of the Vietnamese Communists, a prospect that seemed unlikely in the absence of an escalation of such magnitude that it could provoke a Chinese intervention.[38] The Honolulu declarations, moreover, seemed to make the United States a hostage of its South Vietnamese client's desires. When the point was raised with Kennan, he observed that "they have their own axes to grind," which were "not entirely the same as ours." Indeed the Honolulu declarations gave Kennan "a very, very uneasy feeling."[39]

Instead of entangling itself ever more tightly in an alliance with Saigon, the Democratic critics proposed that the United States take steps to involve as many other countries as possible in promoting a reconciliation between all the warring factions. On this point no senator was more emphatic and more concrete than Morse. "We have reached a point," the Oregonian explained to Rusk, "where this conflict can never be solved bilaterally between the United States, the Vietcong, and the North Vietnamese." Morse was therefore "pleading for us to use our great influence" to get other countries involved. To enlist "80 or 85 countries" in an effort to settle the conflict, Morse advocated the intervention of the United Nations. The starting point would be to bring the matter before the Security Council, but if it refused to take action, the General Assembly could then be convened. According to Morse, the potential for such a strategy to succeed had already been demonstrated by U.N. peacekeeping actions in other parts of the world, including interventions that had enjoyed the cooperation of the Soviet Union. Although self-determination might not be practicable in the near future in South Vietnam, Morse believed that at least the fighting could be halted, preferably under a "protectorate" or "trusteeship" that would last from five to ten years.[40]

The other Democratic critics were less specific about the mechanisms that might bring about a settlement, although virtually all of them advocated some form of international conference that—through the involvement of other countries—would tend to depolarize the conflict. Irrespective of the actions of other countries, the critics wanted the United States to avoid substantial escalation of the war and actively promote the resolution of the conflict through negotiations between all the concerned parties. Although the critics refused to describe concretely the steps that might lead to such a result, they indicated their support for a popular election to determine the future of South Vietnam. And, although the critics were reticent about predicting the outcome of such an election, they clearly implied that, irrespective of its outcome, such an election could provide an honorable basis for the withdrawal of the United States from Vietnam.[41]

IV

The different positions on negotiations of the administration and its Democratic critics point to one of the most substantial differences between them: the critics, unlike the administration, were willing to accept the communization of South Vietnam. Underlying this difference were widely divergent assessments of the stakes in Vietnam and, more generally, the priorities and principles that should guide American foreign policy.

Pell and Fulbright were perhaps the most forthright in raising the possibility that a Communist Vietnam would not necessarily be inimical to America's interests. Pell asked Gavin to speculate about whether in the future Vietnam might be united under a nationalist Communist regime led by Ho Chi Minh that would be a counterweight to Chinese power in a manner comparable to Tito's opposition to Moscow. Although Gavin declined to predict how Ho might behave in the future, he took the occasion to praise the Yugoslavian government and declare that "the best thing we ever did was to allow that government to come into being and demonstrate that this man could bring into being an independent government of his own free of Stalin, and defying him." Pell asked a similar question of Kennan. The former ambassador indicated that he was "puzzled" about different things he read about Vietnamese identity, but noted that he suspected "that these people think of themselves as quite different from Chinese, and there are strong nationalist streaks in their outlook."[42]

Fulbright broached this issue with a quotation from Kennan, in which he had predicted that "there is every likelihood that a Communist regime in South Vietnam would follow a fairly independent course." He then elicited lengthy testimony from the former ambassador on the importance of not having excessive fear of a regime simply because its leaders call themselves Communists. To this Fulbright commented that a settlement that gave power to the Vietnamese Communists would be undesirable "in the sense that [it would not] be perfection and exactly like we would like it" but that it would nonetheless be "tolerable."[43]

In a colloquy with Taylor, Fulbright further suggested the acceptability, though not the desirability, of a Communist Vietnam. In response to the general's argument that, since the war was being fought to determine whether the South Vietnamese would be "either free or not free," morality forbade a compromise that conceded power to the Communists. Fulbright argued that the logic of Taylor's position would require the United States to fight Communism everywhere it held power: "You can extend that reasoning and say, 'How do you compromise the freedom of 250 million Russians?' Why don't we go over there and free them?" Indeed, if American policy were to be guided by Taylor's principles, the United States would be equally compelled to fight Yugoslavia. After all, Taylor had been "talking about communism," and the government in Belgrade was no less Communist than that in Moscow. And even more directly, Fulbright told Rusk, "If they [the Vietnamese] want to be Communists, just like the Yugoslavs, I do not know why we should object to it."[44]

In the view of Fulbright and several other senators, the concept that Communism was the enemy and that American policy should be devoted to its eradication had played a pernicious role in causing the United States to intervene in Vietnam. In a remarkable exchange with Bell, Fulbright challenged the very notion of a foreign policy guided by the juxtaposed semantic abstractions of "freedom" and "Communism."

> FULBRIGHT: I always thought Communism was rather an abstraction. [If the United States invaded Brazil], wouldn't they be justified in saying this was an invasion of capitalism, or would you say it is an invasion of Americans?

BELL: Well, I do not think, sir, that communism—

FULBRIGHT: I am getting at the semantics.

BELL: I do not think communism and capitalism are that easily related in a semantic sense. I think they are quite different notions.

FULBRIGHT: What is a better word than capitalism? Freedom invades Brazil? This use of language confuses me.

Such "abstract terms," according to Fulbright, were "appropriate for some philosophical dissertation but not for describing actual combat such as that going on in Vietnam."[45]

Instead of a policy guided by opposition to all movements and governments bearing the abstract title "Communist," Fulbright urged an acknowledgment of the great differences among Communists, including the existence of Communists who, like the Yugoslavs, "are not participating in any aggression." Instead of a policy based on the moral opposition of universal categories, American policy in Southeast Asia should be seen "not purely from a moral standpoint, but from a practical one of what can be achieved." And it should be a policy that acknowledged "great differences in the culture and the race and language and so on between this area and other areas where we have become involved."[46]

Pell and Church joined Fulbright in his rejection of anti-Communism as a guiding principle for American policy in the region. For Pell there was simply no such thing as "the international Communist apparatus," referred to by Bell. Church was emphatic that the United States not seek "the suppression of communism in southeast Asia." The economic or political system of South Vietnam was less important than the need to contain China as a great power irrespective of the ideology it professed or the color of its flag. A policy based on the moral opposition of freedom to Communism was particularly absurd in Asia and Africa, continents whose peoples did not share with the United States "a common civilization and commonly held attitudes against communism."[47]

Supplementing Fulbright, Pell, and Church's argument that a Communist but independent Vietnam might not be inimical to American interests, the Democratic critics advanced (or elicited from witnesses) other arguments that challenged the notion that a Communist triumph in Vietnam necessarily would be a disaster. Fulbright asserted that such was the extent of American power and prestige that its credibility would be only temporarily damaged by withdrawal from Vietnam.[48] Indeed, some senators suggested that the war was so unpopular among America's allies—particularly those in Asia—that a withdrawal would actually lead to a net increase in the international stature of the United States.[49] And Church bluntly argued, as he had in the past, that the region was of little strategic and economic importance compared to Europe. The implication was that its loss even to a hostile regime should matter little to the United States.[50]

In more general terms, several senators questioned whether the American interest in South Vietnam was so great as to justify the costs of the war. "Viewing Vietnam in light of our global commitments, and our national capability," declared Clark, "the military realities there today are such that the cost in casualties and money of crushing the enemy, retaking the lost real estate, and pacifying the country are too high to be acceptable." Fulbright elicited agreement from Kennan with General Ridgway's view that although "victory might be achieved in Vietnam," the costs of such a victory "would be completely out of proportion to what could be gained by such an activity." Pell and Gore also asked whether Vietnam rose to the level of being a "vital" national interest." Similarly, Gore asked whether "America's vital interests are necessarily involved in Vietnam."[51]

V

With the conspicuous exception of Morse, the record is bereft of comments or questions from the Democratic critics evincing strong condemnation of American policy for being either illegal or immoral. Rather than explicitly invoking law or morality to attack the intervention in Vietnam, the critics typically posed as opponents of (what seemed to them) the misguided legalism and moralism of the administration and its supporters. While not themselves clearly condemning the administration's actions on such grounds, the Democratic critics posed questions calculated to expose ambiguities in the facts and relevant law, and to explain the paucity of support for the American intervention even among the South Vietnamese.

Whereas the administration defended its policies as an effort to repulse the illegal "aggression" of North Vietnam against its southern neighbor, Church and Fulbright pointed out that in the eyes of many it was the United States that was the outside intruder. While acknowledging that "our purposes there are very different from what the French purposes were," Church wondered whether the Vietnamese peasants were "apt to make a distinction between an American uniform or a French." Church was worried that "by transporting Westerners halfway around the globe to fight against Asians in Asia," the United States might "end up making Ho Chi Minh an Asian hero." As a consequence the Americans would "give added momentum to communism," something Church would "hate to see."[52]

Fulbright also emphasized the widespread perception that the war was a struggle of the Vietnamese against Western domination rather than an effort of the South Vietnamese to repulse aggression from Hanoi. After all, the war "clearly began as a war of liberation from French colonial rule," dating from "the time when indigenous Vietnamese nationalists" united in opposition to French imperialism, "most unfortunately from our point of view," under the leadership of Ho Chi Minh and the Communists. This choice of leadership made it no less a national liberation struggle than the American Revolution of 1776, a point that Fulbright, through leading questions, forced Taylor to concede. The Americans, moreover, were hardly in a position to assume an attitude of moral purity, having supplied the French with $2 billion to defeat this independence movement. After the defeat of the French, Fulbright reminded the witness, the United States continued to play a role that opposed the self-determination of the Vietnamese. Rather than facilitate compliance with the Geneva Accords, the United States actually encouraged Diem to undermine the agreement by failing to comply with its requirement that national unification elections be held in 1956. Like the French who had used Bao Dai as a puppet, the United States during this period sought to impose its will on Vietnam through Diem, a man Fulbright contemptuously referred to as "our boy."[53]

The widespread Vietnamese identification of the Americans with colonialism, and Ho Chi Minh with national liberation, persisted in the post-Diem period. Eliciting with a leading question the admission that the current regime in Saigon was "completely dependent" on American support, Church cross-examined Taylor to force him to concede that the regime did not enjoy "widespread support from the people in the countryside." By contrast, as Taylor also conceded, the Communist cause in Vietnam continued to receive great strength from "the prestige, the nationalist prestige that Ho Chi Minh won as the leader of the revolution in driving out the French." In fact, as Fulbright pointed out to Rusk, in the eyes of the

Vietnamese, the Americans were "obviously intruders" and represented "the old Western imperialism."[54]

The Vietnamese and the Communists, according to Fulbright, were not the only ones who did not share the American characterization of the war as "a clear case of international Communist aggression." Pointing to the failure of the members of the Southeast Asia Treaty Organization to give substantial support to the American intervention, Fulbright opined that this failure—particularly on the part of SEATO's Asian members—could only be explained by their view that the war "was more in the nature of a civil war in which outside parties have become involved." In fact, this view had substantial validity since notwithstanding the administration's characterization of the North Vietnamese as "foreign" invaders, the Geneva Accords, as Rusk conceded under the chairman's cross-examination, had explicitly described the seventeenth parallel as but a temporary division not giving rise to separate nations. Indeed, as Fulbright explained to Taylor, the Vietnamese war "was a war between North and South Vietnam very much, I suppose, like our war between North and South."[55]

When pro-administration senators pointed to Communist atrocities, the critics were quick to decry this effort to undermine a rational discussion of the war through what Church called "the use of such vague and highly emotional terms." After all, "war was a brutal business on all sides." Likewise, Gore, referring to his two grandfathers who fought for the South in the Civil War, emphasized that in his region it was known that "war is hell" with "brutalities on both sides," and that this was "the nature of things when men are fighting to kill each other." Pell took a similar position, questioning whether it mattered to the South Vietnamese if they or their loved ones were "horribly murdered" by the Communists or killed by American "napalm bombing, or some other way." Irrespective of the weapon the result was that "you are just dead." The interjection into the debate of atrocity stories did nothing to help the discussion, Fulbright declared, but "is the kind of inflammatory line which discourages the utilization of whatever little reason we have left."[56]

Fulbright was particularly opposed to the belief in American innocence and moral superiority that seemed to underlie this "inflammatory line." At length Fulbright interrogated Taylor in particular on the actual conduct of America in wars past and present:

Can you imagine in your wildest dreams of a Secretary of the Air Force agreeing to napalm a great city, perhaps a great city like Tokyo, with millions of innocent pure children who love their mothers, and mothers who love their children—just like you love your son—resulting in the death of thousands of people who never did us any harm? Can you imagine any Secretary of the Air Force or any President ordering the burning of these little children right before the eyes of their mothers? . . .

What difference, really morally or any other way do you see between burning innocent little children and [as had been alleged about the Vietnamese Communists] disemboweling innocent citizens? Isn't it only the means you use? . . .

The only implication of this question is that we sometimes think we are the only good people, and I certainly don't think we are a bad people. But I don't see any great distinction between using the weapons we happen to have, and others don't, to kill innocent people . . . such as burning by napalm and the disemboweling with a knife because a knife is all you happen to have.

When Taylor protested that, unlike the Communists, "we are not deliberately attacking civilian populations in South Vietnam," Fulbright replied that "we deliberately drop napalm bombs on villages" and that "it is not by accident that we are doing this."[57]

The comments and questions of Fulbright were tame compared to those of Morse. Trying to impose the discipline of a courtroom cross-examination, Morse pursued and repeatedly trapped pro-administration witnesses with questions on the entire history of U.S. involvement in Southeast Asia, an involvement which already "in 1954, 1955, and 1956 paved the way for the shocking catastrophe that is taking place in Vietnam today."[58] Emphasizing the "sad, sordid record in regard to our alleged support for freedom in South Vietnam," he managed to force admissions or evasions from witnesses that called into question the administration's claim that all immorality and illegality rested on the side of the Communists. Not permitting the witnesses to speak in generalities, Morse created an impression of governmental malfeasance (if not criminality) as he forced them to retreat (or take evasive action) before his questions concerning U.S. compliance with specific provision of the Geneva Accords, the U.N.

Charter, and the SEATO Treaty. Although Fulbright and other Democratic critics (with the partial exception of Gore) refrained from explicitly endorsing these arguments, they also refrained from expressing any opposition to them. Fulbright, moreover, may have added to Morse's prestige by his own respectful references to him during the hearings and by permitting him to substitute as chairman immediately after the lunch recess and immediately before adjournment during the first day of televised hearings. Certainly the administration could have felt little comfort when, in response to Rusk's arguments in support of the legality of American intervention, Fulbright responded, "Mr. Secretary, I wish these things appeared as simple to me as they do to you."[59]

VI

Although Fulbright and other Democratic critics evinced no desire to follow Morse's example and confront the administration in the manner of prosecutors, they did express agreement with Morse on the need to reform American foreign policy and not embark on unilateral actions like that in Vietnam. Echoing Morse's opposition to the United States acting as "the enforcers and policemen of the world," Fulbright asserted that America should "insofar as possible" not take upon itself "the role of world policeman," while Church indicated his opposition to a foreign policy that would "cast ourselves in the role of sentinel for the status quo in the world." Instead of seeking to impose what Fulbright called a "Pax Americana," Gore called for a return to the "principles of collective security to which we committed ourselves in the United Nations Charter." Similarly, Fulbright called for a foreign policy that emphasized "the United Nations and collective security," a policy on which "the Senator from Oregon [Morse] in particular has insisted for a long time" in "finding a solution to the Vietnam problem."[60]

Behind the Democratic critics' opposition to a Pax Americana rested several concerns that were heightened by the escalating conflict in Vietnam. These included anxiety about America's international image, especially in Asia, Africa, and Latin America;[61] doubts about the efficacy of unilateral action in actually containing Communism;[62] fear that such a policy would lead to an imbalance in the allocation of resources abroad and at home;[63] and a concern with the enormous costs of such a policy.[64] Their greatest worry, however, was that this policy of unilaterally suppressing Communist insurgencies—particularly as it was carried out in Vietnam—prevented the United States from addressing the urgent need to improve relations among the superpowers.

Gore and Clark gave particular attention to this concern in their examinations of Kennan. Responding to questions that corresponded to arguments he had made in a speech at Princeton exactly one year before, Kennan testified that the escalation of the war had, as he had predicted, brought to a halt the once-promising movement toward détente between the United States and the Soviet Union. Just as he had predicted at Princeton, the escalation had led the Soviet leadership "to come down strongly against us and to enter into a sort of competition with the Chinese to see who could look most critical of our policies, most dedicated and violent in their defense of the Vietcong." As the Soviets sought to compete with the Chinese in the contest "to see who can look the most anti-American" and "who can appear to be the most violent defender of what they call the national liberation movements," it became impossible for the Soviets and Americans to give constructive attention to a series of problems that were "more important" than Vietnam: disarmament, nuclear weapon proliferation, and Germany, whose division remained "the most important specific political geographic problem of the world."[65]

Kennan expressed agreement with Clark when the senator declared that "the major thrust of our American foreign policy today should be the most difficult task of arriving at an overall détente with the Soviet Union in the interests of world peace." He further agreed that sufficient commonality of interests existed between the two countries as to make it possible "with very skillful diplomacy" for such a détente to be achieved and problems like Germany and nuclear proliferation solved. After all, the Russian people and their leaders "need both peace and reasonably good relations with Western countries almost as much as we need the same from them." Fortunately, the general trend, according to Kennan, was toward a significant improvement in U.S.-Soviet relations since the "days when the so-called containment policy was formed." This progress could not continue, however, until there was "some sort of resolution of the Vietnam conflict."[66]

A few senators offered a similar perspective on the potential for normal relations with China. At the root of the administration's intervention in

Vietnam, according to Fulbright, was the belief that the Communist insurgency there was ultimately an expression of Chinese expansionism. Fulbright rejected this as a false premise, repeatedly making comments and eliciting testimony calculated to show that China—both before and after its revolution—was essentially not an aggressive nation. Indeed, according to Fulbright, it was China that had historically been the victim of foreign aggression, particularly that of the Western imperialists. The escalation of American involvement in Vietnam and other actions by the United States in the vicinity of China's borders, however, had led China to feel insecure and "encircled." As a consequence, the rhetoric of the Chinese had recently become increasingly bellicose, and the danger did, in fact, exist that the Chinese might be provoked to take military action in the region, the very danger that American intervention had been supposed to prevent.[67]

Rather than pursue such a counterproductive policy, Fulbright thought the United States would be better served by seeking détente with China. Pointing to the positive evolution of U.S.-Soviet relations prior to the Vietnam crisis, Clark elicited testimony confirming the thesis that "in due course" China could arrive "at a détente or an adjustment with us." Church, for his part, speculated on the possibility that the "awful prospect" of nuclear war that had compelled the Soviet and American leaders to seek accommodation would induce the Chinese to follow suit. Church believed that the perspective of China's leaders would begin to change when they began "to fully appreciate the totality of destruction that will be visited upon China in the event of nuclear war." The development of better relations with China would not, however, be facilitated by American saber rattling, but through the normalization of relations as had been done with the Soviet Union. "In fact," as Morse reminded his colleagues, the existence of normal diplomatic relations with the Soviet Union "may well have been the primary reason" that at the time of the Cuban missile crisis the world was not "thrown into a holocaust." In response to a question from Clark, Kennan speculated that the day would arrive when a "new generation of Chinese leaders will come" who might be amenable to détente with the United States. For that day to come, American leaders would do well to "look back over the history of international affairs," a history that showed that "the counsels of patience and restraint have been more effective, as a general rule, than the counsels of violence and particularly the unleashing of unlimited violence."[68]

CHAPTER 6

1966: The Hearings:
The President's Friends,
the President's Enemies

Within the hearing room, the administration was at a disadvantage. Its critics outnumbered its defenders. Its defenders, moreover, had poor attendance, were relatively marginal members of the committee, and, unlike the critics, failed to present a coherent line. Thomas Dodd of Connecticut was a rigid cold warrior, an uncritical admirer of Diem, and an opponent of any settlement with the Communists in Vietnam or elsewhere. Stuart Symington of Missouri, a strong advocate of the air force, seemed at times more interested in promoting an expansion of the bombing than in defending the administration's chosen policies. Frank Lausche of Ohio, twenty years before described by John Gunther as having "a disinclination to think abstractly," as "a man of emotion, not of mind," and as "little more than a child as regards foreign policy,"[1] at the time of the hearings seemed capable of doing little more than retelling Communist atrocity stories. And the two southerners, John Sparkman of Alabama and Russell Long of Louisiana—one the son of a tenant farmer, the other of Huey Long, a governor and senator—had little interest in foreign affairs and did little (even when they did attend the hearings) to advance the president's cause.

Whatever hope the administration's supporters might have had of equalizing the relationship of forces within the committee room rested with the Republicans, almost all of whom were at least nominally supportive of the war. Rather than seeing the hearings as an opportunity to form a bipartisan front in time of war, however, the Republicans preferred to voice hawkish criticism of the administration, to dwell on the lack of allied support for the war, to inquire about corruption and waste in the aid program, to emphasize the differences between Eisenhower's policies and those of his Democratic successors, and to describe the theater in which the administration had chosen to commit American lives as "quicksand."[2]

Thus the hearings, as much because of the refusal of the Republicans to abandon their partisan identity as that of the failure of the Democrats to adhere to their own, were dominated by senators hostile to the policies of their president.

I

Perhaps the most valuable service the Democratic defenders rendered to the White House was their effective neutralization of General Gavin, one of the two witnesses who had been expected to offer testimony damaging to the administration. To the disappointment of the Democratic critics, the general proved remarkably pliable under cross-examination. In implicit repudiation of his letter to *Harper's,* Gavin denied that he favored a strategic retreat of American forces into South Vietnam's coastal enclaves or even an end to the bombing. Although opposing an increase in the number of soldiers sent to Vietnam, he did not oppose their entry into the jungle in search of the enemy. Nor did he even oppose some expansion of the air war so long as the bombing was restricted to military targets.[3]

In addition, the administration's supporters delivered short speeches and elicited testimony (especially from pro-administration witnesses) supporting the morality, the legality, and the strategic wisdom of the intervention. Decrying the "effort by innuendo and adroit reasoning to imply that our government is the exploiter," Lausche elicited testimony that it was the Communists who were guilty of aggression and who sought to impose their oppressive rule on the people of South Vietnam. Similarly, Sparkman elicited testimony from Taylor and Rusk that the United States was not intervening in a civil war but rather responding to the call of an ally faced with foreign invasion. Accordingly, Long thought the American intervention was entirely legal pursuant to the SEATO Treaty and under article 51 of the U.N. Charter (right to self-defense). It had been under their authority that Congress had approved the Gulf of Tonkin Resolution, thereby making a "commitment to go to the aid of those countries that are being murdered and killed by Communist aggressors." Likewise, the argument that the United States had violated the Geneva accords was unsustainable because the Communists themselves had been the first to violate them. In any case, it was absurd to insist that the United States adhere strictly to the letter of the law when faced with such a ruthless enemy. "Don't you think," Long asked Taylor, "it would be rather foolish to take on a Communist adversary who is bent on destroying you, and fight him by the Queensberry rules while he is fighting you by the law of nail and clawing out your eyeballs and punching you beneath the belt?"[4]

The administration's supporters gave great emphasis to atrocities committed by the Communists. Referring to tens of thousands of deaths from "guerilla tortures," decapitations, disembowelments, hacking children with knives, and other forms of terror, the senators urged witnesses to reject the notion that the United States and its adversary were morally equivalent.[5] "Would you be willing to make the unqualified statement," queried Long of Taylor, "that you just think our people are just better and more honorable and more moral people than the Communists?" Similarly, after telling of an instance in which the Vietcong disemboweled, before an assembled village, each member of its chief's family, including four children, Symington asked Taylor whether he could imagine in his "wildest dreams, any group of Americans pulling a stunt like that?"[6]

Long was particularly incensed at what he considered to be Fulbright's theory "that the atrocities these people commit in the last analysis are not much different than the things our people have done themselves." Citing a range of historical precedents including the bombing of Hiroshima, Long posed leading questions to confirm that when Americans "killed women and children" it was always as an "unavoidable" and unintended consequence of attacking a military target and enemy combatants. Unlike their adversaries, Americans "were playing by the rules of the game." Indeed, the United States had been guilty of excessive humanitarianism in battle, to the point that in order to minimize civilian casualties it had often jeopardized its military effectiveness. In more general terms, Dodd addressed "the tendency on the part of many people to equate the [American] position with that of the forces of aggressive communism." This was "a basic error" that overlooked what "seems so clear in logic and in historical fact that we are not an aggressive power, that every action we have taken has been a defensive one, a reaction to an aggressive act."[7]

The administration's supporters laid great stress on the consequences of a Communist victory. Dodd predicted that should such a victory take place "[a] terrible blood bath will ensue." Prompted by Dodd, Taylor ominously confessed that "it is very hard to visualize what might be the losses in terms of lives, murders committed on the part of the Communists," but that he thought "Hungary would look like a very mild affair compared to what would take place." Symington was more specific, describing the blood bath as one in which "the Vietcong would put hundreds of thousands of Vietnamese to the sword."[8]

Even worse than the suffering in South Vietnam would be the effect of such a debacle on the plight of other countries. Predicting that the triumph of Communism in Vietnam would bolster the cause of Communism elsewhere, pro-administration senators predicted or elicited testimony predicting new Communist threats in Thailand, Burma, Africa, Latin America, Mid-America, all countries bordering on China and the Soviet Union, and then the next tier of countries.[9] Indeed there was no ultimate limit to where the struggle might have to take place if Vietnam fell. If the United States did not resist Communism in Vietnam, asked Lausche, "Where do we take our stand? Is it on the shores of California or Hawaii . . . ?"[10]

Closely related to this fear of an increased threat of Communist expansion was a concern with the damage to American credibility that would ensue if the United States withdrew from Vietnam. Symington was particularly emphatic on this point, eliciting agreement from Taylor and Rusk that if the United States left Vietnam "on other than an honorable basis . . . all people everywhere will never believe the United States is serious in defending its friends and allies in accordance with either treaties or agreements." In fact, Symington had heard from an unnamed person "high in Government best able to comment" that if the United States so much as recognized the NLF the "Saigon government would promptly fall" and "within a relatively short time there would be riots in West Berlin." Responding to Symington, Rusk confirmed Symington's general concern (without addressing the specific predictions about Saigon and Berlin) and added the further fear that allies who had lost faith in the United States might "persuade the Communist world that these commitments of ours are not serious," a prospect that would be "extremely dangerous."[11]

In contrast to the grave consequences that would result from American withdrawal and Communist victory, the pro-administration senators elicited testimony tending to give a buoyant account of the achievements of the American forces and their allies.[12] Looking to the future, they elicited testimony giving an optimistic cast to the course the war was likely to take if the United States persisted in its present policies. Likewise, they elicited testimony that minimized the risk that American policy would provoke the intervention of China.[13] They also elicited testimony that emphasized the policy's reasonableness, attributing the continuation of the war solely to the intransigence of the Communists.[14] Finally, Symington condemned the administration's critics for showing an insufficient concern for the safety of the American soldiers,[15] for indifference toward the welfare of the South Vietnamese, and, on the whole, for advocating an approach to foreign policy that amounted to conceding "spheres of interest" rather than insisting on the self-determination of all nations, great and small.[16]

For several reasons, the pro-administration senators seem to have had only a very limited success in impeding the Democratic critics. Not the least of these was their poor attendance, which inevitably gave their critics more weight than their numbers would have ordinarily commanded. As the first hearing commenced—amid all the excitement and publicity caused by simultaneous coverage on the national television networks—three of the five supporters of the administration were absent: Long, Symington, and Dodd. Of the two present, one, Sparkman, yielded a substantial part of his time to Delaware Republican John Williams, who had a history of hostility to Johnson dating at least as far back as the Bobby Baker scandal. Predictably Williams used Sparkman's time to elicit testimony damaging to the administration. Later, when Williams own turn came, Sparkman graciously refused his offer to reciprocate.[17] By the beginning of the afternoon session (with television cameras still rolling), Sparkman absented himself completely, leaving (due to Fulbright's late return) Morse, who followed Sparkman in seniority, as the acting chairman. Attendance improved for the second session with General Gavin at the witness table. Only Long was absent for the entire hearing. However, Dodd and Sparkman each participated in only one of the two available rounds of interrogation. For the third session, with Kennan at the witness table, attendance fell once again with two pro-administration senators absenting themselves entirely—Dodd and Long—and two others—Lausche and Sparkman—passing up their opportunity to participate in a second round of questioning. All of the administration's supporters were present at the opening of the fourth hearing with General

Taylor at the witness table. As the hearing progressed, however, they began to melt away. By the second round, Dodd and Lausche were missing and by the third, Sparkman had also absented himself. Finally, with Rusk on the stand for the fifth hearing, Lausche was entirely absent while Sparkman, Long, and Dodd limited their participation to the first round.

Even when these senators were in attendance, their performance was not always helpful to the administration. The two southerners, Long and Sparkman, were hardly equal to the task of posing as "true believers" in a crusade for freedom in Southeast Asia. Despite his energetic marshaling of Communist atrocity stories, at one point Long complained that he "wasn't advised about sending those boys [to Vietnam]" and that had he been asked his opinion prior to the signing of the SEATO Treaty, "I would say I just prefer to keep our boys here." Similarly, Sparkman, after eliciting Kennan's testimony opposing interventions like that in Vietnam, tacitly conceded the correctness of Kennan's fundamental analysis while asserting it was simply too late for the country to change course.[18] Sparkman also undermined the administration by refusing to act as its advocate. Instead of posing leading or argumentative questions to witnesses opposed to the administration, he asked them open questions, thus exempting them from hostile interrogation and, in effect, giving them a platform to expound their views without hindrance.

More commonly, these senators betrayed the administration by momentarily joining the ranks of its hawkish critics. Symington was undoubtedly the worst in this regard. Repeatedly, while ostensibly defending the administration from dovish criticism of the bombing, he actually made comments and elicited testimony calculated to favor an escalation of the air war beyond the limits the administration had placed on it.[19] At one point, he even emotionally referred to a pilot who was "willing to risk his life for his country, but [who] didn't see why he should risk it a couple of times a week bombing targets that would not even have been looked at in Korea; bombing empty barracks or a bus, risking lives in a $2 million airplane bombing targets . . . of relatively little importance."[20] Dodd and Long were less brazen in their hawkishness, but they also, at moments, seemed to pose questions tending to undermine confidence in the restraints the administration had placed in its conduct of the war. Referring to questions he received from "American mothers in my state" about the American policy of not impeding Soviet ships entering Haiphong harbor, Dodd asked, "What do I say to a mother who has a boy in Vietnam when she says to me, 'Senator, I understand that . . . the Soviet Union is shipping oil into Haiphong to supply tanks, guns, or trucks, or whatever oil is needed for. Why don't we stop it?'"[21] And the next day, Long, in a manner better calculated to ingratiate himself with flag-waving constituents than inspire trust in the administration, implored Rusk if he was "going to send these boys," not to "send them over there with their hands tied behind them."[22]

The effectiveness of the administration's supporters was limited in other respects. Within the Foreign Relations Committee, they were relatively marginal figures with little likelihood of commanding attention from other committee members. For the same reason, with the exception of Symington—who held an important position in the Armed Services Committee and had been Truman's secretary of the air force—their views on foreign policy probably received little attention within the Senate as a whole, a body whose members tended to defer to the chairmen of committees and their core memberships.[23] They also, again with the exception of Symington, were not men of backgrounds and connections likely to influence members of the foreign policy elite (and, in turn, members of the broader public under its influence). Nor were they even, once again with the exception of Symington, especially attractive or "telegenic" men who were likely to appeal to the great mass of daytime television viewers.[24] Moreover, two of the pro-administration members—Lausche and Long—by on several occasions attempting to speak out of turn and being confrontational, acted in a manner likely to alienate those who viewed the hearings on television, a "cool medium," which by its nature tends to render ridiculous those who behave in a "heated" fashion.[25] Finally, the record reveals a remarkable lack of discipline and coordination among the administration supporters, and an absence of any effort, on their part, to ally themselves with the one force which could have conceivably tipped the balance of the Foreign Relations Committee against the Democratic critics: the six committee Republicans.[26]

II

Taking at face value their professed support of the general objectives of the war, the committee Republicans[27]—with the idiosyncratic exception of Aiken[28]—might have been expected to ally themselves with the pro-administration Democrats. A perusal of the transcript of the hearings suggests, however, that the Republicans did much more to hurt than help the administration. Although the Republicans did elicit some testimony that helped the president's case, the great majority of their questions were about matters that the administration was hardly eager to discuss—least of all on national television. Moreover, the general tone of their inquiry evinced a hostility toward the administration that could hardly have been calculated to inspire enthusiastic support for the war among their constituents. As a consequence, those who viewed the hearings were likely to conclude that the areas that united the Republicans with the administration were less important than those that divided them.

As they had during the time of Truman and the Korean War, the Republicans accused the administration of lacking clear goals or a coherent strategy. And as during that earlier conflict, the Republicans showed a capacity to move easily between hawkish and dovish positions, all the while attacking the administration for its lack of clarity. The ranking Republican, Bourke Hickenlooper of Iowa, for example, echoed liberal critics of the intervention when he likened the American position in Vietnam to "a person who gets into some quicksand." The main thrust of Hickenlooper's comments, however, was decidedly hawkish as he described the administration's goals as "nebulous" and the only real alternatives for the United States as the pursuit of victory or withdrawal, the latter representing "the line of defeat." Karl Mundt of South Dakota, on the other hand, violently berated an administration witness for failing to include among the goals of the intervention the achievement of world peace, an omission which he described as "a shocking thing." Mundt's own strategic recommendations, however, amounted to a call for stepped-up military intervention.[29]

The Republicans reserved some of their greatest hostility for the non-military aspects of the president's appropriation. Drawing on traditional Republican themes, the senators concentrated on such problems as waste and corruption in the program,[30] its cost to the American taxpayer,[31] its tendency to undermine the self-sufficiency of the South Vietnamese,[32] and its inflationary effect on the South Vietnamese economy.[33] Concern was also expressed about a lack of candor in the projected size of the budget and—particularly by Aiken—on the failure of the government to make available its own investigations into alleged corruption in the program.[34]

Rather than funding a wasteful and inefficient welfare program for Vietnam, Hickenlooper emphasized the need for decisive military action against the Communists. Indeed, the South Dakotan, in an exchange with the administrator of AID, seemed to imply that the Americans should adopt what the senator saw as the militarized approach of their Communist opponents:

> HICKENLOOPER: How do you account for the fact that the Vietcong seem to be quite successful in the countryside and seem to be able to at least secure the passive assistance if not the full assistance of the South Vietnamese living in the countryside if they haven't been helping them any at all, while we have been pouring all this money into that economy?
>
> BELL: The principal reason for Vietcong and North Vietnamese success in the countryside is simple terror. They do it with a gun, Senator, not with aid. . . .
>
> HICKENLOOPER: It is cheaper that way, isn't it?[35]

As had been the case during the MacArthur hearings, the Republicans gave considerable time to criticizing America's ostensible allies, particularly Britain, whose ships continued to trade with the enemy. Williams was particularly incensed at Britain's behavior in light of its insistence that the United States respect its embargo against Rhodesia.[36] More commonly, senators criticized Britain as well as other countries for failing to carry their share of the burden in the actual fighting. Unlike the Democratic critics, who typically argued that this failure was symptomatic of the underlying weakness of the American case for intervention, the Republicans saw the failure as a consequence of the administration's unwillingness to make demands on its allies. The failure was all the more outrageous in light of the prodigious generosity that the United States had shown toward these countries, a generosity which had obviously inspired little gratitude or readiness to help the United States in its hour of need.[37]

Like some of the Democratic critics, several Republicans used the hearings to express not only their concern about Vietnam but about American foreign policy in general. Like their Democratic counterparts, the Republicans' fear that the United States had made an unlimited commitment to Vietnam seemed to exacerbate a more general anxiety that the United States had made an unlimited commitment to opposing Communism throughout the world. Thus Mundt expressed relief when Rusk testified that this anxiety was unfounded: "One thing a lot of Americans are going to be pleased to hear [is that] you said that we are not committed to fight Communist countries every place they emerge."[38]

A desire that the United States not overextend itself internationally was also implied in a colloquy between Kennan and Clifford Case of New Jersey, a former Wall Street lawyer who, unlike Mundt, was considered a liberal internationalist. Case asked Kennan whether in the absence of an enforceable system of international law to ensure "world peace," the United States should "act as Britain once did" or, instead, limit itself to acting where its "immediate security" is concerned. Kennan answered that having gone "beyond the barrier of 60 years," he now found himself "with more and more sympathy for the concepts of foreign policy that prevailed at an earlier time" and become "sort of a neo-isolationist." Case then replied: "You know this may be catching. I am past the barrier too."[39]

Frank Carlson of Kansas, although a supporter of the war, echoed the concern of its Democratic critics that it impeded progress toward better relations with the Soviet Union. To this Kennan expressed agreement, noting that he "felt very strongly about this."[40] Similarly, though at least a nominal supporter of the war, Case used his questioning time in a way helpful to the cause of its opponents and the advocates of a more enlightened foreign policy. Indeed, Case's performance during the hearings may have been as damaging to the administration as that of many of the Democratic critics.

On the first day of the hearings, Case devoted almost all his allotted time to delivering a speech attacking AID administrator David Bell for describing the government's objective in Vietnam as one of fighting "Communist aggression." Announcing a theme that would later be picked up by the Democrats Fulbright and Church, Case argued that "using the adjective 'Communist' is a bad practice . . . because it makes it possible, among other things, for people to say we are trying to fight an ideology with military force, and that is impossible." He also confronted Bell with the ominous predictions of the Aiken-Mansfield report, and he joined Morse in arguing that Secretary of Defense Robert S. McNamara be required to appear before the committee in public session.[41]

By contrast, during his questioning of witnesses critical of the administration, Case adopted a friendly, even ingratiating, tone. He offered no challenge to General Gavin as he testified at length on his concern about the high costs of intervention in Vietnam and the undesirability of escalation.[42] After he welcomed Kennan as "a constituent" and told him that "we in New Jersey are very proud of you," Case, in effect, handed the floor over to Kennan who then delivered an eloquent speech on the necessity of avoiding war between the superpowers, limiting war among the smaller states, and how the interests of world peace can be better served by seeking conciliation among the powers.[43]

Case told Taylor that he did not think "most of us either worry about the legality or the morality of our position." He did not agree with "the more romantic among us" who believe "that a man has the strength of 10 because his heart is pure, and for the United States every war it gets into is fine." The relevant question, he explained, is the "feasibility" of our involvement in Vietnam, including whether the costs of achieving American objectives were reasonable. As Taylor sought to respond, he confronted the general with discrepancies between his claims of military progress and the less optimistic reports made by McNamara. He also accused Taylor of "reasoning in a circle" (when he seemed to use the very difficulties of intervention as an argument for its necessity), and inquired whether the United States was becoming trapped in a spiral of escalation in which the enemy had the initiative.[44]

Finally, on the last day of the hearings, Case emphatically told Rusk that he did not view the Gulf of Tonkin Resolution as a congressional grant of "power of attorney" permitting the president to escalate at will. Case then permitted Rusk to testify without interruption on the necessity of the intervention and to recall his encounters with pacifism as a Rhodes Scholar at Oxford during the late 1930s as Hitler's first aggressions went unchecked. On the second round, however, Case confronted Rusk with Fulbright's accusation that the administration was in fact seeking a victory in Vietnam and with an article in the day's *New York Times* "which suggested that the only way this [war] can be won is by destroying Vietnam."[45]

In contrast to their behavior during the final years of the Truman presidency, the Republican senators refrained from any explicit partisan attacks on the Democratic administration. At several points during the hearings, however, Republicans implicitly suggested that neither the war in Vietnam nor American foreign policy in general were matters for which their party was willing to take bipartisan responsibility. For example, Hickenlooper, on the final day of the hearings, chose to give a short speech in which he explained that "countless mistakes were made by this Government [that is, Democratic administrations] at the end especially of World War II," and that "some mistakes were made in the Korean war." With respect to Vietnam, Hickenlooper similarly laid the blame on the Democrats, and used leading questions to force Taylor to concede that the commitment of troops to that theater had not taken place during the Eisenhower presidency.[46]

Williams, on the other hand, saw the hearings as an opportunity to attack the Democrats for their deficit spending. Referring to Bell's claim that the Saigon regime could control inflation by limiting its spending, Williams—recalling the witness's prior position as budget director—asked whether the South Vietnamese "ever ask you how you reconcile your recommendation that they curtail their deficit with your statement some time back that there was a virtue in a deficit here in this country?" A more ambiguous effort to blend criticism of Democratic policies at home and abroad was made in Aiken's interrogation of Taylor in which the septuagenarian seemed to equate, among other things, universal military conscription and maximum hours legislation with Communism.[47]

III

The Vietnam hearings created what one writer has called "a national sensation." Broadcast live to an audience that may have exceeded 30 million, "the hearings impinged on the lives of virtually all Americans." Millions who did not watch the hearings during their daytime broadcasts witnessed major excerpts—including the most dramatic confrontations—on the six and ten o'clock news.[48] Newspapers gave the hearings front-page coverage. The major newsweeklies, in addition to providing their readers with coverage of the hearings, printed excerpts from the transcripts. The leading liberal magazine, *The New Republic* took the unusual measure of providing all of Kennan's testimony in a special detachable supplement. And columnists reinforced public interest in the hearings by using them as a starting point for expression of their own views on the war.[49] There were even some high schools where, as Gore noted during the hearings, ordinary classes were suspended to permit students (and, incidentally, their teachers) to witness for themselves the discussion of a war that was of particular concern to their generation.[50]

The most important immediate effects of the hearings were the intensification of public interest in the war,[51] and the enhancing of the legitimacy of its critics. Looking back at the hearings, Pell opined that they "made peace a respectable word and showed that disagreement was respectable, too. If such a respectable group of stuffed shirts as the Senate Foreign Relations Committee could question this war, it gave other people the courage to question it."[52] A similar view is held by Norma Becker, then one of the central organizers of demonstrations against the war, who recalls that the hearings served as "a major catalyst" to public discussion of Vietnam. "They certainly opened and widened the parameters of debate and expanded the breadth of forces questioning the official line of the government. Fulbright's credibility was qualitatively different from that of left wing groups."[53]

These recollections are consistent with the conclusions of social scientists and historians who have written about the hearings, emphasizing not only the authority of the senators but that of General Gavin and George Kennan, who lent their prestige to the hearings when they testified as witnesses.[54] It is also consistent with David Halberstam's observation that they were a turning point in the way opponents of the administration were perceived. Whereas, according to Halberstam, television had previously "made the opposition appear to be outcasts, frustrated, angry, and rather beyond the pale," the Fulbright hearings, "were the beginning of a slow but massive educational process, a turning of the tide against the President's will and his awesome propaganda machinery," from which point "dissent was steadily more respectable."[55]

For the Senate itself, the hearings marked a turn toward greater assertiveness. As in the past, Morse framed his assertion of congressional power as a claim of constitutional prerogatives. Baldly accusing the president of conducting an illegal war, he indicted the administration for advancing "the strange argument that we should kill American boys without a declaration of war."[56] Although other senators did not explicitly endorse this constitutional argument, several did identify with Morse's more general assertion that congressional debate on the war was not only permissible but desirable.[57] Fulbright, moreover, criticized himself for failing to insist on a full and thorough discussion of the Gulf of Tonkin Resolution before it was voted upon and for not accepting Wisconsin Democrat Gaylord Nelson's amendment that would have limited the authority of the executive branch once it was approved.[58]

Remarkably, Fulbright, for some twenty years an ardent defender of presidential prerogatives in the field of foreign policy, at the hearings voiced anxieties reminiscent of those expressed by Ohio Republican John Bricker, the nemesis of internationalists, more than a decade before. "I hope," Fulbright told Rusk, "that any future commitments that might bring this country into the war will not be made by unilateral declarations or agreements between ministers, but will be made by treaties submitted to and ratified by the Senate."[59] Minnesota Democrat Eugene McCarthy, likewise, seemed to abandon a position traditionally taken by liberal internationalists when he posed questions challenging the assumption that officers of the executive branch had exclusive access to the information needed to make competent decisions on matters of foreign policy.[60] Several other senators, on the other hand, complained that the executive branch was excessively secretive and withheld information to which Congress and the people should have access.[61]

For all of the senators advocating a greater role for the Senate in the making of foreign policy—including Morse—the preferred method of achieving their goal was not through a direct constitutional challenge to the president, but the arousing of public opinion to put pressure on the White House. For Morse, the hearings were part of "the great debate that across this country is going to take place from now through the election in 1968."[62] Similarly, Gore compared the Senate hearings to the practices of presidents who seek to mobilize popular support for their programs. After telling Kennan that "many of his sentiments" had been repeatedly expressed by senators in executive session meetings of the committee without having "made a dent" on the president's policies, the committee was now trying to "go over the head of the President to the American people, and reach him by way of the American people." There was nothing "particularly un-American about going over the head of someone. After all, Congress had been subjected to this by many Presidents" and, indeed, "the State of the Union message is no longer given to Congress but in the prime hours of the evening by way of TV to the American people."[63]

The immediate response of the president to the hearings was rage, which was quickly followed by defiance.[64] Far from making conciliatory moves toward his critics, he greeted the televised hearings with his own announcement of a trip to Honolulu to confer with the leaders of the Saigon government. The move was widely perceived (and has now been confirmed in memoirs and oral history interviews) as an effort to distract attention from the hearings.[65] At Honolulu, however, the president did more than confer with the leaders of South Vietnam; he made speeches and issued a declaration with them that pledged the United States to the Saigon regime and tacitly endorsed that regime's unwillingness to negotiate with its enemies in the National Liberation Front. To the extent that this declaration made the United States a hostage of its client state, the president's critics interpreted the conference as a confirmation of their worst fears.[66] Nonetheless, the very theatricality of the president's actions and the perception that they were taken to divert attention from the hearings paradoxically confirmed the potential power of Johnson's critics even as he ostentatiously defied them.[67]

   If the Senate hearings were the immediate cause of the Honolulu conference, the conference itself set in motion a chain of events that would affect both Vietnam and the United States. As Frances Fitzgerald has explained, "like almost every other Vietnamese, Ky interpreted the meeting with Johnson as a demonstration of U.S. support and a mandate for him to consolidate power in his own hands." In fact, within weeks of the conference Ky attempted to do precisely this, dismissing his rival, General Thi. The dismissal, in turn, set off "the explosion of long-suppressed anger against the regime and all it stood for," in a quasi-revolutionary revolt led by the Buddhists.[68] Although ultimately suppressed, the process of doing this was slow and painful, exposing as never before the military, political, and moral weakness of the regime to which the United States had pledged its unconditional support. Johnson's response was, of course, further escalation of U.S. involvement as the very weakness of the regime became the argument for an even greater allocation of resources to its defense. But the escalation of American involvement brought with it a growing disillusionment in the Vietnamese war among large numbers of Americans. And with that disillusionment came a rise in protest in the United States, including the spread of dissent within the Senate.[69]

But even before the Buddhist rebellion and its manifold consequences, the president was to suffer a blow closer to home. One of the most attentive viewers of the Fulbright hearings was Robert Kennedy, who two years before had become New York's junior senator. In a state of growing agitation and frustration, Kennedy had watched the hearings, sometimes from the back of the hearing room, at other times on television as he paced the floor of his office—occasionally catching himself "talking back to the screen." Undoubtedly with complex motivations, not the least of which was a heightened sense of discomfort with his self-imposed silence on a major issue that the televised hearings were bringing into the homes of millions of Americans, he now decided to lend his voice to the controversy.[70]

Left to right: Secretary of State Dean Rusk,
Sen. Bourke B. Hickenlooper (R-Iowa), and
Sen. J. William Fulbright (D-Ark.).

Sen. George D. Aiken (R-Vt.),
Sen. J. William Fulbright (D-Ark.),
and Sen. John Jackson Sparkman
(D-Ala.) question witnesses at a
Foreign Relations Committee
hearing.

Seated around the table at an Armed Services Committee meeting (*clockwise*): Sen. John C. Stennis (D-Miss.), Sen. Richard B. Russell (D-Ga.), Sen. Leverett Saltonstall (R-Mass.), Sen. Margaret Chase Smith (R-Maine), and Sen. Harry S. Byrd, Jr. (D-Va.).

A hearing of the Foreign Relations
Committee (*left to right*): Sen. Frank
Church (D-Idaho), unidentified,
Sen. George D. Aiken (R-Vt.), Sen.
Bourke B. Hickenlooper (R-Iowa),
Sen. J. William Fulbright (D-Ark.),
Sen. John J. Sparkman (D-Ala.), and
Sen. Wayne L. Morse (D-Ore.).

Senator Fulbright (D-Ark.) faces
(*left to right*) Col. Forrest I. Rettgers,
Department of Defense, legislative
affairs; David Steiner, aide to Bell;
David E. Bell, administrator for the
Agency for International Development; Rutherford Poats, aide to Bell,
at the witness table. Photograph cour-
tesy of the Senate Historical Office.

Dean Rusk at the Foreign Relations
Committee hearing.

At the joint hearing of the Armed Services and Foreign Relations Committee (*from left to right*): unidentified, Sen. Richard B. Russell (D-Ga.), Sen. J. William Fulbright (D-Ark.), Sen. John Jackson Sparkman (D-Ala.), Sen. Bourke B. Hickenlooper (R-Iowa), Sen. Leverett Saltonstall (R-Mass.), Sen. George D. Aiken (R-Vt.) Sen. Thomas Henry Kuchel (R-Calif.), Sen. J. Strom Thurmond (R-S.C.), unidentified, Sen. Mike Mansfield (D-Mont.), Sen. Margaret Chase Smith (R-Maine), and Sen. John C. Stennis (D-Miss.).

CHAPTER 7

1966: Speech and Silence

I

On Saturday morning, February 19, 1966, less than twenty-four hours after the final televised hearing's adjournment, Robert Kennedy, the junior senator from New York, made his first major address on the Vietnam War.[1] Speaking before a room crowded with news reporters, he prefaced his speech with a lengthy plea for toleration of debate on Vietnam, and described the recent Senate discussions on that subject as part of a tradition of "great debates" in which the Senate had permitted controversial opinions to be heard and sometimes ultimately triumph.

Describing his own position, Kennedy announced his agreement with the administration's present policy which represented a viable alternative to the advocates of precipitous withdrawal and the advocates of escalation. What should be done now, according to Kennedy, was to pursue the policy that "President Johnson has made clear," of seeking a negotiated settlement and demanding "unconditional discussions." In practice this would require that each side be conceded "one irreducible demand." For the Americans this would be a refusal to "turn South Vietnam over to the North." For the North Vietnamese, on the other hand, this would be a rejection of "a settlement which leaves in the south a hostile government, dedicated to the final destruction of all Communist elements, refusing any economic cooperation with the North, dependent on the continued presence of American military power."[2]

Although such a "middle way" entailed risks, these risks were no more than "we do take every day in a hundred countries in every corner of every continent" where, despite the risk of Communist subversion, we refrain from attempting "to occupy these nations." This restraint rests on a "basic faith" that has nearly always been confirmed by the fact that "in the past when the question has been clearly presented men have chosen independence and freedom." Assuming "this basic faith in the aspirations of man," the United States could only reach a settlement by inviting the participation of the National Liberation Front: "whatever the exact status of the National Liberation Front—puppet or independent—any negotiated settlement must accept the fact that there are discontented elements in South Vietnam, Communist and non-Communist, who desire to change the existing political and economic system." Rather, than "kill or repress" these elements, or "turn the country over to them," Kennedy urged that the United States "admit them to a share of the power and responsibility."

This participation of the NLF was "at the heart of the hope for a negotiated settlement." Implementation of such a settlement would "require enormous skill and political wisdom" to prevent participation from becoming domination. It would also require "statesmanship willing to exploit the real differences of ambition and intention and interest between Hanoi and Peking and the Soviet Union." Furthermore, it would require the United States "to take considerable risks in the expectation that social and economic success will weaken the appeal of communism—and that sharing the burden and the satisfaction of helping to guide a nation will attract hostile elements towards a solution that will preserve both the independence of their country and their new-found share of power." And he added: a settlement based on participation of the NLF would require that the United States "be willing to face the uncertainties of election, and the possibilities of an eventual vote on unification" and "be prepared to think about what kind of relationship such a reunited country would have to the United States, to Communist China, and to the Soviet Union."[3]

Kennedy's speech, perhaps even more than the Fulbright hearings, received prominent press coverage. Almost all of it portrayed the speech as critical of the president's policies. The administration itself, despite some initial equivocation,[4] also emphasized its differences with Kennedy, particularly his call for granting the NLF a share of power in South Vietnam, a proposal interpreted as favoring a coalition government that would include the Communists. Vice President Humphrey, then on tour in New Zealand, attacked Kennedy's proposal as "a prescription for the ills of South Vietnam which includes a dose of arsenic," and likened the inclusion of the NLF in a coalition government to placing "a fox in a chicken coop" or "an arsonist in the fire department." Similarly, Undersecretary George Ball, appearing on ABC's *Issues and Answers,* denounced such a coalition as leading inevitably to Communism. And McGeorge Bundy, appearing on NBC's *Meet the Press,* quoted from a 1963 speech by President John Kennedy in which he had condemned "popular fronts throughout the world" and had doubted whether "a democrat can ride that tiger."[5]

On its face, the hostility of the administration to Kennedy's speech appears to have been misplaced or at least disproportionate. The speech, after all, was remarkable for its moderation. It had refrained from criticizing the White House and had, in fact, explicitly endorsed its declared goals in Vietnam. And it had even—through its optimistic references to the project of politically defeating the Communists in South Vietnam—taken a position to the right of men like Fulbright, Gavin, and Kennan, who only days before had spoken openly of the acceptability of a Communist victory. Even the idea of forging a coalition with the Communists—if this, indeed, is what Kennedy was proposing—was merely a call for doing in Vietnam what his brother's administration had already done in Laos. Indeed, the National Security Council meetings at which the Laotian popular front policy was approved were attended by then–Vice President Johnson, Secretary of State Rusk, George Ball, and McGeorge Bundy. And Hubert Humphrey, then assistant majority leader in the Senate, although informed of the policy, never dissented.[6]

The fury with which Kennedy's proposals were met, however, was not wholly irrational. Notwithstanding their own complicity in its creation during the Kennedy presidency, even before Robert Kennedy's speech it would have been difficult to find anyone in the Johnson administration willing to praise the Laotian settlement, much less regard it as a precedent or model to be applied elsewhere, least of all in Vietnam.[7] Moreover, even as the administration refused to renounce the long-term goal of effecting détente with the Communist world, official policy remained averse to the inclusion of Communists in governments within the so-called free world. The prevailing orthodoxy still viewed such coalitions as almost inevitably paving the way for the establishment of Communist dictatorships, an orthodoxy that set the Americans apart from such Europeans as de Gaulle, whose experiences during and since the Second World War suggested the possibility of a range of satisfactory accommodations with Communists and other ostensibly revolutionary forces at home and abroad.[8] Indeed, as if to underline his rejection of the American orthodoxy in favor of the pragmatic approach of de Gaulle, at a post-speech press conference, Kennedy referred positively not only to the Laotian settlement but to the popular fronts that had governed Italy and France after the Liberation.[9]

Notwithstanding his many equivocations, Kennedy's proposals immediately won the praise of the most astute contemporary commentators, who readily discerned the difference between Kennedy's approach and that of the Johnson administration. "The difference between Senator Kennedy and the Administration," wrote I. F. Stone, "is not a mere difference on timing or strategy," but a fundamentally different "view of the war and the nature of the rebellion." Likening Kennedy's statement to "de Gaulle's magnanimous appeal to the Algerian rebels for 'a peace of the brave,'" Stone praised the senator for offering a strategy that could provide the United States a realistic path to termination of its involvement in Vietnam.[10] Walter Lippmann went further, arguing that adoption of Kennedy's proposals could lead to "what in my own view is the only live option we ever had in southeast Asia," a neutral and unified Vietnam "probably under the rule of Ho Chi Minh, who is the one national leader of that country."[11]

Unsurprisingly, antiwar forces within the Democratic Party embraced Kennedy's speech as an affirmation of their own views.[12] For some Democrats, it also represented a turning point in their attitude toward Kennedy, a man they had hitherto viewed with considerable suspicion.[13] Needless to say, Humphrey's vitriolic denunciation of the speech gave added impetus to Kennedy's inroads into Humphrey's natural constituency in the left wing of the party.[14] This was viewed by contemporary observers as presaging a contest in 1972 (the final year of Johnson's anticipated second term) between the two men for the presidential nomination of their party, a contest in which Humphrey would presumably be supported by the White House.[15]

More generally, Kennedy's speech represented a turning point in the process by which he transformed his image[16] and encouraged the belief that a sharp line demarcated the policies pursued by the Johnson administration and those that John Kennedy would have pursued had he lived (or which Robert Kennedy would pursue if he became president).[17] This belief could take a poignant form, as in the letter to Robert Kennedy from a boy shaken at seeing a newspaper photograph of American soldiers forcing

South Vietnamese civilians (including children) to raise their hands over their heads:

> I wonder Sir, if it is true as I can not believe that a Democratic country and powerful as it is to fear from children that none of them are more than 7 years old and at gun point forced them to raise their hands like criminals along with their mothers. I strongly believe that the late beloved president would not like to see such things happening to this so far underdeveloped country or any other country in the whole world because from what books about his biography I read (Profiles in Courage, Boy's Life of John F. Kennedy, John F. Kennedy + the P.T. 109) he loved dearly and affectionately children and peace.[18]

Irrespective of the degree to which, as his young correspondent thought, Robert Kennedy's proposals were truly consistent with the policies of his older brother, the Vietnam controversy seemed to be pushing him into the forefront of the movement against the war.

The potential power of Kennedy's challenge to the administration was derived from several closely related sources: his strategic position as a New York senator, the popular perception of him as his brother's "legitimate heir," his family's fabulous wealth, and, above all, his capacity—inside and outside the Senate—to harness these to an informal but powerful network of supporters. This network, variously described by contemporaries as "the Kennedy underground," "the Kennedy party," "the Kennedy machine," and, especially with respect to the Senate, "the Kennedy bloc," had the potential to provide many senators with the protection needed to break with the White House on the war.[19] Such a bloc, combining and overlapping with the opposition already centered in the Fulbright committee, seemed, indeed, to lay the basis for an antiwar bloc that could potentially encompass a majority of the Senate.

II

The potential was not fulfilled. In many respects, the two highly publicized events, the Fulbright hearings and the Kennedy speech, made February the high-water mark for Senate dissent in 1966. To the disappointment of some liberal intellectuals who had hoped that a coherent opposition would now develop in the Senate, uniting Fulbright, Kennedy, and other opponents of the war, such an opposition never materialized. Rather than fulfilling I. F. Stone's hope of uniting with his brother Edward (D-Mass.) and forming a "nucleus" for Senate dissent,[20] Kennedy, after responding to the attacks on his proposal, went into an extended period of silence on the war and refrained from delivering any major speeches on the subject for more than a year.[21]

Fulbright, the other logical leader for an opposition, likewise, after an initial attempt, abandoned the effort to form a disciplined parliamentary bloc. In response to historian Barbara Tuchman's suggestion that there be an "organized and articulate Opposition" to the war, he confessed that he had already tried to do so "in a rather feeble and ineffectual way" and had found the effort "extremely difficult." It would be futile to continue this effort, he explained, because "the Republicans, with a few minor exceptions, are under the influence of the President so that only a few Democrats have the temerity to speak out against the Administration's policy."[22] Fulbright had already rejected a proposal by another historian, Arthur Schlesinger Jr., that Senate dissenters unite to present a resolution calling for a limitation of the war. Asserting that "the Senate at least at present is overwhelmingly— about 80 to 20—under the spell of the President," Fulbright predicted that any resolution he sponsored that criticized the president's conduct of the war would be defeated and "only strengthen his determination."[23] The same conclusion had been reached by a majority of those attending a meeting two days after Kennedy's speech. At this meeting of Fulbright, Kennedy, and ten other Senate opponents of the war, all but three senators agreed that their cause would be more hurt than helped by a floor vote on a resolution for which they could muster only fifteen votes.[24]

Rather than opposing the president with Senate resolutions, Fulbright thought Johnson would be more likely to moderate his actions in response to public opinion (as expressed in polls indicating "danger in the next election") and through "discussion" of his policies.[25] Fulbright sought to promote such discussion through a number of highly publicized lectures that he delivered during the spring of 1966. The best known of these, the Christian Herter lectures given at Johns Hopkins University, were almost immediately published and widely distributed in expanded form under the provocative title *The Arrogance of Power*. Significant attention in these lectures was given to the war in Vietnam. In addressing the subject, Fulbright enumerated in more explicit terms than he had in the past the concrete steps through which a settlement might be reached. These included an end to the bombing, a general cease-fire, negotiations among the belligerents, free elections, and an international conference to guarantee the results. The overriding goal was the self-determination of the South Vietnamese (including their right, if they chose, to unite with North Vietnam) and the neutralization of all of Southeast Asia.[26]

The major part of Fulbright's attention, however, was devoted to the general trajectory of American foreign policy. Partly because of this, a large portion of the publicity given to the lectures was given over not to his proposals for a Vietnamese settlement but to his sweeping generalizations on the American national character and his provocative assertions on such topics as the inevitability of violent revolution, the achievements of Castro's Cuba, and the need for conciliation with Communist China.[27] Off the lecture circuit, back in the committee room, Fulbright seemed similarly disposed to address Vietnam as only a symptom of larger or more fundamental problems.

In March, the Foreign Relations Committee held hearings on American relations with Communist China. With college professors as witnesses, the hearings had more of the ambience of a convocation among senators than a public forum on the need for the government to change its policies in Asia than a real challenge to American policy.[28] Two months later the committee moved yet further from the uncomfortable subject of the continuing carnage in Vietnam, when it heard testimony from prominent psychiatrists on human nature and the psychological aspects of international relations.[29] In early 1967 the trend continued, as the committee heard testimony from the historian Henry Steele Commager on "Changing American Attitudes toward Foreign Policy," a topic that Fulbright conceded was "broad and rather intangible" and which the witness himself called "almost an amorphous subject."[30] The committee's retreat from a specific focus on Vietnam was met with a predictable neglect from the press, a neglect that contrasted sharply with the generous publicity it had given the Vietnam hearings in February and the speaking tour that had followed them. As the committee's chief of staff complained in a memorandum to Fulbright, the local newspapers in particular were "putting . . . the hearings back with the brassiere ads."[31]

III

Notwithstanding Kennedy's silence and Fulbright's failure to maintain his focus on the war, the continuing crisis in Vietnam and the corresponding growth in public anxiety about the war led many senators to add their voices to the controversy. The Buddhist revolt, creating what Wayne Morse called "a civil war within a civil war,"[32] raised doubts about whether the South Vietnamese actually wanted the Americans to be in Vietnam. It also raised the specter that a new regime might come to power in Saigon that would ask the Americans to leave, thereby undermining the proclaimed rationale for the U.S. intervention. In this context, several senators called upon the United States to honor such a request (if it should be made), and withdraw from Vietnam. Among those taking this position were not only such doves as Stephen Young (D-Ohio), Claiborne Pell (D-R.I.), Vance Hartke (D-Ind.), and Jacob Javits (R-N.Y.), but two powerful senators who were widely perceived as advocates of an escalation of American involvement: Richard Russell of Georgia and John Stennis of Mississippi, the chairman and ranking Democrat, respectively, of the Armed Services Committee.[33]

On *Issues and Answers,* Stennis bluntly told the show's several million viewers that if a duly elected South Vietnamese government "says that they no longer want us there, it seems to me that we are left without a leg to stand on [and] would have to retire."[34] Similarly, Russell took advantage of an interview with *U.S. News & World Report* to express to that magazine's conservative readership his doubts as to whether the United States, even in the absence of such a request, should remain in Vietnam. According to the Armed Services Committee chairman, an American triumph in Vietnam might prove "a Pyrrhic victory" because the Vietnamese "will immediately go to fighting among themselves when we leave." The achievement of a victory, moreover, would require that the Americans "take the whole countryside, and practically make hostages of the South Vietnamese." He was "strongly opposed" to such a policy, as were, in his opinion, "most of the American people."

Russell now proposed that the United States conduct a careful survey of the attitudes of the South Vietnamese and withdraw "if that survey shows that the majority of them are anti-American." Asked by the interviewer whether it would be "disastrous for us to pull out," he replied:

> Not if these anti-American demonstrations continue, no. I have often said that we couldn't just "tuck tail and run" as long as the Vietnamese were fighting at our side—and they have been very courageous in battle. But I don't think you could expect anybody— Americans or anybody else—to stay in a country where it became very apparent that they were not wanted. It's not good manners to stay in another man's house against his wishes.

Asked if such a withdrawal would be "disastrous through all Southeast Asia," Russell answered, "I don't buy this so-called domino theory."[35]

A third member of the Armed Services Committee, its second-ranking Republican, Margaret Chase Smith of Maine,[36] was also raising questions during this period about whether the United States should leave Vietnam in light of the attitude of its people toward the Americans. Although she had hitherto been highly supportive of the intervention, serious doubts were raised by a series of letters she received from a young soldier from her state. In one of the letters, he had described the horrors of combat and its victims; the immorality of Saigon, which was filled with prostitutes and bars; the peasants, who were ready to fight for the enemy; and the South Vietnamese troops, who were "spineless and passive" and unwilling to fight for their own government. In reply, she wondered whether there was any choice but "to conclude that we should get out of Vietnam immediately?" Forwarding her correspondence to the president, she wrote that the letters from "this Maine boy" made "it very difficult for anyone not to have doubts about the justification of our continued effort in Viet Nam."[37]

IV

The statements of Russell, Stennis, and Smith did not signal an immediate abandonment of the war by the leadership of the Armed Services Committee. Nor did it presage an immediate movement of Republicans and conservative Democrats into the camp of those opposed to escalation of the war. The statements were, rather, indicative of a more ambiguous phenomenon, a heightened volatility among such senators as they increasingly combined their support to the soldiers with criticism of the civilian officials who sent them onto the battlefield. Following the pattern of conservative dissent during the Truman administration's intervention in Korea, some criticized the government for not doing enough to win the war, some for not doing enough to end the war, and many voiced criticism combining the two themes. Whatever their ambivalence or inconsistency, these senators made it clear that they were unwilling to identify themselves with the war or use their prestige to build public support for its prosecution.[38]

The equivocal position of these Republicans and conservative Democrats seemed to coincide with the trend in public opinion. The first half of 1966, and particularly the period of the spring Buddhist revolt, corresponded to a significant and enduring decline in public support for the policies of the administration and an increase in support for the proposals of both its hawk and dove critics. According to a Harris survey, for example, Americans polled in December 1965 and May 1966 showed a decline from 65 to 47 percent in the opinion that the administration should simply continue to "hold the line" in South Vietnam. By contrast, support for the view that the United States "carry the ground war into North Vietnam at the risk of bringing Red China into the fighting," jumped from 28 to 38 percent. Likewise, the number of respondents favoring withdrawal of all "support and troops" from South Vietnam more than doubled from 7 to 15 percent. According to Harris, "American public opinion is rising toward increased militancy about the Vietnam war and a 'get it over with' mood. . . . The people show a distaste for what they regard as an indecisive stalemate in which American lives are spent, but they cannot arrive at any firm conclusion about what should be done to end the war."[39] Gallup polls also recorded the volatility of public opinion, particularly its capacity to leap from hawk to dove positions. In June 1965 and again in June 1966 Gallup asked Americans to imagine they were voting "on the question of continuing the war in Vietnam or withdrawing our troops during the next few months." Over this one-year period the percentage of respondents favoring a continuation of the war dropped from 66 to 48 while those favoring withdrawal increased from 20 to 36.[40]

With the approach of the congressional elections, public concern with the war persisted as the number of American solders in Vietnam increased by more than three thousand per week, casualties mounted at a rate of one hundred per week, and the cost of military expenditures reached $1.2 billion per month and promised to rise even further. According to a survey conducted by the Republican National Committee, only 12 percent of Americans thought progress was being made in Vietnam, and a mere 6 percent thought the war was being handled well.[41]

A survey during this period of senatorial attitudes toward the war also registered unhappiness with the president's policies. According to a *Congressional Quarterly* survey in late October 1966, only fifty-four senators remained in the president's camp, while twenty-six had defected to the doves, and twenty to the hawks. Of the sixty-eight Senators in the president's own party, thirty-three remained loyal while twenty-three had become doves and eleven hawks.[42] Thus on the eve of the midterm elections, the president's once much-touted "consensus" had been replaced by a slim majority, with growing opposition on his left and right, and within both parties. At the base of this opposition rested a citizenry increasingly alienated by the president's domestic programs, anxious and frustrated by the war, and confronted in November by a choice of Senate candidates in thirty-two states.

V

Although Vietnam was raised as an issue in most of the Senate election contests of 1966 (and in a few instances was a central issue), the results seem to show the power of incumbency rather than the capacity of any one position on the war to win votes and carry new senators into office. In fact, with the peculiar exception of Illinois, all of the incumbents prevailed in the general election irrespective of their views on Vietnam or those of their opponents.[43] In Rhode Island, for example, Pell, who opposed escalation of the war, turned back a challenge from Ruth Briggs, a retired army colonel, who made Vietnam a central campaign issue and called for an extension of the bombing of North Vietnam.[44] Likewise, in Kentucky, incumbent Republican John Sherman Cooper, an opponent of escalation, defeated John Y. Brown, who had likened Cooper to the "appeasers" who had failed to check Adolf Hitler in the 1930s.[45] In Alaska, Democrat E. L. "Bob" Barlett, another incumbent dove, also prevailed over his hawk opponent, although in this case he was undoubtedly aided by the latter's membership in the John Birch Society.[46] In all three of these contests, the margins of victory were considerable. Pell beat Briggs by taking nearly 68 percent of the total vote, Cooper gathered 64.5 percent, and more than three-quarters of Alaska's voters chose to send Bartlett back to Washington.[47]

Incumbent hawks also, without exception, prevailed. In Texas, Goldwaterite John Tower defeated state Attorney General Waggoner Carr, despite the latter's receipt of strong backing from the White House.[48] Similarly, in other states where Vietnam was a campaign issue, incumbent Republican advocates of escalation prevailed: Iowa, South Dakota, Nebraska, and Colorado.[49] In Mississippi, Democrat James Eastland, after facing the strongest Republican challenge of his career, also triumphed as he proposed that "we should level North Viet Nam and end the war."[50] In all of these elections, like their dove counterparts, the incumbent advocates of escalation won by comfortable margins.

The advantage of incumbency also seemed to show itself in races where Senate supporters of the administration faced challenges from either the left or right. Perhaps the clearest case was in New Hampshire where pro-administration incumbent Thomas J. McIntyre faced Harrison R. Thyng (pronounced "thing"), a much-decorated retired air force brigadier general, who enjoyed the support of William Loeb, publisher of the *Manchester Union Leader*, as well as significant financial backing from conservatives from outside the state. According to Thyng, the war could be ended with ten days of intensive bombing (a position he later modified). In response to Thyng's calls for a drastic escalation of the bombing, McIntyre defended what he characterized as the president's "tempered response to aggression," and described Thyng's proposals as "the quickest way to plunge this nation into World War III."[51] On election day, McIntyre prevailed, taking 54.1 percent of the vote.

The only state where an incumbent lost on election day was Illinois, where Republican Charles Percy unseated administration stalwart Paul Douglas. Percy received attention throughout the country, when in July he proposed that the problems of Vietnam be settled at an all-Asian peace conference, which would include Communist China, at which the countries of Asia themselves would decide how to achieve peace in Vietnam and "begin a new year [*sic*] of Asian regional cooperation, in the military, social, political and economic fields."[52] In order to enhance the self-reliance of the Asian nations, Percy proposed that the United States attend the conference as a passive observer, although he also proposed that the United States retain veto power over its results. In addition, he expressed his view that "if the South Vietnamese government asks us to get out after such a conference, I cannot believe that we would not leave." Other planks of Percy's platform called for additional treaties limiting nuclear weapons and for admission of Communist China to the United Nations if it dropped its demand that Nationalist China (Taiwan) be excluded from the U.N. and if it withdrew its indictment of the United States as the aggressor in the Korean War.[53]

Douglas, whose attitudes on foreign policy bore the imprint of the Cold War liberalism that prevailed among Democrats when he was first elected to the Senate in 1948, opposed Percy as insufficiently hostile to Communism, and characterized his Vietnam proposals as "one-sided" and "half-baked." To this last charge, Percy replied that "anything that was half-baked is fresh and not just a warmed-over idea." He also said that by seeking disengagement from Vietnam he was trying to take "a little of the burden off us" and proposed that the United States stop "trying to police the entire world."[54] On election day Percy won with more than 2.1 million votes, or 55 percent of the votes cast. It should be noted, however, that although Percy gave the war considerable attention during his campaign, most observers believed it to have been but one of several reasons for his electoral triumph. These included Douglas's identification with the administration's positions on civil rights (a problem exacerbated by Martin Luther King's summer campaign against discrimination in Chicago), Douglas's age of seventy-four, and sympathy for Percy after his daughter was murdered just six weeks before Election Day.[55]

Among the small number of elections in which neither candidate was an incumbent, in only one was Vietnam a significant issue: the highly publicized race for the seat of retiring Oregon Democrat Maurine Neuberger. The Democratic contender, Congressman Robert Duncan, unequivocally endorsed the White House's war policies and vehemently attacked his Republican opponent, Governor Mark Hatfield, for, in Duncan's view, taking positions "indistinguishable" from those of Wayne Morse. Hatfield's statements during the campaign, in fact, made him readily distinguishable from Morse. In contrast to the unwavering senior senator, Hatfield seemed to reflect the ambivalence of his party (and many Americans) as he seemed to leap from dove to hawk positions and then back again: opposing the war in the primary, then calling upon the administration to institute a naval blockade of Haiphong, and then strongly criticizing the administration when it bombed oil depots near Hanoi and Haiphong. In the final weeks of his campaign he simply refrained from making any mention of the war during his speeches, although by then (despite his wishes) his candidacy was irrevocably identified with the cause of those opposing escalation of the war.[56] On Election Day he won, with 51.8 percent of the vote, a margin of 24,017 votes, in what turned out to be the only truly close Senate race of the year.

The Oregon race was remarkable not because of the equivocation of Hatfield and his attempt to deemphasize his position on the war, but because despite Hatfield's efforts the war did, in fact, become a major issue. This was not true in the majority of states in which Senate seats were contested. A week before the congressional elections, James Reston observed in the *New York Times* that, with a few notable exceptions, "the moral, political, and economic consequences of the war" were not central issues, and that "these questions are not even being debated by the candidates." Indeed, while taking "a long trip back and forth across this country, this reporter did not hear a single politician discuss the rights or wrongs of the war."[57]

Where Vietnam did intrude as an issue in a contest, this was typically a consequence not of the efforts of the incumbent, but of the challenger. If the most dramatic example was Percy's successful "peace candidacy" in Illinois, the more representative examples were the unsuccessful efforts of hawks in New Hampshire, Rhode Island, Montana, Alaska, Kentucky, and Oklahoma. Moreover, the successful Republican candidates (incumbent or otherwise) as a rule showed temperance in their pronouncements on the war, rarely assuming the stance of either a strong hawk or a strong dove. This was true not only of such moderates as Percy, Hatfield, Edward Brooke (an opponent of escalation who successfully won the seat of retiring Massachusetts Senator Leverett Saltonstall), and Clifford Case of New Jersey (who took a stance on the war barely distinguishable from his opponent Warren Wilentz), but such conservatives as Caleb Boggs in Delaware, Jack Miller in Iowa, John Tower in Texas, and Len Jordan in Idaho.

VI

How can we account for the actions of these senators? How do we explain the effort of incumbent senators to evade discussion of Vietnam (or take equivocal positions on the war) even though it was a major concern of their constituents? Would it not have been more likely for the Senate in an election year to become polarized in response to the war with Republicans, in particular, coalescing into a disciplined pro-escalation party? On the other hand, how do we account for the equivocations of the doves and their reluctance to address the war? In particular, how are we to understand Robert Kennedy, whose seat was presumably safe and, in any case, not up for election until 1970? How do we explain his decision to speak out on the war in February and then retreat from the issue for more than a year?

Remarks by party strategists in 1966 strongly suggest political considerations played a part in the failure of Republican senators to emphasize the war as an election issue and, when addressing the issue, to avoid taking an "extremist" Goldwaterite line. According to Thruston Morton of Kentucky, chairman of the Senate Republican Campaign Committee, "Vietnam is what is worrying the people the most but it's hard to get down as an issue." Although aware of growing anxiety among voters about the war, Republican candidates were not "sure in which direction the anxiety will cut." In addition, Ray Bliss, chairman of the party, wanted to avoid focusing on the war because Republicans were divided on the issue.[58] There was also fear that the president might settle the conflict before the election and therefore make the issue disappear. Thus, party strategists were generally agreed that "not much political capital" was to be gained by emphasizing the war or speaking with precision about how it might be ended.[59] One candidate, when asked about the war, simply replied, "It's a mess," an answer he thought would satisfy voters on both sides of the issue.[60]

The caution of the Republicans was undoubtedly encouraged by their still fresh memory of the Goldwater debacle, as well as the electoral success of Eisenhower. If the Goldwater campaign demonstrated the dangers of hawkish consistency, Eisenhower's first campaign provided a lesson in the advantages of diluting a win-the-war line by mixing it with pacifistic themes. For these Republicans, the 1966 congressional elections were to be a testing ground for the rhetoric that they hoped would bring victory at all levels of government two years later. As early as February 1966, some party strategists were reported to "envision a climatic moment in the 1968 campaign when their candidate proclaims 'I will go to Viet Nam' to end the dirty war."[61] Likewise, one White House functionary feared that the Republicans anticipated using the "'Korean whipsaw': On Mondays, Wednesdays and Fridays, we will be the war party; on Tuesdays, Thursdays and Saturdays, the party of appeasement."[62]

It would be an exaggeration, however, to suggest (as many contemporary journalists did) that either the deemphasis of the Vietnam issue or the apparent retreat from the Goldwater line of 1964 was purely an opportunistic maneuver to curry favor with the electorate. Such a view would probably be fair with respect to races like those in Texas and Colorado, where the moderation of the incumbent Republicans did seem to contradict their previously disclosed strong ideological commitments. Such a view, however, would not be fair with respect to many of the Republicans, who although conservative, cannot be described as true Goldwaterites. These politicians, described by one party functionary as "the American squirearchy," "had little interest in doctrine and general contempt for theory," and "basked in a cheerful politics of patronage and custom." Such men, to a degree not generally appreciated, had been alienated by the Goldwaterites who were "too intellectual," whose theories "smelled too much of the lamp," and whose methods "were too coldly devious for extroverted Squirearchy sensibilities."[63] For such essentially nonideological men, it is meaningless to speak of their failure to take a hard line on Vietnam in 1966 as hypocritical or even inconsistent with their ideals.

Two examples of senators of this stripe were George Aiken of Vermont and Len Jordan of Idaho, both of whom delivered speeches on Vietnam during the campaign season. Aiken has been fondly remembered as "out early on snowy New England mornings, feeding the animals, stacking wood, checking the maple sap runoff," as "a man of sturdy independence with a ready shoulder for a neighbor's bogged down car," and as "a composite of the early American virtues."[64] A farmer and descendant of a family whose ownership of Vermont land predated the Revolution, Aiken received his political education through a lengthy apprenticeship in state politics, starting as a local legislator and finally rising to the governorship. By 1966, an old man and twenty-five-year veteran of the U.S. Senate, he eschewed ideological labels, proudly identifying himself simply as "a Republican." Though not a candidate himself that year, he was an important symbol as the most senior senator of his party, and, indeed, as a man who seemed to personify a conservative but pragmatic brand of Republicanism rooted in the farms and villages of nineteenth-century New England.

Approximately two weeks before the elections, Aiken gave his memorable speech in which he proposed that the United States "declare unilaterally that this stage of the Vietnam war is over—that we have 'won' in the sense that our Armed Forces are in control of most of the field and no potential enemy is in a position to establish its authority over South Vietnam." He proposed that this declaration of victory be accompanied by "the gradual redeployment of U.S. military forces around strategic centers and the substitution of intensive reconnaissance for bombing." The likely consequence of these measures would be the "resumption of political warfare as the dominant theme in Vietnam." Under these circumstances, if the North Vietnamese attacked they would be seen as the aggressors, and the international community would condemn their actions and support a renewed intervention of the Americans. However, if the United States failed to make such a unilateral declaration, there would be "no prospect for political negotiations." Aiken was convinced that this initiative would be supported throughout the world: "There is nobody in the United States or in Europe or in Russia that is at all likely to challenge a statement by the President of the United States that our military forces have discharged their duty in their usual and competent manner and occupy the field as victors."[65]

Like Aiken, Jordan was a prosperous businessman and farmer, born in the last century, who had received his political education in the legislature of a rural state of which he ultimately became governor. In the U.S. Senate—to which he did not come until late in his career—he had distinguished himself by an extremely conservative voting record, including opposition to the Limited Test Ban Treaty of 1963. He also represented a state that, despite its isolationist heritage, included pro-war forces that had coalesced in a campaign to recall Frank Church for his opposition to the escalation of the war. Under these circumstances as a candidate for reelection in 1966, it might have been thought prudent for Jordan to refrain from expressing any strong opinions about the war. Nonetheless, on August 12, 1966, Jordan rose on the Senate floor to deliver a speech titled "The Tragedy of War."

Jordan began his speech by referring briefly to the civilian casualties of Communist terrorism in Vietnam, deaths that he called "part of the tragedy of war." He then referred to the mistaken bombing by American planes of the village of Truong Thanh that killed 26 civilians and wounded 114, casualties that are "also part of the tragedy of war." Condemning as "the most understated reaction I can imagine" the administration's characterization of the incident as an "unfortunate occurrence," he expressed his view that the "killing and maiming of noncombatants underscores the horror of the conflict we are in." According to Jordan, there was a "terrible irony in our involvement," in which "Americans are dying in increasing numbers ostensibly for the freedom of the Vietnamese" while pursuing policies "destined to produce destruction and death among the very people we have sought to save."[66]

The significance of Jordan's speech lies less in what it contributed to the cause of the Senate doves (whose rhetoric it echoed) than as a symptom of a decision by Jordan (and other Republicans cut from the same cloth) not to intervene in the Vietnam debate in the vitriolic, ultra-hawk mode that Johnson had feared. This restraint was not limited to Republicans like Jordan and Aiken who opposed the administration from the left, but even such conservative rural-based "squires" as Minority Leader Everett Dirksen of Illinois and Margaret Smith whose temperate tone helped undercut the development of a hard-right opposition reminiscent of that which developed in the final years of the Truman administration.[67]

The restraint of Senate doves during 1966 was also a consequence of several factors, not the least of which was a concern with public opinion polls that, although evincing growing unhappiness with the war, never showed a majority favoring withdrawal from Vietnam. The inhibiting effect of polls on the expression of dove opinion is suggested circumstantially by the discrepancy between the number of senators opposed to the war and the number who openly expressed their dissent. It is also suggested indirectly by the testimony of those senators who did give voice to their unhappiness with the administration's Vietnam policies.

Interviews with dove senators and their aides conducted three years later by Walter Zelman, then a doctoral candidate in political science, confirm that at least eight senators who openly opposed the administration on this issue did so with a sense that they were increasing, to at least some degree, the danger they would not be reelected. In none of the interviews, moreover, is there any indication that senators who dissented during this period believed that their dissent could actually strengthen their political position or increase their chances for reelection. George McGovern, for example, believed that when he decided to dissent in 1965, he was "making a decision to serve only one term." Wisconsin Democrat Gaylord Nelson, who in 1965 joined Morse and Gruening in voting against a war appropriation, in May 1965 was receiving mail that opposed his position fifteen-to-one. And in Idaho, as already mentioned, Church actually faced a recall movement in response to his opposition to the war.

Zelman also reports that "[u]ndoubtedly, at least several senators refrained from dissenting" because of fear that dissent would hurt their electoral chances. Although conceding that it was "difficult to obtain specific evidence" of such restraint, in an interview with the assistant to Clifford Case, Zelman was able to elicit an admission that the senator, who was up for election in 1966, thought that the "mood" in New Jersey supported the war that year. The senator believed, however, that "after reelection . . . [he] could afford the luxury of rethinking the situation."[68]

The inhibiting effect of public opinion on the expression of dove opinion was reinforced by the social position and political connections of many Senate critics of the war. If provincial conservatives such as Jordan, Dirksen, Aiken, and Smith helped inhibit the development of a powerful hawk opposition in the Senate, a parallel phenomenon inhibited the development of a disciplined and zealous opposition by the doves: their domination by a cosmopolitan elite personified by such patricians as Fulbright, Clark, Pell, Cooper, Case, and the Kennedy brothers. Although the opposition of these senators to the war was, to a large extent, an outgrowth of their intimate ties to a foreign policy elite that itself had become divided over Vietnam, these very same ties served to limit the scope and intensity of their dissent. They did not wish to change the existing power structure, but merely to change its course. Particularly for Fulbright and Robert

Kennedy, the "establishment" was not an alien entity but something that they claimed as their own.

As others have observed, Robert Kennedy's decision to speak out in February was part of a broader strategy of extending and consolidating his base on the left. The content of his speech, however, was entirely within the boundaries of established (though dissenting) elite opinion as expressed by men like Walter Lippmann and Hans Morgenthau. Indeed, the speech was ghost written by Richard Goodwin, who only weeks before had left the employ of the White House,[69] and its most controversial component—the need for eventual power sharing with the Communists—had been affirmed by McNamara and Maxwell Taylor in private conversations with Kennedy shortly before the speech was delivered.[70] As late as December 1966, when journalist Jack Newfield privately urged him to once again speak out on Vietnam, the senator expressed his doubts about the political wisdom of doing so, but said he would again have to consult with McNamara and Taylor to determine what the facts were about the war.[71]

Beyond his ties to such elite figures (and his envelopment by a coterie of advisors whose perspectives as a rule were those of liberal critics rather than radical protesters), Kennedy was further inhibited from dissenting against the war by his unspoken but universally assumed long-term goal of capturing the White House.[72] Although the February speech had been motivated in part by a desire to ingratiate himself with the left and thereby further this ultimate goal,[73] this very ambition also ensured the temperance of the speech, his effort to minimize his difference with the president at press conferences and in television appearances in its immediate aftermath, and his subsequent silence on the war. After all, it would only be useful for Kennedy to gain support on the left if this could be done without alienating other constituencies—mass and elite—that would be equally, if not more, decisive in winning a presidential challenge. A Kennedy victory, in any case, could only come about through the Democratic Party; at a minimum this required that he inhibit any impulses to strike directly at the president who was its leader. Nor was it in Kennedy's interest to prematurely divide the party; the danger of too early a break with the president could leave Kennedy with a mere splinter of the party rather than the major fraction he needed.

Moreover, Kennedy's past and his hoped-for future in the executive branch of government, combined with his lack of deep attachment to his new role as senator, made it almost unthinkable for him to challenge the claimed prerogatives of the president to make war.[74] Likewise, it made it highly unlikely that he would apply his considerable resources to the mounting of a congressional opposition to the war. For Kennedy, the goal was not to limit the powers of the presidency but to bring them into his own hands.[75]

CHAPTER 8

1967: Convergence

By any standard, 1967 was one of the most tumultuous years in American history. Among the more noticeable developments that year were an increasingly visible alienation of young people expressed in a rise in student protests, and ominous signs that an already inflationary economy could spiral into a crisis threatening the stability of the capitalist world. Even more striking was a wave of race riots that swept through the nation's major cities in July, most destructively in Detroit, where thirty-nine were killed, some $500 million in damage was inflicted, and five hundred people were left homeless.

All of these phenomena, however disparate, were seen by contemporaries as linked to the war in Vietnam. The economic troubles and generational rebellion, in particular, were viewed as symptomatic of the war. But many sophisticated observers also connected the riots to Vietnam. The link was not only seen in the war's impingement on spending for programs to alleviate urban poverty (believed to be a major cause of the riots), but a more amorphous feeling that the violence in Vietnam and at home were somehow connected to a global descent into strife and unreason.[1]

The war itself remained the central focus of attention, not only for most Americans but for much of the world. And in 1967, to most observers, the prospect for peace in Vietnam seemed as remote as ever. Despite the rise in draft calls and the commitment of an additional 100,000 Americans to combat (bringing the total to 485,600), the war remained stalemated, and notwithstanding optimistic reports from the American military, it seemed unlikely that a breakthrough would come in the foreseeable future. Meanwhile, the human and economic costs of the war continued to mount.[2]

Public anxiety about the war, already high, rose even further. The most visible expression of this was a sharp increase in the size and breadth of the antiwar movement. In April some four hundred thousand protesters demonstrated in New York, while another seventy-five thousand marched in San Francisco.[3] In October an even more dramatic group of protests took place in the nation's capital, culminating in a highly publicized "march on the Pentagon."[4] The unequivocal views of the demonstrators, however, reflected those of only a minority of the general public which, although deeply troubled by the war, vacillated in its attraction to a range of solutions, including proposals to end it through a major escalation of the bombing. In the Senate, this sentiment was expressed most clearly in August when a subcommittee chaired by John Stennis held hearings on the air war. In their course, the hearing room became, in turn, a platform for the Joint Chiefs of Staff to voice their criticism of the administration's allegedly overly restrictive bombing policy and the site of hostile interrogations of Robert McNamara. Believed by contemporary observers to represent broad currents of public opinion and to have influence over the president's actions, the hawks, more than their dove colleagues, often seemed in 1967 to be the most important force in the Senate.

If the criticism of doves like Fulbright and hawks like Stennis seemed to represent a growing polarization in the Senate, there were also significant developments in 1967 that suggested a contrary tendency toward convergence, as expressed most clearly in an alliance forged, in the wake of Johnson's intervention in the Congo, between Fulbright and Richard Russell (D-Ga.). The most conspicuous consequence of this alliance was a Senate resolution on "national commitments" that sought to inhibit the entanglement of the United States in future Vietnam-type conflicts.

This and other examples of collaboration and convergence of Senate doves with ostensible hawks were symptomatic of the merely equivocal commitment of many Senate conservatives to the war, a commitment that was decisively shaken in the early months of 1968 in the wake of the Tet offensive. The ultimate effect of the offensive on the Senate would be an emerging consensus among senators of both right and left that a way out of Vietnam had to be found.

I

With few exceptions, senators opposed to the war continued to acquiesce when asked to vote for its funding. As before, Morse and Gruening registered their lonely dissent on roll calls, joined sometimes by an idiosyncratic colleague such as the former LaFolleteite Gaylord Nelson or the ancient Stephen Young of Ohio. A slight expansion of the dissenters' ranks took place in response to Morse's proposal that the $22 billion defense appropriation for the 1968 fiscal year be reduced by 10 percent, with the secretary of defense authorized to select the items to be cut. This amendment, which theoretically would have permitted McNamara to cut Vietnam funds, garnered five votes: Morse, Gruening, Fulbright, Stephen Young and Joseph Clark of Pennsylvania.[5] A subsequent amendment proposed by Clark to cut the budget by a mere 5 percent attracted the support of one additional senator: Michigan Democrat Philip Hart.[6]

The decision of most doves to vote for war appropriations was undoubtedly influenced in many cases by their sincere opposition to unilateral withdrawal; they conceded the necessity of funding an American presence in Vietnam in the short term, even while criticizing the administration for not actively seeking a negotiated settlement.[7] It is also likely, however, that their votes were influenced by a strong desire to avoid even the appearance of undermining the efforts of the American soldiers in the field, a desire which, according to one leftist critic, had "much more power than even the communist hordes or the domino theory in deterring antiwar senators from actually doing anything to end the war."[8]

The inclination of most doves not to oppose war appropriations was reinforced by the attitude of the few senators who did. While devoting considerable attention to the preparation of their speeches, little if any effort was made by Morse, Gruening, or Nelson to speak informally with other senators and persuade them to join their cause. Morse, Gruening, and Nelson thus took their place in a long tradition of American dissent that gives the expression of moral rectitude precedence over political efficacy.[9]

In marked contrast to the failure of most doves to oppose specific appropriations for the war was their unanimous support (along with the majority of other senators) for two 1967 measures concerning the war generally: the Clark-Mansfield amendment and the Resolution for U.N. Security Council intervention. The first of these was proposed as a relatively uncontroversial substitute for an amendment offered by Clark on February 23 to the $12.3 billion fiscal 1967 supplemental appropriation for Vietnam. The original amendment would have expressed "the sense of Congress" that the appropriated monies not be used for "military operations in or over North Vietnam or to increase the number of United States military personnel in South Vietnam above 500,000 unless there shall have been a declaration of war in accordance with article 1, section 8 of the Constitution." The amendment further expressed Congress's support for all those "men of good will throughout the world" who were trying to prevent the expansion of the war and seeking its end "through a negotiated settlement which will preserve the honor of the United States, protect the vital interests of this country, and allow the people of South Vietnam to determine the affairs of that nation in their own way."[10]

The amendment had been proposed initially on the floor where it immediately met sharp resistance from several senators, particularly those opposed to any effort to restrict the bombing.[11] It was then withdrawn and another substituted by Mike Mansfield (D-Mont.), which, borrowing language from a "fall back" resolution offered by Clark, deleted any restriction on the military operations, any limitation on the number of men deployed, and any reference to the constitutional powers of Congress. Instead, the substitute amendment declared Congress's "firm intentions to provide all necessary support for members of the Armed Forces of the United States fighting in Vietnam." The substitute also expanded its reference to "men of good will throughout the world" to read "the President of the United States and other men of good will throughout the world." Finally, the amendment declared that Congress supported the Geneva Accords of 1954 and 1962 and "urges the convening of that Conference or any other meeting of nations similarly involved and interested as soon as possible for the purpose of formulating plans for bringing the conflict to an honorable conclusion in accordance with the principles of those accords." The amendment was passed, seventy-two to nineteen.[12]

Later in the year Mansfield once again submitted a resolution as a substitute for a more strongly worded declaration, this time one that Morse had drafted. Morse's original resolution would have declared that the president "should" seek emergency consideration of the Vietnam conflict by the U.N. Security Council, that the United States pledge itself in advance to obey its decision, and that, if the Council failed to act, the United States should "take all steps necessary to assure action on the issue by the General Assembly." The Morse resolution further declared the "objective" of the

United States to be "the immediate cessation of hostilities by all parties" and the taking of "appropriate measures, such as the convening of an international conference, for reaching a permanent settlement that will bring a lasting peace for Southeast Asia."[13] The Mansfield substitute resolution, by contrast, merely asked that the president "consider" taking the matter to the United Nations. It was also silent as to how the United States should respond to a decision of the Security Council, made no mention of the General Assembly, and refrained from making any broad declarations of American objectives. After hearings, the Senate Foreign Relations Committee unanimously voted its approval of the Mansfield substitute. Finally, on November 30, 1967, the resolution was passed by the Senate, eighty-two to zero.[14]

On their face, both the Clark-Mansfield amendment and the Mansfield resolution concerning the U.N. Security Council were so innocuous that their passage can hardly be considered a significant victory for Senate opponents of the war. The Clark-Mansfield amendment, in particular, with its unlimited pledge to "provide all necessary support" for American soldiers, and its uncritical reference to the president's efforts to achieve peace, can be read more as an endorsement of the administration's policies than a criticism of them. Indeed, representatives of the administration indicated that they supported the amendment, and it passed with the support of such pro-war senators as Everett Dirksen (R-Ill.), Thomas Dodd (D-Conn.), Bourke Hickenlooper (R-Iowa), Frank Lausche (D-Ohio), Gale McGee (D-Wyo.), George Smathers (D-Fla.), and Stuart Symington (D-Mo.).

Nonetheless, to dismiss the amendment as a mere endorsement of the status quo would be misleading. By coupling its pledge to supply the needs of American soldiers (but nothing in excess of these needs) with an endorsement of all efforts to bring the war to a negotiated settlement, the resolution implicitly rejected the hawks' call for escalation of the conflict and for fighting until an unambiguous victory was achieved. In fact, by explicitly referring to the Geneva Accords, the resolution implied that an acceptable solution might be ultimately achieved (as suggested by the accords) based on the unification of Vietnam. In any case, the vote on the resolution had the effect of showing, in a test of strength, that the Senate hawks were greatly outnumbered by the combined forces of the doves and pro-administration senators. Thus it sent a signal to the White House that a compromise settlement would be met in the Senate with more support than opposition.

The unanimously passed Mansfield resolution, which merely asked the president to "consider" taking Vietnam to the United Nations, was also more significant than it would seem at first glance. Despite the apparently innocuous nature of the resolution, the administration was deeply disturbed by Mansfield's initiative. Among other fears, the administration worried that if the Security Council rebuffed the United States, in Dean Rusk's words, "Some senators such as Morse would misinterpret this as a repudiation by the world body of the United States policy in Vietnam." In fact, such was the president's aversion to the resolution that it became a subject of extended discussion during at least two high-level meetings.[15]

More important than the rare and generally feckless efforts of doves to act as a legislative force was their use of the Senate as a forum for the discussion of Vietnam. As in the past, the Foreign Relations Committee led the way, convening hearings at which the administration's policies could be discussed and questioned. And, as in the past, the committee's witnesses consisted primarily of government officials and establishment figures whose views placed them, for the time being, in "exile" from the upper echelon of executive-branch policy makers. Among the dissenting witnesses to testify in 1967 were George Kennan, Edwin O. Reischauer, and James Gavin—all three of whom had at one time been "insiders," holding ambassadorships and other positions of official authority. Although these hearings were not televised and did not receive the attention of the 1966 hearings, they nonetheless continued to serve the function of expanding the contours of "responsible" debate on the war and on American foreign policy in general.[16]

As before, the Senate doves acted as a conduit (and escape valve) for the views of members of the "informed public"—especially liberals—who, with increasing numbers and mounting anger, opposed the war.[17] While the doves drew sustenance from these concerned constituencies, the constituencies gained legitimacy from Senate dissent.[18] Militant peace protesters also drew legitimacy from the Senate doves, although, at least in the short run, street demonstrations did more to hurt than to help senators who opposed the war.[19] But it would be an error to describe the antiwar movement of this period as exclusively or even primarily comprising such protesters. By 1967 opposition to the war encompassed the great majority of adult liberals and a significant part of the political center,[20] and a dove senator had to look no further than Walter Lippmann's column in his daily newspaper to be assured that in criticizing the war he was in respectable company.[21]

In fact, for senators with substantial liberal constituencies, opposition to the war had become not merely respectable; it had become increasingly a matter of political survival. In late August, Harry McPherson reported to the president on "a long dispiriting talk with Joe Tydings," a freshman Maryland Democrat whose adoptive father, a victim of McCarthy, had lost his seat in the 1950 mid-term elections. Tydings, according to McPherson, "has been a pretty good supporter up to now" but now considered Vietnam a "political albatross." In speaking to McPherson, Tydings had complained that "people are so frustrated and negative in Maryland that any reasonably good Republican could clobber me this year and probably next," and that "every political advisor I have says the only way I can save myself is by attacking the President." Tydings reported that Birch Bayh of Indiana, Ed Muskie of Maine, Fred Harris of Oklahoma, and Phil Hart of Michigan "all had the same story to tell in their states. It is Vietnam, Vietnam."[22] Other pro-administration liberals who privately expressed concern about the opposition of the electorate to the war included Vance Hartke of Indiana,[23] Harrison Williams of New Jersey,[24] and William Proxmire of Wisconsin.[25]

Conversely, reports of conversations with two senators who had been particularly outspoken in opposition to the war revealed a recent increase in their support. Frank Church (D-Idaho), who thought that public criticism of the administration's domestic programs "relates back directly to Vietnam," found that "for the first time his mail is beginning to reflect anti-Vietnam feelings." He now found "his personal standing" in Idaho was "on the upturn" and was "fairly optimistic at this time."[26] Similarly, Joseph Clark reported "his public criticism of the Administration had greatly enhanced his popularity in Pennsylvania—that he received applause for doing so in both urban and rural Pennsylvania."[27]

II

By the late summer of 1967, Vietnam was not merely a problem for liberal Democrats. Linked to the unpopular tax proposal and other domestic issues, the administration's Vietnam policy was increasingly a liability for senators along the whole spectrum of the president's party. In a confidential discussion, Thomas McIntyre (D-N.H.), a member of the Senate Democratic Campaign Committee, revealed "the feeling on the committee is that of the 23 Democratic senators up for reelection, only 3 are considered safe."[28]

Some of the most alarming reports to the White House came from moderate and conservative Democrats, bastions of the Senate "club" with high seniority and strategic committee assignments. For example, Alan Bible (D-Nev.), a conservative member of the Armed Services Committee, reported that "the Administration is at a low ebb in Nevada at this time." Although "the mail reflects a dissatisfaction over the Tax Bill, poverty programs, and domestic spending in general, the basic problem seems to stem from Vietnam." Bible had been "advised by prominent people in the state that he should disassociate himself more from the Administration."[29] Similarly, Mike Monroney of Oklahoma, a committee chairman who in the past had spoken publicly in support of the president's Vietnam policy, repeatedly complained during 1967 "that his consistent voting record with the Administration will have an adverse effect on him." Monroney expressed "aggravation with the circumstances of the tax bill and the Vietnam War," both of which he felt would be "costly in votes, unless there is a dramatic improvement in the Administration's posture over the next few months."[30] Likewise, Joseph Montoya of New Mexico reported that county chairmen he had spoken with earlier in the week "are alarmed at the low rating in the State of the President and the Democrats."[31]

Another senator interviewed, Jennings Randolph of West Virginia, was described as "a solid Democrat" who had been "basically loyal to the President and the Administration's program." "Aware of a great deal of restlessness throughout the country," Randolph had recently been moved to make a speech, expressing his "increasing reservations as to the determination of the government leaders of South Vietnam in this struggle."[32] Allen Ellender of Louisiana, chairman of the Agriculture Committee and a senior member of the Appropriations Committee, was reported to complain that "he had been misled on the Tonkin Gulf Resolution," and that generally the president "was following too closely the advice of the military."[33] Another informant reported that the hitherto loyal Herman Talmadge of Georgia "seems to be softening on Vietnam. He said that it has begun to appear we are not going to win over there and that he was for winning or getting out—and that this conflict had to be decided before November 1968."[34]

John Pastore of Rhode Island, a member of the Senate establishment with particularly close ties to the president,[35] was also upset about the political effects of the war. "Our problem is Vietnam," said Pastore, "boxes coming back, casualties going up—at home not a good word from anyone for us, and this attitude is reflected in the Senate." He feared that "we are losing good Democrats in droves—a paradox, affluent society that fears riots but fears Vietnam more." Thus it was now believed that "any Republican can do a better job."[36] Daniel Inouye of Hawaii, a self-described "staunch supporter of the President's policies," was receiving mail that showed "a discernable increase in the opposition to our involvement in Vietnam."[37] Meanwhile, according to Inouye, the Senate had descended into "anarchy," a place where "basic animal instincts" were unleashed, and senators were acting like "wild animals when they smell blood," with the weaker ones joining the attack "after the leaders have brought the quarry into bay."[38]

III

If senators and their constituents were increasingly disillusioned with the war, it was hardly inevitable—at least from the vantage point of the summer of 1967—that this disillusionment would redound to the advantage of the doves.[39] In the context of massively destructive riots, violent student protests, and inflation, the president's policies seemed, if anything, likely to incite a movement of rightist reaction.[40] Indeed, in the Senate, the most powerful force seemed to be the conservative hawks who echoed the popular desire to bring the war to an end by winning it rapidly.

The most aggressive senatorial manifestation of this movement took the form, in August, of a series of executive session hearings on air strategy held by John Stennis's Preparedness Investigating Subcommittee of the Armed Services Committee. Responding to friendly questioning and ingratiating comments from the senators, the chairman of the Joint Chiefs of Staff and other military leaders used the hearings to attack bombing restrictions imposed by the civilian leadership: restrictions on the number of bombing targets, restrictions on the pace of the bombing, restrictions on bombing near the Chinese border, restrictions on bombing in the Hanoi-Haiphong area, restrictions on bombing "sanctuary" areas, and restrictions on taking the measures necessary to close Haiphong's harbor.

The sole civilian witness, Robert McNamara, faced what his biographer has called "a kangaroo court."[41] In the face of some seven hours of unrelenting and hostile questioning, the secretary did his best to minimize the degree to which the bombing had been restricted, to minimize the tactical and strategic advantages of extending the bombing, and to maximize the risks of following such a course.[42]

After the hearings, a report issued by the subcommittee received front-page newspaper coverage and excited editorial comment. Siding with the generals, the report called for nothing less than "closing the Port of Haiphong, isolating it from the rest of the country, striking all meaningful targets with a military significance, and increasing the interdiction of the lines of communication from Red China." Thus the subcommittee not only brought into the open the long-standing disagreements between military and civilian leaders but reinforced the already common perception that the administration was not doing all it could to bring the war to a rapid and successful conclusion.[43]

The 1967 hearings of the Preparedness Investigating Subcommittee naturally invite comparison with the Senate hearings held sixteen years before in the wake of Truman's dismissal of General MacArthur.[44] Both sets of hearings took place in the context of an unpopular war that appeared stalemated. Both sets of hearings featured the testimony of generals who complained that plans for aggressive action that could bring the war to a successful conclusion were blocked by civilian leaders who, in turn, had predicted that such a course could lead to a disastrous confrontation with China. In both sets of hearings, senators posed questions which suggested that civilian leaders were somehow acting improperly in not deferring to the recommendations of the armed forces. Both featured protracted and hostile questioning of a controversial civilian leader who was held particularly responsible for undermining the cause of American victory—Dean Acheson in 1951, Robert McNamara in 1967.[45] And both had the immediate effect of weakening a liberal administration that was already showing signs of vulnerability to rightist attack.

Viewed historically, however, the similarities between the two sets of hearings are less important than their differences. The 1951 hearings took place at the very peak of the McCarthy inquisition, in a Washington electrified by accusations that were unleashed against the highest levels of government, especially its foreign policy and military apparatus. With virtually the whole Republican Party aligned with McCarthy, the hearings, unlike those held sixteen years later, were bitterly partisan and tainted by expressions of doubt about the very loyalty of the governing party. The 1951 hearings took place, moreover, in a context of a shattered left, of massive public displays of support for MacArthur's defiance of civilian authority, of a deterioration in American-Soviet relations, and of an increasingly widespread belief that the two countries were destined to go to war with each other. The 1967 hearings, by contrast, took place in a context in which relations with the Soviets had improved, in which McCarthyism had been pushed to the margins of respectable politics,[46] and in which the left was resurgent, drawing new strength from an influx of aggressive young activists unscathed by the fears and inhibitions of the preceding decade. In the wake of the MacArthur dismissal, rightists had publicly hanged effigies of Acheson. If in 1967 any effigies of McNamara were hanged, the executioners would have been left-wing antiwar demonstrators.

IV

There is another reason the Stennis hearings did not become a launching pad for an effective movement favoring escalation of the war: changes in the political culture of the Senate, particularly its so-called conservative coalition of Republicans and southern Democrats. By mid-1967, both components of this coalition, which might have been expected to serve as bases for a pro-war movement, were showing little inclination to play such a role. The southern Democrats, historically a bastion of Senate internationalism, by the late 1960s were showing increasing opposition to

American intervention abroad.[47] Whatever support they still gave to the war was usually provided without enthusiasm. Notably, the senators of the former Confederacy refused to echo the administration's rhetoric that the war was being fought to extend the benefits of the Great Society to Vietnam or even that the war was being fought to contain communism. Instead, they justified the intervention purely on grounds of honor and of the avoidance of the humiliation of defeat.[48] They often coupled these justifications, moreover, with reminders of their own personal opposition to intervention in the past and by otherwise disclaiming any responsibility for involving the United States in the war in the first place.[49] As already seen, during the Buddhist crisis, Russell and Stennis had shown their readiness to abandon the struggle altogether.[50] And such southern Democrats as A. Willis Robertson of South Carolina, Herman Talmadge of Georgia, and Allen Ellender of Louisiana had on other occasions expressed their doubts about the war.[51] This is not to mention the well-known dissent of J. William Fulbright of Arkansas and Albert Gore of Tennessee. Meanwhile, such nominal hawks as John McClellan of Arkansas and Sam Ervin of North Carolina used their positions to cause more difficulties for the White House's effort to build support for the war. McClellan, despite the private imploring of the administration, insisted on conducting an investigation of corruption at the highest levels of the Saigon government.[52] And Ervin, chairing his Subcommittee on the Separation of Powers, invited Fulbright to testify about the encroachments of the executive branch on the war powers of Congress.[53]

The Republican Party was also inhospitable to the growth of a powerful movement for escalation.[54] Rather than uniting behind the program of Barry Goldwater, the GOP fissured into factions favoring a variety of responses to the war. Only minorities within the party could be described as deeply committed to either hawk or dove positions. In May 1967 considerable publicity was given to a "white paper" by the staff of the Senate Republican Policy Committee. Issued under the aegis of the committee's chairman, Bourke Hickenlooper, the paper contained a highly critical history of American involvement in Vietnam. Chronicling first the opportunism of the Truman administration in involving the United States in Indochina (and its failure to insist that France grant it independence), the paper then emphasized the difference between (what the authors described as) the "limited" commitment of Eisenhower and the "open-ended" commitment of his Democratic successors. The authors gave particular emphasis to their view that "Republicans—for two decades—have believed that the United States must not become involved in a land war on the Asian continent" whereas the Democratic administration had done precisely that. And the authors provocatively asked: "Does the Republican Party serve America best by saying that politics stops at the water's edge? That we must rally behind the President? Does bipartisanship mean that Democratic mistakes are Republican responsibilities?" The paper did not, however, indicate how the Republicans proposed to bring the war to an end.[55] The omission was unsurprising in light of the fact that the paper had been prepared at the initiative of Senators Jacob Javits (R-N.Y), Charles Percy (R-Ill.), and Margaret Chase Smith (R-Me.), senators with significantly differing views of the war.[56]

Notwithstanding the many differences within the party, later in the year, a wide array of Republicans—ranging from the conservative Strom Thurmond of South Carolina to the liberal Mark Hatfield of Oregon—cosponsored a resolution submitted by Charles Percy which declared "that the armed forces of the United States should not continue to bear an ever-increasing proportion of the fighting in Vietnam." The resolution also called upon the South Vietnamese and other Asian non-Communist governments to "contribute substantially more manpower and resources to share the military, diplomatic, economic and psychological tasks in Vietnam," and declared that the president "should move with greater determination to obtain commitments of such manpower and resources in support of the effort in Vietnam."[57] To say the least, the resolution—which McNamara described as "nasty"[58]—was received by the administration with displeasure. In addition to its potential to create friction between the United States and its Asian allies, it threatened to weaken and isolate the administration politically. The administration's fear was rooted in reality as the resolution won the support of a wide spectrum of Republicans, while enjoying the sponsorship of a wide range of senators belonging to the president's own party including (from left to right) Clark, Abraham Ribicoff (Conn.), Daniel Brewster (Md.), Randolph, Talmadge, and Harry Byrd Jr. (Va.).

In general, the development of a strong hawk movement among southern Democrats and among Republicans was inhibited by the concerns of their conservative and right-wing constituencies during this period. In contrast to liberals who typically viewed Vietnam as the issue of the day, for conservatives concern about the war was typically subsumed in a larger group of anxieties related to (in their view) a prodigiously liberal regime in Washington, an alarming growth in civil disorders and other forms of lawlessness, and a general deterioration in moral discipline. Whatever apprehension a conservative of this period may have felt about the advance of Communism in Southeast Asia was likely to have been surpassed by the anxieties aroused by the televised images of protest demonstrations and riots and the threat they seemed to pose to his own country.[59]

The cause of South Vietnam, moreover, never assumed the privileged place among conservatives in the 1960s that Nationalist China had enjoyed at the beginning of the preceding decade. Whereas Chiang Kai-shek and his lobby had been enthusiastically embraced by the Republican Party, Diem found affection in a much smaller group of legislators, centered on a handful of Catholic Democratic senators.[60] Needless to say, Diem's successors inspired even less enthusiasm from members of either party.

The relatively marginal position of Vietnam as a conservative cause is further revealed by examining the priorities of the Liberty Lobby during this period. While this rightist organization, with close ties to conservative legislators,[61] devoted considerable resources to an effort to defeat Senate ratification of the Soviet Consular Treaty and lobbied aggressively in opposition to American compliance with the embargo against Rhodesia, it remained all but passive with respect to the war in Vietnam. Indeed, its newsletter's description of the upcoming congressional debate and vote on the 1967 supplemental appropriation for Vietnam seemed to imply a preference that the bill be defeated: "Supplemental War Budget—Noisy debate followed by sheep-like approval of anything LBJ asks."[62] On the other hand, while the Liberty Lobby refused to use its influence to forge congressional support for the war, the liberal Republican Ripon Society and the pacifist Friends Committee on National Legislation made opposition to the war a major focus of their efforts.[63]

Of at least equal importance, senators from both parties who might otherwise have aggressively pushed for an escalation of the war were inhibited by the mounting anxieties of the business community about the war's economic consequences, particularly the growth of the deficit, the trade imbalance and drain on gold, and the mounting danger of serious inflation. Alarming reports from economists of the possibly catastrophic consequences of continuing on the present course, combined with the announced deployment of yet forty-five thousand additional soldiers, helped spread Senate concern about Vietnam beyond the specialized committees charged with foreign and military affairs. And Johnson's surplus tax proposal—which the president himself explicitly linked to the war—served as an additional catalyst ensuring that the congressional discussion of taxing and spending would also become a debate about Vietnam.[64] Needless to say, the debate was hardly conducive to the fulfillment of the president's program either at home or abroad.

V

Concerns about the economy and Vietnam converged with a growing belief among a wide spectrum of senators that the United States was over-extended and excessively prone to intervene abroad. Although, as we have seen, most senators were inhibited from translating this concern into legislation affecting the war in Vietnam, many showed a greater willingness to oppose new interventions as, in the words of one journalist, "No More Vietnams" became "a virtually universal sentiment on Capitol Hill."[65] This noninterventionism was complemented by an increased sensitivity to executive branch incursions on the prerogatives of Congress. Like the new non-interventionism, this concern with constitutional prerogatives was shared by a wide range of senators, including internationalists in the Fulbright mold, who in the past had viewed congressional involvement in foreign affairs as largely an obstacle to the making of good policy.

Both of these tendencies—noninterventionism and concern with congressional prerogatives—were dramatically manifested in early July when Johnson dispatched three transport planes to the Congo. Russell, Fulbright, Clifford Case (R-N.J.), Mansfield, Milton Young (R-N.Dak.) and Stennis immediately took to the Senate floor to protest the action. Although the intervention took place thousands of miles from Southeast Asia, Vietnam was very much on the minds of the protesting senators.

"Vietnam started with a force not much larger than this," said Russell. "This presence can swell, and it will swell. If a few sons of American mothers are killed in the Congo, there will be an irresistible demand in this country that something be done about it." Similarly, Fulbright spoke of the likelihood that the intervention would grow into "a confrontation with other parties." He expressed his hope that "at the very least, such intrusions into other countries will not be made until there has been serious consultation with the Senator from Georgia and other interested Senators. In that way we might be given an opportunity, not just to receive a telephone call but to discuss these matters and possibly, I hope, to impose some restraints on this kind of intervention." Stennis wondered whether the administration had learned anything from its experience in Vietnam: "Certainly . . . if we have not already learned a lesson by going it alone and getting unnecessarily involved on the other side of the world, we never will learn it."[66]

Spurred by this crisis, a few days later Fulbright and Russell privately agreed to work together for passage of a resolution on "national commitments." According to the terms of the resolution, the president would be forbidden from committing the United States to the defense of any other nation in the absence of "affirmative action taken by the executive and legislative branches of the U.S. Government through means of a treaty, convention, or legislative instrumentality specifically intended to give effect to such commitment."[67]

There is a rough symmetry between the effect of the 1967 Congo intervention on conservative senators with that of the 1965 Dominican intervention on their liberal colleagues. Both interventions were relatively minor affairs that aroused what seemed to be a disproportionately large senatorial reaction. In both cases, the strong reaction was a direct consequence of a deep unhappiness with the Vietnam War, which made senators quick to perceive similarities between that war and the new foreign intervention. In both cases, moreover, the administration had damaged its credibility with senators by originally claiming that the intervention was necessary to protect or rescue American citizens, only to have the true reason later revealed. And in both cases, there were aspects of the intervention that seemed to confirm anxieties related to the broader worldview of senators be it liberal or conservative. Sending the Marines into the Dominican Republic seemed to senators like Fulbright to represent a regression to the policies of Dulles who, in his zeal to oppose Communism, placed the United States in the role of crushing genuinely popular movements merely because they included the participation of some Communists. The intervention into the Congo, for its part, seemed to confirm the conservative fear that the State Department was siding with irresponsible forces in black Africa.[68] In his speech, Russell had emphasized that the white mercenaries that the Congolese regime was opposing had not harmed any civilians. By contrast, it had been soldiers of the Congolese army—whose government the administration was intervening to support—who had engaged in a massacre of civilians, including several Europeans.

The Dominican intervention had been the event that provoked Fulbright to make public disagreements he had hitherto kept to himself. Similarly, Russell, who had previously agreed not to speak openly against American policy in Vietnam, when faced with the intervention in the Congo, felt it his duty to make "this public protest" only because his past private criticisms had not been heeded.[69] Just as the Dominican fiasco pushed liberals further from the administration and exacerbated their already-growing anxieties about Vietnam, the Congolese intervention reinforced conservative alienation from the administration. Most significantly, it created conditions propelling conservative senators to make common cause with dove opponents of the Vietnam War in order to bring about a general redirection in foreign policy and to reassert the constitutional powers of Congress.

Of course, a major difference between the two controversies is that in 1965 Fulbright and his allies had had to act in the teeth of the opposition of conservative senators. By contrast, in 1967, the Senate, from left to right, presented a united front in opposition to the administration's latest adventure. Another major difference between 1965 and 1967 was the administration's reaction. After Fulbright spoke out against the invasion of the Dominican Republic, the president's response was intransigent and punitive. After Fulbright and his conservative allies publicly opposed the intervention in the Congo, on the other hand, the president's response was solicitous and reassuring, with Rusk "rushing to Capitol Hill to promise the early withdrawal of planes and men," and the State Department announcing that it had rejected a similar request for help from the embattled Nigerian government.[70]

The causes of the change are undoubtedly to be found in the considerable breakdown of the president's support in the Senate and the relative size and breadth of the opposition to the two interventions; the first was an opposition of Fulbright and the Senate's left, the second an opposition of Fulbright and the Senate's very leadership. Although precipitated by interventions elsewhere, both oppositions were responses to profound unhappiness with the administration's policies in Vietnam. One of the cumulative effects of the Dominican and Congolese adventures was the unification of liberal and conservative senators who were unhappy with the war in Vietnam. But the two adventures did more than that. As evidenced by the Fulbright-Russell bloc for the National Commitments Resolution, the adventures encouraged liberal and conservative senators to doubt the fundamental assumptions that had guided American foreign policy since the beginning of the Cold War.[71]

VI

Meanwhile, public and Senate opposition to the war continued and deepened. "We've almost lost the war in the last two months in the court of public opinion," observed Johnson in late October 1967. "These demonstrators and others are trying to show that we need somebody else to take over the country." The shift this time seemed to redound to the advantage of the doves. "The hawks," said Johnson, "are throwing in the towel."[72] The ranks of the doves, on the other hand, were growing. Perhaps the most significant examples of this development were the defections to the opposition in late 1967 of two highly influential senators who had previously been strong supporters of the war: Missouri Democrat Stuart Symington and Kentucky Republican Thruston Morton.

Originally a strong hawk, Symington's views, in Ward Just's description, "began to crystallize into a paradoxical formulation where American arms could have won the war, but the price now was too high, a game not worth the candle."[73] As early as January 1967, while still holding to his hawk position, Symington noted the "irritation among relatively friendly nations at our continuing unfavorable balance of payments—with the consequent steady drain on our gold supply," a problem that "is directly related to the high and mounting costs of this major ground war in Asia."[74] By the end of the year, having abandoned support of the war entirely, he privately told Jack Valenti that the United States had made three errors in Vietnam: "underestimating the durability of the Vietcong"; a "theory of gradual-

ism [which] has consistently underestimated the Vietcong in Hanoi";
and "overestimating the concept of nationhood in [South] Vietnam. They
couldn't last an hour without us and it is a matter of common knowledge
that most of the top leaders are crooks."[75]

Thruston Morton's conversion to the opposition was proclaimed at a
rally sponsored by the newly formed Business Executives Move for Peace in
Vietnam. "If the President of the United States has been mistaken," Morton
told the assembled executives, "so have I." Recalling Eisenhower's warning
"of too much power and too much influence in the hands of a 'military-
industrial complex,'" Morton stated his belief that "President Johnson was
brainwashed by this power center as early as 1961 when, as Vice President,
he ventured to Saigon on a fact-finding mission." The time had now come
to break with these mistaken policies and seek disengagement from the
conflict. To this end, he proposed that the United States immediately stop
the bombing, refrain from search-and-destroy missions, reduce the size of
its forces and concentrate them in coastal enclaves, and pressure the South
Vietnamese to negotiate with the NLF and carry out internal reforms. He
also wanted the United States to try to create an atmosphere conducive to
discussion among the different factions of Vietnamese and the peoples of
different countries in the region upon whose cooperation a lasting peace
would ultimately depend.

Morton took issue with the president's assertion that the war "is worth
the price." Although the alternatives to the president's policy would "not
be cheap," Morton pointed out that nobody could claim that "the present
policies have not been costly." In fact they had prevented the United States
from pursuing its "number one priority" of reaching "an accord with the
Soviet Union." The war had other costs as well: it created a "crisis of confidence and credibility" that threatened "economic and social progress here
and abroad"; it prevented the United States from responding to a European
"revolution of independence" that "challenges American initiative"; it prevented the United States from responding in Latin America to "a revolution of rising population and rising expectations that threatens the future
of our continent"; and, at home, it contributed to "a dangerous political
polarization," in which "extremists of left and right are poised to destroy
our basic social fabric."[76]

The conversions of Symington and Morton were a significant mile-
stone in the development of Senate dissent against the Vietnam War. Both

were men of moderate views, members of the Senate establishment[77] and leaders of their parties. Symington was the only senator serving on both the Armed Services and Foreign Relations committees. Morton, a ranking member of the Finance Committee, was a former chairman of his party. The *New York Times,* in its front-page report on Morton's speech, described him as "one of the Senate's most influential Republicans."[78] Both had been deeply implicated in the formulation of foreign policy during the Cold War. In addition to their role as senators, each had for a time held positions of responsibility in the executive branch. Symington had been appointed by Truman to be the first secretary of the air force. Morton had served under Dulles as assistant secretary of state for congressional liaison. It was in this capacity that, in 1954, he had tried (unsuccessfully) to persuade Richard Russell to support American intervention to lift the siege at Dien Bien Phu.[79]

The two senators also had similar social backgrounds. Both had come from long-established families of wealth with a history of political leadership. Both had been graduated from Yale in the 1920s, had served in the military in time of war, and both had enjoyed successful careers in industry before becoming involved in politics. (Symington, who, among other things, had manufactured gun turrets for war planes before becoming secretary of the air force, had been described as a member of the "military-industrial establishment."[80]) Both senators had wide-ranging geographic connections as well. Each had strong ties to the east although representing states in the heart of the Mississippi Valley; and the states themselves were geographically, culturally, and politically ambiguous, standing at the border of North and South, slave states at the time of the Civil War that had remained within the Union. And both men—through their connections to constituents, the Senate, their parties, and industry—were highly influential; they were representatives not of one "establishment" but seemed, in some sense, to personify the convergence of several elites: political, senatorial, and social. The abandonment by these men of the cause of military victory in Vietnam therefore represented a significant gain for those opposed to the war and a grave blow to a president who had once hoped to wage that war with a broad consensus.[81] The consensus was soon to suffer still further blows when at the end of January 1968 the Vietnamese Communists launched their Tet offensive.

CHAPTER 9

1968: Another Turn

I

Sir Robert Thompson has remarked that in launching the Tet offensive at the end of January 1968, the North Vietnamese expected "a mass uprising in Saigon. What they got, of course, was a mass uprising in the United States."[1] Although the statement is obviously hyperbolic, it nonetheless points to a fundamental truth: however one might evaluate its military achievements in Vietnam, there can be no doubt that in the United States the offensive decisively tilted the balance in favor of the war's opponents. Extensively covered on television, the offensive brought into American homes a series of images that deeply disturbed an already war-weary public, making them witness to, among other things, the besieging of the American embassy in Saigon by Communists and the summary execution of a suspected Communist by South Vietnamese General Nguyen Ngoc Loan on a Saigon street. If the first of these images strongly suggested that the strength and support of the Communists had been underestimated, the second pointed to the dilemma of means and ends that dogged the effort to crush the Communists. The dilemma seemed to be epitomized in the reported statement of an American officer at the village of Ben Tre that "we had to destroy it in order to save it."[2]

Public support for the administration and the war, already fragile before the offensive, now deteriorated,[3] while elite opinion converged and crystallized in support of disengagement.[4] This transformation of elite opinion crossed all levels and organs of official power and private influence, encompassing Johnson's new secretary of defense, the so-called Wise Men who had previously counseled intervention, and finally, at the end of March, the president himself.

In contrast to early 1966 when Fulbright convened the first televised hearings on Vietnam, the Senate was no longer the most prominent component of elite dissent against the war. By 1968 it was but one of an expanding array of forces opposed to the administration's policies. Although in absolute terms Senate dissent was greater than it had been previously, its relative importance was lessened as opposition—mass and elite—to the war increased to unprecedented levels of size, breadth, and intensity. If in 1966 Senate dissent can be described as having the prominence of a flute in a baroque ensemble, in 1968 it had greater resemblance to a violin in a mighty Wagnerian orchestra, its distinct voice obscured by that of a hundred other instruments playing at fortissimo.

Nonetheless, senators continued to add their voice to the larger debate on Vietnam, and, no less than a violin in the midst of an orchestra, even became at moments distinctly audible. This was particularly true with respect to the economic consequences of the war, which necessarily implicated Congress because its consent was required to enact passage of a tax surcharge to cover the costs of the war (and avoid a widely predicted disaster for the economy) and to enact legislation addressing the mounting gold crisis. This was dramatically illustrated on February 28 when Jacob Javits (R-N.Y), blaming the crisis on "rising levels of expenditure in Vietnam and mounting budget deficits," called for a number of strong measures, including a suspension of gold payments to foreign countries. The proposal, made in a Senate floor speech, predicted that, in the absence of such measures, "there would be some kind of financial or economic Armageddon in this world."[5] Although Javits had prefaced his speech by declaring that he did not speak for the administration and lacked inside knowledge of its plans, his remarks triggered an international gold panic with more than $118 million withdrawn from the gold pool within two days.[6]

Meanwhile, as the casualties and economic anxieties mounted, the Senate floor continued to serve as a forum for debate on the war. In these discussions, the dominant voices were those of the administration's critics.[7] At the same time, senators of both left and right sounded the alarm about the economic effects of the war.[8] The Foreign Relations Committee once again interjected itself into the Vietnam debate by holding two well-publicized sets of hearings, the first—with McNamara in the witness chair—an investigation of the events that led to enactment of the Gulf of Tonkin Resolution, the second—with Rusk in the witness chair—a more general inquiry about the administration's war policies.

Administration critics who hoped for an aggressive investigation of the incidents were disappointed by the Gulf of Tonkin hearings. Members of the Committee exercised what some considered undue restraint in their interrogations of the secretary.[9] McNamara, moreover, was able to exercise control of the hearings when he presented the senators with what he claimed to be intercepts of North Vietnamese messages confirming that the disputed August 4, 1964, attack actually took place. Lacking technical expertise, the senators were forced to rely on McNamara's interpretations of the messages, interpretations that later investigations demonstrated to be inaccurate.[10] The secretary also showed himself, as he had many times in the past, a remarkably polished witness with a capacity to make assertions with a sense of conviction and sound of plausibility even where they only bore a tenuous relationship to the truth.

The hearings, nonetheless, were hardly beneficial to the administration. Although the senators failed to break McNamara as a witness, they certainly did succeed in putting him and the administration on the defensive. It was damaging enough for the administration that the investigation was taking place at all.[11] Due to the president's own repeated assertion that Congress's approval of Tonkin Gulf resolution gave him the authority to intervene in Vietnam, the resolution took on growing importance, as did the claims used to induce senators to give it their vote. By the logic of the president's position, the questioning of the accuracy of these claims became a questioning of the legitimacy of the war itself.[12]

Adding to the damage was the fact that the central issue of the hearings was whether the administration had been truthful, a question which hit the Johnson administration at a particularly vulnerable point because it had already been baited for at least three years as lacking credibility. Thus, the hearings added to the doubts of a public that already was prone to view the administration with skepticism, which is to say nothing of the enormous unhappiness of the public with the war and the growth in hostile feelings toward the president—facts that added to the administration's vulnerability to an investigation that took as its subject the basis on which the president justified the war. Nor is it to mention the particular context of February 1968 when the hearing took place: the shock of Tet and the new crisis concerning the capture of the *Pueblo* spy ship by the North Koreans. These, too, could have only served to make the public more likely to share the doubts expressed by the investigating senators.[13]

Finally, the hearings themselves were remarkable for what they did show. If McNamara always seemed to have an answer to the senators' questions, many of his answers seemed inadequate and invited further inquiry rather than belief. Certain facts, moreover, did come to light despite McNamara's polished performance: that the resolution had been prepared prior to the incidents,[14] that doubts had been expressed by military personnel —including the task force captain who was aboard one of the ships—about whether one of the attacks had taken place,[15] that there was uncertainty as to whether the ships entered waters that the North Vietnamese claimed as their own,[16] and perhaps of even greater importance, that the administration, while claiming that the attacks were "unprovoked" and that the ships were on "routine patrol," had failed to disclose that the ships were engaged in surveillance missions against North Vietnam and had also failed to disclose that these coincided with South Vietnamese raids on North Vietnamese territory conducted with the aid of American-supplied boats.[17] Notwithstanding his general exercise of restraint, Fulbright was able to suggest that the administration was ready to engage in ruthless tactics to inhibit military cooperation with his investigation when he announced that a commander who had spoken to him about the subject had been forcibly committed to a psychiatric ward the following day.[18]

The Gulf of Tonkin hearings, however, paled in comparison to the hearings three weeks later with Rusk as a witness. Broadcast on network television, this was Rusk's first public appearance before the committee since the famous 1966 hearings. The 1968 hearings began one day after the *New York Times* reported General Westmoreland's request for 206,000 additional troops and that a general reassessment of Vietnam policy was taking place at the White House. In addition to the anxieties triggered by these reports—which signaled that a major escalation of the war might be imminent—the hearings were convened in an atmosphere still very much colored by the shock of the Tet offensive, post-Tet weekly American casualty rates exceeding five hundred, the ominous siege at Khe Sanh, a gold panic, and signs that discontent with the war was rising even further.[19]

Fulbright opened the hearings by castigating the administration for defending the war with a series of claims that were not sustained by reality: that the war showed the capacity of the United States to defeat "wars of liberation': that failure to fight in Vietnam would force Americans to fight "closer to home, in Hawaii and even California"; that the struggle to protect the South Vietnamese regime was a struggle for freedom; and that the Gulf of Tonkin Resolution was the "functional equivalent of a declaration of war." What reality did show, according to Fulbright, was something very different than any of the administration's claims: "that, even with an army of a half million men and expenditures which approach $30 billion a year, we cannot win a civil war for a regime which is incapable of inspiring the patriotism of its own people."

In contrast to the hearings two years before when he had defensively emphasized the desirability of public discussion of Vietnam, Fulbright now aggressively attacked the substance of the administration's policies, whose consequences included division among Americans and loss of reputation abroad. In Fulbright's view, the "fate of a small and war-torn Asian nation" had also become "the fate of America, not because it had to be so but because our leaders have made it so." Through the commitment of a half-million young men "to bloody and endless combat in these distant jungles, our leaders have converted a struggle between Vietnamese into a struggle between Americans for possession of the American spirit." The war had led to a "discrepancy between present policies and the traditional values of America." Not long ago, Americans believed that "their principal contribution to the world to be their own example as a decent and democratic society. Now, with our country beset by crises of poverty and race, as we wait and arm ourselves for the annual summer of violence, with our allies alienated and our people divided by the most unpopular war in our history, the light of the American example burns dim around the world."

Even more "alarming" to Fulbright was "the dimming of optimism among the American people," especially the youth, who "having believed too well what they were brought up to believe in, have risen up in a kind of spiritual rebellion against what they regard as the betrayal of traditional American values." Evidence of this rebellion was to be seen "all around us—not just in the hippie movement and in the emergence of an angry 'new left' but in the sharp declines in applications for the Peace Corps, in the turning away of promising students from careers in Government, in letters of protest against the war and troubled consciences about the draft."

Expressing skepticism about the administration's claim that the nation could afford the $30 billion annual cost of the war, Fulbright wondered whether, even if this claim were true, the nation could afford its other costs:

> Can we afford the sacrifice of American lives in so dubious a cause?
> Can we afford the horrors that are being inflicted on the people
> of a poor and backward land? Can we afford the alienation of our
> allies, the neglect of our own deep domestic problems, and the disil-
> lusionment of our youth? Can we afford the loss of confidence in
> our Government and institutions, the fading of hope and optimism,
> and the betrayal of our traditional values?[20]

Several other senators emphasized the war's more tangible costs. Symington reiterated his doubt about whether the United States could "continue the gigantic financial costs incident to this major ground war in Asia" without the American economy becoming "nonviable."[21] Joseph Clark wondered, in light of its limited achievements to date, how much more money the administration planned "to plow" into the pacification program. The war, according to Clark, had "become a cancer" whose "casualties only began on the battlefield." Its victims were both economic and noneconomic: "the programs of the Great Society, the balance of payments, a sound budget, a stable dollar, the world's good will, détente with the Soviet Union, and hopes for a durable world peace."[22] And Claiborne Pell wanted to know if there was a "top price" that the United States was willing to pay to con- tinue in Vietnam.[23]

Pell and Frank Church saw the war as symptomatic of a foreign policy that committed the United States beyond its resources. "We have already spent so lavishly abroad," observed Church, "that by the end of this year we will have spent an incredible $100 billion, or nearly so, on Vietnam alone." In addition to disengaging from Vietnam, Pell suggested that the United States reduce its treaty commitments and "make what we call in business terms general partnerships into more limited partnerships." More broadly, Church argued that the United States needed a foreign policy that created "a rational balance between commitment and capacity."[24]

On the second day of hearings, Fulbright returned to the question of costs by citing an editorial from the *Wall Street Journal,* which he described as "certainly a very responsible and excellent publication." According to the editorial, which Fulbright read aloud, "The Administration is duty bound to recognize that no battle and no war is worth any price, no matter how ruinous, and that in the case of Vietnam it may be failing for the simple reason that the whole place and cause is changing from within." Clifford Case, a former Wall Street lawyer, had similarly been influenced by another conservative publication, the *Telegraph* of London, which had recently printed an editorial by Peregrine Westhorne, hitherto a supporter of the war. In the editorial, which Case quoted at length, Westhorne revealed that he no longer found it possible "to be certain that fighting on—at such a terrible cost in degradation—will prove a less debilitating exercise for the United States than suffering the humiliation of withdrawal." Case said his own position was "almost exactly" that of Westhorne. Case, like Westhorne, was particularly concerned that America could only achieve its ends in Vietnam at the expense of "more destruction in South Vietnam and more and more degradation at home."[25]

A similar position was taken by Albert Gore. "Our leaders and people are determined and proud," observed the senior senator from the Volunteer State. "They would find a humiliation" if the United States conceded its inability to achieve its goals in Vietnam. Nonetheless, the time had come for Americans "to measure this disagreeable possibility alongside the possible disastrous consequences of a wider war which military leaders represent as necessary for the achievement of victory." It was now incumbent on all Americans "to guard their vanities and to suppress their ambitions, and to take and support such action as appears in the long-term best interest of the country."[26]

Pell, when addressing the costs of the war, was the only senator to relate the suffering it caused the Vietnamese to the damage it did to American "moral values." For Pell, the United States had to address the "basic question" of whether it was "more important to continue the killing to attain the objectives so the people who are killed will lie in graveyards that are in non-Communist territory" or to abandon its objectives so as to stop the suffering. Rusk, in responding, noted that "I have never myself personally tried to put these great matters strictly on moral ground, because I feel it is for providence to make moral judgments." He was also disturbed that Pell seemed more ready to condemn the Americans than the Communists for their misdeeds. Pell replied, "I would agree with you that both sides have lost moral values, but I wonder if we haven't lost the most because we started from a higher moral plane."[27]

As before, the anxiety of the doves about an American escalation of
the conflict was exacerbated by their fear that it would simply lead the
Communists to increase their own involvement even further. China with
its vast population, in particular, presented the frightening possibility that
an escalation pushed too far could provoke a general war of unspeakable
proportions on the Asian mainland. "In Asia," Church warned, "there are
vast populations that are waiting to engulf us." It was likely, moreover, that
if American solders remained in Vietnam they would continue to carry a
disproportionate burden of the fighting and casualties. Referring to the statistics of the previous year showing American casualties in excess of those
suffered by the South Vietnamese army, Church said "when it reaches that
point I think the policy is sick." The success of the Communists during the
Tet offensive would not have been possible but for significant support for
them among the South Vietnamese. In fact, corruption and incompetence
were so pervasive in South Vietnam and its army, that "they have lost the
capacity to command the respect of the people."[28]

Case agreed with Church's assessment of South Vietnam and went a
step further, suggesting that, under these circumstances, South Vietnam
had actually forfeited its right to exist. According to Case, "There [was] no
such thing as a right of a country to exist apart from its willingness and
ability to preserve its own existence." Rusk responded by saying that the
implication of this "startled" him as it seemed to suggest that aggression
could be tolerated and because it was inconsistent with the whole frame-
work of international law set forth in the U.N. Charter. Case, however,
remained steadfast, asserting that "the primary qualification of a nation
is its ability to exist by itself" and that "it is error . . . to think there is
anything in the status quo at any particular time that we are required to
enforce."[29]

Gore too evinced a readiness to abandon official orthodoxy when he
complained that American policy was "based upon almost exclusively western values. One man, one vote, a constitution, democracy." Gore wanted
to know if the United States had any right "to assume that the Vietnamese
people want them or appreciate them or attach any particular importance
to them?"[30] Other issues raised by committee doves included whether the
administration had made adequate efforts to initiate peace talks,[31] whether
the administration was willing to abide by the Geneva Accords,[32] whether

the conflict was a civil war,[33] whether the incidents in the Gulf of Tonkin had been provoked by the United States,[34] whether the United States was in effect a hostage of its client state,[35] whether the SEATO pact actually required the United States to be in Vietnam,[36] and whether the Senate would be consulted prior to any decision to escalate the war.[37] The last inquiry, pursued with unusual zeal by the chairman, yielded only equivocal answers.[38]

Two senators who were not doves, as in the past, refused to comport themselves in a manner helpful to the administration. Frank Carlson, a nominal supporter of the war, echoed its critics when he expressed his fear that in attempting to save the people of South Vietnam, the United States was actually destroying their country. The Kansas Republican confronted Rusk with a statement by a former head of the International Voluntary Services that the Americans in the eyes of many Vietnamese "have become foreign invaders with too many troops and too much money" and that "our policies are creating more Vietcong than we are able to kill." Carlson also expressed his disagreement with the official position that the Tet offensive had ended in a victory for the Americans, and noted the discrepancy between government accounts of the war and those of reporters who were "much more pessimistic."[39]

Another Republican, John Williams of Delaware, a thoroughly reactionary senator with a deep and abiding hostility toward the president, also refused to give Rusk any comfort. Forming a united front with some of the doves, he called attention to the lack of effort by the other member nations of SEATO. He also inquired about the availability of official reports on corruption in South Vietnam. And then, returning to a favorite conservative theme, he vehemently attacked Great Britain for permitting her flagships to trade with Hanoi, while hypocritically insisting that other nations abide by its embargo of Rhodesia. "It is a little hard for us," said Williams, "to explain to our constituents why some of our former [!] allies are trading with North Vietnam at a time when American boys are dying there."[40]

Senators actually trying to help the administration (or its beleaguered witness) were scarce. Ranking Democrat John Sparkman of Alabama, during a brief round of questioning, elicited testimony of Communist intransigence with respect to negotiations and a record of violating truces. However, when Sparkman tried to get Rusk to emphasize the treachery

involved in the recent violation of the Tet truce, Rusk balked; the secretary
was more interested in refuting the charge that the Americans were taken
by surprise by the offensive due to poor intelligence than in scoring points
against Hanoi for launching a surprise attack. Rusk responded similarly to
questions posed by Lausche on the same theme.[41]

The administration may have felt some small comfort when Bourke
Hickenlooper complained that "every time I pick up a paper or magazine
or news magazine, of some kind . . . there is a picture of a child or a poor
woman or somebody injured by the Americans or killed by the Americans,"
and that there was a lack of publicity on the atrocities committed by the
Communists.[42] On the other hand, it is possible—as is the risk in libel liti-
gation—that even in complaining about these pictures he was spreading
their message. In any case, Hickenlooper refrained from asking any questions or offering any other comments that might have helped Rusk make
his case for the administration's policies.

Frank Lausche seemed to make more of an effort to help the administration. To this end, he posed a series of rather pedantic leading questions
on U.S. treaty obligations and various charges made against the United
States, including "making prostitutes of the women of South Vietnam"
and "committing atrocities and cruelties by design and plan." In addition,
Lausche called for an end to public hearings on Vietnam because "[h]earings
are usually held with a view to taking action," whereas no concrete legislative proposal was contemplated by the committee.[43]

Lausche then, to the discomfort of the committee doves, proposed
that "instead of talking and talking" about Vietnam, they submit to the
Senate for a vote resolutions embodying their views.[44] The response to this
proposal revealed the persistent anxiety of many doves about mounting a
legislative challenge to the administration. Fulbright said that "personally,
I am ready to take action now, and would do so on the floor, but I think a
degree of education is necessary, and that is what these hearings are for."
Vermont Republican George Aiken said he thought the onus should be
on supporters of the administration to submit a resolution of *their* views.
Gore said he thought a resolution would only lead "to a stalemate between
the President and Senate"; what was needed was "teamwork" between the
two branches of government. And Mike Mansfield said he thought that
since sense of the Senate resolutions had no "validity," "you get back to

the basic point that under our system of government the buck stops at the White House. He has the final say."[45]

In addition to Lausche (and perhaps Sparkman), there were probably only two other senators on the committee who still unequivocally supported the war: South Dakota Republican Karl Mundt and Connecticut Democrat Thomas Dodd. On the defensive in early 1968,[46] they criticized the administration for failing, in Dodd's words, "to give the people an adequate reason for us paying so high a price in blood and treasure in Vietnam."[47] This failure was a consequence of what the senators suggested was the contradiction between the administration's call for Americans to take up arms against Communism in Vietnam while simultaneously pursuing détente and an end to the Cold War.

Mundt, a highly conservative senator who had been close to Joseph McCarthy, was clearly shaken by the amount of controversy that now surrounded the war. "Never before," said Mundt, "in all the wars that I have studied, have we had quite this degree of divisiveness, quite this extent of debate in public places, in Congress and around the country by prominent people as we are having in connection with this war." Mundt disputed those who claimed that this dissension was due to "the fact that it isn't God that is dead, it's patriotism that is dead." On the contrary, he believed that "basically our people are as patriotic as they have been in previous wars." The cause of the dissension was not a lack of patriotism but the failure of the administration to convince the American people that the war was nothing less than "the cutting edge" and "fighting front" in the "global contest between communism . . . and the desire of the people of the free world to live in their own way without being the victims of aggression."[48]

Mundt was also full of contempt for the way the Democratic administration tried to justify the war by stressing free elections and public works projects for the Vietnamese, and asked Rusk if the administration was conducting "a war or a WPA project?" He also attacked the administration for its "indefensible policy" of issuing licenses to American firms to trade with various Communist countries. Many of the materials acquired by the Communists through this trade were then used to help the cause of Hanoi. This policy, according to Mundt, not only undermined the military struggle in Vietnam but caused among the American people "a complete sense of bewilderment as to what this is all about."[49]

Dodd endorsed Mundt's criticism of the administration's failure to explain the war as a struggle against international Communism. "In a larger sense," Dodd asked, "isn't this really a global conflict between the free world and the Communist world? Isn't that what it really is all about?"[50] In answering Mundt and Dodd, Rusk assumed the role of a liberal advocate of an enlightened and realistic foreign policy. Eschewing the crude bifurcation of the world into free and Communist camps, Rusk insisted on making distinctions between different Communist countries and refused to reduce the Vietnamese insurgency to an expression of what Dodd called "a worldwide conspiracy."[51] There were "some important differences evolving among the Communist countries in tactics, in internal structure, in their degree of liberty with which they open up the minds of the people in their society." Rusk therefore was "a little reluctant" to consider Communism "solely a world movement concentrating in this point in time [on South Vietnam]."[52] American policy could not be based on a blanket opposition to Communism but on opposition to all powers that seek to impose their will by force in violation of the U.N. Charter.[53]

The March 1968 hearings were undoubtedly more helpful to those opposing than those supporting the administration's policies, and, in particular, were a cause of concern at the White House.[54] Their degree of influence on public opinion, however, is difficult to estimate because of the great and still ascending concern about the war that predated the hearings and undoubtedly would have continued even if they had not been held. The section of the public that was likely to have been most attentive to the hearings, moreover, would have been diverted from a particular focus on the Foreign Relations Committee hearings by Johnson's unexpectedly poor showing in the New Hampshire primary, which coincided with the second day of hearings; four days later came the still more diverting entry of Robert Kennedy into the race for the nomination of his party.[55]

Less difficult to measure than the influence of the hearings is what they show about the changes that had recently taken place in elite opinion. The extended readings by dissenting senators of editorials from the *Wall Street Journal* and the London *Telegraph* were among the clearest signs of this process. Likewise, a sense of the extent to which the business community had turned against the war was revealed when, during the hearings, the stock market suddenly surged upwards. Tellingly, the cause for this upturn was a false report that Rusk had testified that the United States was willing to stop the bombing of North Vietnam in order to bring about peace talks.[56]

For the Senate itself the hearings were symptomatic of a new level of isolation for the administration's supporters. These senators, who now perceived themselves as a minority, spoke with a defensiveness traditionally associated with dissidents espousing unpopular causes or, following the politician's credo of caution, simply remained silent. Conversely, the hearings marked a turning point in the growth of those forces in the Senate opposed to the war. "The long and implacable attack by an erstwhile small Senate minority on the national commitment to military resistance to Communist aggression upon South Vietnam," complained pro-Johnson columnist William S. White immediately after the hearings, "is gaining adherents in the Senate and in the country." According to White, himself a strong supporter of the White House, "it can no longer be said that this is only a rump rebellion embracing only a handful gathered about Sens. J. William Fulbright, Robert F. Kennedy and Eugene McCarthy." The change was made "altogether plain" not only by "the baiting of Secretary Dean Rusk before the Foreign Relations Committee" but by the "demonstrable disinclination of members who really agree with him to say so."[57]

Less than three weeks later, on March 31, the president himself seemed to capitulate to the doves. Addressing the nation that night on television, Johnson stated he was "prepared to move immediately to peace through negotiations" and that, "tonight, in the hope that this action would lead to early talks [he was] taking the first step to deescalate the conflict." To this end, Johnson was ordering "our aircraft and naval vessels to make no attacks on North Vietnam, except in the area north of the demilitarized zone where the continuing enemy buildup directly threatens allied forward positions and where the movements of their troops and supplies are clearly related to that threat," thus exempting from attacks an area that "includes almost 90 percent of North Vietnam's population and most of its territory." Echoing arguments previously made by his critics, he justified this "unilateral" de-escalation by calling attention to the "men on both sides of the conflict" who would be "lost" if the war continued. Only a political settlement could "save the lives of brave men—and . . . save the lives of innocent women and children." At the same time, Johnson referred to the need for the South Vietnamese themselves to bear a greater share of the fighting. And at greater length, he spoke of the economic problems caused by war, abroad and at home. Among the latter was a deficit that "just must be reduced," and could only be addressed by passage of a new "tax bill" (whose content he neglected to supply) and by "expenditure control." The principal theme of the speech, however, was the need to reach a settlement with the enemy, even though no one could "foretell the precise terms of an eventual settlement." Implying a readiness to compromise, Johnson claimed that the American "objective in South Vietnam has never been the annihilation of the enemy." Finally, so as to prevent domestic politics from interfering with his pursuit of peace, Johnson pledged that he would neither seek nor accept the nomination of his party for a second term as President.[58]

II

Declassified White House meeting notes reveal what has long been suspected: that Johnson was deeply concerned about dissension in the Senate, particularly during the final two years of his presidency. The President's concern took several forms. With respect to dove criticism, Johnson repeatedly expressed his belief that it created doubt about American unity and perseverance and therefore emboldened the enemy.[59] He also revealed his anxiety about the effect of such criticism on public opinion. At one high-level meeting, for example, Johnson displayed an article from the *Christian Science Monitor* on the views of several dissenting senators. "This," said Johnson, "is the type of thing which the American people are seeing everyday. We need to get them more information of a factual nature."[60]

Johnson took an active interest in hearings conducted by the Foreign Relations Committee. He personally took part in deliberations about how to respond to Fulbright's demands for public testimony from Rusk,[61] and when a second set of televised hearings did ultimately take place, the president was among the viewers.[62] He also actively monitored the committee's effort to investigate the true circumstances surrounding the Gulf of Tonkin Resolution.[63] As is well known, the Senate's vote for the Resolution continued to be used by the president as a parry against the thrusts of the Senate doves.[64] The vehemence and frequency with which he cited the vote is itself an indication of the degree to which he valued the imprimatur of Senate approval for his policies. In the same vein, the president's habit of making derogatory references to Fulbright should be presumed to reflect, albeit in distorted form, the degree to which Johnson wished he still had the senator's support.[65]

Johnson's concern about Senate opinion is also demonstrated by the resources he devoted to the "friendly five" canvas of congressional attitudes toward the war.[66] Lawrence O'Brien, director of the White House's Office of Congressional Relations under Kennedy and Johnson, believed that the results of the survey had considerable impact on Johnson, particularly with respect to the doubts expressed by senators who hitherto had been loyal to him. According to O'Brien, "It didn't much impress Johnson to learn that, say, Senator McGovern was talking against the war, because he'd been against it for a long time. But when someone like [John] Pastore [D-R.I.] questioned the war, someone who's been a staunch supporter of ours, the President had to be impressed with the seriousness of the situation."[67]

At least through 1967, the president's concern with dove criticism seems to have been at least equaled by his fear of the hawks. There is probably no clearer example of senatorial influence on Johnson than his response to the Stennis Committee's hearings on the air war. On the day following the release of the committee's report condemning restrictions on the bombing, Johnson called an unscheduled press conference where he denied the existence of significant differences between the military and civilian leaderships. As if to make reality confirm to his claims, over the course of the following weeks, he approved fifty-two of the fifty-seven previously denied targets. According to Phillip D. Davidson, who then directed military intelligence in Vietnam, the president's conduct represented in effect a capitulation to the hawks and a rebuff to McNamara whose "resignation (or dismissal) was now assured."[68] In late 1967 at a meeting with civilian and military advisors, Johnson spoke of the difficulties caused by the Stennis hearings. More generally, White House meeting notes for that year show the president's persistent concern with anticipated hawk criticism (as well as anticipated dove criticism) during his discussions with these advisors on whether to limit or extend the bombing.[69]

Without explicitly surrendering claims of executive prerogative, the president's behavior during this period shows a growing timidity in his dealings with the Senate. In a meeting with congressional leaders in which

Fulbright directly confronted Johnson, what is striking is the almost complete unwillingness of the other senators present to come to the president's
defense. Indeed, the tone of the confrontation is not that of a "consensus
president" batting away the criticism of an unrepresentative gadfly, but that
of an unpopular leader who assumes that the opposition openly expressed
by Fulbright is silently shared by many of the other congressional leaders.[70] Similarly, in reviewing Johnson's handling of the Congo intervention,
one is struck by the speed and sensitivity with which he responded to
Fulbright and Russell's criticism. If the intervention itself was symptomatic of Johnson's continued readiness to use force without congressional
approval, his response to the criticism was a sign of a heightened awareness of the political dangers that such actions entailed.

The president's anxiety with respect to the Senate continued in
early 1968. Under the shock of the Tet offensive, the leaked report of
Westmoreland's request for 206,000 more troops, and yet further loss of
public support for the war, the president appears to have felt increasingly
vulnerable to senatorial criticism. The sense of vulnerability was exacerbated by a looming economic crisis (which seemed to threaten a collapse
of the dollar and international monetary system), the floundering of his tax
bill, and proposals to escalate dramatically the intervention in the wake of
Tet, including a possible call-up of the reserves and an extension of tours
of duty. All of these developments increased the president's dependence on
Congress at precisely the moment when its members would have had the
greatest interest in displaying their independence from him.

A long distance had been crossed since the days when a docile Senate
had rapidly passed the Gulf of Tonkin Resolution. At a meeting of senior
foreign policy advisors in early March 1968, Johnson expressed his fear
of seeking Senate approval for an expansion of the war: "In the Senate
we face a real problem. Anything that requires authority may result in a
filibuster."[71] Three weeks later, the president stated that he "wouldn't be
surprised if they repealed the Tonkin Gulf Resolution."[72]

The problems for the president seemed to increase geometrically: the
Foreign Relations Committee conducted its investigations of the Gulf of
Tonkin incidents and interrogated Dean Rusk for two days on national
television; with an eye on the November elections, Republican criticism
became more vocal; Eugene McCarthy made an unexpectedly strong

showing as a peace candidate in the New Hampshire primary; and in the wake of the primary, Johnson's old nemesis, Robert Kennedy, declared his own candidacy. Meanwhile, the president's Vietnam policies faced new challenges from two other Democratic senators: Robert Byrd of West Virginia and Edward Kennedy of Massachusetts.

Byrd's break with the White House, like the defections of Morton and Symington, was undoubtedly symptomatic of a growing sense of despair among senators about the course of the war. Byrd, the secretary of the Senate Democratic Conference and a longtime Johnson loyalist, had until the Tet offensive been a consistent supporter of the war. Tet changed him. At a meeting of Democratic leaders at the White House, he confronted the president with his criticisms: "1. That we had poor intelligence. 2. That we were not prepared for these attacks. 3. We underestimated the morale and vitality of the Viet Cong. 4. We over-estimated the support of the South Vietnamese government and its people." Byrd noted that "I have never caused you any trouble on this matter on the Hill. But I do have serous concerns about Vietnam." Later, after the president and others tried to paint a more optimistic picture of what happened during the offensive, Byrd persisted, "Something was wrong over there." Contrary to the claim of the administration, the Communists had been successful since "their objective was to show they could attack all over the country and they did."[73]

Later in the day, at a meeting with his principal foreign policy advisors, Johnson asked them to review Byrd's criticisms. Johnson told his advisors that he was "alarmed at this." He was also alarmed "that the attitude expressed by Senator Byrd seemed to be reflected by much of the comments heard in Washington not only by politicians but by the press." A discussion on Byrd's criticisms then ensued with opinions expressed by Walt Rostow, George Christian, General Wheeler, and McNamara, the last of whom commented, "I am very disturbed about what the President said about the [Democratic] leadership, especially Senator Byrd."[74]

The administration seemed even more alarmed by criticisms made by Edward Kennedy. As chairman of the Subcommittee on Refugees and Escapees of the Judiciary Committee, Kennedy had initially called attention to the plight of the enormous number of South Vietnamese civilians who had been forced to flee their native villages due to the war, often as a consequence of American-supported military action. Now Kennedy extended his criticism by castigating the Saigon regime for failing to lessen the American burden by mobilizing its own young people and, more broadly, for its corruption. These criticisms seemed to strike a sensitive nerve, as they became a subject of no fewer than nine high-level meetings involving the president (as well as an eighteen-page telegram from Ellsworth Bunker, the American ambassador to South Vietnam, to Rusk). The potency of Kennedy's criticisms on Johnson undoubtedly owed much to the context of post–Tet offensive crisis in which they were made and the anxieties the president associated with the Kennedy name. The president himself attributed their importance to what he claimed to be their deleterious effects. Thus, at a March 26, 1968, meeting with Generals Wheeler and Craighton Abrams, Johnson complained that the political and economic "panic" of the last three days was "caused by Ted Kennedy's report on corruption and the ARVN and GVN being no good."[75]

Although these meeting notes show the president's persistent and mounting concern about Senate criticism, they hardly suggest that such criticism was the immediate cause of the president's decision at the end of March to limit the bombing and seek disengagement from Vietnam through a negotiated settlement. As many historians have pointed out, the immediate influences brought to bear on the president during this period were largely from outside of Congress, most notably his new secretary of defense, Clark Clifford, and an unofficial body of "wise men" who had previously supported the war. The Senate critics can, however, be credited with helping to forge the political environment within which the president and his advisors conducted their discussions. Moreover, as Clark Clifford's biographers have pointed out, the secretary's own rethinking of his position on Vietnam and decision to use his influence to change the president's course took place under the impetus of aggressive pressure from Fulbright to testify publicly before the Foreign Relations Committee. "Certainly," as Townsend Hoopes has written, "the idea of having to defend a highly dubious enterprise before informed and vehement critics, and under the klieg lights for the benefit of a national television audience, was a prospect calculated to concentrate the mind wonderfully."[76] More broadly, the Senate contributed to the president's March decision by casting its threatening shadow over his deliberations. It was less what the Senate did during this period than fear of what the Senate might do in the future if, instead of seeking disengagement, the president had followed the advice of the military and drastically escalated the war. As Harry McPherson observed, "If the street demonstrations could not convince the President to alter his course, word that Congress no longer supported it could. Along the armature between the Capitol and the White House, the current flowed—not, this time, from President to Congress to country but in reverse."[77]

III

The president's dramatic announcement at the end of March marked a turning point in American policy in Southeast Asia. Although failing to declare with specificity what he thought the United States should do in Vietnam, by its emphasis on the goal of peace and the importance of South Vietnamese self-reliance, the speech implicitly signaled a change in policy favoring American disengagement from that country. The speech also clearly, if implicitly, signaled a rejection of any proposals for significant escalation of American intervention there. The goal now was to get out of Vietnam. How this goal was to be reached, however, remained unclear.

The initial response of senators, particularly the doves, was highly favorable, even effusive.[78] Disappointment soon set in among the war's critics, however, when it became clear in the weeks and months that followed that the president, although committed to disengagement, also remained committed to avoiding a Communist victory—at least a Communist victory immediately following an American withdrawal.

By seeking disengagement while refusing to cede victory to the other side, Johnson, in effect, adopted a position that many of the doves themselves had long advocated. In fact, for years the doves argued for such a policy, rhetorically framing it as the golden mean between dangerous calls for escalation and irresponsible calls for immediate withdrawal.[79] This formula, however, had been supplemented, albeit equivocally and irregularly, with suggestions of a bolder approach. Fulbright and Case, in particular, sometimes using sympathetic witnesses rather than their own speeches, had suggested that a "Yugoslavian solution" in Vietnam—that is, the victory of Ho Chi Minh, a Vietnamese "Tito"—would not necessarily be detrimental to American interests. In the wake of Tet such a position was likely to have, if anything, added attraction. Indeed, as we saw, at the

March hearings, Gore himself had implied that the only realistic option was in effect to concede victory to the enemy. He had voiced his hope that the hearings would "have a disciplining and conditioning effect upon public opinion in preparation for the concessions we must make and settlement we must accept."[80]

In private, Robert Kennedy was even more explicit. When an advocate of withdrawal reported to Kennedy that, in an argument with Averill Harriman, the latter had said, "Your friend Bobby is not for cut-and-run as you are," Kennedy replied, "Little does he know." In other conversations Kennedy simply emphasized the necessity of withdrawal without proposing any conditions. "I'd get out of there in any possible way," he told Thomas Watson of IBM. The war was "an absolute disaster" and "it's worse to be there than any of the shame or difficulty one would engender internationally by moving out. And so, with whatever kind of apologies and with whatever kind of grace I could conjure up, I'd get out of there in six months with all the troops the United States has."[81]

Notwithstanding their disappointment with the persistence of the war, the Senate doves found their strategic position significantly improved because of the president's speech. Before the speech, Senate debate on the war was tripartite, with the president occupying the central position flanked by doves and hawks. After March 31, debate shifted to the left, largely revolving around differences on the speed of disengagement and the means through which it was to be accomplished.[82] The president's speech, moreover, represented a victory not just for the doves but for the broader group of senators favoring a more restrained foreign policy. Although it would be an exaggeration to see that date as marking a return to isolationism, in the following period there was a perceptible shift in the emphasis of American foreign policy. This included an effort to limit the direct intervention of American military forces abroad, a corresponding effort to encourage other "surrogate" powers to further American interests, and, less tangibly, a relative loss in the self-confidence (what Fulbright had called "arrogance") that had characterized the American attitude toward its world mission during the preceding years of the "American century." Of particular interest to the doves, the turn of March 31 inaugurated new opportunities for détente with the Communist world, although these were not to be pursued energetically until the Nixon presidency.[83]

The long-range effect of the events of 1968 on the balance of power between Congress and the executive branch in the area of foreign affairs is less clear. Certainly during the Nixon and Ford presidencies there is evidence of a new assertiveness in Congress. This can be seen particularly in the Senate where the Hatfield-McGovern "end-the-war" amendment was able to garner some forty-two votes and the Cooper-Church amendment, prohibiting the employment of American ground troops beyond the borders of Vietnam, was able to win majority approval and become enacted into law.[84] The War Powers Act, which originated in the Senate, also represented an effort by Congress to recoup some of the power that had been usurped by claimed presidential prerogatives, although, by its express terms, the act was not applicable to Vietnam. Moreover, as former senator Thomas Eagleton (D-Mo.) has pointed out, in only partially limiting presidential power, the act had the effect of ceding a part of the power reserved exclusively to Congress by the Constitution.[85] Congress also played an important role, more through its inaction than any initiative, when it refused in 1975 to heed President Ford's call to save the regime in Saigon from its final collapse.[86]

In more recent years, there have also been displays of congressional assertiveness, as legislators have insisted on having extended discussions and votes concerning executive-branch-initiated interventions against Iraq[87] and Yugoslavia. Unsurprisingly, the issues raised in these debates bear a resemblance to those raised about Vietnam: diplomatic alternatives to war, the efficacy of intervention, the degree of support from other nations, the role of the United Nations and international law, and, of course, the competing constitutional claims of Congress and president. Compared at least to the early discussion of Vietnam, fewer senators seem to be inhibited from at least expressing their doubts or (if not of the president's party) of being accused of undermining the goal of bipartisan consensus. Certainly, compared to Vietnam, the opposition to the Kosovo war was remarkable, with the majority of senators of both parties combining to table a resolution that would have authorized the president to "use all necessary force and other means" by a vote of 78 to 22.[88]

This assertiveness has usually had, however, a strong partisan dynamic, and has not represented an effective challenge to the executive branch's capacity to inflict violence abroad at will. The Kosovo vote, after all, did not stop Clinton from bombing Belgrade. Nor did the war arouse the type of intense indignation and aggressive action among Clinton's adversaries that his perjury had, notwithstanding the fact that it was waged in direct defiance of Congress and international law.[89] If during the Clinton years many members of Congress showed a willingness to push some of their constitutional prerogatives to the limit, these did not include their power to decide between war and peace.

Unsurprisingly, with the Republican administration's intervention into Iraq, Democratic senators have been the principal dissenters. Senate criticism of the war, like criticism among the American people, has emerged and spread more rapidly than during the Vietnam War. In addition, public opposition in the Senate to the war in Iraq, unlike opposition to the Vietnam War, has not been the preserve of marginal figures. Indeed, Robert Byrd, the Senate's president pro tempore at the time Iraq was invaded, has been the opposition's leading figure and has attacked the war with arguments similar to those employed by Morse and Gruening forty years before.[90] But, as in during the early years of the Vietnam War, senators of both parties have typically tended toward passivity, equivocation, and evasiveness.

CONCLUSION

I

As may be readily surmised from the preceding pages, the great majority of senators of the Vietnam era were cautious in both thought and deed. Few were imaginative or inclined to muse or speculate about difficult problems, particularly if the problems were ones that did not seem to demand immediate attention. Nor were many prone to court danger to their careers by entering controversies whose issue was uncertain. Certainly, at the beginning of 1965 when the Eighty-ninth Congress convened, few senators had ever given significant thought to American policy in Southeast Asia. Later in the year, as the American intervention escalated and the war took on a sense of urgency, few senators evinced a desire to address the war openly, and even fewer had concrete proposals of their own on how the conflict might be ended. It was not an issue on which they were eager to innovate or lead, and to the extent votes had to be cast and speeches delivered, they sought to imitate and follow those they had imitated and followed in past controversies. For an influential minority of senators, disproportionately represented on the Foreign Relations Committee, this approach meant following the lead of the White House and espousing the views of newspaper columnists, such as Walter Lippmann and the Alsop brothers, and the editorial writers of prestigious newspapers like the *New York Times*. This changed with Vietnam.

Vietnam divided the elite "leaders of opinion" and with it the senators who had followed them. It created for the first time since World War II a significant division between senators who considered themselves internationalists and the executive branch of government. The war also encouraged the continuation of a long-term trend of decline in support by southern senators for military interventions in the Third World, and it reawakened and reinforced the skepticism among many Republican senators toward the whole postwar enterprise of asserting American influence throughout the world. The convergence of all of these groups by 1968 in support of ending American involvement in Vietnam was made all but inevitable by the growing consensus in the business community that the war had to end.

Deference to this community, whether centered on Wall Street or Main Street, in the final analysis was the most potent force that made possible the emergence of a new Senate consensus on this issue.

Unsurprisingly, the core of the post-Tet consensus for withdrawal was made up largely of the same forces that had opposed escalation three years before. These 1964–65 opponents of escalation had included a preponderance of the shapers of elite opinion—among others, the most influential columnist in the country, Walter Lippmann; the editorial pages of the *New York Times, Wall Street Journal,* and *Washington Post;* and the lion's share of academic experts on East Asia and foreign affairs. In the Senate, it had included the majority leader, the majority of the Senate Foreign Relations Committee, and the chairman of the Senate Armed Services Committee, who was also the leader of the Southern Caucus and de facto chairman of the Appropriations Committee.

The post-Tet opposition featured these same forces (some of which had become temporarily silent or had been brought into the president's camp after he had committed himself to escalation), as well as new elements that had not opposed escalation in 1964 and early 1965. The most conspicuous of these, and the most decisive with respect to changing the president's course, were official and unofficial advisors to the White House, above all, the secretary of defense and the so-called Wise Men. These elite dissensions were given added impetus by mass opinion, hitherto equivocal and labile, which now swung unambiguously against the war. And they were encouraged still further by an awareness of the breadth of international opposition to the war, which included the Soviet Union, all the countries of Eastern Europe, all the advanced capitalist countries (with the solitary exception of Australia), the secretary-general of the United Nations, and virtually the entire postcolonial world, including most of the countries of Southeast Asia, the very "dominoes" for whose defense the war was supposedly waged.

As discussed in detail in the preceding chapter, the president was also significantly affected by the persistence, renewal, and extension of opposition in the Senate. In this body the most significant opposition to emerge after early 1965 came ironically from the same parties whom the president had hoped to appease or politically disarm by escalating the war and saving the regime in Saigon: Robert Kennedy and the Republicans. The Republicans, it was feared, would greet the victory of Vietnamese

Communism with attacks comparable to those launched against previous Democratic administrations for their failure to vanquish Communism in China and Korea, and, more recently, in Cuba. At the same time, Kennedy would, in Johnson's view, have been able to mobilize vast constituencies in the aftermath of such a victory, accusing him of betraying the legacy of his older brother. As it turned out, neither Robert Kennedy nor the Republicans could be effectively appeased. Kennedy, from complex motives, joined the doves. The Republicans, for their part, while refraining from the frontal attacks to which they had subjected Truman, were quite willing to engage in a damaging low-intensity political warfare against Johnson, alternately criticizing him for not doing enough to win the war and for not doing enough to achieve peace.

The failure of the Republican senators to offer Johnson effective support in his Vietnam policy was particularly damaging to him. Having lost significant support from his own party for pursuing policies deemed to resemble those proposed by Barry Goldwater, the president needed compensatory support from the Republicans. Their failure to provide this left Senate support for his policies in the hands of such relatively marginal Democrats as the politically vulnerable Gale McGee of Wyoming and the recently censured Tom Dodd of Connecticut, hardly a satisfying situation for a president who had aspired to govern by consensus.

II

As has been stressed, the Senate critics of administration policy were not as a rule original thinkers. Nor did they aspire to originality. Like judges compelled to justify their decisions by claiming their consistency with the decisions of courts higher than their own, these senators rarely expressed an opinion in the Vietnam debate without ostentatiously proclaiming its accord with some other authority, particularly those of a venerated columnist or the editorial page of a respected newspaper.[1] On the other hand, the Senate doves can be described as purveyors of a cluster of concerns, ideas, and proposals that would not have gained as much influence and legitimacy had they not used their prestigious position to disseminate them.

First among these was the constant warning of the dangers of escalation —above all, the danger that it could provoke a general war with China and even the Soviet Union. They also insisted, contrary to official optimism, that neither the military nor the political efforts—the so-called pacification campaign—were succeeding in Vietnam. At the same time, they argued that neither an expansion of the bombing nor an increase in ground forces were likely to lead to a reversal of this trend. Aligning themselves with the so-called Never Again Club, the Senate doves cited the opposition of such well-known soldiers as Omar Bradley and Douglas MacArthur to the United States committing itself to a war on the Asian mainland. And with respect to Vietnam in particular, the invoked the authority of such retired generals as James Gavin, Matthew Ridgway, and David Shoup, and called attention to their proposals, particularly the enclave strategy proposed by Gavin (and endorsed by Ridgway), that seemed to offer a way for the United States to limit its expenditure of resources and ultimately extricate itself from the conflict.

They further challenged the administration's characterization of the war as a struggle to defend democracy and independence in South Vietnam. Rather, they pointed to widespread corruption in Saigon and the unwillingness of many South Vietnamese to fight for their own country. Likewise, notwithstanding the administration's prediction that a Communist victory in South Vietnam would lead to its triumph elsewhere, the Senate doves repeatedly pointed to the refusal of the non-Communist countries of Asia to contribute significantly to the military effort. More fundamentally, Fulbright, Gore, and Morse, insisted on challenging the official version of Vietnam's history, including the American claim to have honored the Geneva Accords.

With increasing explicitness, dissenting senators also challenged the administration's claim that the conflict was a war between two nations rather than a civil war. Some doves even openly questioned whether U.S. interests would be especially damaged by the unification of Vietnam under the leadership of Ho Chi Minh, a "national Communist" they likened to Yugoslavia's Tito. They emphasized that, instead, the real danger came from the damaging effects of the war on American life, including the war's drain on the resources needed to address pressing domestic problems, and the war's major contribution to the increasing alienation of young people. And the Senate doves consistently criticized the war for the damage it did to America's economic position and moral standing abroad and for the way the war made it impossible for the administration to reach its professed goal of establishing détente with the Soviet Union.

III

As would be expected of a critique emanating from Walter Lippmann and other members of the foreign policy establishment, the arguments articulated by the Senate doves differed in some respects from those advanced by the organizers of the militant protest movement against the war. In contrast to the leadership of the protest movement, in which Marxists, radical pacifists, and other opponents of the "status quo" predominated, the Senate doves commonly argued that the United States should disengage itself from Vietnam because the war threatened the stability of the established order. Indeed the Senate doves, far from seeing the war as serving the needs of the American capitalists, under the impetus of the gold crisis and other ominous signs, saw a particular urgency in ending the war, lest its continuation bring about a collapse of the capitalist economy. Moreover, unlike the militant organizers, who entertained a spectrum of attitudes toward the Communist adversary (including the view that it was not an adversary), the Senate doves, like the Senate hawks, were, without exception, anti-Communists. And while radical pacifists condemned the war because of the intrinsic evil of violence, the Senate doves framed their arguments in terms of the relative benefits and costs of continuing the fighting.

The differences between the senators and the militants, however, can be overstated. The senators, while not embracing the radical critique of the Vietnam War as symptomatic of the fundamental structure of American capitalism, frequently did link the war to a foreign policy that insisted on maintaining an "American Empire," which was likened to that of imperial Rome and imperialist Britain. Their cost-benefit analysis of the war, moreover, was not merely an exercise in cold-blooded pragmatism; the Senate doves' analysis of "costs" encompassed the human suffering inflicted by the war, and a review of their private communications reveal that senators, no less than other Americans of the period, could become genuinely disturbed when confronted with evidence of the war's worst horrors.[2] Likewise, the legal arguments of the Senate's most consistent doves, Morse and Gruening, found an echo among the antiwar protesters who condemned the intervention as unlawful and its perpetrators as war criminals. Indeed, when the Senate dissenters invoked the U.N. Charter, they opened the door to radical arguments that challenged the legitimacy of not only the war in Vietnam but of a long list of Cold War military interventions that had been conducted in contravention of the Charter. Similarly, when the dissenters (following Lippmann) invoked the Geneva Accords' characterization of the seventeenth parallel as merely a temporary "demarcation" line and cited Vietnam-wide elections required by the Accords, they echoed arguments made at college teach-ins that "questioned the very legitimacy of the South Vietnamese State."[3]

It should also be noted that the differences between the dove senators and the leadership of the antiwar movement are easier to discern than their differences with the movement's rank and file. Among the latter, where coherent ideological commitments were relatively rare, it is likely that very few discerned a difference between their own strongly felt but inarticulate aversion to the war and the views expressed by the Senate doves. On the other hand, the Senate doves did differ from many of the protestors on the efficacy and desirability of mass action as a means of effecting change. But even on this point there turns out to have been more in common than one might expect between the dissenting senators and the militants. If the discomfort of the senators toward massive demonstrations was partly a natural outgrowth of their own elite position in the social and political structure, many of the radicals themselves, especially those on the college campuses, preferred small, if sometimes dramatic, protests to ones that would readily invite the involvement of ordinary adults with jobs and family responsibilities. Like the establishment dissenters, the ultra-lefts typically relegated such ordinary men and women to the role of sympathetic spectators rather than active participants. Thus, in apparent confirmation of Leninist theory, the two movements had elitist affinities that betrayed the superior social origins of their leaders, the one disproportionately upper class, the other disproportionately middle class.[4]

Of course the opposition to the war cannot be reduced to two movements: one of elites, the other in the streets. By the late 1960s opposition to the war was expressed through the whole continuum of institutions and social strata. All of these components of dissent had porous boundaries, overlapped with others, and interacted in complex ways. Their complexity is such that it is impossible to ascertain with precision the effect of any one component on the larger population, or even to other components of the opposition. This is certainly true of Senate dissent. Nonetheless, at least

three general observations about its distinctive contribution to the movement against the war are possible.

The most obvious point is the relative authority of senators. Notwithstanding their failure to exercise their constitutional powers, when senators spoke they had vastly greater chances of being listened to attentively
than citizens outside of government, or even persons holding offices upon
which the constitutional power to make war was not conferred. As such,
senators, at least from 1966 when the televised hearings took place, played
a decisive role in ensuring that voices opposed to the war were audible and
accessible to people throughout the United States. Although the effect of
these voices on the larger population cannot be precisely ascertained, it may
be assumed that they at least created doubt with respect to the wisdom of
the government's policies. It may also be assumed that for many Americans
the voices of senators questioning the war were more likely to spread
doubt than the voices of other Americans, such as student protesters who
had also raised their voices against the war.

In addition, the authority of senators played a special role with respect
to members of the military and foreign policy establishments. As the president and his inner circle became more intransigent, more secretive, and less
willing to consider opposing opinions, dissenting retired soldiers, former
officials, and leading scholars with relevant expertise naturally gravitated
to the Senate. In the Senate, especially in the hearing room of the Foreign
Relations Committee, they found a place where they could be listened to
with the deference to which they felt entitled and from which they could
efficiently disseminate their views to a larger audience.

In a certain sense, the invitations issued by Fulbright to such men
(generally selected from lists presented to him by his chief of staff, who
was himself a bona fide member of the foreign policy establishment)[5] confirmed rather than challenged the hierarchy through which debate on foreign policy had taken place prior to the Vietnam controversy; the witnesses
invited to Capitol Hill were the same men whose counsel had once been
welcomed at the Pentagon, Foggy Bottom, or the White House. However,
precisely in confirming the old hierarchy Fulbright helped to ensure that
the debate on Vietnam encompassed the full range of elite opinion, that
the contours of legitimate discourse about Vietnam would be defined by a

relatively large "central committee" of leading citizens rather than the small "politburo" that controlled the main levers of executive power.

Finally, note should be made of the special role of the Senate dissenters in providing continuity to the opposition. Reflecting divisions within the left, the protest movement against the war never had a unified leadership or even a durable structure. The movement lacked continuity—for extended periods, such as 1966, it became relatively inactive—and some of its components actually tried to liquidate or transform it into a multi-issue coalition that would subordinate Vietnam to a general program, presumably centered around the concerns of black militants.[6] In some respects a parallel phenomenon took place in the Senate in 1966 after the Fulbright hearings and Robert Kennedy's speech: for the remainder of the year Kennedy became virtually silent about the war, and Fulbright diluted his public opposition to the war by subsuming it within a general campaign for a more enlightened foreign policy.

In the long run, however, senators could not avoid Vietnam. If nothing else, the Senate's constitutional role in the appropriation of monies ensured that its members would be repeatedly forced to face the war. This role became even more pronounced when the effects of the war on the economy and Johnson's surtax proposal forced senators and committees not ordinarily concerned with foreign policy to discuss and debate the war. The issue of race, moreover, which had a tendency to pull activists away from the antiwar movement, ironically had the effect in the Senate of pushing southern senators—naturally averse to the sacrifice of American blood and treasure in defense of nonwhite governments—into alliance with the doves.[7] Indeed, as the radical protest movement fragmented and lost its focus on Vietnam, the Senate dissenters grew stronger, more cohesive, and more persistent in their opposition.

IV

The nuclear age is distinguished not only by the weapons with which war can be waged but by the instruments with which peace can be established. The two traits were revealed at the outset of the age almost simultaneously; the United States incinerated Hiroshima nine days after the Senate ratified the Charter of the United Nations.

The U.N. Charter is no ordinary treaty, and it was certainly not regarded as such by the eighty-nine senators who gave it their approval. Its text, with its general prohibition of international violence, subject to only the narrowest exceptions, was justifiably regarded as an effective outlawing of war. Behind its complex structure and burdensome procedures was a simple premise: that nations can and must settle their differences peaceably through negotiation and compromise. The idea was given a sense of urgency by Hiroshima, whose flattened buildings and charred corpses suggested what, on a far greater scale, could result if nations continued to act in the old way.

These powerful hopes and fears have been themes in every postwar Senate debate about the use of violence abroad. The Vietnam controversy was unique only in the manner in which they were combined. The distinctiveness of the Vietnam dissension was a consequence of the peculiar features of the time in which escalation took place. As during the Korean War, senators were afraid an increase and extension of American attacks would provoke a general war involving China and ultimately the Soviet Union, two powers which, despite bitter differences, had never renounced their military pact. If anything, the sense of foreboding was greater than it had been in 1950. By 1965 China had exploded a nuclear device, and atomic weaponry and the arsenals of the superpowers had developed so far as to virtually guarantee that a Soviet-American conflagration would presage the end of civilization itself.

If senators in 1965 may have been more fearful than during the Korean intervention, they certainly were more hopeful of the possibilities of peaceably resolving conflicts than at any previous time during the Cold War. This was more than wishful thinking: their hopes were supported by remarkable developments of the immediate past—above all, the successful negotiations that had led the Soviet Union and the United States to bind themselves to the Limited Test Ban Treaty and a number of lesser agreements that similarly evinced a future trajectory of further disarmament and détente between the great adversaries. If Kennedy and Khrushchev had been able to survive the near-death experience of the Missile Crisis and go on to forge these agreements, it was hardly unrealistic to expect that a local conflict, such as that in Vietnam, could also be resolved through negotiation and compromise. These hopes were stimulated by Johnson himself when he repeatedly renounced the goal of victory in Vietnam and proclaimed that his sole objective there was an amicable settlement. The professions of Johnson seemed all the more sincere coming in the wake of his magnificently successful campaign for the White House, in which he made the avoidance of nuclear war the highest priority.

Into this volatile mixture of heightened fear about the consequences of war and growing hopes about the prospects for peace came the reality of Vietnam. The first explosion came from Senate liberals and international-ists, their responses accelerated by the Dominican fiasco and by signals from opinion leaders to whom they had paid deference in the past. More reactions soon followed, first from the core of the Senate's Republicans, then from the leader of the Southern Caucus (this time with the Congo acting as a catalyst), and by the end of 1967 from such bastions of the Senate establish-ment as Stuart Symington and Thruston Morton. After Tet, the discrete explosions were united into a single great flame. It was not new for senators to oppose a war. What lacked precedent was its intensity and the speed with which it spread through the Senate chamber and encompassed both parties and every significant group within them. Such was the consequence of wag-ing America's greatest war against Communism in a time when Americans fervently wanted—and reasonably expected—the secure and lasting peace that can only come through compromise and conciliation.

APPENDIX I

Senators Serving, 1964–1968

The Arabic numerals following each entry represent percentage ratings given by Americans for Democratic Action (ADA), as published in the *Congressional Quarterly Weekly Report,* 22 (October 23, 1964): 2548; 24 (February 25, 1966): 474; 24 (November 4, 1966): 2766; 26 (April 26, 1968): 917; and 26 (November 22, 1968): 3197. The letters "NA" are inserted where a rating, due to the senator's dates of service, is unavailable. The roman numeral that follows indicates which of three classes of seats was occupied by the senator: "I" denotes a seat that faced election in 1964, "II" a seat that faced election in 1966, and "III" a seat that faced election in 1968.

Aiken, George David. R-Vt. (8/30/92–11/19/84). Served January 10, 1941, to January 3, 1975.
61. 35. 65. 54. 43. III

Allot, Gordon Llewellyn. R-Colo. (1/2/07–1/17/89). Served January 3, 1955, to January 3, 1973.
24. 6. 15. 8. 14. II

Anderson, Clinton Presba. D-N.Mex. (10/23/95–11/11/95). Served January 3, 1949, to January 3, 1973.
67. 59. 65. 31. 21. II

Baker, Howard Henry, Jr. R-Tenn. (11/15/25). Served January 3, 1967, to January 3, 1985.
NA. NA. NA. 23. 21. II

Bartlett, Edward Lewis (Bob). D-Alaska. (4/20/04–12/11/68). Served January 3, 1959, to death.
74. 76. 80. 46. 57. II

Bass, Ross. D-Tenn. (3/17/18–1/9/73). Served November 4, 1964, to January 3, 1967.
NA. 76. 50. NA. NA. II

Bayh, Birch Evan. D-Ind. (1/22/28). Served January 3, 1963, to January 3, 1981.
86. 94. 80. 62. 50. III

Beall, J. Glenn. R-Md. (6/5/94–1/14/71). Served January 3, 1953, to January 3, 1965.
26. NA. NA. NA. NA. I

Bennett, Wallace Foster. R-Utah. (11/13/98–12/19/93). Served January 3, 1951, to December 20, 1974.
   3. 12. 0. 0. 0. III

Bible, Alan Harvey. D-Nev. (11/20/09–9/12/88). Served December 2, 1954, to December 17, 1974.
   39. 47. 40. 23. 14. III

Boggs, James Caleb. R-Del. (5/15/09–3/26/93). Served January 3, 1961, to January 3, 1973.
   33. 35. 50. 23. 43. II

Brewster, Daniel Bough. D-Md. (11/23/23). Served January 3, 1961, to January 3, 1969.
   81. 82. 80. 77. 57. III

Brooke, Edward William, III. R-Mass. (10/26/19). Served January 3, 1967, to January 8, 1979.
   NA. NA. NA. 77. 86. II.

Burdick, Quentin Northrop. D-N.Dak. (6/19/08–9/8/92). Served August 8, 1960, to death.
   88. 88. 90. 62. 64. I

Byrd, Harry Flood, Sr. D-Va. (6/10/87–10/20/66). Served March 4, 1933, to November 10, 1965.
   4. NA. NA. NA. NA. I

Byrd, Harry Flood, Jr.[1] Va. (12/20/14). Served November 12, 1965, to January 2, 1983.
   NA. 0. 5. 8. 0. I

Byrd, Robert Carlyle. D-W.Va. (1/15/18). Served January 3, 1959, to date.
   52. 35. 35. 23. 21. I

Cannon, Howard Walter. D-Nev. (1/26/12–3/5/02). Served January 3, 1959, to January 3, 1983.
   51. 59. 35. 38. 29. I

Carlson, Frank. R-Kan. (1/23/93–5/30/87). Served November 29, 1950, to January 3, 1969.
   28. 6. 5. 15. 7. III

Case, Clifford Philip. R-N.J. (4/16/04–3/5/82). Served January 3, 1955, to January 3, 1979.
   81. 94. 95. 100. 100. II

Church, Frank Forrester. D-Idaho. (7/25/24–4/7/84). Served January 3, 1957, to January 3, 1981.
   86. 88. 55. 92. 43. III

Clark, Joseph Still. D-Pa. (10/21/01–1/12/90). Served January 3, 1957, to January 3, 1969.
   100. 100. 100. 92. 93. III

Cooper, John Sherman. R-Ky. (8/23/01–2/21/91). Served November 6, 1946, to January 3, 1949; November 5, 1952, to January 3, 1955; November 7, 1956, to January 3, 1973.
   53. 24. 15. 46. 71. II

Cotton, Norris H. R-N.H. (5/11/00–2/24/89). Served November 8, 1954, to December 31, 1974.
   6. 12. 5. 23. 29. III

Curtis, Carl Thomas. R-Neb. (3/15/05–1/24/00). Served January 1, 1955, to January 3, 1979.
   5. 6. 0. 0. 7. II

Dirksen, Everett McKinley. R-Ill. (1/4/96–9/7/69). Served January 3, 1951, to death.
   28. 6. 5. 8. 7. III

Dodd, Thomas Joseph. D-Conn. (5/15/07–5/24/71). Served January 3, 1959, to January 2, 1971.
   78. 94. 75. 54. 50. I

Dominick, Peter Hoyt. R-Colo. (7/7/15 to 3/18/81). Served January 3, 1963, to January 2, 1975.
   17. 6. 15. 15. 29. III

Douglas, Paul Howard. D-Ill. (3/26/92–9/24/76). Served January 3, 1949, to January 3, 1967.
   96. 100. 85. NA. NA. II

Eastland, James Oliver. D-Miss. (11/28/04–2/19/86). Served June 30, 1941, to September 28, 1941; January 3, 1943, to December 27, 1978.
   3. 0. 0. 8. 0. II

Edmondson, J. Howard. D-Okla. (9/27/25–11/17/71). Served January 8, 1963, to November 3, 1964.
   42. NA. NA. NA. NA. II

Ellender, Allen Joseph. D-La. (9/24/90–7/27/72). Served January 3, 1937, to July 27, 1972.
   16. 18. 20. 23. 7. II

Ervin, Samuel James, Jr. D-N.C. (9/27/96–4/23/85). Served June 5, 1954, to December 31, 1974.
   11. 0. 5. 15. 0. III

Fannin, Paul Jones. R-Ariz. (1/29/07–1/13/02). Served January 3, 1965, to January 3, 1977.
NA. 6. 0. 0. 7. II.

Fong, Hiram Leung. R-Hawaii. (10/15/06–8/18/04). Served August 21, 1959, to January 3, 1977.
37. 53. 55. 31. 43. I

Fulbright, James William. D-Ark. (4/9/05–2/9/95). Served January 3, 1945, to December 31, 1974.
36. 41. 50. 38. 14. III.

Goldwater, Barry Morris. R-Ariz. (1/1/09–5/29/98). Served January 3, 1953, to January 3, 1965, January 3, 1969, to January 3, 1987.
0. NA. NA. NA. NA. III

Goodell, Charles Ellsworth. R-N.Y. (3/16/26–1/21/87). Served September 10, 1968, to January 3, 1971.
NA. NA. NA. NA. NA. I

Gore, Albert Arnold. (12/26/07–12/5/98). Served January 3, 1953, to January 3, 1971.
69. 65. 75. 54. 43. I

Griffin, Robert Paul. R-Mich. (11/6/23). Served May 11, 1966, to January 2, 1979.
NA. NA. 24. 31. 43. II

Gruening, Ernest. D-Alaska. (2/6/87–6/26/74). Served January 3, 1959, to January 3, 1969.
67. 82. 85. 62. 64. III

Hansen, Clifford Peter. R-Wyo. (10/16/12). Served January 3, 1967, to December 31, 1978.
NA. NA. NA. 8. 7. II

Harris, Fred Roy. D-Okla. (11/13/30). Served November 4, 1964, to January 2, 1973.
NA. 76. 60. 62. 57. II

Hart, Philip Aloysius. D-Mich. (12/10/12–12/26/76). Served January 3, 1959, to death.
96. 100. 85. 92. 86. I

Hartke, Rupert Vance. D-Ind. (5/31/19–7/27/03). Served January 3, 1959, to January 3, 1977.
75. 65. 60. 46. 50. I

Hatfield, Mark Odem. R-Oreg. (7/12/22). Served January 3, 1967, to January 3, 1997.
NA. NA. NA. 54. 71. II

Hayden, Carl Trumbull. D-Ariz. (10/2/77–1/25/72). Served March 4, 1927, to January 3, 1969.
42. 29. 5. 15. 7. III

Hickenlooper, Bourke. R-Iowa (7/21/96–9/4/71). Served January 3, 1945, to January 3, 1969.
17. 6. 0. 0. 0. III

Hill, Joseph Lister. D-Ala. (12/29/94–12/21/84). Served January 11, 1938, to January 2, 1969.
25. 12. 10. 15. 7. III

Holland, Spessard Lindsey. D-Fla. (7/10/92–11/6/71). Served September 25, 1946, to January 2, 1971.
14. 6. 5. 15. 0. I

Hollings, Ernest Frederick. D-S.C. (1/1/22). Served November 8, 1968, to January 3, 2004.
NA. NA. NA. 8. 14. III

Humphrey, Hubert Horatio. D-Minn. (5/27/11–1/13/78). Served January 3, 1949, to December 29, 1964; January 3, 1971, to death.
97. NA. NA. NA. NA. I

Hruska, Roman Lee. R-Neb. (8/16/04–4/25/99). Served November 8, 1954, to December 12, 1976.
5. 0. 0. 0. 7. I

Inouye, Daniel Ken (9/7/24). D-Hawaii. Served January 3, 1963, to date.
75. 82. 75. 62. 64. III

Jackson, Henry Martin. D-Wash. (5/31/12–9/9/93). Served January 3, 1953, to death.
82. 71. 80. 69. 57. I

Javits, Jacob Koppel. R-N.Y. (3/18/04–3/7/86). Served January 9, 1957, to January 3, 1981.
89. 94. 90. 77. 86. III

Johnston, Olin DeWitt Talmadge. D-S.C. (11/18/96–4/18/65). Served January 3, 1945, to death.
25. NA. NA. NA. NA. III

Jordan, Benjamin Everett. D-N.C. (9/8/96–3/15/74). Served April 19, 1958, to January 3, 1973.
17. 12. 0. 8. 0. II

Jordan, Leonard Beck. R-Idaho. (5/15/99–6/30/83). Served August 6, 1962, to January 2, 1973.
8. 0. 0. 8. 21. II

Keating, Kenneth Barnard. R-N.Y. (5/18/00–5/5/75). Served January 3, 1959, to January 3, 1965.
67. NA. NA. NA. NA. I

Kennedy, Edward Moore. D-Mass. (2/22/32). Served November 6, 1962, to date.
92. 94. 100. 92. 71. I

Kennedy, Robert Francis. D-N.Y. (11/20/25–6/6/68). Served January 3, 1965, to death.
NA. 94. 100. 100. NA. I

Kuchel, Thomas Henry. R-Calif. (8/15/10–11/21/94). Served January 2, 1953, to January 3, 1969.
72. 41. 45. 38. 50. II

Lausche, Frank John. D-Ohio (11/14/95–4/21/90). Served January 3, 1957, to January 3, 1969.
26. 29. 5. 8. 21. III

Long, Edward Vaughn. D-Mo. (7/18/08–11/6/72). Served September 23, 1960, to December 27, 1968.
70. 76. 80. 62. 50. III

Long, Russell Billieu. D-La. (11/3/18–5/9/03). Served December 31, 1948, to January 3, 1987.
17. 65. 45. 23. 0. III

McCarthy, Eugene Joseph. D-Minn. (3/29/16–12/10/05). Served January 3, 1959, to January 3, 1971.
90. 82. 90. 62. 21. I

McClellan, John Little. D-Ark. (2/25/96–11/23/77). Served January 3, 1943, to death.
6. 6. 0. 15. 0. II

McGee, Gale William. D-Wyo. (3/17/15–4/9/92). Served January 3, 1959, to January 3 1977.
76. 82. 90. 77. 57. I

McGovern, George Stanley. D-S.Dak. (7/19/22). Served January 3, 1961, to January 3, 1981.
94. 94. 85. 92. 43. III

McIntyre, Thomas James. D-N.H. (2/20/15–8/8/92). Served November 7, 1962, to January 3, 1979.
81. 88. 50. 69. 50. II

McNamara, Patrick Vincent. D-Mich. (10/4/94–4/30/66). Served January 3, 1955, to death.
97. 94. NA. NA. NA. II

Magnuson, Warren Grant. D-Wash. (4/12/05–5/20/89). Served December 14, 1944, to January 3, 1981.
78. 71. 75. 69. 36. III

Mansfield, Michael Joseph. D-Mont. (3/16/03–10/15/01). Served January 3, 1953, to January 2, 1977.
80. 76. 85. 54. 29. I

Mechem, Edwin Leard. R-N.Mex. (7/2/12–11/27/02). Served November 30, 1962, to November 3, 1964.
0. NA. NA. NA. NA. I

Metcalf, Lee Warren. D-Mont. (1/28/11–1/12/78). Served January 3, 1961, to death.
90. 82. 70. 77. 79. II

Miller, Jack Richard. R-Iowa (6/6/16–8/29/94). Served January 3, 1961, to January 3, 1973.
21. 12. 10. 8. 14. II

Mondale, Walter Frederick. D-Minn. (1/5/28). Served December 30, 1964, to December 30, 1976.
NA. 94. 95. 92. 86. II

Monroney, Almer Stillwell Mike. D-Okla. (3/2/02–2/13/80). Served January 3, 1951, to January 3, 1969.
64. 71. 50. 31. 21. III

Montoya, Joseph Manuel. D-N.Mex. (9/24/15–1/5/78). Served November 4, 1964, to January 3, 1977.
NA. 82. 75. 54. 36. I

Morse, Wayne Lyman.[2] Oreg. (10/20/00–7/22/74). Served January 3, 1946, to January 3, 1969.
78. 88. 90. 92. 79. III

Morton, Thruston Ballard. R-Ky. (8/19/07–8/14/82). Served January 3, 1957, to January 3, 1969.
22. 12. 5. 31. 21. III

Moss, Frank Edward. D-Utah (9/23/11–7/29/03). Served January 3, 1959, to January 3, 1977.
86. 88. 80. 77. 79. I

Mundt, Karl Earl. R-S.Dak. (1/3/00–8/16/74). Served December 31, 1948, to January 3, 1973.
10. 0. 5. 15. 0. II

Murphy, George Lloyd. R-Calif. (4/04/02–5/3/92). Served January 1, 1965, to January 2, 1971.
NA. 0. 5. 0. 14. I

Muskie, Edmund Sixtus. D–Maine. (3/38/14–3/26/96). Served January 3, 1959,
   to May 7, 1980.
   89. 82. 85. 62. 79. I

Neuberger, Maurine Brown. D-Oreg. (1/9/07–2/22/00). Served November 9,
   1960, to January 3, 1967.
   93. 76. 95. NA. NA. II

Nelson, Gaylord Anton. D-Wisc. (6/4/16–7/3/05). Served January 8, 1963, to
   January 3, 1981.
   100. 94. 100. 92. 71. III

Pastore, John Orlando. D-R.I. (3/17/07–7/15/00). Served December 19, 1950, to
   December 28, 1976.
   90. 94. 80. 62. 79. I

Pearson, James Blackwood. R-Kans. (5/7/20). Served January 3, 1962, to December 23, 1978.
   23. 6. 5. 15. 21. III

Pell, Claiborne de Borda. D-R.I. (11/22/18). Served January 3, 1961, to January 3,
   1997.
   90. 94. 90. 92. 79. II

Percy, Charles Harting. R-Ill. (9/27/19). Served January 3, 1967, to January 3,
   1985.
   NA. NA. NA. 38. 79. II.

Prouty, Winston Lewis. R-Vt. (9/1/06–9/10/71). Served January 3, 1959 to
   death.
   39. 29. 35. 38. 43. I

Proxmire, William. D-Wisc. (11/11/15–12/15/05). Served January 3, 1959, to
   January 3, 1989.
   86. 88. 85. 77. 64. I

Randolph, Jennings. D-W.Va. (3/8/02–5/8/98). Served November 5, 1958, to
   January 3, 1985.
   74. 76. 70. 69. 64. II

Ribicoff, Abraham Alexander. D-Conn. (4/09/10–2/22/98). Served January 3,
   1963, to January 3, 1981.
   92. 94. 90. 85. 86. III

Robertson, A. Willis. D-Va. (5/27/87–11/1/71). Served November 25, 1946, to
   December 30, 1966.
   5. 0. 5. NA II

Russell, Donald Stuart. D-S.C. (2/22/06–2/22/98). Served April 22, 1965, to
   November 5, 1966.
   NA. 0. 10. NA. NA. III

Russell, Richard Brevard, Jr. D-Ga. (11/2/97–1/21/71). Served January 12, 1933, to death.
  17. 6. 5. 8. 0. II

Salinger, Pierre Emil George. D-Calif. (6/14/25–10/16/04). Served August 5, 1964, to December 31, 1964.
  100. NA. NA. NA. NA. I

Saltonstall, Leverett. R-Mass. (9/1/92–6/17/79). Served January 4, 1945, to January 3, 1967.
  26. 35. 10. NA. NA. II

Scott, Hugh Doggett, Jr. R-Pa. (11/11/00–7/21/94). Served January 3, 1959, to January 3, 1977.
  51. 65. 45. 46. 57. I

Simpson, Milward Lee. R-Wyo. (11/12/87–6/17/93). Served November 7, 1962, to January 3, 1967.
  0. 0. 0. NA. NA. II

Smathers, George Armistead. D-Fla. (11/14/13). Served January 3, 1951, to January 3, 1969.
  25. 41. 10. 31. 7. III

Smith, Margaret Chase. R-Maine. (12/14/97–5/29/95). Served January 3, 1949, to January 3, 1973.
  52. 59. 55. 23. 36. II

Sparkman, John Jackson. D-Ala. (12/20/99–11/16/85). Served November 6, 1946, to January 3, 1979.
  40. 24. 15. 8. 0. II

Spong, William Belser, Jr. D-Va. (9/29/20–10/8/97). Served December 31, 1966, to January 3, 1973.
  NA. NA. NA. 23. 29. II

Stennis, John Cornelius. D-Miss. (8/3/01–4/23/95). Served November 5, 1947, to January 3, 1989.
  5. 0. 0. 0. 0. I

Symington, Stuart. D-Mo. (6/26/01–12/14/88). Served January 3, 1953, to December 27, 1976.
  87. 59. 55. 54. 0. I

Talmadge, Herman Eugene. D-Ga. (8/9/13–3/21/02). Served January 3, 1957, to January 3, 1981.
  14. 14. 0. 8. 0. III

Thurmond, James Strom.[3] S.C. (12/5/02–6/26/03). Served November 7, 1956, to January 3, 2003.
  2. 0. 0. 0. 0. II

Tower, John Goodwin. R-Tex. (9/29/25–4/5/91). Served June 15, 1961, to January 3, 1985.

    0. 0. 5. 8. 0. II

Tydings, Joseph Davies. D-Md. (5/4/28). Served January 3, 1965, to January 3, 1971.

    NA. 94. 85. 77. 86. I

Walters, Herbert S. D-Tenn. (11/17/91–8/17/73). Served August 27, 1963, to November 3, 1964.

    11. NA. NA. NA. NA. II

Williams, Harrison Arlington, Jr. D-N.J. (12/10/19–11/17/01). Served January 3, 1959, to March 11, 1982.

    92. 82. 95. 77. 86. I

Williams, John James. R-Del. (5/17/04–1/11/88). Served January 3, 1947, to December 31, 1970.

    13. 6. 5. 23. 21. I

Yarborough, Ralph Webster. D-Tex. (6/8/03–1/27/96). Served April 2, 1957, to January 3, 1971.

    66. 71. 90. 62. 57. I

Young, Milton Ruben. R-N.Dak. (12/6/97–5/31/83). Served March 12, 1945, to January 3, 1981.

    17. 0. 5. 0. 0. III

Young, Stephen Marvin. D-Ohio. (5/4/89–12/1/84). Served January 3, 1959, to January 3, 1971.

    87. 88. 85. 77. 93. I

NOTES

    1. Formally resigned from Democratic Party on March 17, 1970, but remained as an Independent in Democratic Caucus.

    2. Served as Republican to October 24, 1952, and then as an Independent (in Democratic Caucus) to February 17, 1955, when he became a Democrat.

    3. Served as a Democrat before September 16, 1964.

APPENDIX II

Membership of the Foreign Relations Committee, 1964–1968

88th Congress

Service Dates of Committee Chair: February 25, 1963–January 8, 1965
Service Dates of Majority Members: February 25, 1963–January 8, 1965
Service Dates of Minority Members: February 25, 1963–January 15, 1965

MAJORITY

RANK, NAME	PARTY	STATE	YEARS IN SENATE	YEARS IN COMMITTEE	
Chr, Fulbright, J. William	Dem	Ark.	19	1	5
2nd, Sparkman, John J.	Dem	Ala.	17	13	
3rd, Humphrey, Hubert H., Jr.	DFL	Minn.	15 (1)*	11	
4th, Mansfield, Michael J.	Dem	Mont.	11	11	
5th, Morse, Wayne L.	Dem	Ore.	19	9	
6th, Long, Russell B.	Dem	La.	15	7	
7th, Gore, Albert A.	Dem	Tenn.	11	5	
8th, Lausche, Frank J.	Dem	Ohio	7	5	
9th, Church, Frank F.	Dem	Idaho	7	5	
10th, Symington, W. Stuart	Dem	Mo.	11	3	
11th, Dodd, Thomas J.	Dem	Conn.	5	3	
12th, Smathers, George A.	Dem	Fla.	13	1	

MINORITY

RANK, NAME	PARTY	STATE	YEARS IN SENATE	YEARS IN COMMITTEE
RM, Hickenlooper, Bourke B.	Rep	Iowa	19	17
2nd, Aiken, George D.	Rep	Vt.	25	12
3rd, Carlson, Frank	Rep	Kans.	13	5
4th, Williams, John J.	Rep	Del.	17	4
5th, Mundt, Karl E.	Rep	S.Dak.	15	1

NOTE
* Member's first period of service on the committee.

CHANGES

MAJORITY

Humphrey, Hubert J., Jr.	Dem	Minn.	December 29, 1964, resigned, elected vice-president

89th Congress

Service Dates of Committee Chair: January 8, 1965–January 11, 1967
Service Dates of Majority Members: January 8, 1965–January 11, 1967
Service Dates of Minority Members: January 15, 1965–January 16, 1967

MAJORITY

			———YEARS IN———	
RANK, NAME	PARTY	STATE	SENATE	COMMITTEE
Chr, Fulbright, J. William	Dem	Ark.	21	16
2nd, Sparkman, John J.	Dem	Ala.	19	14
3rd, Mansfield, Michael J.	Dem	Mont.	13	12
4th, Morse, Wayne L.	Dem	Ore.	21	10
5th, Long, Russell B.	Dem	La.	17	9
6th, Gore, Albert A.	Dem	Tenn.	13	6
7th, Lausche, Frank J.	Dem	Ohio	9	6
8th, Church, Frank F.	Dem	Idaho	7	5
9th, Symington, W. Stuart	Dem	Mo.	13	4
10th, Dodd, Thomas J.	Dem	Conn.	7	4
11th, Smathers, George A.	Dem	Fla.	15	2
12th, Clark, Joseph S.	Dem	Penn.	9	1
13th, Pell, Claiborne	Dem	R.I.	5	1

MINORITY

RM Hickenlooper, Bourke B.	Rep	Iowa	21	19
2nd Aiken, George D.	Rep	Vt.	25	12
3rd Carlson, Frank	Rep	Kans.	15	6
4th Williams, John J.	Rep	Del.	19	5
5th Mundt, Karl E.	Rep	S.Dak.	15	1
6th Case, Clifford P.	Rep	N.J.	11	1

CHANGES

Smathers, George A.	Dem	Fla.	April 26, 1965, moved to Judiciary
McCarthy, Eugene J.	DFL	Minn.	April 26, 1965, replaced Smathers
Long, Russell B.	Dem	La.	March 25, 1966, moved to Commerce
McGee, Gale W.	Dem	Wyo.	March 25, 1966, replaced Long

DEPARTURES FROM COMMITTEE

MAJORITY

Moved to Banking and Currency	McGee, Gale W.

MINORITY

None

90th Congress

Service Dates of Committee Chair: January 11, 1967–January 14, 1969
Service Dates of Majority Members: January 11, 1967–January 14, 1969
Service Dates of Minority Members: January 16, 1967–January 14, 1969

MAJORITY

			YEARS IN	
RANK, NAME	PARTY	STATE	SENATE	COMMITTEE
Chr, Fulbright, J. William	Dem	Ark.	23	18
2nd, Sparkman, John J.	Dem	Ala.	21	16
3rd, Mansfield, Michael J.	Dem	Mont.	15	14
4th, Morse, Wayne L.	Dem	Ore.	23	13
5th, Gore, Albert A.	Dem	Tenn.	15	8
6th, Lausche, Frank J.	Dem	Ohio	11	8
7th, Church, Frank F.	Dem	Idaho	11	8
8th, Symington, W. Stuart	Dem	Mo.	15	7

9th, Dodd, Thomas J.	Dem	Conn.	9	7
10th, Clark, Joseph S.	Dem	Penn.	11	3
11th, Pell, Claiborne	Dem	R.I.	7	3
12th, McCarthy, Eugene J.	DFL	Minn.	9	2

MINORITY

RM, Hickenlooper, Bourke B.	Rep	Iowa	23	21
2nd, Aiken, George D.	Rep	Vt.	27	14
3rd, Carlson, Frank	Rep	Kans.	17	8
4th, Williams, John J.	Rep	Del.	21	7
5th, Mundt, Karl E.	Rep	S.Dak.	19	4
6th, Case, Clifford P.	Rep	N.J.	13	3
7th, Cooper, John Sherman	Rep	Ky.	15	1

NOTE
Rankings on this committee were adjusted on September 12, 1968, with John J. Williams (R–Del.) moving from fourth to seventh minority rank and Mundt, Case, and Cooper moving up a rank.

DEPARTURES FROM SENATE

	MAJORITY	MINORITY
Defeated for Reelection	Clark, Joseph S., D-Pa. Morse, Wayne L., D-Ore.	None
Defeated for Renomination	Lausche, Frank J., D-Ohio	None
Retired None	Carlson, Frank, R-Kans. Hickenlooper, Bourke B., R-Iowa	

DEPARTURES FROM COMMITTEE

	MAJORITY	MINORITY
Moved to Govt. Operations	McCarthy, Eugene J., DFL-Minn	None

SOURCE: *U.S. Senate Historical Office.*

APPENDIX III

Membership of the Armed Services Committee, 1965–1968

89th Congress

Service Dates of Committee Chair: January 8, 1965–January 11, 1967
Service Dates of Majority Members: January 8, 1965–January 11, 1967
Service Dates of Minority Members: January 15, 1965–January 16, 1967

MAJORITY

RANK, NAME	PARTY	STATE	YEARS IN SENATE	YEARS IN COMMITTEE
Chr, Russell, Richard B.	Dem	Ga.	32	32
2nd, Stennis, John C.	Dem	Miss.	18	14
3rd, Byrd, Harry Flood	Dem	Va.	32	32
4th, Symington, W. Stuart	Dem	Mo.	12	12
5th, Jackson, Henry M.	Dem	Wash.	12	11
6th, Ervin, Samuel J.	Dem	N.C.	11	10
7th, Cannon, Howard W.	Dem	Nev.	7	6
8th, Byrd, Robert C.	Dem	W.Va.	7	4
9th, Young, Stephen M.	Dem	Ohio	7	2
10th, Inouye, Daniel K.	Dem	Hawaii	3	2
11th, McIntyre, Thomas J.	Dem	N.H.	3	1
12th, Brewster, Daniel B.	Dem	Md.	3	1

MINORITY

Chr, Fulbright, J. William	Dem	Ark.	23	18
RM, Saltonstall, Leverett	Rep	Mass.	21	21
2nd, Smith, Margaret Chase	Rep	Maine.	17	13
3rd, Thurmond, J. Strom	Rep	S.C.	10	7

| 4th, Miller, Jack R. | Rep | Iowa | 5 | 1 |
| 5th, Tower, John G. | Rep | Tex. | 4 | 1 |

NOTES
J. Strom Thurmond (R–S.C.) served previously on this committee as a Democrat in the 88th Congress. John C. Stennis (D-Miss.) was moved to second rank on the committee ahead of Harry Flood Byrd (D-Va.).

CHANGES

MAJORITY

| Byrd, Harry Flood | Dem | Fla. | November 10, 1966, resigned and retired |
| Byrd, Harry Flood, Jr. | Dem | Va. | January 15, 1966, replaced Byrd Sr. |

DEPARTURES FROM SENATE

	MAJORITY	MINORITY
Retired	None	Saltonstall, Leverett, R-Mass.

90th Congress

Service Dates of Committee Chair: January 11, 1967–January 14, 1969
Service Dates of Majority Members: January 11, 1967–January 14, 1969
Service Dates of Minority Members: January 16, 1965–January 14, 1967

MAJORITY

| | | | ——YEARS IN—— | |
RANK, NAME	PARTY	STATE	SENATE	COMMITTEE
Chr, Russell, Richard B.	Dem	Ga.	34	34
2nd, Stennis, John C.	Dem	Miss.	20	16
3rd, Symington, W. Stuart	Dem	Mo.	15	14
4th, Jackson, Henry M.	Dem	Wash.	15	13
5th, Ervin, Samuel J.	Dem	N.C.	13	13
6th, Cannon, Howard W.	Dem	Nev.	9	8
7th, Byrd, Robert C.	Dem	W.Va.	9	7
8th, Young, Stephen M.	Dem	Ohio	9	4
9th, Inouye, Daniel K.	Dem	Hawaii	5	4

10th, McIntyre, Thomas J.	Dem	N.H.	5	3
11th, Brewster, Daniel B.	Dem	Md.	5	3
12th, Byrd, Harry Flood, Jr.	Dem	Va.	2	1

MINORITY

RM, Smith, Margaret Chase	Rep	Maine.	19	15
2nd, Thurmond, J. Strom	Rep	S.C.	12	9
3rd, Miller, Jack R.	Rep	Iowa	7	3
4th, Tower, John G.	Rep	Tex.	6	3
5th, Pearson, James B.	Rep	Kans.	5	1
6th, Dominick, Peter H.	Rep	Colo.	5	1

NOTE

J. Strom Thurmond (R–S.C.) served previously on this committee as a Democrat.

DEPARTURES FROM SENATE

	MAJORITY	MINORITY
Defeated for Reelection	Brewster, Daniel B., D-Md.	None

DEPARTURES FROM COMMITTEE

	MAJORITY	MINORITY
Moved to Judiciary	Byrd, Robert C., D-W.Va.	None
Moved to Finance	None	Miller, Jack R., R-Iowa
Moved to Appropriations	None	Pearson, James B., R-Kans.

Charter of the United Nations, Preamble and Chapters VI–VIII

June 26, 1945, 59 Stat. 1031, T.S. 993, 3 Bevans 1153, entered into force October 24, 1945.

Preamble

WE THE PEOPLES OF THE UNITED NATIONS DETERMINED
to save succeeding generations from the scourge of war, which twice in our lifetime has brought untold sorrow to mankind, and

to reaffirm faith in fundamental human rights, in the dignity and worth of the human person, in the equal rights of men and women and of nations large and small, and

to establish conditions under which justice and respect for the obligations arising from treaties and other sources of international law can be maintained, and

to promote social progress and better standards of life in larger freedom,

AND FOR THESE ENDS
to practice tolerance and live together in peace with one another as good neighbors, and

to unite our strength to maintain international peace and security, and

to ensure by the acceptance of principles and the institution of methods, that armed force shall not be used, save in the common interest, and

to employ international machinery for the promotion of the economic and social advancement of all peoples,

HAVE RESOLVED TO COMBINE OUR EFFORTS TO
ACCOMPLISH THESE AIMS

Accordingly, our respective Governments, through representatives assembled in the city of San Francisco, who have exhibited their full powers found to be in good and due form, have agreed to the present Charter of the United Nations and do hereby establish an international organization to be known as the United Nations.

Chapter VI
Pacific Settlement of Disputes

ARTICLE 33

1. The parties to any dispute, the continuance of which is likely to endanger the maintenance of international peace and security, shall, first of all, seek a solution by negotiation, enquiry, mediation, conciliation, arbitration, judicial settlement, resort to regional agencies or arrangements, or other peaceful means of their own choice.

2. The Security Council shall, when it deems necessary, call upon the parties to settle their dispute by such means.

ARTICLE 34

The Security Council may investigate any dispute, or any situation which might lead to international friction or give rise to a dispute, in order to determine whether the continuance of the dispute or situation is likely to endanger the maintenance of international peace and security.

ARTICLE 35

1. Any Member of the United Nations may bring any dispute, or any situation of the nature referred to in Article 34, to the attention of the Security Council or of the General Assembly.

2. A state which is not a Member of the United Nations may bring to the attention of the Security Council or of the General Assembly any dispute to which it is a party if it accepts in advance, for the purposes of the dispute, the obligations of pacific settlement provided in the present Charter.

3. The proceedings of the General Assembly in respect of matters brought to its attention under this Article will be subject to the provisions of Articles 11 and 12.

ARTICLE 36

1. The Security Council may, at any stage of a dispute of the nature referred to in Article 33 or of a situation of like nature, recommend appropriate procedures or methods of adjustment.

2. The Security Council should take into consideration any procedures for the settlement of the dispute which have already been adopted by the parties.

3. In making recommendations under this Article the Security Council should also take into consideration that legal disputes should as a general rule be referred by the parties to the International Court of Justice in accordance with the provisions of the Statute of the Court.

ARTICLE 37

1. Should the parties to a dispute of the nature referred to in Article 33 fail to settle it by the means indicated in that Article, they shall refer it to the Security Council.

2. If the Security Council deems that the continuance of the dispute is in fact likely to endanger the maintenance of international peace and security, it shall decide whether to take action under Article 36 or to recommend such terms of settlement as it may consider appropriate.

ARTICLE 38

Without prejudice to the provisions of Articles 33 to 37, the Security Council may, if all the parties to any dispute so request, make recommendations to the parties with a view to a pacific settlement of the dispute.

Chapter VII
Action with Respect to Threats to the Peace,
Breaches of the Peace, and Acts of Aggression

ARTICLE 39

The Security Council shall determine the existence of any threat to the peace, breach of the peace, or act of aggression and shall make recommendations, or decide what measures shall be taken in accordance with Articles 41 and 42, to maintain or restore international peace and security.

ARTICLE 40

In order to prevent an aggravation of the situation, the Security Council may, before making the recommendations or deciding upon the measures provided for in Article 39, call upon the parties concerned to comply with such provisional measures as it deems necessary or desirable. Such provisional measures shall be without prejudice to the rights, claims, or position of the parties concerned. The Security Council shall duly take account of failure to comply with such provisional measures.

ARTICLE 41

The Security Council may decide what measures not involving the use of armed force are to be employed to give effect to its decisions, and it may call upon the Members of the United Nations to apply such measures. These may include complete or partial interruption of economic relations and of rail, sea, air, postal, telegraphic, radio, and other means of communication, and the severance of diplomatic relations.

ARTICLE 42

Should the Security Council consider that measures provided for in Article 41 would be inadequate or have proved to be inadequate, it may take such action by air, sea, or land forces as may be necessary to maintain or restore international peace and security. Such action may include demonstrations, blockade, and other operations by air, sea, or land forces of Members of the United Nations.

ARTICLE 43

1. All Members of the United Nations, in order to contribute to the maintenance of international peace and security, undertake to make available to the Security Council, on its call and in accordance with a special agreement or agreements, armed forces, assistance, and facilities, including rights of passage, necessary for the purpose of maintaining international peace and security.

2. Such agreement or agreements shall govern the numbers and types of forces, their degree of readiness and general location, and the nature of the facilities and assistance to be provided.

3. The agreement or agreements shall be negotiated as soon as possible on the initiative of the Security Council. They shall be concluded between the Security Council and Members or between the Security Council and groups of Members and shall be subject to ratification by the signatory states in accordance with their respective constitutional processes.

ARTICLE 44

When the Security Council has decided to use force it shall, before calling upon a Member not represented on it to provide armed forces in fulfillment of the obligations assumed under Article 43, invite that Member, if the Member so desires, to participate in the decisions of the Security Council concerning the employment of contingents of that Member's armed forces.

ARTICLE 45

In order to enable the United Nations to take urgent military measures Members shall hold immediately available national air-force contingents for combined international enforcement action. The strength and degree of readiness of these contingents and plans for their combined action shall be determined, within the limits laid down in the special agreement or agreements referred to in Article 43, by the Security Council with the assistance of the Military Staff Committee.

ARTICLE 46

Plans for the application of armed force shall be made by the Security Council with the assistance of the Military Staff Committee.

ARTICLE 47

1. There shall be established a Military Staff Committee to advise and assist the Security Council on all questions relating to the Security Council's military requirements for the maintenance of international peace and security, the employment and command of forces placed at its disposal, the regulation of armaments, and possible disarmament.

2. The Military Staff Committee shall consist of the Chiefs of Staff of the permanent members of the Security Council or their representatives. Any Member of the United Nations not permanently represented on the Committee shall be invited by the Committee to be associated with it when the efficient discharge of the Committee's responsibilities requires the participation of that Member in its work.

3. The Military Staff Committee shall be responsible under the Security Council for the strategic direction of any armed forces placed at the disposal of the Security Council. Questions relating to the command of such forces shall be worked out subsequently.

4. The Military Staff Committee, with the authorization of the Security Council and after consultation with appropriate regional agencies, may establish regional subcommittees.

ARTICLE 48

1. The action required to carry out the decisions of the Security Council for the maintenance of international peace and security shall be taken by all the Members of the United Nations or by some of them, as the Security Council may determine.

2. Such decisions shall be carried out by the Members of the United Nations directly and through their action in the appropriate international agencies of which they are members.

ARTICLE 49

The Members of the United Nations shall join in affording mutual assistance in carrying out the measures decided upon by the Security Council.

ARTICLE 50

If preventive or enforcement measures against any state are taken by the Security Council, any other state, whether a Member of the United Nations or not, which finds itself confronted with special economic problems arising from the carrying out of those measures shall have the right to consult the Security Council with regard to a solution of those problems.

ARTICLE 51

Nothing in the present Charter shall impair the inherent right of individual or collective self-defense if an armed attack occurs against a Member of the United Nations, until the Security Council has taken measures necessary to maintain international peace and security. Measures taken by Members in the exercise of this right of self-defense shall be immediately reported to the Security Council and shall not in any way affect the authority and responsibility of the Security Council under the present Charter to take at any time such action as it deems necessary in order to maintain or restore international peace and security.

Chapter VIII
Regional Arrangements

ARTICLE 52

1. Nothing in the present Charter precludes the existence of regional arrangements or agencies for dealing with such matters relating to the maintenance of international peace and security as are appropriate for regional action, provided that such arrangements or agencies and their activities are consistent with the Purposes and Principles of the United Nations.

2. The Members of the United Nations entering into such arrangements or constituting such agencies shall make every effort to achieve pacific settlement of local disputes through such regional arrangements or by such regional agencies before referring them to the Security Council.

3. The Security Council shall encourage the development of pacific settlement of local disputes through such regional arrangements or by such

regional agencies either on the initiative of the states concerned or by reference from the Security Council.

4. This Article in no way impairs the application of Articles 34 and 35.

ARTICLE 53

1. The Security Council shall, where appropriate, utilize such regional arrangements or agencies for enforcement action under its authority. But no enforcement action shall be taken under regional arrangements or by regional agencies without the authorization of the Security Council, with the exception of measures against any enemy state, as defined in paragraph 2 of this Article, provided for pursuant to Article 107 or in regional arrangements directed against renewal of aggressive policy on the part of any such state, until such time as the Organization may, on request of the Governments concerned, be charged with the responsibility for preventing further aggression by such a state.

2. The term enemy state as used in paragraph 1 of this Article applies to any state which during the Second World War has been an enemy of any signatory of the present Charter.

ARTICLE 54

The Security Council shall at all times be kept fully informed of activities undertaken or in contemplation under regional arrangements or by regional agencies for the maintenance of international peace and security.

APPENDIX V

South East Asia Resolution (Gulf of Tonkin Resolution)

Joint Resolution of U.S. Congress: Public Law 88-408, August 7, 1964, Approved on August 10, 1964

To promote the maintenance of international peace and security in southeast Asia.

Whereas naval units of the Communist regime in Vietnam, in violation of the principles of the Charter of the United Nations and of international law, have deliberately and repeatedly attacked United States naval vessels lawfully present in international waters, and have thereby created a serious threat to international peace; and

Whereas these attacks are part of a deliberate and systematic campaign of aggression that the Communist regime in North Vietnam has been waging against its neighbors and the nations joined with them in the collective defense of their freedom; and

Whereas the United States is assisting the peoples of southeast Asia to protect their freedom and has no territorial, military or political ambitions in that area, but desires only that these peoples should be left in peace to work out their own destinies in their own way: Now, therefore, be it

Resolved by the Senate and House of Representatives of the United States of America in Congress assembled, That the Congress approves and supports the determination of the President, as Commander in Chief, to take all necessary measures to repel any armed attack against the forces of the United States and to prevent further aggression.

Sec. 2.   The United States regards as vital to its national interest and to world peace the maintenance of international peace and security in southeast Asia. Consonant with the Constitution of the United States and

the Charter of the United Nations and in accordance with its obligations under the Southeast Asia Collective Defense Treaty, the United
States is, therefore, prepared, as the President determines, to take all
necessary steps, including the use of armed force, to assist any member or protocol state of the South-east Asia Collective Defense Treaty
requesting assistance in defense of its freedom.

Sec. 3.   This resolution shall expire when the President shall determine that
the peace and security of the area is reasonably assured by international conditions created by action of the United Nations or otherwise, except that it may be terminated earlier by concurrent resolution of the Congress.

SOURCE: *Department of State Bulletin,* August 24, 1964, 268.

APPENDIX VI

Multilateral Asia Collective Defense Treaty (SEATO Treaty)

BY THE PRESIDENT OF THE UNITED STATES OF AMERICA

A PROCLAMATION

WHEREAS the Southeast Asia Collective Defense Treaty and a Protocol relating thereto were signed at Manila on September 8, 1954 by the respective Plenipotentiaries of the United States of America, Australia, France, New Zealand, Pakistan, the Republic of the Philippines, the Kingdom of Thailand, and the United Kingdom of Great Britain and Northern Ireland;

WHEREAS the texts of the said Treaty and the said Protocol, in the English language, are word for word as follows:

Southeast Asia Collective Defense Treaty

The Parties to this Treaty,

Recognizing the sovereign equality of all the Parties,

Reiterating their faith in the purposes and principles set forth in the Charter of the United Nations and their desire to live in peace with all peoples and all governments,

Reaffirming that, in accordance with the Charter of the United Nations, they uphold the principle of equal rights and self-determination of peoples, and declaring that they will earnestly strive by every peaceful means to promote self-government and to secure the independence of all countries whose peoples desire it and are able to undertake its responsibilities,

Desiring to strengthen the fabric of peace and freedom and to uphold the principles of democracy, individual liberty and the rule of law, and to promote the economic well-being and development of all peoples in the treaty area,

Intending to declare publicly and formally their sense of unity, so that any potential aggressor will appreciate that the Parties stand together in the area, and

Desiring further to coordinate their efforts for collective defense for the preservation of peace and security,

Therefore agree as follows:

ARTICLE I

The Parties undertake, as set forth in the Charter of the United Nations, to settle any international disputes in which they may be involved by peaceful means in such a manner that international peace and security and justice are not endangered, and to refrain in their international relations from the threat or use of force in any manner inconsistent with the purposes of the United Nations.

ARTICLE II

In order more effectively to achieve the objectives of this Treaty, the Parties, separately and jointly, by means of continuous and effective self-help and mutual aid will maintain and develop their individual and collective capacity to resist armed attack and to prevent and counter subversive activities directed from without against their territorial integrity and political stability.

ARTICLE III

The Parties undertake to strengthen their free institutions and to cooperate with one another in the further development of economic measures, including technical assistance, designed both to promote economic progress and social well-being and to further the individual and collective efforts of governments toward these ends.

ARTICLE IV

1. Each Party recognizes that aggression by means of armed attack in the treaty area against any of the Parties or against any State or territory

which the Parties by unanimous agreement may hereafter designate, would endanger its own peace and safety, and agrees that it will in that event act to meet the common danger in accordance with its constitutional processes. Measures taken under this paragraph shall be immediately reported to the Security Council of the United Nations.

2. If, in the opinion of any of the Parties, the inviolability or the integrity of the territory or the sovereignty or political independence of any Party in the treaty area or of any other State or territory to which the provisions of paragraph 1 of this Article from time to time apply is threatened in any way other than by armed attack or is affected or threatened by any fact or situation which might endanger the peace of the area, the Parties shall consult immediately in order to agree on the measures which should be taken for the common defense.

3. It is understood that no action on the territory of any State designated by unanimous agreement under paragraph 1 of this Article or on any territory so designated shall be taken except at the invitation or with the consent of the government concerned.

ARTICLE V

The Parties hereby establish a Council, on which each of them shall be represented, to consider matters concerning the implementation of this Treaty. The Council shall provide for consultation with regard to military and any other planning as the situation obtaining in the treaty area may from time to time require. The Council shall be so organized as to be able to meet at any time.

ARTICLE VI

This Treaty does not affect and shall not be interpreted as affecting in any way the rights and obligations of any of the Parties under the Charter of the United Nations or the responsibility of the United Nations for the maintenance of international peace and security. Each Party declares that none of the international engagements now in force between it and any other of the Parties or any third party is in conflict with the provisions of this Treaty, and undertakes not to enter into any international engagement in conflict with this Treaty.

ARTICLE VII

Any other State in a position to further the objectives of this Treaty and to contribute to the security of the area may, by unanimous agreement of the Parties, be invited to accede to this Treaty. Any State so invited may become a Party to the Treaty by depositing its instrument of accession with the Government of the Republic of the Philippines. The Government of the Republic of the Philippines shall inform each of the Parties of the deposit of each such instrument of accession.

ARTICLE VIII

As used in this Treaty, the "treaty area" is the general area of Southeast Asia, including also the entire territories of the Asian Parties, and the general area of the Southwest Pacific not including the Pacific area north of 21 degrees 30 minutes north latitude. The Parties may, by unanimous agreement, amend this Article to include within the treaty area the territory of any State acceding to this Treaty in accordance with Article VII or otherwise to change the treaty area.

ARTICLE IX

1. This Treaty shall be deposited in the archives of the Government of the Republic of the Philippines. Duly certified copies thereof shall be transmitted by that government to the other signatories.

2. The Treaty shall be ratified and its provisions carried out by the Parties in accordance with their respective constitutional processes. The instruments of ratification shall be deposited as soon as possible with the Government of the Republic of the Philippines, which shall notify all of the other signatories of such deposit.(2)

3. The Treaty shall enter into force between the States which have ratified it as soon as the instruments of ratification of a majority of the signatories shall have been deposited, and shall come into effect with respect to each other State on the date of the deposit of its instrument of ratification.

ARTICLE X

This Treaty shall remain in force indefinitely, but any Party may cease to be a Party one year after its notice of denunciation has been given to the Government of the Republic of the Philippines, which shall inform the Governments of the other Parties of the deposit of each notice of denunciation.

ARTICLE XI

The English text of this Treaty is binding on the Parties, but when the Parties have agreed to the French text thereof and have so notified the Government of the Republic of the Philippines, the French text shall be equally authentic and binding on the Parties.

UNDERSTANDING OF THE UNITED STATES OF AMERICA

The United States of America in executing the present Treaty does so with the understanding that its recognition of the effect of aggression and armed attack and its agreement with reference thereto in Article IV, paragraph 1, apply only to communist aggression but affirms that in the event of other aggression or armed attack it will consult under the provisions of Article IV, paragraph 2.

In witness whereof, the undersigned Plenipotentiaries have signed this Treaty.

Done at Manila, this eighth day of September, 1954.

(1) TIAS 3170; 6 UST 81-86. Ratification advised by the Senate February 1, 1955; ratified by the President February 4, 1955; entered into force February 19, 1955.

(2) Thailand deposited its instrument of ratification December 2, 1954; the remaining signatories (the United States, Australia, France, New Zealand, Pakistan, the Philippines, and the United Kingdom) deposited their instruments February 19, 1955.

SOURCE: *American Foreign Policy, 1950–1955,* Basic Documents, vols. 1 and 2, Department of State Publication 6446, *General Foreign Policy Series* 117 (Washington, D.C.: GPO, 1957).

NOTES

INTRODUCTION

1. *Congressional Record* (hereafter *"CR"*) 116 (September 1, 1970), 30682.

2. Robert Mann, *A Grand Illusion: America's Descent into Vietnam* (New York: Basic Books, 2001), 669–70; compare Thomas J. Knock, "'Come Home America'; The Story of George McGovern," in *Vietnam and the American Political Tradition: The Politics of Dissent,* ed. Randall B. Woods (Cambridge: Cambridge University Press, 2003), 82–84.

3. U.S. Const., art. I, sec. 8.

4. Ibid., art. II, sec. 2. The provision is framed in positive terms: "He [the president] shall have Power, by and with the Advice and Consent of the Senate, to make Treaties, provided two-thirds of the Senators present concur."

5. Ibid., art. II, sec. 4.

6. *CR* 97 (January 5, 1951), 54–60.

7. Ibid., 55.

8. Cecil Crabb Jr., *Bipartisan Foreign Policy: Myth or Reality?* (Evanston, Ill.: Row, Peterson, 1957), 59.

9. Thomas J. McCormick, *America's Half-Century* (Baltimore: Johns Hopkins University Press, 1989), 87.

10. Crabb, *Bipartisan Foreign Policy,* 86.

11. With respect to this attitude, speeches made by conservative Senate opponents of the proposed Marshall Plan are particularly revealing. See, for example, *CR* 94 (March 5, 1948), 2189 (George Malone [R-Nev.]).

12. Quotations from John W. Spanier, *The Truman-MacArthur Controversy and the Korean War* (Cambridge, Mass.: Belknap, 1959), 155. The sense of alienation was mutual. Citing Acheson's letters to his daughter during his days as a congressional liaison, Walter Isaacson and Evan Thomas depict him "poking about the halls of Congress like an anthropologist sampling native customs" (*The Wise Men* [New York: Simon & Schuster, 1986], 394).

13. Senate Committee on Foreign Relations, *Nomination of John Foster Dulles,* 83rd Cong., 1st Sess., 1953, 10. See Carl Solberg, *Riding High: America in the Cold War* (New York: Mason and Lipscomb), 222.

14. Solberg, *Riding High,* 225–27.

15. For a more detailed account of the Truman and Eisenhower years, see Gary Steven Stone, "The Senate and the Vietnam War" (Ph.D. diss., Columbia University, 2000), chap. 1.

16. Larry Berman, *Planning a Tragedy* (New York: Norton, 1982), 6, 128.

17. It might be added that Johnson himself contributed to the administration's troubles when he libelously red-baited Leland Olds and blocked his reappointment to the chairmanship of the Federal Power Commission. See Robert A. Caro, *The Years of Lyndon Johnson: Master of the Senate* (New York: Vintage, 2002), chap. 11.

18. Lisa McGirr, *Suburban Warriors* (Princeton, N.J.: Princeton University Press, 2001), 63–71 and *passim;* Randall Bennett Woods, *Fulbright: A Biography* (Cambridge: Cambridge University Press, 1995), 278–89; *CR* 108 (September 20, 1962), 2002–3.

19. Compare McGirr, *Suburban Warriors,* 81–110.

20. See Fredrik Logevall, *The Origins of the Vietnam War* (Harlow, Eng.: Pearson/ Longman, 2001); Logevall, *Choosing War* (Berkeley: University of California Press, 1999). I was unaware of these brilliant works (or even of the existence of their author) until the final draft of this book was almost completed. To say the least, my confidence in the validity of my thesis increased when I learned that Logevall had reached many of the same conclusions that I had reached, using largely different sources and working with a different perspective and focus.

21. See Logevall, *Origins of the Vietnam War,* chap. 6; *Choosing War,* 412–13.

22. David Kaiser, *American Tragedy: Kennedy, Johnson and the Origins of the Vietnam War* (Cambridge: Harvard University Press, 2000), 1; James T. Patterson, *Grand Expectations: The United States, 1945–1974* (New York: Oxford University Press, 1996), 603; compare Alton Frye and Jack Sullivan, "Congress and Vietnam: The Fruits of Anguish," in *American Society and the Future of American Foreign Policy,* ed. Anthony Lake, 194–215 (New York: New York University Press, 1976).

23. Gary W. Reichard, "Divisions and Dissent: Democrats and Foreign Policy, 1952–1956," *Political Science Quarterly* 93 (1978): 51–72, reprinted in Joel H. Silbey, ed., *To Advise and Consent: The United States Congress and Foreign Policy in the Twentieth Century.* (Brooklyn: Carlson, 1991), 1:273–94); Patterson, *Grand Expectations,* 603; Solberg, *Riding High,* 466; Terry Dietz, *The Republicans and Vietnam, 1961–1968* (Westport, Conn.: Greenwood, 1986), 119, citing with approval Walter Zelman, "Senate Dissent and the Vietnam War, 1964–1968" (Ph.D. diss., University of California, Los Angeles, 1971), 163.

24. For example, Tristram Coffin, *Senator Fulbright: Portrait of a Public Philosopher* (New York: Dutton, 1966).

25. See Paul Douglas, *In the Fullness of Time* (New York: Harcourt, Brace, 1971), 577–94.

26. Logevall, *Origins of the Vietnam War,* chap. 6; *Choosing War,* 412–13; see also Kaiser, *American Tragedy,* 6.

27. Cf. Logevall, *Origins of the Vietnam War,* 91.

28. Doris Kearns [Goodwin], *Lyndon Johnson and the American Dream* (New York: Harper, 1976); Kaiser, *American Tragedy,* 5–6.

29. See Woods, *Fulbright,* 279–300.

30. Kaiser, *American Tragedy,* 6.

31. The creation of a truly comprehensive study of all senators of the period, tracing the range of influences upon them, would require a collaborative effort sustained over several years comparable to the project that resulted in Sir Lewis Namier and John Brooke, *The History of the House Parliament: The House of Commons, 1754–1790,* 2 vols. (London: London Parliament Trust of Her Majesty's Stationery Office, 1964).

32. Thomas Powers, *Vietnam: The War at Home, Vietnam and the American People, 1964–1968* (New York: Grossman, 1973).

33. Charles DeBenedetti, with Charles Chatfield, *An American Ordeal: The Antiwar Movement of the Vietnam Era.* (Syracuse, N.Y.: Syracuse University Press, 1990).

34. Among the reasons that SDS is an especially bad object to place at the center of an account of the antiwar movement is the fact that SDS, choosing to involve itself with other issues, turned away from the antiwar movement soon after it began in 1965.

CHAPTER 1

1. *CR* 99 (June 30, 1953), 7780.

2. For the Senate, this transformation was marked by the proposal of Truman for aid to Greece and Turkey, undemocratic countries, which he claimed were threatened by international Communism. Claude Pepper (D-Fla.) voiced his opposition by making what he apparently considered a *reductio ad absurdum* argument about where the new policy might lead: "What would our people back home have said if it had been believed that we were supporting the French Army that was in Indonesia [*sic*], shooting down with modern weapons of war the natives who are seeking to lift themselves out of their slavery to emancipation as a new people?" *CR* 93 (April 10, 1947), 3285.

3. Interestingly the original Goldwater amendment was tougher than the substitute amendment subsequently offered by Kennedy. Compare *CR* 99 (June 30, 1953), 7610 (Goldwater amendment) with *CR* 99 (July 1, 1953), 7783 (Kennedy amendment). See *CR* 99 (July 1, 1953), 7784 (Dirksen); 7782 (Goldwater).

4. *CR* 99 (July 1, 1953), 7781.

5. Ibid., 7639. On Robertson, see Harry McPherson, *A Political Education: A Washington Memoir* (1972; Boston: Houghton Mifflin, 1988), 53.

6. *CR* 99 (July 1, 1953), 7636.

7. *CR* 99 (June 30, 1953), 7659.

8. Ibid.

9. *CR* 99 (July 1, 1953), 7754; *CR* 99 (July 1, 1953), 7784.

10. *CR* 99 (June 30, 1953), 7611.

11. For example, ibid., 7637.

12. Ibid., 7638. On Case, see McPherson, *Political Education,* 71.

13. *CR* 99 (July 1, 1953), 7780; *CR* 99 (July 1, 1953), 7782; *CR* 99 (June 30, 1953), 7611; *CR* 99 (June 30, 1953), 7638.

14. *CR* 99 (June 30, 1953), 7623–25, quotation at 7623; *CR* 99 (June 30, 1953), 7625; *CR* 99 (June 29, 1953), 7570; *CR* 99 (July 1, 1953), 7781; *CR* 99 (June 30, 1953), 7637.

15. For example, *CR* 99 (June 30, 1953), 7606 (Russell Long); 7647–73 (Langer, combining radical critique of American foreign policy with extremely hostile examination of European powers, especially Britain).

16. See William C. Gibbons, *The U.S. Government and the Vietnam War: Executive and Legislative Roles and Relationships* (Princeton: Princeton University Press, 1984–86), vol. 1:87–95, and sources cited therein. The account of Johnson's desk banging comes from a December 4, 1978, Congressional Research Service interview with Albert Gore to whom Johnson related the meeting on the day it took place. According to Gore, Johnson claimed to have banged on Eisenhower's desk. Actually the meeting was at the State Department and the president was absent (191). The Gibbons work cited was the first of four volumes prepared, without a named author, under the aegis of the Congressional Research Service for the Senate Committee on Foreign Relations and published by the

United States Government Printing Office ("GPO"). Each volume (referred to as a "part") was subsequently published, with the same pagination, but with Mr. Gibbons as the named author, by Princeton University Press ("PUP"). The first part was published by the GPO in April 1984 and by PUP in 1986, the second by the GPO in December 1984 and by PUP in 1986, the third by the GPO in December 1988 and by PUP in 1989, and the fourth by the GPO in June 1994 and by PUP in 1995.

17. On February 9, 1954, John C. Stennis (D-Miss.) responded to the decision to send aircraft technicians, by expressing his fear that "step by step we are getting into a war in Indochina," and predicting that such a war "could result in involving us further on an enormous, and, I believe, an endless scale." He demanded that proponents of intervention "advocate a larger army, the increased taxes that will be necessary to maintain it, and a call for men each month under the Selective Service Act" (CR 100, 1550–52).

18. Ibid. (April 14, 1954), 5111 (Mansfield); (April 15, 1954), 5218–19 (Morse); 5289–91 (Lehman and Humphrey).

19. Compare, for example, CR 100 (April 26, 1954), 5477: Edwin Johnson predicting that "[s]uch a war could last 10 years, or it could touch off and spawn a world war which would have to be fought for 100 years without victory. It could drive the brown and Malay races into the arms of the Communists in a solid front against the white race in a death struggle which eventually would destroy all civilization. These are some of the uncalculated risks of the proposal to fight in Indochina." Johnson also characterized the struggle of the Vietminh as a just war, in accordance with the ideals of the American and French revolutions and Bolivar, against colonialism. CR 100 (April 26, 1954), 5478. See also Mansfield at CR 100 (April 14, 1954), 5115: If the United States intervenes in Indochina there would be a "50-50 chance" of Chinese intervention in Indochina and Korea; "Then we shall be on the mainland of Asia whether we like it or not, and the net result will be that we may not only be engaged in a war for a long, long time, but in the meantime, even Western Europe, its industrial potential as well as its people, will fall prey to Communist aggression"; Malone at CR 100 (April 14, 1954) (North Atlantic Pact faulted for making America servant of Old World imperialists and America's pursuit of policies that only give colonial countries "the choice of Communism or a continuation of their colonial status"); Kennedy at CR 100 (April 6, 1954), 4674–75 (emphasizing anticolonial dimension of anti-French struggle and danger of U.S. supporting France); Gillette at CR 100 (April 5, 1954) (same); Stennis at CR 100 (April 6, 1954), 4681 (emphasizing dangers of unilateral action).

20. CR 100 (April 19, 1954), 5281 (Flanders); CR 100 (April 6, 1954), 4679 (Dirksen); CR 100, 4680 (Jackson).

21. CR 103 (March 1, 1957), 2873–74.

22. See Robert A. Caro, The Years of Lyndon Johnson: Master of the Senate (New York: Vintage, 2002), chap. 22.

23. David M. Oshinsky, A Conspiracy So Immense (New York: Free Press, 1983), 349–505.

24. Richard O. Davies, Defender of the Old Guard: John Bricker and American Politics (Columbus: Ohio State University Press, 1993), 157. On the constitutional issues that the Bricker amendment was meant to address, see 156; Gerald Gunther, Cases and Materials on Constitutional Law, 9th ed. (Mineola, N.Y.: Foundation Press, 1975), 273–75, and authorities cited therein. See also Congressional Quarterly Almanac (1954), 254–62.

25. See the moving letter from a "Montana mother" inserted by Mike Mansfield *CR* 100 (April 5, 1954), 4551–52. See also public opinion polls cited and discussion in Ralph B. Levering, *The Public and American Foreign Policy, 1918–1978* (New York: Morrow, 1978), 92–119, and Lawrence S. Wittner, *Rebels against War: The American Peace Movement, 1941–1960* (New York: Columbia University Press, 1969), 243–44 (describing large favorable mail response to November 15, 1957, manifesto of National Committee for a Sane Nuclear Policy printed in the *New York Times*).

26. See Stephen Ambrose, *Rise to Globalism,* 5th ed. (New York: Penguin, 1988), 149: "Brinksmanship held the line. In the process, however, it had scared the wits out of people around the world, perhaps even members of the Eisenhower administration itself, with good reason."

27. Gary W. Reichard, "Divisions and Dissent: Democrats and Foreign Policy, 1952–1956," *Political Science Quarterly* 93 (1978): 51–72, *passim,* surveys Democrats and influential elite foreign-policy criticism during the Eisenhower years; on the influential role in Washington of columnists like Lippmann and Reston, see William L. Rivers, *The Opinionmakers* (Boston: Beacon, 1965); on the particular relationship of senators and journalists during the 1950s, see William S. White, *Citadel: The Story of the United States Senate* (New York: Harper, 1956), 167; Donald R. Matthews, *U.S. Senators and Their World* (Chapel Hill: University of North Carolina Press, 1960), 197–217. See also Robert O. Keohane, "Realism, Neorealism, and the Study of World Politics," in *Neorealism and Its Critics,* ed. Robert O. Keohane (New York: Columbia University Press, 1986), 9–10.

28. *CR* 100 (April 9, 1954), 4971 (Morse); (April 6, 1954), 4677–78 (Kennedy).

29. See Kennan interview by Louis Fischer (March 23, 1965), esp. 2–26, John F. Kennedy Library. The Kennan-Kennedy correspondence is appended to the interview transcript. John Kennedy speech quoted in Arthur M. Schlesinger Jr., *Robert Kennedy and His Times* (Boston: Houghton Mifflin, 1976), 416. On the Reith lectures and the reaction to them, see Anders Stephanson, *Kennan and the Art of Diplomacy* (Cambridge, Mass.: Harvard University Press, 1989), pp. 151–52.

30. Quoted in William Appleman Williams, *The Tragedy of American Diplomacy* (1959; New York: Norton, 1972), 10–12.

31. Michael Foley, *The New Senate: Liberal Influence on a Conservative Institution, 1959–1972* (New Haven, Conn.: Yale University Press, 1980), pp. 25–27. The senators listed as liberals meet Foley's rather stringent test, a test which, for example, excludes Mansfield and Church, and includes only three Republicans for the entire period under study.

32. Minutes of early meetings and related documents concerning this organization are located in the Joseph S. Clark Papers, Historical Society of Pennsylvania, Box 24-W (B). On the United World Federalists and Grenville Clark, see Jon A. Yoder, "The United World Federalists: Liberals for Law and Order," in *Peace Movements in America,* ed. Charles Chatfield, 95–115 (New York: Schocken, 1973); Gerald T. Dunne, *Grenville Clark, Public Citizen* (New York: Farrar, Straus, 1986).

33. See Randall Bennett Woods, *Fulbright: A Biography* (Cambridge, Eng.: Cambridge University Press, 1995), 250–52.

34. See Thomas J. McCormick, *America's Half-Century* (Baltimore: Johns Hopkins University Press, 1989), 120.

35. Thanks to the insertion of Wayne Morse, the texts of the Formosa and Middle East Resolutions, as well as the Cuba and Gulf of Tonkin resolutions (discussed later), are conveniently set forth side-by-side at *CR* 110 (August 6, 1964), 18428–29.

36. For Stennis's remarks on sending of technicians to Indochina, see *CR* 100 (February 9, 1954), 1550–52. For Langer on Iran, see *CR* 99 (June 30, 1953), 7653. To date these are the only Senate remarks I have found criticizing U.S. policy toward Mossadegh. With respect to Guatemala, Langer was the only senator to cast a dissenting vote when the Senate passed 69-1 Lyndon Johnson's concurrent resolution supporting the OAS in taking "appropriate action to prevent any interference by the international Communist movement in the affairs of the states of the Western Hemisphere" (*CR* 100 [June 25, 1954], 8921–27).

37. Kennan interview, 7.

38. See E. W. Kenworthy, "The Fulbright Idea of Foreign Policy," *New York Times Magazine,* May 10, 1959, 10–11, 74–78. Compare Senate Committee on Foreign Relations, *What Is Wrong with American Foreign Policy,* 86th Cong., 1st sess. (Hans Morgenthau, witness), with Committee on Foreign Relations, Senate, hearings Situation in Vietnam, 86th Cong., 1st sess. (Washington, D.C.: G.P.O., 1959).

39. See answers of Fulbright to questions posed by James Reston on television program *Meet the Press,* June 7, 1959, emphasizing the need for a "very tough" president who can impose his will on Congress. Extensively quoted in James A. Robinson, *Congress in Foreign Policy: A Study in Legislative Influence and Initiative* (Homewood, Ill.: Dorsey, 1962), 213–14.

40. J. William Fulbright, "American Foreign Policy in the Twentieth Century under an Eighteenth-Century Constitution," *Cornell Law Quarterly* 47 (1961): 1–2, 7–8.

41. In his foreword to Joseph S. Clark et al., *The Senate Establishment* (New York: Hill and Wang, 1963), 5.

42. Clark, in ibid., 25–27.

43. Szilard to Fulbright, May 28, 1963, attached to cover memorandum Carl Marcy to Fulbright, June 7, 1963, Marcy Chronological Files, Records on the Committee on Foreign Relations RG 46, National Archives.

44. Council for a Livable World memorandum "Persons Interested in Pragmatic Measures to Ease International Tensions," quoted in *Washington Report,* November 30, 1964, 1, copy located in Box 21-W, Clark Papers.

45. *Council for Abolishing War Washington Bulletin* 1, no. 1 (November–December 1962), copy in folder "Szilard," Box 25-W (A), Clark Papers. The *Bulletin* notes that as of November 6, 1962, the Council had received a total of $79,318.65. A breakdown by candidate is then given.

46. *Washington Report,* November 30, 1964, 1, copy located in Box 21-W, Clark Papers. A tenth victorious Senate candidate, Quentin N. Burdick (D-N.Dak.) returned the money given to him. According to this newsletter of the conservative American Security Council, the Council for a Livable World's performance was "impressive." Contributions for 1964, according to CLW's Colonel Crosby, were "about $78,000," some of which went to House candidates.

47. Democratic senators outside the states of the former Confederacy voted 43-2. See Mary Milling Lepper, *Foreign Policy Formulation: A Case Study of the Nuclear Test Ban Treaty of 1963* (Columbus, Ohio: Merrill, 1971).

48. Gibbons, *U.S. Government and the Vietnam War* 2:127; *CR* 108 (October 10, 1962), 22961. Morse also revealed that he had "complete confidence in the strong leadership of our great President in connection with the military defense and security of this Republic" (*CR* 108 [October 10, 1962], 22961).

49. Gibbons, *U.S. Government and the Vietnam War* 2:166–69; LeRoy Ashby and Rod Gramer, *Fighting the Odds: The Life of Senator Frank Church* (Pullman: Washington State University Press, 1994), 169–71.

50. Marcy to Fulbright, August 14, 1961, Marcy Chronological Files, RG 46, National Archives.

51. *CR* 108 (September 20, 1962), 2002–3.

52. See Woods, *Fulbright*, 280–83; Ashby and Gramer, *Fighting the Odds*, 162–66. See also Rowland Evans and Robert Novak, *Lyndon B. Johnson: The Exercise of Power* (New York: New American Library, 1966), 457; Allen J. Matusow, *The Unraveling of America: A History of Liberalism in the 1960s* (New York: Harper, 1986), 137.

53. See transcripts of November 24, 1963, telephone conversation of Bill Moyers and Eugene V. Rostow, and November 25, 1963, telephone conversation of Lyndon Johnson and Joseph Alsop, Johnson Library, esp. at 1, 4; Mrs. J. H. Ragsdale to Fulbright, November 25, 1963, Fulbright papers, Ser. 1:1, Box 2; McPherson, *Political Education*, 212; Evans and Novak, *Lyndon B. Johnson*, 302; Porter McKeever, *Adlai Stevenson: His Life and Legacy* (New York: Morrow, 1986), 539.

54. Galbraith to Fulbright, January 29, 1964, Fulbright papers, Ser. 88:1, Box 7.

55. Fulbright to Galbraith, February 24, 1964, Fulbright papers, Ser. 88:1, Box 7.

56. *CR* 110 (March 25, 1964), 6227–31. The White House dissociated itself from the Cuba remarks but, in the words of Fulbright's biographer, was "generally pleased" with the speech (Woods, *Fulbright*, 334–39). Within seven days of delivering the speech Fulbright received over fifteen thousand letters (Haynes Johnson and Bernard Gwertzman, *Fulbright the Dissenter* [Garden City, N.Y.: Doubleday, 1968]), 187.

57. McNamara to Johnson, March 16, 1964, *Pentagon Papers,* New York Times edition (Toronto: Bantam, 1971), 278–79, Gravel edition, (Boston: Beacon, 1971), 3:501–2.

58. George C. Herring, *America's Longest War,* 2nd ed. (New York: Knopf, 1986), 116–19.

59. See *Pentagon Papers* (New York Times ed.), 259–70; (Gravel ed.), 3:183–87; Herring, *America's Longest War,* 119–21; Gibbons, *U.S. Government and Vietnam War,* 2:280–309. The Senate debate on the Gulf of Tonkin Resolution is discussed in the next chapter.

60. Fulbright to McNamara, May 23, 1964, Foreign Relations Committee Chairman's Correspondence, RG 46, National Archives, Box 2.

61. Dutton to McGeorge Bundy, June 2, 1964, National Security File, Country File: Vietnam, microfilm frames 4–066 to 4–069.

CHAPTER 2

1. *CR* 110 (August 5, 1964), 18127–28.

2. This view was offered by an employee of the influential Rand Institute of International Affairs even at a time when Indonesian Maoism was near its peak. John Gittings, "China's Military Strategy," *The Nation* 200 (January 18, 1965), 43–46.

3. See David S. Myers, *Foreign Affairs and the 1964 Presidential Election in the United States* (Meerut, India: Sadhna Prakashan, 1972).

4. Anthony Austin, *The President's War: The Story of the Tonkin Gulf Resolution and How the Nation Was Trapped in Vietnam* (Philadelphia: Lippincott, 1971), 82. See also Eugene C. Windchy, *Tonkin Gulf* (Garden City, N.Y.: Doubleday, 1971), 23. On what actually transpired in the Gulf, see Edwin Moise, *Tonkin Gulf and the Escalation of the Vietnam War.* (Chapel Hill: University of North Carolina Press, 1996). On the Senate and the Test Ban Treaty, see Mary Milling Lepper, *Foreign Policy Formulation: A Case Study of the Nuclear Test Ban Treaty of 1963* (Columbus, Ohio: Merrill, 1971), esp. 88–113.

5. P.L. 88-408.

6. *CR* 110 (August 6, 1964), 18427. The vote for the resolution in the House of Representatives was even more overwhelming: 416-0.

7. James T. Patterson, *Grand Expectations: The United States, 1945–1974* (New York: Oxford University Press, 1996), 603.

8. *CR* 110 (August 6, 1964), 18411.

9. Ibid., 18420.

10. See, for example, *CR* 110 (August 5, 1964), 18299–30 (Glen Beall); *CR* 110 (August 6, 1964), 18399 (McGovern, Allen Ellender); 18407–8 (Gaylord Nelson); 18420 (Jennings Randolph); 18423 (Robert Byrd).

11. Gibbons, *U.S. Government and the Vietnam War* 2:287; *New York Times,* August 4, 1964.

12. *CR* 110 (August 6, 1964), 18402–3.

13. Ibid., 18408.

14. Ibid., 18403; 18404.

15. Ibid., 18369. This syndicated column was published August 6, 1964.

16. *CR* 110 (August 6, 1964), 18403.

17. Ibid., 18406; 18406; 18406, 18416–17; 18406 (McGovern); *CR* 110 (August 7, 1964), 18457 (Javits).

18. *CR* 110 (August 7, 1964), 18412. The senator's "once again" referred to Korea, and he reminded his colleagues that "in excess of 90 percent of the soldiers who died in South Korea, other than South Koreans, were American"; 18412; 18412, 18404; 18417.

19. *CR* 110 (August 5, 1964), 18129–30 (Beall); *CR* 110 (August 6, 1964), 18412 f. (Hickenlooper); 18414–15 (Kuchel); 18462 (Dirksen); *CR* 110 (August 7, 1964), 18456 (Keating).

20. *CR* 110 (August 6, 1964), 18404; 18408. On the controversial granting by Truman of "sanctuary" in Korea by restricting military action against certain areas, particularly with respect to the Chinese forces, see Bernard Brodie, *War and Politics* (New York: Macmillan, 1973), 66–69.

21. *CR* 110 (August 6, 1964), 18420; 18416–17.

22. Ibid., 18147; for example, ibid. (Cooper).

23. The Senate's sole Quaker, Paul Douglas (D-Ill.), had actually joined the Marines as a private in 1942 at the age of fifty. Serving in the South Pacific, he was twice wounded, awarded the Bronze Star for "heroic achievement," and finally discharged in 1946 as a lieutenant colonel. During the Vietnam controversy he was a strong supporter of the president, and after his electoral loss to Charles Percy in 1966 headed a committee to build public support for the war.

24. *CR* 110 (August 6, 1964), 18418; 18417.

25. Ibid., 18417.

26. Ibid., 18416.

27. Ibid.

28. Ibid., 18420; 18414.

29. *CR* 110 (August 7, 1964), 18459; 18422; 18410.

30. Ibid., 18407.

31. Ibid., 18411. See Caroline F. Ziemke, "Richard Russell and the 'Lost Cause' in Vietnam, 1954–1968," *Georgia Historical Quarterly* 72 (1988): 30–77.

32. *CR* 110 (August 7, 1964), 18418; 18415; 18414.

33. *CR* 110 (August 5, 1964), 18133; *CR* 110 (August 7, 1964), 18488.

34. *CR* 110 (August 7, 1964), 18470.

35. Ibid., 18448.

36. *CR* 110 (August 5, 1964), 18136; 18135. The article, datelined from Saigon for the previous day, was by Seymour Topping and titled "Kanh Warned of Plots Seeks to Bolster Regime."

37. *CR* 110 (August 7, 1964), 18443; *CR* 110 (August 6, 1964), 18437.

38. *CR* 110 (August 6, 1964), 18437; 18449; *CR* 110 (August 5, 1964), 18138; 18138; *CR* 110 (August 7, 1964), 18449; 18448.

39. "Unmeasured Response," *New Republic,* August 22, 1964, 3–4. *The Nation,* which Gruening himself had edited forty years before, was more critical. See *The Nation* 199 (August 24, 1964), 61. On the other hand, *The Reporter,* a liberal magazine widely read in government circles during this period, offered no editorial comment on the Tonkin Gulf events or resolution. Likewise on the left, no commentary was offered by the socialist *Dissent,* and no dissent offered by the American Jewish Committee's *Commentary.*

40. Despite (or, perhaps, because of) Johnson's large lead in opinion polls, the editors of the *New Republic* counseled its readers against complacency and repeatedly warned of the grave danger posed by a Goldwater victory. See TRB, *The New Republic,* September 5, 1964; see also *New Republic,* September 25, 1964, 14 (collecting twenty-five frightening quotations of Goldwater); compare *The Nation* 199 (August 10, 1964), 41 (similar Goldwater quotations). On the especially acute fears of Church and Fulbright, see David F. Schmitz, "Congress Must Hold the Line: Senator Frank Church and the Opposition to the Vietnam War and Imperial Presidency," in *Vietnam and the American Political Tradition: The Politics of Dissent,* ed. Randall B. Woods (Cambridge: Cambridge University Press, 2003), 126; Woods, *Fulbright; A Biography* (Cambridge: Cambridge University Press, 1995), 353.

41. In subsequent years the Supreme Court would repeatedly refuse to review chal lenges to the constitutionality of the war, although in several cases there were dissents from this refusal, most notably by Potter Stewart and William O. Douglas. In *Holtzman v. Schlesinger,* 414 U.S. 1304, 1316, 1321 (1973), a district court enjoined air raids over Cambodia, the injunction was stayed by the Court of Appeals, and Thurgood Marshall denied a petition to vacate the stay. Douglas then vacated Marshall's stay, but Marshall, later the same day after consulting with the other justices, had the stay reinstated. See also *DaCosta v. Laird,* 405 U.S. 979 (1972); *Massachusetts v. Laird,* 400 U.S. 886 (1970); *Velvel v. Nixon,* 396 U.S. 1042 (1970); *Holmes v. United States,* 391 U.S. 936 (1968); *McArthur v. Clifford,* 393 U.S. 936 (1968); *Mora v. McNamara,* 389 U.S. 934 (1967). As the war escalated, legal arguments against the war were treated respectfully and in some cases embraced by scholars writing in prestigious law journals. See, for example, N. H. Alford Jr. and R. A. Falk, "Legality of

the United States Participation in the Viet Nam Conflict: A Symposium," *Yale Law Journal* 75 (1966): 1085–1160; Note, "Congress, the President, and the Power to Commit Forces to Combat," *Harvard Law Review* 81 (1968): 1771–1805.

42. Taped telephone interview with Herbert Jolovitz, April 11, 1995. Joseph Clark's legislative aide, Harry Schwartz, recalls that Clark (who was not himself up for reelection in 1964) voted for the resolution to support the president's election bid. Taped telephone interview, May 24, 1995. A colleague advanced the same rationale in an effort to persuade Morse to support the resolution. Gibbons, *U.S. Government and the Vietnam War,* 304; Joseph C. Goulden, *Truth Is the First Casualty* (Chicago: Rand McNally, 1969), 49.

43. "Foreign Policy," resolution adopted by ADA, 17th Annual National Convention, Washington, D.C., May 15, 16, and 17, 1964. This and other ADA resolutions were inserted, with a flattering message to the convention from President Johnson, at *CR* 110 (May 27, 1964), 12113–22. The insertion was made by Joseph Clark, himself a member the ADA national board of directors. The passage quoted appears at 12114 and refers specifically to the "normalization" of U.S.–Soviet relations, but is representative of the general attitude of the resolution to current policy and ADA's goals.

44. George F. Kennan, "Polycentrism and Western Policy," *Foreign Affairs* 42 (January 1964): 171–83; Ambassador George C. McGhee, "East-West Relations," speech delivered before German Foreign Policy Society at the Redoute, Bad, Godesberg, Feb. 18, 1964; Grayson Kirk, "World Perspectives, 1964," *Foreign Affairs* 43 (October 1964): 1–14. Fulbright, "Old Myths and New Realities" speech with inserted transcript of McGhee speech at *CR* 110 (March 25, 1964), 6227–35. On the press coverage of Fulbright's speech, see Woods, *Fulbright,* 336. On the speaking tour, see Haynes Johnson and Bernard M. Gwertzman, *Fulbright the Dissenter* (Garden City, N.Y.: Doubleday, 1968), 189.

45. Quoted in Woods, *Fulbright,* 337.

46. Minutes of Group Meeting of Informal Committee of Members of Congress for World Peace Through the Rule of Law, July 15, 1959, Joseph S. Clark Papers, Box 24-W(B).

47. Robert W. Kastenmeier to Claude Desautels, January 12, 1962, Clark Papers, Box 24-W(B). The description of past activities is made in the context of a letter confirming the conversation of Representative Kastenmeier's legislative assistant, Gar Alperovitz, with Desautels of the White House about the possibility of President Kennedy addressing a meeting of the organization.

48. See, for example, McGeorge Bundy, "The Presidency and the Peace," *Foreign Affairs* 42 (April 1964): 353–65 (emphasizing continuity of Kennedy and Johnson administrations and their shared devotion to promoting world peace); *accord* Walter Lippmann columns appearing February 5, 1964; March 24, 1964; April 21, 1964; July 28, 1964.

49. See Allen J. Matusow, *The Unraveling of America* (New York: Harper, 1986), 147.

50. Galbraith speech, "The Conservative Myth and the Liberal Task," delivered in Phoenix Arizona, n.d. [1964]. The speech is attached to a letter, Galbraith to Fulbright, March 5, 1964, Fulbright Papers, Ser. 88:1, Box 7.

51. See 1964 foreign policy resolution of the Americans for Democratic Action inserted at *CR* 110 (May 27, 1964), 12113–22.

52. Quoted in Johnson and Gwertzman, *Fulbright the Dissenter,* 186.

CHAPTER 3

1. On March 30, 1965, the chief of staff of the Foreign Relations Committee reported to its chairman that a "clear majority of the Committee (nine according to my account) agree with the Lippmann column of this morning and with the [Hans] Morgenthau article in the New Republic [calling for disengagement from Southeast Asia]. At least four other members probably agree. I suspect that if the issue were drawn and there were a vote on sending an additional 300,000 men to Vietnam as McNamara hinted last week, the Committee would be even more numerous in opposition. Yet everyone is silent." Carl Marcy to Fulbright, March 30, 1965, Marcy Chronological Files, Senate Foreign Relations Committee, Record Group 46, National Archives.

2. On Russell's status in the Senate, see Gibbons, *U.S. Government and the Vietnam War* 3:435; Paul Douglas, *In the Fullness of Time: The Memoirs of Paul H. Douglas* (New York: Harcourt, Brace, 1972), 227; George E. Reedy, *The U.S. Senate* (New York: Crown, 1986), 86; David M. Barrett, *Uncertain Warriors: Lyndon Johnson and His Vietnam Advisers* (Lawrence: University Press of Kansas, 1993), 37 (noting that, among other powers, Russell was "de facto chairman" of the Appropriations Committee because of the age and illness of Chairman Carl Hayden [D-Ariz.]).

3. Fulbright to McNamara, March 23, 1964, Senate Foreign Relations Committee, Chairman's Correspondence, Box 2, RG 46, National Archives. Mansfield's opposition to U.S. policy in Vietnam during this period is set forth in numerous memoranda and letters to Johnson. These and the replies drafted by McGeorge Bundy and others are located in National Security File, Name File, Mansfield, Johnson Library. On Russell's advice, see Gibbons, *U.S. Government and the Vietnam War* 2:397–98; Michael R. Beschloss, ed., *Taking Charge: The Johnson White House Tapes, 1963–1964* (New York: Simon & Schuster, 1997), 400–403 (tape of June 11, 1964).

4. See Robertson to Lawrence O'Brien, March 27, 1964, inserted by Morse at *CR* 110 (May 18, 1964), 11218; *CR* 111 (February 17, 1965), 2874–75 (Ellender questioning Thomas Dodd [D-Conn.]).

5. See Terry Dietz, *Republicans and Vietnam, 1961–1968* (Westport, Conn.: Greenwood, 1986); compare Cecil V. Crabb Jr., *Bipartisan Foreign Policy: Myth or Reality?* (Evanston, Ill.: Row, Peterson, 1957); Norman A. Graebner, *The New Isolationism: A Study in Politics and Foreign Policy since 1950* (New York: Ronald, 1956); Gary W. Reichard, "Divisions and Dissent: Democrats and Foreign Policy, 1952–1956," *Political Science Quarterly* 93 (1978): 51–72; reprinted in *To Advise and Consent: The United States Congress and Foreign Policy in the Twentieth Century,* ed. Joel Sibley, 1:273–94 (Brooklyn: Carlson, 1991); Malcolm E. Jewell, *Senatorial Politics and Foreign Policy* (1962; Westport, Conn: Greenwood, 1974). For the different definitions of bipartisanship, see David N. Farnsworth, *The Senate Committee on Foreign Relations* (Urbana: University of Illinois Press, 1961), 155–58. An overview of Dirksen's response to the Vietnam escalation is given in Edward L. Schapsmeier and Frederick H. Schapsmeier, *Dirksen of Illinois* (Urbana: University of Illinois Press, 1985), 167, 199–209.

6. See I. F. Stone's reference to Robert Kennedy and his brother, Edward (D-Mass.), as "the possible nucleus of a liberal opposition against Johnson." "The Form of Democracy," *I. F. Stone's Weekly,* May 17, 1965, 4.

7. George Gallup, *The Gallup Poll* (New York: Random House, 1972), 1962.

8. Ibid., 1942, 1945, 1976.

9. The League for Industrial Democracy was dominated by the Socialist Party–Social Democratic Federation. On the SP-SDF's influence in the civil rights and labor movements during this period, see Gary Stone, "The Divided Center: Michael Harrington, American Social Democracy, and the Vietnam War" (M.A. thesis, Columbia University, 1991).

10. Fred Halstead, *Out Now!* (New York: Monad, 1978), 24–91; Dodd quoted at p. 90 from *Time,* October 29, 1965. In May, Dodd had presided over hearings on radical participation in protest movements; Senate Committee on the Judiciary, Subcommittee on the Administration of the Internal Security Act and Other Internal Security Laws, *Communist Youth Program,* 89th Cong., 1st sess., 1965. Despite the witnesses' tendency to see the protests in conspiratorial terms, the hearings' emphasis on the leading role of the far left in the antiwar movement of this period is confirmed by writers sympathetic to the movement including Halstead, *Out Now!* and Charles DeBenedetti, with Charles Chatfield, *An American Ordeal: The Antiwar Movement of the Vietnam Era* (Syracuse, N.Y.: Syracuse University Press, 1990).

11. On the November March, see Halstead, *Out Now!* 93–120; DeBenedetti, *American Ordeal,* 131–32.

12. See remarks of McGovern at 111 *CR* (February 17. 1965), 2878–79. For examples of Aiken's candor, see quotations in Gibbons, *U.S. Government and the Vietnam War* 3.301.

13. On the attitude of senators toward those who write them see Donald R. Matthews, *U.S. Senators and Their World* (Chapel Hill: University of North Carolina Press, 1960), 219–24. In addition to providing personalized responses to letters from lawyers, professors, and other "VIPs," the offices of Senators Fulbright and Robert Kennedy kept tabulations of the opinions expressed in all mail and telegrams concerning Vietnam. See, for example, Marcy to Fulbright, March 1, 1965, Marcy Chronological Files, Senate Foreign Relations Committee, RG 46, National Archives. For an illustration of the complex of pressures, elite and popular, falling on a major senator critical of the war yet not ready to break with the administration, see Norvill Jones to Fulbright, April 23, 1965, Fulbright Papers, Ser. 48:11, Box 35.

14. For a useful survey of many of these influences immediately before the Vietnam controversy, see William L. Rivers, *The Opinionmakers* (Boston: Beacon, 1965).

15. Undoubtedly liberal senators derived their ideas from liberal sources. See Allen J. Matusow, *The Unraveling of America: A History of Liberalism in the 1960s* (New York: Harper, 1986), 379. The degree to which they acted upon these ideas, however, was typically determined by signals from the center. A particularly clear example is Joseph Clark, a leader of the ADA, who treated the *New Republic* as his "bible" (taped telephone interview with Harry K. Schwartz, May 24, 1995). It was not the *New Republic* but a speech by George Kennan calling for stepped-up efforts to reach détente, however, that caused a surge of enthusiasm at Clark's office and whose transcription was inserted into the *Congressional Record* with the unusual request that "it be printed in ordinary type, not in the small unreadable type in which insertions are usually printed." Harry K. Schwartz to Clark, March 12, 1965, Clark Papers, Box 24-W(A).

16. See Morton H. Halperin, *Bureaucratic Politics and Foreign Policy* (Washington, D.C.: Brookings, 1974), 19; Thomas J. McCormack estimates that this elite of "in-and-

outers," individuals who "move back and forth between the public and private sectors, as though on a perpetual shuttle" as comprising two-thirds of the foreign policy establishment (*America's Half-Century* [Baltimore: Hopkins University Press, 1989]), 13.

17. See Fredrik Logevall, *Choosing War: The Last Chance for Peace and the Escalation of the War in Vietnam*. (Berkeley: University of California Press, 1999), 361–62 (surveying press divisions).

18. Titled "Vietnam Dialog: Mr. Bundy and the Professors," the debate took place at George Washington University on June 21, 1965, and was broadcast live on CBS-TV. Other participants were Zbigniew K. Brzezinski, Edmund O. Clubb, Guy J. Paulker, and John D. Donoghue. William Proxmire (D-Wisc.) referred to the debaters on both sides as "highly qualified American experts" and had the entire transcript inserted in the *Congressional Record* (*CR* 111 [June 30, 1965], 15396–401). The Morgenthau dinner is described in David F. Schmitz, "Congress Must Draw the Line: Senator Frank Church and the Opposition to the Vietnam War and Imperial Presidency," in Randall B. Woods ed., *Vietnam and the American Political Tradition: The Politics of Dissent* (Cambridge: Cambridge University Press, 2003), 127.

19. *CR* 111 (April 22, 1965), 8284–92.

20. William S. White, *Citadel: The Story of the U.S. Senate* (1956; Boston: Houghton, Mifflin, 1968), 167.

21. Quoted in Rivers, *Opinionmakers,* 57.

22. *CR* 103 (July 11, 1957), 11307.

23. *CR* 110 (September 22, 1964), 22540. Fulbright inserted, after his tribute, a similarly effusive editorial from that morning's *New York Times* titled "Lippmann at 75."

24. For example, *CR* 93 (April 10, 1947), 3289 (Claude Pepper [D-Fla.]); *CR* 100 (May 7, 1954), 6214 (Herbert Lehman); *CR* 110 (February 5, 1964), 2108 (Humphrey); *CR* 110 (March 23, 1964), 6005 (Smathers); *CR* 110 (July 21, 1964), 16364 (Paul Douglas [D-Ill.])

25. For example, column for July 31, 1964, inserted by Paul Douglas, *CR* 110 (July 21, 1964), 16364: "One of the ablest observers upon the public scene is Mr. Walter Lippmann, who for many years has turned his penetrating intelligence upon the problems of the Nation and of the world. . . . I believe we would all profit from reading Mr. Lippmann's article and considering the significant points he brings out."

26. Column for August 6, 1964, inserted by Church, *CR* 110 (August 6, 1964), 18369 ("The article shows such unusual perception and displays such insight and wisdom that I commend it to my colleagues in the Senate").

27. For example, column for March 5, 1964, inserted by George McGovern (D-S.Dak.), *CR* 110 (March 5, 1964), 4482; column for April 21, 1964, inserted by Gruening, *CR* 110 (April 21, 1964) 8602; column for May 21, 1964, inserted by E. L. "Bob" Bartlett (D-Alaska), *CR* 110 (May 21, 1964), 11566 ("as so often in the past, Walter Lippmann has admirably untangled some of the confusion now general on the situation in southeast Asia") and Eugene McCarthy (D-Minn.), *CR* 110 (May 22, 1964), 11725–26 (including extensive discussion of its contents); column for June 2, 1964, inserted by Morse, *CR* 110 (June 2, 1964), 12399 ("In the one enlightenment of the editorial section of the Washington Post, one finds today that Walter Lippmann is again calling for the only legal and responsible handling of our policy in Vietnam").

28. Lippmann's column for April 1, 1965, used perhaps the best ploy for attaining the Senate's attention: flattery of one of its members—in this case John Sherman Cooper

(R-Ky.), who had given a speech criticizing the administration for setting terms for "nego-tiation" that amounted to a call for Communist surrender. As if to reciprocate on behalf of his colleague, Bartlett prefaced his insertion of the column by noting that "consistently over the darkening months of the Vietnam crisis, Walter Lippmann has spoken in clear and reasoned tones. He has not simplified the complex nor has he avoided the unpleas-ant. Our policymakers would not dismiss what this wise man says" (CR 111 [April 1, 1965], 6622). Actually, while Bartlett was outside the chamber, Clark had already taken the floor to insert the article as well as that of March 30 (CR 111 [April 1, 1965], 6546–47). The latter was presumably widely read in the Foreign Relations Committee. As referred to in n. 1 above the committee's chief of staff in a memorandum asserted that, despite their failure to speak out openly, nine committee members agreed with the column. A week later (April 5), when the April 12, 1965, issue of Newsweek hit the newsstands with a Lippmann article on Vietnam, McGovern inserted the article and praised Lippmann as "the clearest and most persistent commentator on the deepening Vietnamese crisis" and as one who "has clearly exposed the fallacies of our Vietnam policy and the dangers of our present course" (CR 111 [April 5, 1965], 6962–63). Shortly thereafter, Morse took the floor and announced that "in today's issue of Newsweek . . . the incomparable Walter Lippmann really made my speech for me today in opposition to the shocking American war and its continuation in Asia." Morse then read almost the entire article into the Record (6877–78).

29. Randall Bennett Woods, Fulbright: A Biography (Cambridge: Cambridge University Press, 1995), 358, 367.

30. Frank Church, "We Are In Too Deep in Asia and Africa," The New York Times Mag-azine, February 14, 1965, 30–31, 84, 86; LeRoy Ashby and Rod Gramer, Fighting the Odds: The Life of Senator Frank Church (Pullman: Washington State University Press, 1994), 192.

31. Gibbons, U.S. Government and the Vietnam War 3:137.

32. CR 111 (February 18, 1965), 3188–89.

33. CR 111 (February 17, 1965), 2869–72.

34. Ibid., 2878–79; 2877–78.

35. CR 111 (February 18, 1965), 3190.

36. CR 111 (February 19, 1965), 3245–46. In this speech, Gruening quoted extensively from a February 10, 1965, New York Times editorial titled "What Price Vietnam?" He also inserted James Reston's column for that day ("A Time for Reflection on Vietnam") and quoted from an advertisement in the February 19, 1965, New York Times ("Vietnam: America Must Decide Between a Full-Scale War and a Negotiated Truce") sponsored by a large number of prominent individuals.

37. CR 111 (February 24, 1965), 3520. This speech was interrupted by comments by Gale McGee who argued that, even accepting the facts as given by Gruening to be true, the United States had no viable alternative but to oppose Communism in Vietnam. The colloquy between the two senators degenerated into a contest of juxtaposed John Kennedy quotations, McGee thrusting with "We shall never fear to negotiate freely, but we shall never negotiate freedom" and Gruening parrying with "We shall never negotiate from fear, but we shall never fear to negotiate" (3521).

38. CR 111 (February 17, 1965), 2885–88.

39. John M. Goshko, "Dodd Ties Security to Vietnam War, Rejects Negotiating," Washington Post, February 24, 1965, A2.

40. *CR* 111 (February 23, 1965), 3349–57. On the American Friends of Vietnam see Robert Scheer and Warren Hinckle, "The 'Vietnam Lobby,'" *Ramparts,* July 1965, 16–24.

41. These included: Russell Long (D-La.), *CR* 111 (February 17, 1965), 2811 (emphasizing bipartisan unity in face of Communist aggression); Mike Monroney (D-Okla.), 2811–12 ("I believe the people are now awaking to the hard facts, and are now beginning to see the South Vietnam struggle in terms of the cold war; for indeed it is the principal battlefront of the cold war"); Dirksen, *CR* 111 (February 18, 1965), 3146–47 (emphasizing need for patriotism and courage); Saltonstall, 3147 (emphasizing need to "retaliate" since "our boys are being killed," and asserting that U.S. "relationships" abroad would suffer if negotiations began); George Smathers (D-Fla.), 3148–49 ("the Vietcong, the Hanoi regime, the Communist Chinese, and Soviet Russia have demonstrated not the usefulness, but the futility of conducting another Geneva-type conference at the present time"); Frank Lausche (D-Ohio), 3150–51 (Munich analogy, domino theory, futility of negotiating with Communists or including them in coalition governments which inevitably lead to communization, memories of Communists in Cleveland at time of Hitler-Stalin pact); Paul Douglas, *CR* 111 (February 23, 1965), 3376–77 (profuse praise of Dodd speech, explicit endorsement of domino theory); Peter Dominick (R-Colo.), 3377–78 (describing Vietnam as a "contest of willpower"); Karl Mundt (R-S.Dak.), 3377–78 (emphasizing agreement with Dodd on need for more "political warfare" and faulting State Department for its "stubborn reluctance" to provide the needed training for this); John Tower (R-Tex.), 3377–78 ("stringent action" in Southeast Asia needed to deter Communists elsewhere); Fred Harris (D-Okla.), 3380 (endorsing Dodd's proposals, especially emphasis on political warfare). Jacob Javits (R-N.Y.) was more critical, calling on the president to clarify his program, make more of an effort to involve other allied countries in the war, and asking whether the South Vietnamese were truly willing to fight for their government, 3378–3380.

42. *CR* 111 (February 17, 1965), 2874–75 (Symington); *CR* 111 (February 23, 1965), 3376–77 (Ellender).

CHAPTER 4

1. See John M. Goshko, "Party Lines Break on Viet Policy," *Washington Post,* February 18, 1965, 1, 4.

2. Michael Beschloss, ed., *Reaching for Glory: Lyndon Johnson's Secret White House Tapes, 1964–1965* (New York: Simon & Schuster, 2001), 185 (explanatory footnotes omitted); see also 195, 351 (Johnson to McNamara).

3. *CR* 111 (February 18, 1965), 3146. See also short speech of Leverett Saltonstall at 3147. Russell Long inserted the statement by the Joint Senate-House Leadership at *CR* 111 (February 17, 1965), 2811. The question of Dirksen's support was discussed on the same day in separate telephone calls between Dirksen and Johnson, and between Johnson and McGeorge Bundy (Beschloss, *Reaching for Glory,* 182–83, 186–87).

4. See Jack Newfield, *Robert Kennedy: A Memoir* (New York: Dutton, 1969), 122; Arthur M. Schlesinger Jr., *Robert Kennedy and His Times* (Boston: Houghton Mifflin, 1978), 731.

5. The executive branch during this year also failed to mobilize sympathetic senators who would have been willing to give speeches inside and outside the Senate chamber in

support of the war. As if the goal was more to quiet the Vietnam debate than win it, the president did not respond enthusiastically to George Smathers' communication that he knew twenty-five senators who would gladly give a speech supporting the administration's policies if they could find the time to write one "or if someone would supply them with one." Smathers to Johnson, May 27, 1965, WHCF, ND 19/CO 312, Johnson Library, Box 215. See also Smathers to Johnson, August 6, 1965, WHCF, ND 19/CO 312, Johnson Library, Box 216. In the same vein, it is likely that McGeorge Bundy heeded the advice of John J. McCloy and Robert Lovett—men whose advice was rarely not heeded—when they forcefully cautioned him of the danger that statements issued publicly by supporters of the administration could excite renewed opposition from its opponents. McCloy to Bundy, July 29, 1965, WHCF, ND 19/CO 312, Johnson Library, Box 216.

6. Taped telephone interview with Jack Stempler, assistant secretary of defense for congressional affairs, September 27, 1994; interview with Jean Lewis, White House Office of Congressional Relations, Arlington, Virginia, September 10, 1995.

7. This is not to suggest that McNamara, in particular, was unimpressive as a witness. In fact, his memory and command of facts could have an almost overpowering effect on his hearers. Overpowering his inquisitors, however, was not the same thing as truly winning them to his cause and could, over the course of time, create resentment (Stempler interview). It may have been McNamara's aggressive use of quantitative data that prompted Carl Marcy to suggest that the Foreign Relations Committee receive "the unvarnished facts—facts not embroidered with charts and high power salesmanship." Marcy to Fulbright, March 30, 1965, Marcy Chronological Files, Senate Foreign Relations Committee, RG 46, National Archives.

8. See, for example, Congressional Briefing, February 25, 1965, transcript from tape, Congressional Briefings on Vietnam, Johnson Library, Box 1.

9. See Rowland Evans and Robert Novak column in the *Washington Post,* May 4, 1965, A14.

10. Quoted in Randall Bennett Woods, *Fulbright: A Biography* (Cambridge: Cambridge University Press, 1995), 365. In his autobiography, McGovern recalls that as he departed from the White House he "literally trembled for the future of the nation" (*Grassroots* [New York: Random House, 1977], 104–5).

11. Gibbons, *U.S. Government and the Vietnam War,* 128–29; LeRoy Ashby and Rod Gramer, *Fighting the Odds: The Life of Senator Frank Church* (Pullman: Washington State University Press, 1994), 194–96. Ashby and Gramer estimate that the confrontation only took a half hour. Gibbons' account is based on the Library of Congress, Congressional Research Service interview with Church, July 5, 1983.

12. See Nigel Bowles, *The White House and Capitol Hill* (Oxford: Clarendon, 1987), 66–114 and *passim;* Doris Kearns, *Lyndon Johnson and the American Dream* (New York: Harper, 1976), 10–11. See also Jean P. Lewis, "President Johnson Surveys the Congress," (Georgetown University paper for senior seminar in history, May 1990), 44. Compare comments of Clark Clifford quoted in Barbara Kellerman, *The Political Presidency* (New York: Oxford University Press, 1984), 25.

13. The documentary record and oral histories suggest that Johnson's deprivation of patronage in retaliation for Vietnam dissent was limited and unsystematic. In my taped telephone interview with George McGovern (June 28, 1993), for example, he recalled only one instance (a judicial appointment) in which might he have been denied patron-

age. Compare Stanley Karnow, *Vietnam: A History* (New York: Viking, 1983), 485 (patronage deprived from Vance Hartke [D-Ind.]); taped telephone interview with Mace Broide, administrative assistant to Vance Hartke, April 10, 1995 (same); Woods, *Fulbright,* 368.

14. Memorandum of Senator Morse's Conversation with the President, Thursday, June 17, 11:30, Marcy Chronological Files, Senate Foreign Relations Committee, RG 46, National Archives. This account of his conversation was transmitted on the same day to the chief of staff of the Foreign Relations Committee, who immediately drafted a remarkable speech for Johnson announcing that he was enlisting the United Nations to resolve the Vietnamese conflict. The speech, of course, was never given. A memorandum introducing the speech, "Memorandum for the President on United States Policies in Vietnam," and the draft of the speech are at the same location.

15. Public Papers of the President: Lyndon Johnson, 1965 (Washington, D.C.: GPO, 1966), bk. 1, 394–99.

16. See Karnow, *Vietnam,* 418 (emphasizing Johnson's desire to undercut senatorial critics as a major motive for the Hopkins speech). On the congressional response to the speech, see McGeorge Bundy to Johnson, April 10, 1965 (showing pleasure of hawks and doves—except Morse—with speech). NSF Files of Gordon Chase, Johnson Library, Box 9.

17. Gibbons, *U.S. Government and the Vietnam War* 3:219, quoting from Church Oral History, May 1, 1969, Johnson Library.

18. Kathleen J. Turner, *Lyndon Johnson's Dual War: Vietnam and the Press* (Chicago: University of Chicago Press, 1985), 126–27.

19. Jack Valenti, notes of NSC meeting, May 16, 1965, Meeting Notes File, Johnson Library; Gibbons, *U.S. Government and the Vietnam War* 3:256.

20. Gibbons, *U.S. Government and the Vietnam War* 3:257. In an executive session of the Foreign Relations Committee on June 3, 1965, Pell asked Rusk (who did not know that Pell had learned of the "feeler") whether he had received any such contact. Rusk, in general terms, denied that any significant communication had been received. Pell refrained from embarrassing the secretary with specific follow-up questions.

21. See William Safire, *Safire's Political Dictionary* (New York: Random House, 1978), 147–48; James Deakin, *Lyndon Johnson's Credibility Gap* (Washington, D.C.: Public Affairs, 1968).

22. Compare Donald A. Ritchie, *Pat Holt: Chief of Staff, Foreign Relations Committee, Oral History Interviews* (Washington, D.C.: Senate Historical Office, 1980), 177; Rowland Evans and Robert Novak, *Lyndon B. Johnson: The Exercise of Power* (New York: New American Library, 1966), 515, 519–20.

23. *CR* 111 (May 5, 1965), 9497 (Albert Gore [D-Tenn.]). See also, for example, similar remarks of Church (9500). For contemporary skepticism concerning the claimed emergency, see Howard Margolis, "LBJ Fund Request Reflects Increased National Commitment," *Washington Post,* May 5, 1965, A10; Bundy MS, chap. 25, pp. 18–19, Johnson Library, quoted in Gibbons, *U.S. Government and the Vietnam War* 3:242.

24. *CR* 111 (May 5, 1965), 9492.

25. Tom Wicker, "Johnson Policies: A Survey of Support," *New York Times,* June 14, 1965, 1, 14.

26. Marcy to Fulbright, July 22, 1965, Marcy Chronological Files, Senate Foreign Relations Committee, RG 46, National Archives.

27. Gibbons, III, p. 433. Ned Kenworthy apparently had called Lippmann and asked the columnist to use his influence with Fulbright to call such a meeting. Ibid.

28. Mansfield to Johnson, July 27, 1965, WHCF, ND 19/C0 312, Box 216, Johnson Library.

29. Public Papers of the President: Lyndon Johnson, 1965, bk. 2, pp. 794–803.

30. George Herring, *America's Longest War: The United States and Vietnam: 1950–1975* 2nd ed. (New York: Knopf, 1986), 143.

31. Marcy to Fulbright, August 17, 1965, Marcy Chronological Files, Senate Foreign Relations Committee, RG 46.

32. J. William Fulbright, "American Foreign Policy in the Twentieth Century Under an Eighteenth-Century Constitution," *Cornell Law Quarterly* 47 (1961): 1–13.

33. *CR* 111 (June 15, 1965), 13656–58; Woods, *Fulbright,* 371–72; Howard Margolis, "Fulbright Would Ease Viet Stand," *Washington Post,* June 16, 1965, 1, 20; "The Road Past North C Pier . . . ," *Newsweek,* June 28, 1965, 19–20; "Speech by Senator Fulbright Promises New Flexibility in America's Vietnam Policy," (London) *Times,* June 17, 1965. Sander Vanocur, who interviewed Fulbright on the *Today* show, seemed also to assume that the senator represented the views of the White House. WRC-TV and NBC Network "Today Show," June 15, 1965, Fulbright Papers, Ser. 72 Box 25. Compare "Why Not Peace Through Elections," *I. F. Stone's Weekly,* June 21, 1965, 4, 11 (scathing attack on Fulbright for timidity of his criticisms and his failure to break with the administration).

34. See Marcy to Fulbright, May 19, 1965, Marcy Chronological Files, Senate Foreign Relations Committee, RG 46, National Archives (efforts to prevent Edward Kennedy [D-Mass.], chairman of the Subcommittee on Refugees and Escapees of the Judiciary Committee, from holding hearings on the problem of refugees in South Vietnam and Cambodia). A few months later, Fulbright informed Jennings Randolph (D-W.Va.) and Jacob Javits (D-N.Y.) that it was the "consensus" of his committee not to hold either public or executive session hearings on a resolution the two senators had proposed concerning American intervention in Vietnam. Fulbright to Randolph and Javits, July 13, 1965 (Marcy Chronological Files, Senate Foreign Relations Committee, RG 46, National Archives). In July Edward Kennedy did begin hearings on the refugee crisis. Senate Committee on the Judiciary, Subcommittee to Investigate Problems Connected with Refugees and Escapees, *Refugee Problems in South Vietnam and Laos,* 89th Cong., 1st sess., 1965. The Kennedy Committee, however, generally restricted questioning to the immediate problems of refugees and the administration of relief to them.

35. *CR* 111 (September 15, 1965), 23835–65.

36. *CR* 111 (September 16, 1965), 24168 (Smathers); 24169–73 (Dodd): *CR* 111 (September 17, 1965), 24221–23 (Lausche); *CR* 111 (September 21, 1965), 24558–59 (Russell); Woods, *Fulbright,* 385–88. The syndicated Kraft column as well as the Lippmann column for September 28, 1965; the Marquis Childe column of September 27, 1965; and an article by Andrew Kopkind, "The Speech Maker: Fulbright as the Arkansas de Tocqueville," *New Republic,* October 10, 1965, all defending Fulbright, were inserted by Clark at *CR* 111 (October 7, 1965), 26237–40. In an interesting speech Karl Mundt, a member of the Foreign Relations Committee, indicated his support for the invasion but defended Fulbright's conduct of the hearings (*CR* 111 [September 17, 1965], 24222–23).

37. *Cf.* Evans and Novak, *Lyndon B. Johnson,* 529; Robert Mann, *A Grand Illusion: America's Descent into Vietnam* (New York: Basic Books, 2001), 470–75.

CHAPTER 5

1. CBS failed to broadcast the second hearing in which George Kennan testified, a decision that led to the resignation of the president of its news division, Fred Friendly. David Halberstam, *The Powers That Be* (New York: Dell, 1979), 697–706. See comments of Ernest Gruening (D-Alaska) and Albert Gore (D-Tenn.), the text of Friendly's resignation letter, and a *New York Times* editorial addressing the affair at *CR* 112 (February 16, 1966), 3030–41. A preliminary hearing with Secretary of State Dean Rusk as principal witness took place on January 28 and was not televised live but was filmed and shown for three and five minutes on the CBS and NBC evening news, respectively. The footage "was the most dramatic film from the Congress in years" (Halberstam, *Powers That Be,* 702). To avoid confusion, all citations to the preliminary hearing indicate parenthetically the absence of live television coverage.

2. *New York Times,* February 20, 1966, 1E.

3. *Newsweek,* February 21, 1966, 21. The Foreign Relations Committee used the president's request for a $415 million supplemental authorization of funds for the foreign aid program (of which $275 million was to be spent on Vietnam) as the occasion for its more far-reaching review of Vietnam policy. See Carl Marcy to Fulbright, January 7, 1966 (anticipating request and proposing it be used as starting point for full hearings on Vietnam) (Marcy Chronological Files, Senate Foreign Relations Committee, RG 46, National Archives). The aid request is reflected in the official citation of the hearings: Senate Committee on Foreign Relations, *Supplemental Foreign Assistance Fiscal Year—Vietnam,* 89th Cong., 2d sess., 1966 (hereafter *"Vietnam Hearings"*).

4. See "Senate's Vietnam Debate, Isn't," *Wall Street Journal,* February 10, 1966; Andrew J. Glass, "The Great Debate on Viet Opens in Senate," *New York Herald-Tribune,* February 1, 1966, 3.

5. For Fulbright it was the very loudness of the proclamations of pacific intentions that suggested that the administration was not truly interested in negotiating a compromise with the enemy. The way to a settlement was "the old-fashioned way of going to [the Communists] privately" (*Vietnam Hearings,* 668 [Rusk at witness table]).

6. The full text of the letter is quoted in Gibbons, *U.S. Government and the Vietnam War* 4:156. The fifteen Democrats were: E. L. Bartlett (Alaska), Quentin Burdick (N.Dak.), Frank Church (Idaho), Joseph Clark (Pa.), Gruening, Vance Hartke (Ind.), Eugene McCarthy (Minn.), George McGovern (S.Dak.), Lee Metcalf (Mont.), Wayne Morse (Ore.), Gaylord Nelson (Wisc.), Maurine Neuberger (Ore.), William Proxmire (Wisc.), Harrison Williams (N.J.), and Stephen Young (Ohio). A sixteenth Democrat who had been out of the country, Frank Moss (Utah), sent the president a separate letter identifying himself with the fifteen. Moss to Johnson, February 7, 1966, WHCF, ND 19/CO 312, Box 219, Johnson Library.

7. Mansfield, Aiken, Edmund S. Muskie (D-Maine), Daniel K. Inouye (D-Hawaii), and J. Caleb Boggs (R-Del.), *The Vietnam Conflict: The Substance and the Shadow* (Washington, D.C.: GPO, 1966). The entire report and related correspondence and appendices were inserted at *CR* 112 (January 29, 1966), 1511–22. See "Mansfield Report: Real Danger of Bigger War," *U.S. News & World Report,* January 17, 1966, 11 (describing report as "One of the gloomiest reports to come out of the Vietnam war").

8. Oberdorfer's intelligence was shared with Henry H. Wilson of the White House's Office of Congressional Relations and then conveyed by Wilson to the president in a

memorandum. Wilson to Johnson, February 18, 1966, WHCF, FG 431/F, Box 342. The president agreed that the Stennis speech had done great damage. See Gibbons, *U.S. Government and the Vietnam War* 4:253, citing February 19, 1966, meeting notes. The significance of the Stennis speech to the senators is indicated by its insertion into the record (*Vietnam Hearings*, 714–18).

9. Gibbons, *U.S. Government and the Vietnam War* 4:223.

10. *Wall Street Journal*, January 18, 1966, 18.

11. In addition to Rusk, Fulbright had wanted McNamara to appear, and his refusal to do so became itself an issue of contention. See, for example, lead editorial, "The Senate Inquiry," *Washington Post*, February 7, 1966, A16. Others from the executive branch refusing to testify but not arousing significant controversy were Joint Chiefs of Staff chairman Gen. Earle Wheeler and Undersecretary of State George Ball. With respect to witnesses critical of the war, Fulbright would have preferred General Matthew Ridgway to Gavin. See Fulbright to Ridgway, February 11, 1966; Ridgway to Fulbright, February 19, 1966, Ser. 48:17, Box 43, Fulbright Papers. Ridgway had served as commander of U.N. forces during the Korean War and as army chief of staff at the time of the defeat of the French in Indochina. In his latter capacity, he had energetically opposed the proposed intervention of American forces in Indochina in 1954. Gavin had been chief of plans and operations for the Department of the Army and had conducted the feasibility study on which Ridgway had based his recommendation. The Gavin article appeared in *Harper's*, February 1966. The editor's introduction described it as "the first basic criticism of the administration's Vietnam policy by a major military figure." The full text is inserted at *Vietnam Hearings*, 232–34.

12. I. F. Stone criticized the committee for not confronting Taylor with the highly critical and pessimistic report he had written after his tour of South Vietnam in October 1961. The report had emphasized, among other things, that the Communists were aided by the unpopularity of the Saigon regime and that drastic reforms would be necessary if it was to survive: "Gen. Taylor knows better than most men that the Vietnamese war was no simple Communist plot or foreign invasion" (*I. F. Stone's Weekly*, February 28, 1966, 1).

13. The Democratic critics were: Fulbright (chairman) and (in order of committee seniority) Mansfield, Wayne Morse (Ore.), Gore, Frank Church (Idaho), Clark, Pell, and McCarthy. Consistent with his past practice of remaining publicly loyal to the president, Mansfield did not participate in the hearings, although, in fact, his desire that the United States disengage from Vietnam was by then well known. McCarthy is given little attention in this discussion because of his poor attendance and very limited participation when present.

14. On February 16, Richard Russell, chairman of the Armed Forces Committee, had taken the Senate floor to announce that as many as 300,000 Americans were already in Vietnam. This was a quantity, as Taylor conceded in response to a leading question from Gore, that approximated the peak of American involvement in Korea (*Vietnam Hearings*, 472). Russell's protégé, John Stennis, the ranking Democrat on the Armed Services Committee, as already mentioned, had recently noted the possibility of 600,000 Americans in Vietnam. And Stuart Symington (D-Mo.), the third-most-senior Democrat on the Armed Services Committee, dramatically pointed out that the 600,000 "figure did not originate with [Stennis]" but "came from some of the highest military authority" (*Vietnam Hearings*, 375).

15. At one point during the hearings Fulbright confronted Taylor with the government's own statistics to assail the administration's claim to be making progress in the war. According to the Pentagon, in January 1965 there were 103,000 so-called Vietcong; 19,000 new infiltrators throughout the year; and 35,000 VC killed or captured in the same period. "This would, I believe, leave about 76,000. Their present estimates are that there are 236,000 which would indicate they had recruited 160,000 during the course of 1965. This would seem to be inconsistent with the theory that we are killing ever increasing numbers, and thereby making progress. Is that true?" The general's response was evasive, arguing in essence that the growth of the VC was cause for greater intervention (ibid., 543).

16. For example, ibid., 321 (Clark with Gavin at witness table) (citing Lippmann). For comments by other Democrats evincing concern that the United States had embarked on a course of unlimited and spiraling escalation with the consequent loss of initiative to the enemy, see 251 (Gore with Gavin at witness table assenting); 494 (Pell with Taylor at witness table); 523–25, 554 (Gore with Taylor at witness table).

17. Ibid., 512–13 (Morse confronting Taylor); 98–99 (Fulbright confronting Bell).

18. See ibid., 222 (Morse with Bell at witness table); 411 (Gore with Kennan at witness table); 282 (Clark with Gavin at witness table). Both Gore and Clark cited President Kennedy's dictum that "in the final analysis it is their war. They are the ones who have to win it or lose it."

19. Ibid., 211 (Bell at witness table); see also 252 (Gore with Gavin at witness table assenting).

20. Ibid., 282–83.

21. Ibid., 100. Bell answered: "Well, Senator, I was in the Marine Corps in World War II, and we did go into the jungle to fight the Japanese and we did quite well."

22. Ibid., 500; 235 (Fulbright); 266 (Church); 325–27 (Eisenhower); 324–25 (Ridgway read aloud); 560 (Ridgway endorses Gavin testimony).

23. Ibid., 165–67 (Morse questioning Bell on corruption profiteering, and fairness of South Vietnamese taxation policies); 192 (Morse confronting Bell with report from a "very reliable source" about profiteering and enormous black market in Saigon); 215 (Morse confronting Bell with article from *New York Times Magazine* on black market; calls for an investigator to go to Vietnam); 187 (Fulbright questioning Bell on allegation that South Vietnamese send U.S. currency to bank accounts in France and Switzerland); 190 (Fulbright confronting Bell with "rumor" that import licenses could be bought as a commodity in South Vietnam"); 190 (Fulbright replying to Bell's assurance that corruption was prosecuted in South Vietnamese courts with sarcastic question: "And they have a very efficient judicial system, haven't they?"); 152 (Clark questioning Bell on extent which aid used as leverage to promote reforms in past eleven years: "I suggest to you because of the failure of various governments to make the desperately needed social and economic reforms that we have precious little to show for our $2,700 million and I will ask you to comment on that"); 97–98 (Fulbright asking Bell about popularity of Saigon government); 444 (Fulbright asking Taylor how he knows that South Vietnamese prefer Saigon regime); 536–37 (Church questioning Taylor on relative popularity of Ky regime and Communists); 541 (Pell asking Taylor why North Vietnamese seem more enthusiastic about Ho regime than South Vietnamese about Ky regime).

24. Ibid., 219–22 (Morse confronting Bell with article in *Wall Street Journal* describing disruptive effect of U.S. presence on South Vietnamese economy); 121–22 (Gore questioning

Bell on why an area once called "the rice basket of Asia" needs now to import rice and evincing general concern that the aid program fostered dependency of South Vietnam).

25. Ibid., 113 (with Bell at witness table); 152; 174–75. Pell prefaced his statement by referring to an article citing the head of South Vietnam's medical aid program, Major General James W. Humphreys Jr., as finding that civilian casualties exceeded military casualties of the war. The general found that both sides in the conflict made an ordinary practice of attacking villages "it believed occupied by the other" and that "many thousands" of civilians were killed or wounded as the war continued to be waged, as a rule, in civilian populated area. Pell inserted the article at 175–76. Lewis Gulick, "Vietnam Medical Aid to Increase—U.S. General Cites Civilian Casualties," (Washington) *Evening Star,* January 6, 1966.

26. The belief that the intervention in Vietnam carried with it the risk of a general war with China was by no means limited to the Senate doves. In a private conversation with Lyndon Johnson on May 20, 1964, Richard Russell (D-Ga.) warned that American involvement in Vietnam would "eventually lead to a ground war and a conventional war with China." Michael R. Beschloss, ed., *Taking Charge: The Johnson White House Tapes, 1963–1964* (New York: Simon and Schuster, 1997), 363.

27. *Vietnam Hearings,* 412 (Kennan at witness table).

28. Ibid., 252 (Gavin at witness table). Gavin's response was hardly reassuring: "It takes little in the way of thought to see how this [a third world war] could come about. Let us put it this way . . . a Chinese intervention, volunteers, regulars, a reopening of Korea and we could have a major affair on our hands, and where world war III could occur."

29. Ibid., 303 (Gavin at witness table). Gavin replied that Gore's scenario was "absolutely right" if he was suggesting a situation in which North Vietnam was occupied even if the Chinese border itself was not violated. Gore added, "The gravity of this issue impels us to be candid." Ibid.

30. Ibid., 267.

31. Ibid., 371; 248; 513–14 (Taylor at witness table countering that Soviet ambassador's assertions were mere bluff). See also 249 (Morse eliciting testimony from Gavin on danger posed by a blockade of North Vietnam, that could lead to the sinking of a Russian ship); compare Morse questioning Gen. Collins on danger arising from sinking a British or Soviet ship during a blockade of North Korea. U.S. Senate Committee on Armed Services and Committee on Foreign Relations, *Military Situation in the Far East,* 82d Cong., 1st sess., 1951 (*MacArthur Hearings*), 1341–42.

32. *Vietnam Hearings,* 195.

33. Ibid., 473, 527 (Gore with Taylor at witness table); 534–35 (Church with Taylor at witness table); 562. See also 661 (Fulbright with Rusk at witness table: "I do not think this dispute is worthy of an escalation that would result in a confrontation with China and a world war"); 666 (Fulbright with Rusk at witness table: "It is in one sense a rather minor controversy. In an other sense it seems be the trigger that could result in a world war and I do not want that to happen"); 672 (Morse with Rusk at witness table: "Our motives are of the best—I don't question my country's motives—I simply say the policy you are following is not the best, because it is making war, and you can't make war in 1966 and not endanger mankind in a nuclear war not too far away").

34. Ibid., 663 (Rusk at witness table); 668 (Rusk at witness table). See also 669: "Normally in the old days that is the way [diplomacy] used to be done—not on the front pages of every capital in the world. It used to be done in a different way."

35. Ibid., 668; 562.

36. Ibid., 545 (with Rusk at witness table); 526 (with Taylor at witness table); 497 (responding to question from Fulbright); 527 (responding to question from Gore); 545 (responding to question from Fulbright).

37. Ibid., 668;, 661.

38. Ibid., 387–88 (Fulbright with Kennan at witness table); 577–79 (Fulbright with Rusk at witness table); 400 (Morse with Kennan at witness table). The article, Drew Middleton, "Honolulu Parley Stirs Doubts at U.N.," *New York Times,* February 10, 1966, was inserted by Fulbright at *Vietnam Hearings, 390–91.* Gore inserted the Lippmann column for the same date at 428–29. Kennan himself cited both articles with approval, respectively, at 388 and 428.

39. *Vietnam Hearings, 389.*

40. Ibid., 670–72.

41. See ibid., 545 (Fulbright with Taylor at witness table); 561 (Fulbright with Rusk at witness table); 661 (same); and following section.

42. Ibid., 322; 372.

43. Ibid., 337–38.

44. Ibid., 545, 666.

45. Ibid., 160–61.

46. Ibid., 161; 337 (with Kennan at witness table).

47. Ibid., 209; 133 (Bell at witness table); 356–57. It is interesting to note that, despite their controversial content, these two discussions—one on the "semantics" of anti-Communism, the other on the acceptability of a Communist Vietnam—received no mention in newspapers covering the hearings. At least this is suggested by a review of the five New York dailies and the leading newspaper for the cities of Philadelphia, Washington, Cleveland, Chicago, St. Louis, and Los Angeles. The same omission is found in the secondary literature.

48. Ibid., 666 ("We are certainly strong enough and decent enough and good enough in every respect to withstand any compromise that is at all reasonable").

49. Ibid., 416–17 (Church with Kennan at witness table); 347 (Gore with Kennan at witness table).

50. Ibid., 356 (Church eliciting testimony from Kennan contrasting strategic interest of United States in containing Communism in Europe with that present in Asia). In the private conversation of Richard Russell with Johnson, cited above, the president asked: "How important is it [Vietnam] to us? Russell answered: "It isn't important a damn bit with all these new missile systems." The president went on to point to the SEATO Treaty. Russell in turn pointed out that the United States was the only treaty signatory "paying any attention to it!" To this Johnson conceded, "Yeah, I think that's right." Beschloss, *Taking Charge, 364.*

51. *Vietnam Hearings, 321* (with Gavin at witness table agreeing that costs had reached point of "doubtful acceptability"); 338. Fulbright was paraphrasing, not quoting, Ridgway.

See *also* ibid., 668–69 (same point made with Rusk at witness table); 542 (with Taylor at witness table citing Gulf of Tonkin Resolution as proof that Congress answered the question in the affirmative in 1964); 302 (Pell with Gavin at witness table denying such a vital interest); 251 (Gore quoting Gavin).

52. Ibid., 416–17 (Kennan at witness table assenting and analogizing effects of American 1918 intervention in Russia).

53. Ibid., 651 (Rusk at witness table); 441; 443; 502 (Taylor at witness table).

54. Ibid., 536-37. See also Pell asking Taylor "why can we not arouse the same fervor in the South Vietnamese that apparently Ho Chi Minh does in the North Vietnamese?" (ibid., 541); 666.

55. Ibid., 650; 667; 443. Fulbright immediately followed this comment with two rhetorical questions: "But we still consider ourselves one country, even though we had a war, didn't we? The more powerful side prevailed, didn't it?"

56. Ibid., 133 (Bell at witness table); 553–54 (Taylor at witness table); 496 (Taylor at witness table); 546 (Taylor at witness table).

57. Ibid., 544–45. The ellipses here delete some exchanges between Fulbright and Taylor in which the general was forced to concede the fact that Tokyo was firebombed.

58. Ibid., 670 (with Rusk at witness table). On Morse's personality and Senate style, see A. Robert Smith, *The Tiger in the Senate: The Biography of Wayne Morse* (Garden City, N.Y.: Doubleday, 1962), 31.

59. *Vietnam Hearings,* 502 (Taylor at witness table); 217 (questioning Bell on unlawful American use of territory to prosecute war); 455–57 (questioning Taylor on violations of Geneva Accords); 509–11 (questioning Taylor on his claim that intervention permitted under U.N. Charter and SEATO Treaty); 670 (berating Rusk for illegality of war, especially U.S. violation of Geneva Accords); 605–6 (Gore telling Rusk that he frankly does not understand how SEATO Treaty can require intervention in light of the statements of three presidents); 582. In mock self-deprecation the chairman then added: "I am sure it is due to my own obtuseness but we will pursue this later."

60. Ibid., 214 (with Bell at witness table); 651 (with Rusk at witness table); 417 (with Kennan at witness table); 8 (Kennan at witness table during preliminary hearing not televised live); 192 (Bell at witness table); 252 (with Gavin at witness table). He made the same point at 123 (with Bell at witness table); 651 (Rusk at witness table).

61. Ibid., 347 (Gore with Kennan at witness table), for example.

62. Ibid., 417 (Church with Kennan at witness table), for example.

63. Ibid., 251 (Gore with Gavin at witness table), for example.

64. Ibid., 417 (Church with Kennan on the witness table), for example; see also 540 (Pell with Taylor at witness table).

65. Ibid., 346 (responding to questions from Gore). Compare 369 (similar testimony in response to questions from Clark). The Princeton speech, the Walter E. Edge Lecture, was the cause of considerable excitement in Clark's office when its transcript was first received; Clark had then had it entered into the *Congressional Record* with the unusual request it "be printed in ordinary type, not the small almost unreadable type in which insertions are usually printed" (*CR* 111 [April 1, 1965], 6547). Clark also had it inserted in the hearing record. *Vietnam Hearings,* 359–66.

66. *Vietnam Hearings,* 369–70.

67. Ibid., 287–89 (with Gavin at witness table); 391–93 (with Kennan at witness table).

68. Ibid., 370 (with Kennan at witness table); 268 (with Gavin at witness table); 294 (with Gavin at witness table). Morse implied that "normal diplomatic relations" included admission of China to the United Nations when in a sentence immediately after one describing U.S.-Soviet diplomatic relations as "normal," he noted that the two countries "had discussed problems . . . at the United Nations" (293); 371.

CHAPTER 6

1. *Inside U.S.A.* (New York: Harper, 1947), 429. Gunther's remarks are made in the context of a generally admiring portrait of the man (422–30). On his subsequent career, see Neal R. Peirce, *The Megastates of America* (New York: Norton, 1972), 304–5.

2. The "quicksand" metaphor was used by no lesser senator than Bourke Hickenlooper, the committee's ranking Republican (*Vietnam Hearings,* 673 [Rusk at witness table]). The performance of the committee Republicans during the hearings is described more fully below.

3. Ibid., 238 (under questioning by Sparkman, Gavin concedes he only calls for a temporary bombing halt); 239 (under questioning by Sparkman concedes that bombing of Haiphong area might be appropriate); 258, 261 (under questioning by Lausche affirms his support for U.S. involvement in Vietnam); 270–72 (under strong cross-examination by Symington concedes he is not seeking an end to the bombing, an end to the escalation of the ground war, and does not favor an end to active efforts to pursue enemy rather than remain in coastal enclaves; accuses *Harper's* editors of distorting his views in introduction to his letter by calling him an advocate of enclave strategy); 280–81 (under questioning by Dodd concedes that withdrawal of American forces would hurt South Vietnamese morale and that South Vietnam a victim of aggression by Communists); 304–5 (under questioning by Lausche concedes fall of Vietnam would be likely to be followed by Communist challenges elsewhere); 307 (under questioning by Lausche concedes necessity of bombing all military targets); 316 (under questioning by Symington concedes that expansion of defense perimeter, rather than avoidance of offensive actions, will lead to reduction in vulnerability of American troops); 320 (under questioning by Symington tacitly concedes that he had been inaccurate in accusing United States of taking a purely military approach to Vietnam; praises Edward Lansdale's current work in South Vietnam); 321 (under questioning by Symington concedes need for better bombing targets).

4. Ibid., 475 (with Taylor at witness table); 445–46 (Taylor); 582 (Rusk); 464 (with Taylor at witness table); 515–16 (with Taylor at witness table); 600 (with Rusk at witness table); 465 (with Taylor at witness table); 553 (with Taylor assenting).

5. Ibid., 114 (Lausche asking Bell for "number of orphans and dead that resulted from guerilla tortures"); 127–28 (Lausche asking Bell about decapitations, kidnapping of children, other examples of "reign of terror"); 466 (Long asking Taylor about killings of noncombatant men, women, and children); 551 (Long with Taylor at witness table; cutting "a little child to pieces in front of the mother and father"); 555 (Symington reminding Taylor of funeral they attended in 1961 of anti-Diemist official horribly tortured to death for having voted once against North Vietnamese interests).

6. Ibid., 551. Taylor replied: "They certainly are behaving that way in South Vietnam"; 531.

7. Ibid., 550–51 (with Taylor at witness table); 630 (with Rusk at witness table).

8. Ibid., 493; 420 (with Kennan at witness table).

9. Ibid., 205–6 (Lausche questioning Bell; Thailand and Burma, South America and Mid-America); 447 (Sparkman questioning Taylor; speculating on spread of threat to Africa and Latin America); 517–18 (Long questioning Taylor; states bordering Soviet Union and China and states bordering them).

10. Ibid., 129 (with Bell at witness table). See also 486 (Symington reading from Churchill's *The Gathering Storm* with Taylor at witness table).

11. Ibid., 677–78.

12. Ibid., 128–29 (Lausche questioning Bell; increasing territory under allied control); 483 (Symington questioning Taylor; no South Vietnamese defections); 491 (Dodd questioning Taylor; increase in enemy defections).

13. Ibid., 127 (Lausche questioning Bell); 532 (Symington questioning Taylor); 676–77 (Symington questioning Rusk).

14. Ibid., 129 (Lausche questioning Bell); 351 (Lausche questioning Kennan); 375 (Symington questioning Kennan); 582–85 (Sparkman questioning Rusk); 626–27 (Symington questioning Rusk); 677 (Symington questioning Rusk).

15. Ibid., 420 (Kennan at witness table); 555 (Taylor at witness table).

16. Ibid., 378 (Kennan at witness table); 627–28.

17. Williams's questioning focused on black-marketeering in Saigon, obviously a vulnerable point for the administration. Nonetheless, when Williams apologized "for using the Senator's time," Sparkman replied: "I think they were very good follow-up questions and I was glad to yield" (ibid., 102–4). Sparkman's failure to take advantage of Williams's offer to reciprocate "for having used a good bit of the time" is at 123.

18. Ibid., 597 (Rusk at witness table); 381. Sparkman similarly made no substantive objection when Kennan offered testimony suggesting that the maintenance of a client state is not necessarily beneficial to its patron, be it the United States and South Vietnam or the Soviet Union and Cuba.

19. Ibid., 271 (Gavin at witness table); 317 (Gavin at witness table); 375–78 (Kennan at witness table); 419–20 (Kennan at witness table).

20. Ibid., 321 (Gavin at witness table).

21. Ibid., 491 (Taylor at witness table). See Wilson to Johnson, Feb. 18, 1966, WHCF, FG 431/F. Box 342, Johnson Library. "He [Don Oberdorfer] says that Symington works, but that he is obviously more interested in plugging for the Air Force than for the Administration generally, and that everything he says is directed towards constantly pushing for big bombing raids and other Air Force activities."

22. *Vietnam Hearings*, 598. When Rusk assured the senator that "there was too much power immediately available in the area" for a debacle like Dien Bien Phu to take place, Long was not satisfied. Long: "We have the power, if we use it. That is what I am talking about and that is what I would like to hear you say" (598–99).

23. See Wilson memorandum: "He [Don Oberdorfer] says that it is his observation that the Administration is not really very well represented in the Committee—that Long is

regarded by other members as being not really a Foreign Relations Committee man—that he just doesn't attend Committee meetings very often; that Sparkman is not particularly valuable, and that he also has seldom attended meetings; that the most effective advocate of the Administration position is Lausche." On the influence of committee chairmen, see Donald R. Matthews, *U.S. Senators and their World* (Chapel Hill: University of North Carolina Press, 1960), pp. 159–62. It should also be noted that for Long, who had recently ascended to the chairmanship of the Finance Committee, there may have been special problems of status within the Senate. See Joseph M. Bowman to Barefoot Sanders, August 24, 1967 (reporting on meeting with Long): "He feels that he is not treated by the Senate leadership with the same respect that other Senate Committee chairmen are treated. He still feels that he is regarded as a 30-year old freshman Senator nobody took too seriously" (Personal Papers of Barefoot Sanders, Box 12, Johnson Library).

24. On the growing importance of physical appearance for politicians during the period of the hearings, see William L. Rivers, *The Opinionmakers* (Boston: Beacon, 1966), 94–95. Of twelve senators listed by Rivers as very handsome, three (Clark, Church, and McCarthy) were among the Democratic critics and only one (Symington) among its defenders. The author also lists Fulbright as one of the three most "distinguished looking" senators, a label that should also, in my opinion, be applied to Gore. John Gunther does describe Lausche as having "considerable (political) sex appeal for women," but this is based on observations made twenty years before the hearings. *Inside U.S.A.,* 429.

25. See *Vietnam Hearings,* 113 (Lausche interrupting Morse; Bell at witness table); 442 (Long interrupting Fulbright with Taylor at witness table). Even *Time,* which was strongly pro-administration in its coverage of the hearings, treated Long as an embarrassment. See "The War," *Time,* February 25, 1966. See also Millard Durham to Fulbright, February 20, 1966, Ser. 48:18, Box 47, Fulbright Papers (disparaging description of Long's performance). The classic statement on television as a "cool medium" is roughly contemporary with the hearings. Marshall McLuhan, *Understanding Media: The Extensions of Man* (New York: McGraw-Hill, rev. paperback ed., 1964), 22–32, 308–37.

26. One searches the Johnson Library in vain for documents showing efforts by the White House itself to take even so modest a step as to encourage better attendance by its supporters at the hearings. One does find, however, with no evidence of White House response, reports that Long, Hickenlooper, and Symington were eager to be helpful. There is also a report that Symington worked with Taylor in preparation for his appearance. See Mike Manatos to Johnson, February 16, 1966, WHCF, ND 19/CO 312, Box 219, Johnson Library.

27. They were, in order of committee seniority: Hickenlooper, Aiken (Vt.), Frank Carlson (Kans.), John J. Williams (Del.), Karl Mundt (S.Dak.), and Clifford P. Case (N.J.).

28. See Aiken speech and colloquy with other senators *CR* 112 (January 31, 1966), 1576–84; syndicated column of Marquis Childs, "More Ornithology, Owl in the Senate," *Washington Post,* February 8, 1966, A12.

29. *Vietnam Hearings,* 673 (Rusk at witness table); 453 (Taylor at witness table); 673 (Rusk at witness table); 136 (Bell at witness table); 481–82 (Taylor at witness table).

30. Ibid., 102–4, 123–24 (Williams questioning Bell; black marketeering); 198 (Aiken questioning Bell; black-marketeering); 461 (Aiken questioning Taylor; black marketeering); 519 (Carlson questioning Taylor; failure to carry out past projections). Williams, in

particular, seems to have viewed the hearings as essentially a corruption investigation. On Williams, see *Congressional Quarterly Weekly Report* 24 (July 22, 1966), 1555–56; Harry McPherson, *A Political Education* (1972; Boston: Houghton Mifflin, 1988), 80; On Williams as an antagonist to Johnson, see McPherson, *Political Education,* 80–81; Michael R. Beschloss, ed., *Taking Charge: The Johnson White House Tapes, 1963–1964* (New York: Simon and Schuster, 1997), for example, 158, 175 ("Son-of-a-bitching Williams"), 356–57 ("He's a mean vicious man. . . . emotionally unbalanced and he's so goddamned interested").

31. Ibid., 104 (Hickenlooper questioning Bell); 137 (Mundt [Iowa] questioning Bell; amount requested "in my part of the world is considered quite a chunk of money"); 132–34 (Case questioning Bell; concern about future costs). See also 19 (Williams questioning Bell at preliminary hearing not televised live); 118 (Carlson questioning Bell at preliminary hearing not televised live; concern about open-ended authorization).

32. Ibid., 104–5 (Hickenlooper questioning Bell).

33. Ibid., 519 (Carlson questioning Taylor). See also 11 (Hickenlooper questioning Bell at preliminary hearing not televised live); 11 (Williams questioning Bell at preliminary hearing not televised live).

34. Ibid., 10 (Hickenlooper inquiring of Rusk or Bell about lack of candor on budget; at preliminary hearing not televised live); 117 (Case questioning Bell about reasonableness of budget request); 198–99 (Aiken questioning Bell regarding failure to disclose investigation reports).

35. Ibid., 106. Hickenlooper's questioning ironically pushed Bell to deemphasize the Communists' use of terror. Thus Bell referred to "a rather astute and effective propaganda campaign" waged by the Communists, and the existence of "real grievances and problems in the countryside which they have attempted to exploit," including "serious problems of landownership and tenancy" (106).

36. Ibid., 41 (with Rusk at witness table during preliminary hearing not televised live). Compare Senate Committee on Armed Services and Committee on Foreign Relations, *Military Situation in the Far East,* 82d Cong., 1st sess., 1951; *Vietnam Hearings,* 599 (Harry P. Cain [R-Wash.] with George Marshall at witness table; British trade with Chinese while we fight them in Korea); 1699 (H. Alexander Smith [R-N.J.] with Admiral Sherman at witness table; same); 1762 (Leverett Saltonstall [R-Mass.] with Dean Acheson at witness table; differences of United States with Britain and other allies regarding sanctions against China); 2684 (Morse [R-Ore.] with Louis Johnson at witness table; "deplore" British trade with "Red Chinese"); 3099 (Hickenlooper with General O'Donnell at witness table; asking whether Russian jets used against Americans in Korea were modeled on those sold or given to Russians by British).

37. *Vietnam Hearings,* 508 (Hickenlooper with Taylor at witness table; "so-called allies" do not do enough); 40 (Aiken questioning Rusk at preliminary hearing not televised live; question of Britain's contribution); 602 (Carlson with Rusk at witness table). Fulbright and Gore intervened in alliance with Mundt, the chairman recalling his criticism of Australia for the small size of its contribution and recalling the State Department's criticism of him for doing so openly. Fulbright suggested that if the Department truly wanted increased allied help it should have praised rather than criticized this effort to shame Australia into doing more (68–72). Pell, and Fulbright elsewhere, however, took the position, more logical for opponents of the war, that the lack of allied support was evidence not of ingrati-

tude but of substantive disagreement with America's policy (539 [Pell with Taylor at witness table]); 650 (Fulbright with Rusk at witness table). Compare *MacArthur Hearings*, 951 (Cain with Gen. Bradley at witness table; lack of British and French help despite membership in NATO); 1626 (Hickenlooper with Adm. Sherman at witness table; fear that United States, by assuming major burden in fight against Communists, will encourage its allies to be passive and dependent on United States); 1784 (Smith with Acheson at witness table; allies do not help enough); 2515 (Cain with General Wedemeyer at witness table; concern regarding failure of allies to give "equality of sacrifice"); 3035 (Cain with Gen. Barr at witness table; concern regarding failure of allies to give "equality of sacrifice").

38. *Vietnam Hearings*, 595–96 (Aiken questioning Rusk; extent of global commitments); 459 (Aiken questioning Taylor; referring to Japanese and French in Indochina): "I think it is in both cases a matter of biting off more than you can chew. The question is where do we stop biting?"; 611.

39. Ibid., 387.

40. Ibid., 414.

41. Ibid., 129–32; 164.

42. Ibid., 269–71.

43. Ibid., 378–80.

44. Ibid., 486–89.

45. Ibid., 619–22; 683–84.

46. Ibid., 673 (Rusk at witness table). The "mistakes" referred to were presumably those set forth in the standard Republican indictment of the Democrats during the McCarthy era: treachery at Yalta, connivance in the victory of Chinese Communism, etc.; 450.

47. Ibid., 17 (preliminary hearing not televised live); 515.

48. Randall Bennett Woods, *Fulbright: A Biography* (Cambridge: Cambridge University Press, 1995), 405.

49. For excerpts see *Newsweek*, February 28, 1966, 19–20 (Rusk and Taylor); *U.S. News & World Report*, February 28, 1966, 40–42 (Rusk and Taylor); *Time*, February 18, 1966, 20 (Kennan; captioned "From Containment to Isolation"); *New Republic*, February 26, 1966, 19–30 (Kennan). An only slightly abridged version of the transcript (with an introduction by Fulbright and commentary by Morse) soon found its way into bookstores as Frank M. Robinson and Earl Kemp, eds., *The Truth about Vietnam* (San Diego: Greenleaf Classics, 1966). For syndicated columns see Joseph Alsop (February 23, 1966); Doris Fleeson (February 7, 1966); Joseph Kraft (February 18, 1966); Max Lerner (February 21, 1966); Walter Lippmann (February 10 and 15, 1966); Mary McGrory (February 16, 18, and 21, 1966); Murrey Marder (February 5, 1966); James Reston (February 9, 14, and 20, 1966); James Wechsler (February 16, 1966). On press coverage of the hearings generally, see Woods, *Fulbright*, 409; Eugene Brown, *J. William Fulbright: Advice and Dissent* (Iowa City: University of Iowa Press, 1985), 77–79; Francesca Constance Morgan, "Unlikely Rebel: J. William Fulbright, His 1966 Hearings and Their Impact on American Politics" (Harvard University undergraduate thesis, 1990), 85–86 and *passim*.

50. *Vietnam Hearings*, 554 (with Taylor at witness table). A week before he had reported that his office had been "flooded with telephone calls" as he was "sure this is true of every member" (ibid., 410 [with Kennan at witness table]).

51. See discussion of mail in transcript of Fulbright's February 21, 1966 press conference, 11–13; Ser. 72, Box 25. Among the letters are several with recognizable names. See, for example, Clayton Fritchey to Fulbright, February 9, 1966 Ser. 48: 18, Box 48; Julia B. Foraker (granddaughter of Senator Jos. B. Foraker [R-Ohio]) to Fulbright, May 30, 1966, same location; Helen Gahagan Douglas to Fulbright, May 16, 1966, Ser. 48: 17, Box 47, Fulbright Papers. *Cf.* "Senate Letters 30 to 1 Against War," *St. Louis Post-Dispatch,* February 12, 1966, p. 1. Compare also large and remarkable group of letters sent to Morse and printed at *CR* 112 (February 16, 1966), 3048–89. Fulbright himself, in the wake of the hearings, became the recipient of 736 speaking invitations and was greeted with a standing ovation when in March he addressed the delegates to the National Conference on Higher Education. Melvin Small, *Johnson, Nixon, and the Doves* (New Brunswick, N.J.: Rutgers University Press, 1988), 80. On particular growth of concern among members of the so-called attentive public, See Brown, *J. William Fulbright,* 58; Woods, *Fulbright,* 411.

52. CRS interview, January 24, 1979, quoted in Gibbons, *U.S. Government and the Vietnam War* 4:249. Pell added, "I really think our committee was more responsible than any other single individual or body of individuals in turning public opinion around on that war."

53. Telephone interview, July 15, 1998. On Becker, see Fred Halstead, *Out Now!* (New York: Monad, 1978), 76–78, 89.

54. Woods, *Fulbright,* 405, 410; Walter Zelman, "Senate Dissent and the Vietnam War, 1964–1968" (Ph.D. diss., University of California–Los Angeles, 1971), 230; Lee Riley Powell, *J. William Fulbright and America's Lost Crusade* (Little Rock, Ark.: Rose, 1984), 179; Brown, *Fulbright,* 75; William C. Berman, *William Fulbright and the Vietnam War* (Kent, Ohio: Kent State University Press, 1988); Small, *Johnson, Nixon, and the Doves,* 80; Kathleen J. Turner, *Lyndon Johnson's Dual War* (Chicago: University of Chicago Press, 1985), 156; Donald Ritchie, *Oral History Interviews: Pat Holt* (Washington: Senate Historical Office, 1983), 203.

55. David Halberstam, *The Powers That Be* (New York: Dell, 1979), 706.

56. *Vietnam Hearings,* 138 (Bell at witness table). See also 511 (Taylor at witness table): "This President of ours cannot justify under the Constitution sending a single American boy to his slaughter."

57. Ibid., 413 (Carson with Kennan at witness table); 412 (Gore with Kennan at witness table); 225 (Fulbright with Gavin at witness table); 384 (Aiken with Kennan at witness table); 512 (Pell with Taylor at witness table).

58. Ibid., 652 (Rusk at witness table).

59. Ibid.

60. Ibid., 373 (Kennan at witness table).

61. For example, ibid., 138 (Clark questioning Bell on classified map depicting Communist strength in South Vietnam); 198 ff. (Aiken questioning Bell; challenging classification of General Accounting Office reports on corruption investigations).

62. Ibid., 548 (Taylor at witness table).

63. Ibid., 410.

64. See Woods, *Fulbright,* 411; Berman, *William Fulbright and the Vietnam War,* 56; A. J. Langguth, *Our Vietnam* (New York: Simon and Schuster, 2000), 420. Johnson directed that the FBI monitor the television broadcasts and compare statements of Fulbright and Morse, in particular, with the "Communist Party line." A few weeks later he directed the

agency to monitor several antiwar senators for contacts with foreign embassies, especially that of the Soviet Union. At the president's initiative the agency's assistant director also paid visits to Senators Dirksen (R-Ill.) and Hickenlooper to discuss Fulbright and Morse. See Robert Mann, *A Grand Illusion: America's Descent into Vietnam* (New York: Basic Books, 2001), 494; Gibbons, *U.S. Government and the Vietnam War* 4:228–30 and sources cited therein.

65. See, for example, *New York Times,* February 5, 1966, 1; Woods, *Fulbright,* 403; Small, *Johnson, Nixon, and the Doves,* 78.

66. See text of declaration and Morse's comments at *Vietnam Hearings,* 400–401.

67. See Small, *Johnson, Nixon, and the Doves,* 78–79: "If the Honolulu Conference and its attendant policy statements and publicity was indeed fabricated only to distract attention from the Senate hearings, then once again antiwar criticism had influenced policy."

68. Frances Fitzgerald, *Fire in the Lake* (New York: Vintage, 1973), 373.

69. On the sharp decline in public support for the war that accompanied the period of the Buddhist revolt and its suppression—a loss that would never be recovered except during transient intervals—see Gibbons, *U.S. Government and the Vietnam War* 4:334–42 and accompanying graphs.

70. Arthur M. Schlesinger Jr., *Robert Kennedy and His Times* (Boston: Houghton Mifflin, 1978), 735; *Time,* March 4, 1966, 26.

CHAPTER 7

1. Citations to the speech are from the text inserted by Joseph Clark (D-Pa.) at *CR* 112 (March 14, 1966), 5617–19. This is the only unabridged version of the speech available in printed form. Jack Newfield, who witnessed the speech, recalls that "in the front row was I. F. Stone, resembling a professor watching his unruly but favorite pupil reading his prize-winning essay" (*Robert Kennedy: A Memoir* [New York: Dutton, 1969], 125).

2. Ibid.

3. Ibid., 5618–19.

4. See Jeff Shesol, *Mutual Contempt: Lyndon Johnson, Robert Kennedy, and the Feud That Defined a Decade* (New York: Norton, 1998), 289; Arthur Schlesinger Jr., *Robert Kennedy and His Times* (Boston: Houghton, Mifflin, 1978), 737.

5. Shesol, *Mutual Contempt,* 290; Schlesinger, *Robert Kennedy and His Times,* 737–39.

6. See Clayton Fritchey, "The Record on Kennedy's Proposal," *Washington (D.C.) Star,* February 25, 1966, inserted by Clark at *CR* 112 (March 14, 1966), 5620–21.

7. See Senate Committee on Foreign Relations, *Foreign Assistance Act of 1968, Part 1—Vietnam,* 90th Cong., 2d sess., 1968, 162 (testimony of Rusk).

8. See *The Complete War Memoirs of Charles de Gaulle,* trans. Jonathan Griffin (New York: Simon and Schuster, 1964), 779–83.

9. Transcript of press conference held by Senator Robert F. Kennedy, at 5:00 P.M., Senate Office Building, Washington, D.C., February 22, 1966. This transcript, as well as that of other press conferences and television interviews of Kennedy (and his attackers) in the aftermath of his speech are conveniently collected in the Adam Walinsky Papers, Box 17, JFK Library.

10. *I. F. Stone's Weekly,* February 23, 1966.

11. Lippmann column for February 22, 1966, in the *Washington Post,* inserted by Clark immediately after the text of Kennedy's speech at *CR* 112 (March 14, 1966), 5619–20.

12. See, for example, Sanford Gottlieb, "A Transitional Government in Vietnam: Bridging the Gap," February 23, 1966 (expanding on Kennedy proposal for power sharing and noting the author's own earlier proposal along similar lines in pacifist Norman Cousins's *Saturday Review*), Walinsky Papers, Box 16, JFK Library. See also lavish praise for speech in Norman Thomas to Robert Kennedy, February 21, 1966; Martin Luther King Jr. to Robert Kennedy, March 21, 1966: "Only the heavy pressures of our Chicago project and the intense voter registration campaign in the south could have delayed me in writing to applaud your statement on Viet Nam. . . . Former President Kennedy, your great brother, carried us far in new directions with his concept of world diversity; your position advances us to the next step which requires us to reach the political maturity to recognize and relate to all elements produced by the contemporary colonial revolutions" (RFK Senate Papers: Subject File, 1966, Box 47, JFK Library).

13. See William V. Shannon, *The Heir Apparent* (New York: Macmillan, 1967), 108.

14. See *I. F. Stone's Weekly,* February 28, 1966 (rhetorically juxtaposing Kennedy, who had become a "liberal," with Humphrey who had become a "war monger"); editorial, *New Republic,* March 15, 1966, 5 (favorably comparing Kennedy to Humphrey); editorial, *The Nation* 202 (March 7, 1966), 253 (supporting Kennedy statement, but faulting him for equivocations). See also William V. Shannon, "The Making of President Robert Kennedy," *Harper's,* October 1966, 67.

15. Shannon, "Making of President Robert Kennedy," 62–63.

16. On the liberal revulsion toward Robert Kennedy, see Schlesinger, *Robert Kennedy and His Times,* 669.

17. The sentiment that the succession from John Kennedy to Lyndon Johnson was somehow improper probably dates from the time of the former's assassination (see Shannon, *Heir Apparent,* 4). The uproar in response to public readings of Barbara Garson's play *MacBird* (Berkeley, Calif.: Grassy Knoll Press, 1966) was symptomatic of the sensitivities surrounding the question of the "legitimacy" of the succession. See Victor S. Navasky in the *New York Times,* December 18, 1966, D8. The idea of an illegitimate succession (and a wrongly deprived "heir") undoubtedly drew some of its strength from its deep roots in American and European political culture. See Marcus Raskin, "JFK," in "AHR Forum: JFK and the Culture of Violence," *American Historical Review* 97 (1992): 487–99.

18. Perikles-Platon Vastardis to Robert Kennedy, May 12, 1966, RFK Senate Papers, Senate Correspondence: Subject File, 1966, Box 48, JFK Library. The senator referred the letter and picture to the Pentagon which ultimately replied to Kennedy with a letter explaining, among other things, that "a hand grenade thrown by a child can be just as deadly as one thrown by a grown up." See Kennedy to Vastardis, June 1, 1966; June 25, 1966; Arthur Sylvester, assistant secretary of defense, to Robert Kennedy, June 10, 1966, RFK Senate Papers, Senate Correspondence: Subject File, 1966, Box 48, JFK Library. Among the distinctive and moving features of the Robert Kennedy correspondence files is the large volume of mail from idealistic children and adolescents.

19. Allen J. Matusow, *The Unraveling of America* (New York: Harper, 1986), 383; Ralph de Toledano, *R.F.K: The Man Who Would Be President* (New York: Putnam's, 1967), 314–15; See also Shannon, "Making of President Robert Kennedy," 63–65.

20. *I. F. Stone's Weekly,* May 18, 1965. In the aftermath of the speech, the editors of the dovish *St. Louis Post-Dispatch* (February 27, 1966) vainly proposed that Kennedy proposals be embodied in a Senate resolution. See *I. F. Stone's Weekly,* March 7, 1966.

21. See scathing attack on Kennedy titled "While Others Dodge the Draft, Bobby Dodges the War," in *I. F. Stone's Weekly,* October 24, 1966; compare Evan Thomas, *Robert Kennedy: His Life* (New York: Simon & Schuster, 2000), 316.

22. Fulbright to Tuchman, August 17, 1966, Ser. 88:1, Box 10, Fulbright Papers.

23. Fulbright to Schlesinger, March 15, 1966, Ser. 88:1, Box 9, Fulbright Papers.

24. Gibbons, *U.S. Government and the Vietnam War;* Senate Committee on Foreign Relations, Comm. Print 103–83 (Washington, D.C.: GPO, 1994), 4:255–57. The dissenters were Wayne Morse (D-Oreg.), Eugene McCarthy (D-Minn.), and Albert Gore (D-Tenn.).

25. Fulbright to Schlesinger, March 15, 1966, Ser. 88:1, Box 9, Fulbright Papers.

26. *The Arrogance of Power* (New York: Random House, 1966), 188–97.

27. Ibid., 22; 69–70; 99; see also 81: "[Communism's] doctrine has redeeming tenets of humanitarianism. . . . some countries are probably better off under communist rule than they were under preceding regimes. . . . some people may even want to live under communism"; 153–56.

28. U.S. Senate, Committee on Foreign Relations, Hearings, *U.S. Policy with Respect to Mainland China* (Washington, D.C.: GPO, 1966).

29. U.S. Senate, Committee on Foreign Relations, Hearings, *Psychological Aspects of International Relations* (Washington, D.C.: GPO, 1966).

30. U.S. Senate, Committee on Foreign Relations, Hearings, *Changing American Attitudes Toward Foreign Policy* (Washington, D.C.: GPO, 1967), 2–3.

31. Gibbons, *U.S. Government and the Vietnam War* 4:584.

32. *CR* 112 (April 5, 1966), 7635.

33. *CR* 112 (April 14, 1966), 8153 (Javits); *CR* 112 (April 18, 1966), 8224–25 (Young); *CR* 112 (April 20, 1966), 8611 (Pell); *New York Times,* April 18, 1966 (Stennis, Javits, Hartke) p. 4.

34. Ibid. "If a Saigon Regime Asks U. S. to Leave, It Must."

35. *U.S. News & World Report,* May 2, 1966, 56.

36. With the retirement of Leverett Saltonstall of Massachusetts at the end of the year, Smith would become the senior Republican on the committee.

37. Tony Geishauser to Smith, April 25, 1966; May 20, 1966; Smith to Geishauser, May 27, 1966; Smith to Johnson, June 1, 1966, WHCF, ND 19/CO 312, Box 221, Johnson Library. The same folder includes another letter from Smith to Geishauser, another letter from Smith to Johnson, several internal memoranda from Pentagon and White House officials on how to cope with Smith's letters, a draft reply, and the actual reply finally sent to Smith by Walt Rostow on July 5, 1966. Rostow's reply challenges the soldier's low opinion of the commitment of the South Vietnamese army, emphasizing their high level of casualties.

38. In August 1966 the Preparedness Investigating Subcommittee of the Armed Services Committee (including Stennis, Stuart Symington [D-Mo.], and Smith), held a series of hearings on *Worldwide Military Commitments* (Washington, D.C.: GPO, 1966). These hearings provided an opportunity for the cross-examination (again) of Dean Rusk and for Stennis and Symington to note their concern about the extent of present and

possible future commitments. Stennis, in particular, expressed doubts about the legal basis for the involvement in Vietnam (101–3 and *passim*).

39. Quoted in Gibbons, *U.S. Government and the Vietnam War* 4:336. But see Tristram Coffin to Adam Walinsky, August 26, 1966, paraphrasing a Time-Life reporter who examined the effect of the war on a small town in Ohio: "When I first went door-to-door polling opinions, I found only a small minority, perhaps a quarter, favoring withdrawal. But as I came to know the people and drink with them and be accepted by them, I discovered that most people wanted to get out. The view constantly heard was, 'I don't think it's worth the life of a single American boy.'" When asked to account for the discrepancy, the reporter replied: "People are afraid to appear unpatriotic or a beatnik; and a casual poller will get the kind of answer they think is in conformity with majority opinion. They are also afraid of the mighty power of the Federal Government, and think it might be used against them individually if they profess an anti-Government stand on the issue." At the top of the letter are some cryptic notations including "Senator: Do you think him reliable? A. If he is, it's an important letter." Further notations in Kennedy's handwriting are illegible to me. Walinsky Papers, Box 18, JFK Library.

40. Gibbons, *U.S. Government and the Vietnam War* 4:336.

41. John Curry, "Impact of Vietnam on Elections Likely to Be Light," *New York Times*, October 20, 1966, 1, 27.

42. *Congressional Quarterly Weekly Report* (hereafter "*CQWR*") 24 (October 28, 1966): 2661.

43. In a few primaries "peace candidates" appeared as challengers; all were defeated. As will be discussed below, hawk challengers, although in several instances winning primaries, ultimately fared no better. A synopsis of election and primary contests is given in *CQWR* 24 (July 22, 1966): 1487–1522.

44. *CQWR* 24 (July 22, 1966): 1533.

45. *CQWR* 24 (October 7, 1966): 2358. See also Curry, "Impact of Vietnam on Elections Likely to Be Light," 27.

46. *CQWR* 24 (October 14, 1966): 2433.

47. All official election results for 1966, including vote breakdowns by congressional district, are set forth in *CQWR* 25 (May 12, 1967): 746–70.

48. See *CQWR* 24 (October 7, 1966): 2370.

49. See *CQWR* 24 (September 9, 1966): 1959; *CQWR* 24 (October 21, 1966): 2537 (Iowa); *CQWR* 24 (October 21, 1966): 2534 (South Dakota); *CQWR* 24 (October 14, 1966): 2440 (Colorado).

50. *CQWR* 24 (October 7, 1966): 2361.

51. Curry, "Impact of Vietnam on Elections Likely to Be Light," 27; *CQWR* 24 (September 30, 1966): 2273.

52. Jerry E. Mandel, "A Critical Analysis of the Form of Communication in Charles H. Percy's 1966 Senatorial Campaign," (Ph.D. diss. [speech], Perdue University, 1968), 48–49 and *passim*.

53. *CQWR* 24 (October 21, 1966): 2509.

54. Ibid.

55. See Mandel, "Critical Analysis," 54–58. See also Paul Douglas's own account of the contest, *In the Fullness of Time* (New York: Harcourt, Brace, 1971), 577–94. Of Percy's use of Vietnam in his campaign, Douglas writes: "Without openly attacking the war as such,

my opponent dwelt on the lengthening casualty lists and the hardships experienced by our soldiers. As Senators Fulbright and Morse attacked our Vietnam policy in the most vitriolic terms, I knew that they were gathering support. Several prominent rabbis, hitherto friendly to me, now came out in open opposition to the Vietnam war naturally intensified as casualty lists mounted and boys were brought home for burial. Percy's Vietnam proposals were confused but embodied opposition to the war. As a Quaker and long-time supporter of collective security, I was astonished, baffled, and hurt to find the label of 'hawk' pinned on me by his followers" (583–84).

56. *CQWR* 24 (October 14, 1966): 2449; *CQWR* 24 (November 4, 1966): 2712.

57. James Reston, "Washington: The Elections and Vietnam," *New York Times,* October 30, 1966, IV:10E.

58. Curry, "Impact of Vietnam on Elections Likely to Be Light," 1, 27.

59. John Herbers, "Riots, War and Economy Looming as Major Election Issues for Both Parties," *New York Times,* October 2, 1966, 74.

60. Richard Dudman, "Presidents Johnson, Ho Agree Viet Nam Is Issue in Elections," *St. Louis Post-Dispatch,* November 6, 1966, 14A.

61. James A. Wechsler, "GOP Non-Policy," *New York Post,* February 3, 1966, 26.

62. John Roche to Lawrence O'Brien, February 6, 1967, NSF Name File, Roche Memos, Johnson Library, quoted in Gibbons, *U.S. Government and the Vietnam War* 4:603.

63. James Reichley, "The American Squirearchy," *Harper's,* February 1966, 98–107. At the time he wrote the article, Reichley was the legislative secretary to Governor Scranton of Pennsylvania.

64. Harry McPherson, *A Political Education* (1972; Boston: Houghton Mifflin, 1988), 69.

65. *CR* 112 (October 19, 1966), 27523–24. See Mark A. Stoler, "What Did He Really Say? The 'Aiken Formula' for Vietnam Revisited," *Vermont History* 46 (1978): 100–108.

66. *CR* 112 (August 12, 1966), 19177–78.

67. In late September Dirksen inserted into the *Congressional Record* "The Temper of Our Times—An Analysis by the Senate Republican Policy Committee Staff on Issues of the Day," a document that he thought "warrants study by everyone." Far from inciting hawkish sentiment, when the document addresses the war it seems to appeal to pacifistic feelings: "In Place of Peace—War . . . One remembers the sight of the pitiful young wife clinging to her boyish husband on a railroad platform in Wilmington, Ill., as he was leaving for Ft. Sam Houston in San Antonio to join the army. . . . Even more, one recalls another reporter's story in North Carolina about watching a mother and father waiting silently in a railroad station for a train bringing home the body of their son, killed in Vietnam" (second ellipsis in original; undated quotation from *Los Angeles Times*) (*CR* 112 [September 26, 1966, 23811).

68. Zelman, "Senate Dissent and the Vietnam War," 172.

69. Richard N. Goodwin, *Remembering America* (Boston: Little, Brown, 1988), 453–55.

70. Shesol, *Mutual Contempt,* 288.

71. Newfield, *Robert Kennedy,* 128.

72. An interesting exercise for one seeking to understand the motivations of Robert Kennedy is to contrast his behavior during this period with that of his brother, Edward, a senator whose "genetic makeup" (figuratively and literally) was so similar. See the insightful article by Meg Greenfield, "The Senior Senator Kennedy," *The Reporter,* December 15, 1966, 19–24.

73. See footnote 14, this chapter.

74. See Betty Dowling (Boston) to Robert Kennedy, July 6, 1966; Robert Kennedy to Betty Dowling, July 22, 1966, RFK Senate Papers, Senate Correspondence: Subject File, 1966, Box 49. On Kennedy's generally negative attitude toward the Senate and its members, see Adam Walinksy interviewed by Thomas F. Johnston, 2nd interview (November 30, 1966), RFK Oral History Project, 50–52; Joseph Kraft interviewed by Roberta Greene (March 7, 1966), RFK Oral History Project, 16. See also quotation of Theodore Sorensen in Garry Wills, *The Kennedy Imprisonment* (New York: Pocket Books, 1983), 186.

75. See Shannon, "Making of President Robert Kennedy," 62–63.

CHAPTER 8

1. See Richard P. Stebbins, *The United States in World Affairs, 1967* (New York: Simon and Schuster for the Council on Foreign Relations, 1968), 1–3. See also *CR* 113 (August 9, 1967), 21226–27 (Fulbright); *CR* 113 (April 17, 1967), 9800–9802 (Clark speech inserted by Gruening).

2. In 1967, 9,377 American soldiers were killed and 62,024 were wounded. This brought the cumulative total of killed and wounded since 1961, respectively, to 16,021 and 99,762.

3. See Fred Halstead, *Out Now!* (New York: Monad, 1978), chap. 10.

4. The confrontations at the Pentagon were preceded by a much larger and peaceful rally of some one hundred thousand at the Lincoln Memorial, the largest crowd to congregate in Washington against the war up until that time. See Halstead, *Out Now!*, chap. 11. See also Norman Mailer, *The Armies of the Night* (New York: New American Library, 1968).

5. *CR* 113 (August 22, 1967), 23471.

6. Ibid., 23498. The appropriation subsequently passed with only Morse, Gruening, and Stephen Young dissenting (23502).

7. On May 17, 1967, sixteen Senate critics of the president's policies issued to the North Vietnamese government a declaration that in the absence of a negotiated settlement they "remain steadfastly opposed to any unilateral withdrawal of American forces from South Vietnam." Inserted and discussed by Frank Church (D-Idaho) at *CR* 113 (May 17, 1967), 13011–13.

8. John Rothschild, "Cooing Down the War: The Senate's Lame Doves," *Washington Monthly*, August 1971, 6–19, quotation at 13.

9. In my interview with Nelson in which he proudly recalled his vote against the 1965 supplemental, he admitted that he had made no effort at all to lobby or otherwise persuade any of his colleagues to join him, which contrasted with the strenuous effort made to compose the text of the speech in which he told the president, "Obviously you need my vote less than I need my conscience" (*CR* 111 [May 6, 1965], 9759). A recording of the interview is available at the Wisconsin Historical Society.

10. *CR* 113 (February 23, 1967), 4295.

11. Ibid., 4723–24.

12. *CR* 113 (February 28, 1967), 4938; 4948.

13. *CR* 113 (September 11, 1967), 25957; S.R. 44-90.

14. *CR* 113 (October 25, 1967), 30023; *CR* 113 (November 30, 1967), 34364.

15. Quoted in Gibbons, *U.S. Government and the Vietnam War* 4:917. Rusk's statement was made at the September 12, 1967, Tuesday Lunch in the presence of the president, McNamara, General Harold Johnson, and George Christian (917).

16. Fulbright's view of these hearings is explicated in Senate Committee on the Judiciary, Subcommittee on the Separation of Powers, *Separation of Powers,* 90th Cong., 2d sess., 1967, 51–52 (Seth Tillman reading report by Fulbright).

17. See ibid., 50.

18. Examples abound of liberals bolstering their own opposition to the war by citing Senate dissent. See, for example, *Nation* 204 (April 3, 1967), 439; *Nation* 204 (May 8, 1967), 578–79; *Nation* 204 (May 15, 1967), 610–11; *Nation* 204 (May 22, 1967), 642–43; Jay Neugeboren, "Disobedience Now," *Commonweal* 86 (June 16, 1967), 367–70; *Commonweal* 86 (June 30, 1967), 403–6; *New Republic,* July 27, 1967, 5–7, at 7; *Commonweal* 86 (July 28, 1967), 459–60.

19. See Halstead, *Out Now!* 600 and *passim*. For examples of pro-war senators using the protests as an easy target, see *CR* 113 (April 17, 1967), 9804–7 (Robert Byrd [D-W.Va.] and Hugh Scott [R-Pa.]); ibid., 9830–31 (Strom Thurmond [R-S.C.]); *CR* 113 (April 18, 1967), 9915 (Robert Byrd); *CR* 113 (April 20, 1967), 10241–42; *CR* 113 (April 24, 1967), 10568 (Russell Long [D-La.]); *CR* 113 (October 19, 1967), 29484–85 (Robert Byrd); *CR* 113 (October 20, 1967), 29548–57 (Robert Byrd, Stennis, and Herman Talmadge [D-Ga.]); *CR* 113 (October 23, 1967), 29660–61 (Robert Byrd). Compare *CR* 113 (October 23, 1967), 29661 (Mansfield disassociating himself from protesters). But also compare *CR* 112 (April 25, 1966), 8871 (insertion of Fulbright speech to students at Johns Hopkins describing their protests as "a moral and intellectual improvement on the panty raids of the 1950s").

20. See petitions and other materials evincing spread of dissent inserted by Gruening at *CR* 113 (January 16, 1967), 537–45.

21. Lippmann's syndicated column appeared, among other places, in the *Washington Post,* which Fulbright once proclaimed in the Senate to be "the most widely read newspaper in this body—except for local papers" (*CR* 114 [March 7, 1968], 5645). Dissenters continued the practice of invoking the authority of Lippmann and regularly inserting his columns relating to Vietnam. Such was the eagerness of the doves to call attention to Lippmann's views that sometimes the same column was inserted by different senators— for example, *CR* 113 (January 17, 1967), 629 (insertion by Clark of column titled "Alternatives"), 660 (insertion by Morse of same column); *CR* 113 (April 27, 1967), 11044 (insertion by Fulbright of column titled "Intervention of the General"); *CR* 113 (May 2, 1967), 11428–29 (insertion by Morse of same column); *CR* 113 (May 4, 1967), 11790 (insertion by Fulbright of column titled "The Honored Dead"), 11797 (insertion by Gruening of same column). The formidable status of Lippmann was indirectly acknowledged when McGee, a supporter of the president's policies, inserted a column by Howard K. Smith attacking him, "A Colleague's Appraisal of Walter Lippmann" (*CR* 113 [May 15, 1967], 12554).

22. Harry McPherson to Johnson, August 25, 1967, WHCF, ND 19/CO 312, Johnson Library, Box 228. For corroboration of Tydings's statement on Hart, see report of private

conversation in John L. Sweeny to Barefoot Sanders, August 25, 1967. These conversations, and others discussed in this chapter above, were conducted pursuant to the so-called Friendly Five survey by which various executive-branch officials were assigned to initiate supposedly private discussions in the late summer of 1967 with members of Congress with whom they were on friendly terms and to then report back on their contents. See Jean F. Lewis, "President Johnson Surveys the Congress" (paper, senior seminar in history, Georgetown University, 1990).

23. Charles D. Roche to Barefoot Sanders, August 25, 1967, Papers of Barefoot Sanders, Johnson Library, Box 12.

24. Townsend memorandum, n.d. [late August 1967], Papers of Barefoot Sanders, Johnson Library, Box 12.

25. Ken Gray to Barefoot Sanders, August 25, 1967, Papers of Barefoot Sanders, Johnson Library, Box 12.

26. Townsend memorandum, n.d, [late August 1967], Papers of Barefoot Sanders, Johnson Library, Box 12.

27. John L. Sweeny to Barefoot Sanders, August 25, 1967, Papers of Barefoot Sanders, Johnson Library, Box 12.

28. Andrew I. Hickey to Barefoot Sanders, August 25, 1967, Papers of Barefoot Sanders, Johnson Library, Box 12.

29. Ira Whitlock to Barefoot Sanders, August 25, 1967, Papers of Barefoot Sanders, Johnson Library, Box 12.

30. Richard C. Darling to Barefoot Sanders, August 25, 1967, Papers of Barefoot Sanders, Johnson Library, Box 12.

31. James R. Jones to Barefoot Sanders, August 25, 1967, Papers of Barefoot Sanders, Johnson Library, Box 12.

32. Samuel Merick to Barefoot Sanders, August 25, 1967, Papers of Barefoot Sanders, Johnson Library, Box 12; CR 113 (August 18, 1967), 23253–54.

33. Thomas R. Hughes to Barefoot Sanders, n.d. [late August 1967], Papers of Barefoot Sanders, Johnson Library, Box 12.

34. Joseph M. Bowman to Barefoot Sanders, August 24, 1967, same location.

35. See Ross K. Baker, *Friend and Foe in the U.S. Senate* (New York: The Free Press, 1980), 1–2, quoting an anonymous description of Pastore as one of the Johnson loyalists "who would walk across hot coals for him."

36. Larry O'Brien to Johnson, August 25, 1967, Papers of Barefoot Sanders, Johnson Library, Box 12.

37. Townsend memorandum, n.d. [late August 1967], Papers of Barefoot Sanders, Johnson Library, Box 12.

38. Jack Stempler to Barefoot Sanders, August 25, 1967, Papers of Barefoot Sanders, Johnson Library, Box 12.

39. Opinion surveys are interesting but cryptic. A poll taken in May and June 1967 found a tie at 48 percent between Americans who felt they did and did not "have a clear idea of what the Vietnam war is all about—that is what we are fighting for." George H. Gallup, *The Gallup Poll, 1935–1971* (New York: Random House, 1972), 3:2068. In mid-July when interviewees were asked if they favored a proposal to send one hundred thousand more troops to Vietnam, 40 percent approved, 49 percent disapproved, and 11 percent had no opinion. The same survey found that the president's handling of the war was

approved by only 33 percent, and disapproved by 52 percent, while 15 percent had no opinion (3:2074).

40. Compare Allen J. Matusow, *The Unraveling of America* (New York: Harper, 1986), 385.

41. Deborah Shapley, *Promise and Power: The Life and Times of Robert McNamara* (Boston: Little, Brown, 1993) 428. Shifting metaphors, Shapley also described the scene in the hearing room as "Christians and lions" (429).

42. Senate Committee on Armed Services, Preparedness Investigating Subcommittee, *Air War against North Vietnam,* 90th Cong., 1st sess., 1967.

43. The *New York Times,* September 1, 1967, covered the report on the front page, devoted its lead editorial to the report ("Generals Out of Control"), and reprinted its entire text.

44. Senate Committee on Armed Services and Committee on Foreign Relations, *Military Situation in the Far East,* 82d Cong., 1st sess., 1951.

45. See editorial, *New York Times,* September 1, 1967.

46. A sense of the degree to which times had changed since the 1950s is revealed in the debate on proposals made in 1967 to abolish the Subversive Activities Control Board. See *CR* 113 (October 23, 1967), 29716 (Daniel Brewster [D-Md.]); *CR* 113 (August 15, 1967), 22598 (William Proxmire [D-Wisc.]). Of course, to say that McCarthyism declined is not to say that it died. See Samuel C. Dunlop III to Richard Russell, April 28, 1967; Russell to Dunlop, May 3, 1967 (discussing "Reds" in State Department). Records of the Armed Services Committee, 90th Cong., General Correspondence, RG 46, Box 970, National Archives.

47. Compare Alfred O. Hero, *The Southerner and World Affairs* (Baton Rouge: Louisiana State University Press, 1965); Thomas A. Becnel, *Allen Ellender of Louisiana* (Baton Rouge: Louisiana State University Press, 1995), chap. 14 (emphasizing subject's foreign policy heterodoxy after World War II).

48. Compare remarks during debate on Gulf of Tonkin Resolution. *CR* 110 (August 7, 1964), 18411. See Caroline F. Ziemke, "Richard Russell and the 'Lost Cause' in Vietnam, 1954–1968," *Georgia Historical Quarterly* 72 (1988): 30–77, at 37–38; Michael Scott Downs, "A Matter of Conscience: John C. Stennis and the Vietnam War" (Ph.D. diss., Mississippi State University, 1989, emphasizing motivation of simple patriotism and "southern code of honor").

49. For example, *CR* 110 (August 7, 1964), 18411 (Russell); Senate Committee on Foreign Relations, *Supplemental Foreign Assistance Fiscal Year 1966—Vietnam,* 89th Cong., 2d sess., 1966, 597 (Russell Long).

50. See above, chap. 7, sec. III.

51. Robertson to Lawrence O'Brien, March 27, 1964, inserted by Morse at *CR* 110 (May 18, 1964), 11218; *CR* 111 (February 17, 1965), 2874–75 (Ellender questioning Thomas Dodd [D-Conn.]); Joseph M. Bowman to Barefoot Sanders, August 24, 1967, Papers of Barefoot Sanders, Johnson Library Box 12 (on Talmadge).

52. Senate Committee on Government Operations, Permanent Subcommittee on Investigations, *Improper Practices, Commodity Import Program, U.S. Foreign Aid, Vietnam,* 90th Cong., 1st sess., 1967. See July 25, 1967, Notes of the President's Luncheon Meeting with Secretary Rusk, Secretary McNamara, Walt Rostow and George Christian, Tom Johnson Notes of Meetings, Johnson Library, Box 1.

53. Senate Committee on the Judiciary, Subcommittee on the Separation of Powers, *Separation of Powers*, 90th Cong., 2d sess., 1967.

54. See Richard Scott, "Republicans and the Vietnam Debate," *Manchester Guardian Weekly*, October 19, 1967.

55. Inserted at *CR* 113 (May 9, 1967), 12030–41.

56. See Terry Dietz, *Republicans and Vietnam, 1961–1968* (Westport, Conn.: Greenwood, 1986), 117–18.

57. *CR* 113 (October 5, 1967), 28038.

58. Notes of the President's Meeting with Secretary Rusk, Secretary McNamara, Mr. Rostow, CIA Director Helms, and George Christian, October 3, 1967, Tom Johnson Notes of Meetings, Johnson Library, Box 1. Discussion of the resolution was initiated by Johnson.

59. See Michael William Flamm, "'Law and Order': Street Crime, Civil Disorder, and the Crisis of Liberalism" (Ph.D. diss., Columbia University, 1998).

60. See Robert Scheer and Warren Hinckle, "The Vietnam Lobby," *Ramparts,* July 1965, pp. 16–24. See also *I. F. Stone's Weekly,* January 11, 1965, praising an earlier article by Robert Scheer, "Hang Down Your Head, Tom Dooley," *Ramparts,* January–February 1965 for revealing "the extent to which this war from the beginning has been Cardinal Spellman's war." *Cf.* Gregory Allen Olsen, "Mike Mansfield's Ethos in the Evolution of United States Policy in Indochina" (Ph.D. diss., University of Minnesota, 1988), chap. 3.

61. See William W. Turner, *Power on the Right* (Berkeley, Calif.: Ramparts, 1971), 158–59.

62. *Liberty Letter,* January 1967.

63. See *CR* 113 (October 26, 1967), 30272–77 (Ripon Society); Charles Harker, acting executive secretary, Friends Committee on National Legislation to Clark, January 17, 1968, Clark Papers, Box 18(C), Historical Society of Pennsylvania.

64. See, for example, argumentative questions posed to official witnesses defending the president's tax surcharge proposal at a February 5, 1968, meeting of the Joint Economic Committee. Senate Joint Economic Committee, *The 1968 Economic Report of the President,* 90th Cong., 2d sess., 1968, 27 (Javits), 40–41 (Percy). See also Senate Committee on Appropriations, Subcommittee on Department of Defense and Committee on Armed Forces, *Supplemental Defense Appropriations and Authorizations, Fiscal Year 1967,* 90th Cong., 1st sess., 1967, esp. comments of Symington (95). On the tax surcharge, see Nigel Bowles, *The White House and Capitol Hill* (Oxford: Clarendon Press, 1987), chap. 6.

65. Don Oberdorfer, "Noninterventionism, 1967 Style," *New York Times Magazine,* September 17, 1967, 29–31, 102–12, quotation at 102.

66. *CR* 113 (July 10, 1967), 18094–96. Milton Young, for his part, blamed the Congo intervention on the administration's misguided insistence in following the policy initiated "after World War II" of seeking "to police the whole world" (18096).

67. Quoted in Gibbons, *U.S. Government and the Vietnam War* 4:810.

68. See July 13, 1967, Notes of the President's Meeting with the National Security Council Staff, Tom Johnson Notes of Meetings, Johnson Library, Box 1. Compare Stebbins, *United States in World Affairs,* 238–44. On the attitude of southern senators to the regimes of black Africa see Harry McPherson, *A Political Education* (1972; Boston: Houghton Mifflin, 1988), 53; Hero, *Southerner and World Affairs,* 187–91.

69. *CR* 113 (July 10, 1967), 18094–95.

70. Oberdorfer, "Noninterventionism," 31.

71. Compare William S. White, "U.S. Promises to Free World Challenged by Attack on Policy," *Washington Post,* March 13, 1968, A21.

72. Notes of the President's Meeting with Secretary Rusk, Secretary McNamara, Walt Rostow, George Christian, General Wheeler, October 23, 1967, Tom Johnson Notes of Meetings, Johnson Library, Box 1.

73. "Stu Symington: The Path of a High Level Defector," *Washington Post,* April 7, 1969, A20. See A. J. Langguth, *Our Vietnam* (New York: Simon & Schuster, 2000), 432.

74. *CR* 113 (January 23, 1967), 1191. The words quoted are from a speech titled "Vietnam—The High Price."

75. Valenti to Watson, December 14, 1967, Office Files of Marvin Watson, Johnson Library, quoted in Gibbons, IV, p. 831n.

76. Inserted by Gruening at *CR* 113 (September 28, 1967), 27131–32.

77. See Clayton Fritchey, "Who Belongs to the Senate's Inner Club?" *Harper's,* May 1971, 104–7.

78. *New York Times,* September 28, 1967.

79. A description of Morton's 1954 conversation with Russell is in Oberdorfer, "Noninterventionism," 32. On Morton and Symington generally see Sara Judith Smiley, "The Political Career of Thruston B. Morton: The Senate Years, 1956–1968" (Ph.D. diss., University of Kentucky, 1975); Ward Just, "Stu Symington: The Path of a High-Level Defector," *Washington Post,* April 7, 1969, A20; Flora Lewis, "The Education of a Senator," *Atlantic Monthly,* December 1971, p. 55–64. I am indebted to Joseph R. L. Sterne, then a congressional reporter for the (Baltimore) *Sun* for his suggestion that I focus on Symington as a figure in the story of the Vietnam Senate controversy. My understanding of Symington has also benefited from a May 2, 1995, taped telephone interview with Harriet Robnett, who had served as his legislative assistant.

80. Just, "Stu Symington."

81. Gruening believed that Morton's speech, in particular, had considerable influence on senators who had hitherto refrained from publicly expressing their doubts about the war. Interview of Gruening cited in Walter Arnold Zelman, "Senate Dissent and the Vietnam War, 1964–1968" (Ph.D. diss., University of California–Los Angeles, 1971), 272. See Don Oberdorfer, "The Wobble on the Hill," *New York Times Magazine,* December 17, 1967 (describing Morton's speech as "an instant sensation" because the senator was viewed "as a political weathervane and because of the forthrightness of his confession of error"). On the president's excited response to Morton's speech See Gibbons, *U.S. Government and the Vietnam War* 4:828.

CHAPTER 9

1. W. Scott Thompson and Donaldson D. Frizzell, eds., *The Lessons of Vietnam* (New York: Crane Russek, 1979), 100, quoted in Melvin Small, *Johnson, Nixon, and the Doves* (New Brunswick, N.J.: Rutgers University Press, 1988), 133.

2. See Stanley Karnow, *Vietnam: A History* (New York: Viking, 1983), 523–49; Pell to Rusk, February 2, 1968, Senate Committee on Foreign Relations, Marcy Chronological File, RG 46, National Archives.

3. See "69% in Poll Back a Pullout in War," *New York Times,* March 13, 1968. According to a Gallup survey conducted in late February, 49 percent of the respondents thought the involvement in Vietnam had been a mistake (compared to 41 percent who thought it had not been a mistake). The same survey found that only 33 percent of Americans thought the United States and its allies were making progress in Vietnam. George H. Gallup, *The Gallup Poll, 1935–1971* (New York: Random House, 1972), 3:2109. See also Robert Dallek, *Flawed Giant: Lyndon Johnson and His Times, 1961–1973* (New York: Oxford University Press, 1998), 526 (citing Gallup and Harris polls during this period finding public disapproval of the president's Vietnam policies to be, respectively, 50 and 62 percent).

4. Contemporary sources during this period abound with illustrations showing the spread and breadth of this opposition. See, for example, the authorities discussed, quoted, and inserted by Gruening at *CR* 114 (March 13, 1968), 6341–48.

5. *CR* 114 (February 28, 1968), 4548–51, quotations at 4548.

6. See *New York Times,* March 2, 1968, 45: "The Senator had emphasized that he was speaking only for himself, but the European markets seemed either not to have understood this or else chose to believe his remarks had more significance." See also Gabriel Kolko, *Anatomy of a War* (New York: Pantheon, 1985), 314.

7. See, for example, *CR* 114 (February 7, 1968), 2504 (Hugh Scott [R-Pa.]); *CR* 114 (February 14, 1968), 2977 (Harry S. Byrd, Jr. [D-Va.]); 2980–81 (Hartke); *CR* 114 (February 19, 1968), 3361–62 (James Pearson [R-Kans.]); *CR* 114 (February 21, 1968), 3805–11 (Church) and esp. *CR* 114 (March 7, 1968), 5644–67 (discussion with unusually wide participation including Fulbright, Jack Miller [R-Iowa], Hatfield, Javits, Church, Hartke, John Tower [R-Tex.], Nelson, Lausche, Mansfield, Stennis, McGovern, Clark, Hart, Gore, Claiborne Pell (D-R.I.), and Gruening). A speech by McGee, one of the few senators during this period willing to speak unequivocally in support of administration policy, is at *CR* 114 (February 7, 1968), 2513–14.

8. See comment of Dirksen after speeches by John Williams (R-Del.) and Javits: "Once more I salute a tremendously liberal senator from New York and one whom I could properly recognize as a very conservative, the Senator from Delaware, and how closely they see this problem and how closely they come in their recognition of what the remedy must ultimately be" (*CR* 114 [January 31, 1968], 1707).

9. William Berman, *William Fulbright and the Vietnam War* (Kent, Ohio: Kent State University Press, 1988), 94–95.

10. Deborah Shapley, *Promise and Power: The Life and Times of Robert McNamara* (Boston: Little, Brown, 1993), 454–56.

11. As is the rule in such matters, even prominent reporting of McNamara's denials had the effect of reinforcing public awareness of the accusations and keeping the issue on the front pages. See, for example, coverage in *Washington Post,* February 21, 1968 (front page); *New York Times,* February 21, 1968 (front page); February 22, 1968 (front page); February 25, 1968 (front page); February 24, 1968 (front page). See also *New York Times,* February 24, 1968, 28, editorial captioned "Half-Truths about Tonkin."

12. Senate Committee on Foreign Relations, *The Gulf of Tonkin, The 1964 Incidents,* 90th Cong., 2d sess., 1968, 52 (hereafter "*1968 Gulf of Tonkin Hearings*").

13. See Randall Bennett Woods, *Fulbright: A Biography* (Cambridge: Cambridge University Press, 1995), 476.

14. *1968 Gulf of Tonkin Hearings,* 83 (Morse).

15. Ibid., 54.

16. Ibid., 37 (Morse), 48 (Fulbright).

17. For example, ibid., 37 (Case), 40–42 (Fulbright), 45–46 (McCarthy), 45–46, 49–50, 83 (Morse).

18. Ibid., 78. McNamara denied knowledge of the hospitalization: "I think it would be a monstrous act if we sent a man to a psychiatric ward even if he told a falsehood to the committee, and I can't believe it was done" (78). Fulbright's biographer refers to the hospitalization as the senator's "ace in the hole." Woods, *Fulbright,* 478.

19. Concern about the gold crisis, in particular, by mid-March was especially intense. Coverage of the crisis moved from the financial pages to the front and editorial pages. See, for example, *Washington Post,* March 15, 1968 (banner headline fully stretched across front page: "London Shuts Markets in Gold Crisis"); *St. Louis Post-Dispatch,* March 14, 1968 (lead article on front page in large letters: "RUSH FOR GOLD RISES SHARPLY, THREATENS WORLD MONEY SYSTEM"); *Washington Post,* March 9, 1968 (lead editorial); *St. Louis Post-Dispatch,* March 12, 1968 (lead editorial); *New York Times,* March 12, 1968 (editorial).

20. Senate Committee on Foreign Relations, *Foreign Assistance Act of 1968, Part 1— Vietnam,* 90th Cong., 2d sess., 1968, 8–10.

21. Ibid., 98–99.

22. Ibid., 180; 191.

23. Ibid., 203.

24. Ibid., 104; 129; 104.

25. Ibid., 136; 94; 92; 93.

26. Ibid., 206.

27. Ibid., 202–3.

28. Ibid., 165; See also 126 (Pell); 81; 87.

29. Ibid., 149.

30. Ibid., 44.

31. Ibid., 151–52 (Aiken), 194 (Cooper).

32. Ibid., 79 (Gore pointing out contradiction between administration's claim of willingness to abide by Geneva Accords—which do not acknowledge permanent division of Vietnam—and administration's insistence on South Vietnamese self-determination).

33. See comment by Gore at ibid., 45: "Through thousands of years the Vietnamese have been one people. Perhaps they feel they have a right to move about within their own country."

34. Ibid., 138 (Fulbright).

35. See questions posed by Case at ibid., 91–92.

36. Ibid., 129 (Pell), 206 (Gore).

37. For example, ibid., 140 (Fulbright).

38. Ibid., 138.

39. Ibid., 163–65; 37–38.

40. Ibid., 50–51.

41. Ibid., 152–55; 56.

42. Ibid., 156.

43. Ibid., 56–57.

44. Ibid., 58, 141.

45. Ibid., 141–43.

46. It is a sign of the changing times that in referring to the war as part of the struggle against world communism, Dodd said, "I know this is considered a little old fashioned" (ibid., 199). And a little later he conceded: "I know I am on the minority side. I think. I know" (ibid., 209).

47. Ibid., 96.

48. Ibid., 58; 174.

49. Ibid., 74; 62.

50. Ibid., 108.

51. Ibid., 199.

52. Ibid., 118.

53. Ibid., 174; See also ibid., 174–75.

54. See discussion in sect. II below.

55. March 1968 was undoubtedly a period of "accelerated history." The leak of Westmoreland's request for 206,000 additional troops appeared in the *New York Times* for Sunday, March 10. The hearings, colored by anxieties stemming from the leak, were convened the next morning and continued through the following day (Tuesday, March 12), the day of the now-famous primary. Kennedy's announcement was officially made on March 16. The eclipse of the hearings can be measured in the coverage of the *New York Times*. The first day of hearings were granted the lead article at the right side of the front page; on the next morning, however, the New Hampshire primary was given this honored position as coverage of the hearings, titled in a more modest type-size, was moved to the far left side of the page. By the next day, the press was already giving front-page coverage to speculations about Robert Kennedy's intentions, coverage that was itself surpassed only by headlines about the gold crisis with a tone bordering on the apocalyptic. See, for example, *St. Louis Post-Dispatch,* March 14, 1968.

56. Philip Greer, "Rusk Testimony Sends Stock Averages Higher," *Washington Post,* March 12, 1968, D6. The article was commented on and inserted by Hartke at *CR* 114 (March 13, 1968), 6357–58.

57. William S. White, "U.S. Promises to Free World Challenged by Attack on Policy," *Washington Post,* March 13, 1968, A21.

58. *Public Papers of the President: Lyndon Johnson, 1968–1969* (Washington, D.C.: GPO, 1970, bk. 2.

59. See Notes of the President's Meeting with Jim Lucas, August 24, 1967 ("If all these people [Bishop Sheen, Fulbright, other members of Congress] wanted to help their President, they could come here and say to me privately what they are saying to the press. Its looks as though they are talking to Ho, not to me"); Notes of the President's Meeting with Chalmers Roberts of the Washington Post, October 13, 1967 (assenting to opinion of Roberts that "[a]11 of this discontent must be a factor in the thinking of Hanoi and Peiping"); Notes of the President's Meeting with Secretary Rusk, Secretary McNamara, Mr. Rostow, CIA Director Helms, and George Christian, October 3, 1967 ("This [Vietnamese Communist] Ph.D. also said, 'How can we believe anything Johnson says if his own people don't believe him?'"); Meeting with Congressional Leaders, January 31, 1968 ("I ask you to measure your statements before you make them. The greatest source of Communist propaganda statements is our own statements"). Tom Johnson Notes of Meetings, Johnson Library, Box 1. *Cf.* Notes of the President's Meeting with his Foreign Policy Advisers at the Tuesday Luncheon, March 19, 1967, Tom Johnson Notes

of Meetings, Johnson Library, Box 1, Clark Clifford commenting: "The enemy may feel he is doing so well politically that he need not do anything militarily. They see:

"—Debate in the Senate

"—The New Hampshire Primary

"—Quarrels over the war in Congress."

60. November 21 [1967] Meeting with Saigon Advisers, Tom Johnson Notes of Meetings, Johnson Library, Box 1.

61. Notes of the President's Meeting with Secretary Rusk, Secretary McNamara, General Wheeler, CIA Director Helms, Walt Rostow, George Christian, October 17, 1967 ("I do not think they have to have it televised"): Notes of the President's Meeting with Senior Foreign Policy Advisers, February 9, 1968, Tom Johnson Notes of Meetings, Johnson Library, Box 1: "We should deal with this as privately as possible. Attention and recognition is what he wants. . . . I will tell them . . . we are willing to give them all the facts, but not make a television show of it."

62. Notes of the President's Meeting with his Foreign Policy Advisers at the Tuesday Lunch, March 13, 1968, Tom Johnson Notes of Meetings, Johnson Library, Box 1 (viewing examination of Rusk by Dodd, Pell, Gore, and Fulbright). See also Notes of the President's Meeting with Foreign Policy Advisers, March 11, 1968, Tom Johnson Notes of Meetings, Johnson Library, Box 1.

63. Notes of the President's Meeting with Foreign Policy Advisers, February 20, 1968. At this meeting, among other things, Johnson asked McNamara which senators "took the lead in opposing and defending you?" McNamara replied: "Senator Lausche was on our side. Senator Morse did the most damage trying to prove we provoked the incident. Senator McCarthy was very nasty personally. Senator Cooper was decent. Senator Mundt did not find the opening he wanted. Sparkman was marginally helpful. So was Senator Mansfield and Senator Hickenlooper on one occasion." Later in the meeting Johnson commented to McNamara, "I suppose you have a better case on the fact that the attack occurred than on the charge we did not provoke the attack."

64. See, for example, Notes on the President's Meeting with Helen Thomas and Jack Horner, August 25, 1967, Tom Johnson Notes of Meetings, Johnson Library, Box 1.

65. See Dallek, *Flawed Giant,* 369–70.

66. See Jean P. Lewis, "President Johnson Surveys the Congress" (paper, senior seminar in history, Georgetown University, 1990).

67. Lawrence O'Brien, *No Final Victories* (Garden City, N.Y.: Doubleday, 1974), 214. O'Brien, then postmaster general, had personally conducted the interview with Pastore.

68. *Vietnam at War* (Novato, Calif.: Presidio, 1988), 464–65.

69. See, for example, Notes of the President's Meeting with Secretary McNamara, Undersecretary Katzenbach, George Christian, Walt Rostow, Joe Califano at the Tuesday Luncheon, August 8, 1967, Tom Johnson Notes of Meetings, Johnson Library, Box 1.

70. The Fulbright-Johnson exchange is described in Meeting of the President on July 25, 1967, with the Senate Committee Chairmen, Tom Johnson Notes of Meetings, Johnson Library, Box 1.

71. Memorandum of the President's Meeting with Senior Policy Advisers, March 4, 1968, Tom Johnson Notes of Meetings, Johnson Library, Box 1.

72. Notes of the President's Meeting with General Earle Wheeler, Joint Chiefs of Staff, and Craighton Abrams, March 26, 1968, Tom Johnson Notes of Meetings, Johnson Library, Box 1.

73. Notes of President's Meeting with the Democratic Congressional Leadership, February 6, 1967, Tom Johnson's Notes of Meetings, Johnson Library, Box 1.

74. Notes of the President's Meeting with Senior Policy Advisers, February 6, 1967, Tom Johnson Notes of Meetings, Johnson Library, Box 1.

75. Notes of the President's meeting with General Earle Wheeler, JCS and Craighton Abrams, March 26, 1968, Tom Johnson Notes of Meetings, Johnson Library, Box 1.

76. Douglas Frantz and David McKean, *Friends in High Places: The Rise and Fall of Clark Clifford* (Boston: Little, Brown, 1995), 230–31; Townsend Hoopes, *The Limits of Intervention* (New York: McKay, 1970), 198. Fulbright only relented in his pressure for Clifford to testify when he confided to the senator that his own views had changed and that a reassessment of the war was taking place at the Pentagon and White House. Communication between Clifford and Fulbright was facilitated by the fact that they were golfing companions. Frantz and McKean, *Friends in High Places,* 231.

77. Harry McPherson, *A Political Education* (1972; Boston: Houghton Mifflin, 1988), 436. See Kolko, *Anatomy of a War,* 320: "the conviction during March that Congress would no longer support escalation undoubtedly . . . weighed heavily in his calculations"; David M. Barrett, *Uncertain Warriors: Lyndon Johnson and His Vietnam Advisers* (Lawrence: University Press of Kansas, 1993), 111.

78. See, for example, Mike Manatos to Johnson, April 4, 1968, WHCF, ND 19/CO 312, Box 232, Johnson Library; See also Dallek, *Flawed Giant,* 530.

79. For example, *CR* 113 (February 27, 1967), 4607–20 (Clark); *CR* 112 (March 14, 1966), 5617–19 (Robert Kennedy).

80. Senate Committee on Foreign Relations, *Foreign Assistance Act of 1968, Part 1— Vietnam,* 90th Cong., 2d sess., 1968, 206.

81. All quotations from Arthur Schlesinger Jr., *Robert Kennedy and His Times* (Boston: Houghton Mifflin, 1978), 844.

82. See Gallup surveys summarized in Dallek, *Flawed Giant,* 570.

83. See Thomas J. McCormick, *America's Half-Century* (Baltimore: Johns Hopkins University Press, 1989), 155. See remarks of McGovern prior to insertion of Max Frankel, "Can We End the Cold War?" *New York Times Magazine,* January 27, 1967; *CR* 113 (January 6, 1967), 2683.

84. For a comprehensive survey of congressional resolutions concerning the war in the Nixon period, see *Congress and the Nation* (1969–73), 3:899–931. Of eighty-four roll call votes concerning the war in 1966–72, over eighty of these took place after Nixon's inauguration (3:900).

85. PL 93–148. See Anne-Marie Scheidt, "Origins and Enactment of the War Powers Resolution, 1970–73" (Ph.D. diss., State University of New York at Stony Brook, 1989); Thomas F. Eagleton, *War and Presidential Power: A Chronicle of Congressional Surrender* (New York: Liveright, 1974), arguing that Act is an abdication of congressional power.

86. See P. Edward Haley, *Congress and the Fall of South Vietnam and Cambodia* (Rutherford, N.J.: Dickinson University Press, 1982).

87. Although on January 12, 1991, Congress authorized the first Iraq war, the vote in the Senate was narrow and the debate—which included explicit references to Vietnam— was remarkable for the aggressive opposition of a broad range of Democratic senators. See *Congressional Quarterly Almanac* 46 (1990): 726–56. On October 11, 2002, the resolu-

tion on the second Iraq war passed 77-23. Democrats voted 29-21, Republicans 48-1. For Senate debate on Kosovo see *CR* 145 (May 3, 1999), 4514–47.

88. See *Congressional Quarterly Almanac* 54 (1999): S-23. The division on intervention in Yugoslavia was also expressed indirectly on a cloture vote to end debate on an amendment proposed by Trent Lott (R-Miss.) that would have prohibited funding military operations in any part of that country in the absence of an explicit authorization by Congress. The vote, which took place on March 23, 1999, was 55-4 for the motion (a majority, but short of the two-thirds needed for cloture), the Republicans voting 54-0 for the motion. The amendment was later withdrawn. *CQWR* 57 (March 27, 1999): 752.

89. See "Editorial Comments: NATO's Kosovo Intervention," *American Journal of International Law* 94 (1999).

90. See, e.g., *CR* 149 (Jan. 29 2003): 1712–19 (Byrd).

CONCLUSION

1. The authorities senators invoked when discussing their general political philosophies were typically statesmen of generations past. See David F. Schmitz, "Congress Must Draw the Line: Senator Frank Church and the Opposition to the Vietnam War and the Imperial Presidency," in *Vietnam and the American Political Tradition: The Politics of Dissent,* ed. Randall B. Woods (Cambridge: Cambridge University Press, 2003), 122 (influence on Church of William Borah and Franklin Roosevelt); Kyle Longley, "The Reluctant 'Volunteer': The Origins of Albert A. Gore's Opposition to the Vietnam War," in *Vietnam and the American Political Tradition,* ed. Woods, 220, 225 (influence on Gore of Cordell Hull, William Jennings Bryan, Woodrow Wilson, and Franklin Roosevelt); Randall Bennett Woods, *Fulbright: A Biography* (Cambridge: Cambridge University Press, 1995), 246 (influence on Fulbright of Woodrow Wilson).

2. See J. William Fulbright to Richard Russell, May 23, 1967, and accompanying letters from soldiers, Senate Armed Services Committee, RG 46, National Archives, Box 970. It is interesting that Fulbright believed that Russell should see these deeply disturbing letters.

3. Kai Bird, *The Color of Truth* (New York: Simon & Schuster, 1998), 327 (describing April 1965 conversation in which Lippman made argument to McGeorge Bundy).

4. See Peter Camejo, *Liberalism, Ultraleftism, and Mass Action* (New York: Monad pamphlet, 1972).

5. For example, Marcy to Fulbright, January 3, 1967; January 12, 1967; May 16, 1967; Marcy Chronological File, RG 46, National Archives. The chief of staff's membership in the Council on Foreign Relations is recorded in its annual reports (1964–68).

6. The best account of the internal disputes of the antiwar movement, including the debate on multi- versus single-issue approaches remains Fred Halstead, *Out Now!* (New York: Monad, 1978).

7. Supporters of the war have argued that even Fulbright's opposition to the war stemmed from his indifference to the plight of brown-skinned peoples. See Harry McPherson interviewed by T. H. Baker (Johnson Library Oral History, interview two, September 19, 1968), 10.

BIBLIOGRAPHY

My most valuable sources were also the most accessible: *The Congressional Record* and the transcripts of public hearings. In their use, I have taken particular guidance and inspiration from I. F. Stone, whose work on a shoestring budget and under pressure of weekly deadline has shown just how much can be learned from sources that are readily available if one is willing to read them carefully and critically. I was also able to find much of value in Senate committee records at the National Archives and among the large number of Senate-related documents at the Lyndon Baines Johnson Library. My visits to Austin would have been even more productive if they had not predated the transcription of many relevant telephone conversations that are now available there and whose further release in coming years can be expected to require many researchers—including me—to modify their conclusions.

Several sources offered little specific information about actions and events, but did much to educate me about the political culture that provided their context. The scholarly apparatus of this book does not do justice to the degree to which my views were shaped by the days I spent immersed in the work of contemporary journalists ranging from the *Dan Smoot Report* to the editorial pages of the *Wall Street Journal*. Needless to say, the contrasting perspectives that these sources offered gave me something of the feel of both travel through time and travel to different worlds. Likewise, interviews with those who served in the Senate and those who knew them, including several individuals not cited, did much to give depth to my picture of the Senate during the 1960s. Private collections of senators were valuable for the same reason, although to a lesser extent. Several of those I sampled (admittedly but a small fraction of the total that are now open) corroborated Anna K. Nelson's lament that many private collections of the recent past are "dominated by variations of the constituent form letter and offer very little about the personal views of the senator or representative" ("The Researchers Dilemma," in Robert H. Davidson and Richard C. Sachs, eds., *Understanding Congress: Research Perspectives* [Washington, D.C.: GPO, 1991], 64). Among the books listed, I owe a special debt to the works of William C. Gibbons, Randall Bennett Woods, Cecil V. Crabb, G. William Domhoff, and (especially) Carl Solberg.

I have excluded from this bibliography all specific citations to material inserted into the *Congressional Record,* material appended to published transcriptions of hearings, specific citations to archival documents, subdivisions of papers at the Lyndon Baines Johnson Library, subdivisions of papers at the John F. Kennedy Library other than the Robert F. Kennedy Senate Papers, citations to specific congressional authorizations and appropriations, most international agreements, and most short articles, columns, and editorials appearing in magazines and newspapers.

I. Legal Authorities

A. JOINT RESOLUTIONS

Cuba Resolution, P.L. 87-733.

Formosa Resolution, P.L. 84-4.

Middle East Resolution, P.L. 85-7.

Southeast Asia (Gulf of Tonkin) Resolution, P.L. 88-408.

B. SUPREME COURT ORDERS AND DISSENTS

DaCosta v. Laird, 405 U.S. 979 (1972).

Holmes v. United States, 391 U.S. 936 (1968).

Holtzman v. Schlesinger, 414 U.S. 1304 (1973).

Massachusetts v. Laird, 400 U.S. 886 (1970).

McArthur v. Clifford, 393 U.S. 1002 (1968).

Mora v. McNamara, 389 U.S. 934 (1967).

Velvel v. Nixon, 396 U.S. 1042 (1970).

C. OTHER LEGAL AUTHORITIES

Southeast Asia Collective Defense Treaty, 6 U.S.T. 81.

Treaty Banning Nuclear Weapons Tests in the Atmosphere, in Outer Space, and Under Water (Limited Test Ban Treaty), 14 U.S.T. 1313.

United Nations Charter, 59 Stat. 1031.

United States Constitution.

War Powers Act, P.L. 93–148.

II. Other Official Publications

Congressional Record.

Public Papers of the President: Lyndon Johnson, 1965. Washington, D.C.: GPO, 1966, bk. 1.

U.S. Congress. Joint Economic Committee. *The 1968 Economic Report of the President.* 90th Cong., 2d sess., 1968.

U.S. Congress. Senate. Committee on Appropriations. Subcommittee on Department of Defense and Committee on Armed Forces. *Supplemental Defense Appropriations and Authorizations, Fiscal Year 1967.* 90th Cong., 1st sess., 1967.

U.S. Congress. Senate. Committee on Armed Services, Preparedness Investigating Subcommittee. *Air War Against North Vietnam.* 90th Cong., 1st sess., 1967.

U.S. Congress. Senate. Committee on Armed Services and Committee on Foreign Relations. *Military Situation in the Far East.* 82d Cong., 1st sess., 1951.

U.S. Congress. Senate. Committee on Foreign Relations. *Changing American Attitudes toward Foreign Policy.* 90th Cong., 1st sess., 1967.

———. *Foreign Assistance Act of 1968, Part 1—Vietnam, Hearings.* 90th Cong., 2d sess., 1968.

———. *The Gulf of Tonkin: The 1964 Incidents.* 90th Cong., 2d sess., 1968.

———. *Nomination of John Foster Dulles to Be Secretary of State.* 83rd Cong., 1st sess., 1953.

———. *Nomination of Lincoln Gordon to Be Assistant Secretary of State for Inter-American Affairs.* 89th Cong., 2d sess., 1966.

———. *Psychological Aspects of International Relations.* 89th Cong., 2d sess., 1966.

———. *Supplemental Foreign Assistance Fiscal Year 1966—Vietnam.* 89th Cong., 2d sess., 1966.

———. *U.S. Commitments to Foreign Powers.* 90th Cong., 1st sess., 1967.

———. *The U.S. Government and the Vietnam War: Executive and Legislative Roles and Relationships.* Committee print 103-83. Washington, D.C.: GPO, 1994, pt. IV. Prepared at direction of Committee on Foreign Relations by the Congressional Research Service, Library of Congress. The volume shall be republished by Princeton University Press with William C. Gibbons of the Congressional Research Service credited as author.

———. *U.S. Policy with Respect to Mainland China.* 89th Cong., 2d sess., 1966.

———. *What Is Wrong with Our Foreign Policy?* 86th Cong., 1st sess., 1959.

U.S. Congress. Senate. Committee on Government Operations, Permanent Subcommittee on Investigations. *Improper Practices, Commodity Import Program, U.S. Foreign Aid, Vietnam.* 90th Cong., 1st sess., 1967.

U.S. Congress. Senate. Committee on the Judiciary. Subcommittee on the Administration of the Internal Security Act and Other Internal Security Laws. *Communist Youth Program.* 89th Cong., 1st sess., 1965.

———. Subcommittee to Investigate Problems Connected with Refugees and Escapees. *Refugee Problems in South Vietnam and Laos.* 89th Cong., 1st sess., 1965.

———. Subcommittee on the Separation of Powers, *Separation of Powers.* 90th Cong., 2d sess., 1967.

III. Archives

Clinton P. Anderson Papers, Library of Congress.

Clifford P. Case Papers, Rutgers University at New Brunswick, N.J.

Joseph S. Clark Papers, Historical Society of Pennsylvania, Philadelphia.

J. William Fulbright Papers, University of Arkansas, Fayetteville.

Jacob Javits Papers, State University of New York at Stony Brook.

Lyndon Baines Johnson Library, University of Texas, Austin.

Records of the Senate Armed Services Committee, RG 46, National Archives, Main
  Building, Washington, D.C.

Records of the Senate Committee on Foreign Relations, RG 46, National Archives, Main
  Building, Washington, D.C.

Records of the Senate Committee on the Judiciary, RG 46, National Archives, Main
  Building, Washington, D.C.

Robert F. Kennedy Senate Papers, John F. Kennedy Library, Boston.

IV. Books and Articles

Acheson, Dean. *Present at the Creation.* New York: Norton, 1969.

Alford, N. H., Jr., and R. A. Falk. "Legality of the United States Participation in the
  Viet Nam Conflict: A Symposium." *Yale Law Journal* 75 (1966): 1085–1160.

Ambrose, Stephen. *Eisenhower.* Vol. 2. New York: Simon and Schuster, 1984.

———. *Rise to Globalism.* 5th ed. New York: Penguin, 1988.

Ashby, LeRoy, and Rod Gramer. *Fighting the Odds: The Life of Senator Frank Church.*
  Pullman: Washington State University Press, 1994.

Austin, Anthony. *The President's War: The Story of the Tonkin Gulf Resolution and How the
  Nation Was Trapped in Vietnam.* Philadelphia: Lippincott, 1971.

Bailey, Thomas A. *A Diplomatic History of the United States.* 9th ed. Englewood Cliffs, N.J.:
  Prentice Hall, 1974.

Baker, Ross K. *Friend and Foe in the U.S. Senate.* New York: The Free Press, 1980.

Baltzell, E. Digby. *The Protestant Establishment* New York: Vintage. 1966 [1964].

Barrett, David M. *Uncertain Warriors: Lyndon Johnson and His Vietnam Advisers.* Lawrence:
  University Press of Kansas, 1993.

Becnel, Thomas A. *Allen Ellender of Louisiana.* Baton Rouge: Louisiana State University
  Press, 1995.

Berman, Larry. *Planning a Tragedy.* New York: Norton, 1982.

Berman, William C. *William Fulbright and the Vietnam War.* Kent, Ohio: Kent State
  University Press, 1988.

Beschloss, Michael R., ed. *Reaching for Glory: Lyndon Johnson's Secret White House Tapes,
  1964–1965.* New York: Simon and Schuster, 2001.

———. *Taking Charge: The Johnson White House Tapes, 1963–1964.* New York: Simon and
  Schuster, 1997.

Bird, Kai. *The Color of Truth.* New York: Simon & Schuster, 1998.

Bohlen, Charles E. *The Transformation of American Foreign Policy.* New York: Norton, 1969.

Bowles, Nigel. *The White House and Capitol Hill.* Oxford: Clarendon, 1987.

Brinkley, Alan. "Minister without Portfolio." *Harper's,* February 1983, 30–46.

Brinton, Crain. *Anatomy of Revolution.* New York: Vintage, 1965.

Brodie, Bernard. *War and Politics.* New York: Macmillan, 1973.

Brown, Eugene. *J. William Fulbright: Advice and Dissent.* Iowa City: University of Iowa Press, 1985.

Bundy, McGeorge. "The Presidency and the Peace." *Foreign Affairs* 42 (April 1964): 353–65.

Burns, James MacGregor. Foreword to Joseph S. Clark et al., *The Senate Establishment.* New York: Hill and Wang, 1963.

Camejo, Peter. *Liberalism, Ultraleftism, and Mass Action.* New York: Monad (pamphlet), 1972.

Carleton, William G. *The Revolution in American Foreign Policy.* 2nd ed. New York: Random House, 1967 [1954].

Caro, Robert A. *The Years of Lyndon Johnson: Master of the Senate.* New York: Vintage, 2002.

Cheever, Daniel S., and H. Field Haviland Jr. *American Foreign Policy and the Separation of Powers.* Cambridge, Mass.: Harvard University Press, 1952.

Church, Frank. "We Are in Too Deep in Asia and Africa." *The New York Times Magazine,* February 14, 1965, 30–31, 84.

Clark, Joseph S., et al. *The Senate Establishment.* New York: Hill and Wang, 1963.

Coffin, Tristram. *Senator Fulbright: Portrait of a Public Philosopher.* New York: Dutton, 1966.

Colegrove, Kenneth W. *The American Senate and World Peace.* New York: Vanguard, 1944.

"Congress, the President, and the Power to Commit Forces to Combat." *Harvard Law Review* 81 (1968): 1771–1805.

Crabb, Cecil V., Jr. *Bipartisan Foreign Policy: Myth or Reality?* Evanston, Ill.: Row, Peterson, 1957.

Dahl, Robert A. *Congress and Foreign Policy.* New York: Norton, 1964.

Dallek, Robert. *Flawed Giant: Lyndon Johnson and His Times, 1961–1973.* New York: Oxford University Press, 1998.

Davidson, Phillip B. *Vietnam at War.* Novato, Calif.: Presidio, 1988.

Davies, Richard O. *Defender of the Old Guard: John Bricker and American Politics.* Columbus: Ohio State University Press, 1993.

Deakin, James. *Lyndon Johnson's Credibility Gap.* Washington, D.C.: Public Affairs, 1968.

DeBenedetti, Charles (Charles Chatfield, assisting author). *An American Ordeal: The Antiwar Movement of the Vietnam Era.* Syracuse, N.Y.: Syracuse University Press, 1990.

de Gaulle, Charles. *The Complete War Memoirs of Charles de Gaulle.* Translated by Jonathan Griffin. New York: Simon and Schuster, 1964.

de Toledano, Ralph. *R.F.K: The Man Who Would Be President.* New York: Putnam's, 1967.

Dietz, Terry. *Republicans and Vietnam, 1961–1968.* Westport, Conn.: Greenwood, 1986.

Divine, Robert A. *A Second Chance: The Triumph of Internationalism in America during World War II.* New York: Atheneum, 1967.

Domhoff, G. William. *The Higher Circles.* New York: Vintage, 1970.

———. *Who Rules America?* Englewood Cliffs, N.J.: Prentice Hall, 1967.

Douglas, Paul. *In the Fullness of Time: The Memoirs of Paul H. Douglas.* New York: Harcourt, Brace, 1971.

Dunne, Gerald T. *Grenville Clark, Public Citizen.* New York: Farrar, Straus, 1986.

Eagleton, Thomas F. *War and Presidential Power: A Chronicle of Congressional Surrender.* New York: Liveright, 1974.

"Editorial Comments: NATO's Kosovo Intervention." *American Journal of International Law* 94 (1999).

Elkins, Stanley. *Slavery.* 2nd ed. Chicago: University of Chicago Press, 1968.

Evans, Rowland, and Robert Novak. *Lyndon B. Johnson: The Exercise of Power.* New York: New American Library, 1966.

Fairlie, Henry. "Political Commentary." *The Spectator* 195 (September 29, 1955): 379–81.

Farnsworth, David N. *The Senate Committee on Foreign Relations.* Urbana: University of Illinois Press, 1961.

Fitzgerald, Frances. *Fire in the Lake.* New York: Vintage, 1973.

Foley, Michael. *The New Senate: Liberal Influence on a Conservative Institution, 1959–1972.* New Haven, Conn.: Yale University Press, 1980.

Frantz, Douglas, and David McKean. *Friends in High Places: The Rise and Fall of Clark Clifford.* Boston: Little, Brown, 1995.

Fritchey, Clayton. "Who Belongs to the Senate's Inner Club?" *Harper's,* May 1971, 104–7.

Frye, Alton, and Jack Sullivan. "Congress and Vietnam: The Fruits of Anguish." In *American Society and the Future of American Foreign Policy,* edited by Anthony Lake, 194–215. New York: New York University Press, 1976.

Fulbright, J. William. "American Foreign Policy in the Twentieth Century under an Eighteenth-Century Constitution," *Cornell Law Quarterly* 47 (1961): 1–13.

———. *The Arrogance of Power.* New York: Random House, 1966.

Gaddis, John Lewis. *Strategies of Containment.* New York: Oxford University Press, 1982.

Gallup, George H. *The Gallup Poll, 1935–1971.* Vol. 3. New York: Random House, 1972.

Garson, Barbara. *MacBird.* Berkeley, Calif.: Grassy Knoll Press, 1966.

Gibbons, William C. *The U.S. Government and the Vietnam War: Executive and Legislative Roles and Relationships.* 4 Vols. Princeton, N.J.: Princeton University Press, 1984–95.

Gibson, Hugh. *The Road to Foreign Policy.* Garden City, N.Y.: Doubleday, 1944.

Gibson, James William. *The Perfect War: The War We Couldn't Lose and How We Did.* New York: Vintage, 1988.

Gitlin, Todd. "Counter-Insurgency: Myth and Reality in Greece." In *Containment and Revolution: Western Policy toward Social Revolution: 1917 to Vietnam,* edited by David Horowitz. London: Blond, 1967.

Gittings, John. "China's Military Strategy." *The Nation* 200 (Jan. 18, 1965): 43–46.

Goodwin, Richard N. *Remembering America.* Boston: Little, Brown, 1988.

Goulden, Joseph C. *Truth Is the First Casualty.* Chicago: Rand McNally, 1969.

Graebner, Norman A. *The New Isolationism: A Study in Politics and Foreign Policy since 1950.* New York: Ronald, 1956.

Greenfield, Meg. "The Senior Senator Kennedy." *The Reporter,* December 15, 1966, 19–24.

Grimmett, Richard F. "Who Were the Senate Isolationists?" *Pacific Historical Review* 42 (Nov. 1973): 479–98; reprinted in *To Advise and Consent: The United States Congress and Foreign Policy in the Twentieth Century,* edited by Joel Silbey, 1:183–202. Brooklyn: Carlson, 1991.

Guinsberg, Thomas N. *The Pursuit of Isolationism in the United States Senate from Versailles to Pearl Harbor.* New York: Garland, 1982.

Gunther, Gerald. *Cases and Materials on Constitutional Law.* 9th ed. Mineola, N.Y.: Foundation Press, 1975.

Gunther, John. *Inside U.S.A.* New York: Harper, 1947.

Halberstam, David. *The Best and the Brightest.* New York: Random House, 1972.

———. *The Powers That Be.* Paperback ed. New York: Dell, 1979.

Haley, P. Edward. *Congress and the Fall of South Vietnam and Cambodia.* Rutherford, N.J.: Dickinson University Press, 1982.

Halperin, Morton H. *Bureaucratic Politics and Foreign Policy.* Washington, D.C.: Brookings, 1974.

Halstead, Fred. *Out Now!* New York: Monad, 1978.

Hero, Alfred O. *The Southerner and World Affairs.* Baton Rouge: Louisiana State University Press, 1965.

Herring, George C. *America's Longest War: The United and Vietnam: 1950–1975.* 2nd ed. New York: Knopf, 1986.

Hodgson, Godfrey. *America in Our Time,* 111–33. Garden City, N.Y.: Doubleday, 1976.

Hoopes, Townsend. *The Limits of Intervention.* New York: McKay, 1970.

Howe, Irving. *Socialism and America.* San Diego: Harcourt Brace Jovanovich, 1985.

Hull, Cordell. *The Memoirs of Cordell Hull.* New York: Macmillan, 1948, vol. II.

Isaacson, Walter, and Evan Thomas. *The Wise Men.* New York: Simon and Schuster, 1986.

Jewell, Malcolm E. *Senatorial Politics and Foreign Policy.* Westport, Conn.: Greenwood, 1974 [1962].

Johnson, Haynes, and Bernard M. Gwertzman. *Fulbright the Dissenter.* Garden City, N.Y.: Doubleday, 1968.

Johnson, Robert David. "Ernest Gruening and the Tonkin Gulf Resolution." *Journal of American–East Asian Relations* 12 (1993): 111–35.

Johnson, Robert David. *The Peace Progressives and American Foreign Policy.* Cambridge, Mass.: Harvard University Press, 1995.

Just, Ward. "Stu Symington: The Path of a High Level Defector." *Washington Post,* Apr. 7, 1969, A20.

Kaiser, David. *American Tragedy: Kennedy, Johnson, and the Origins of the Vietnam War.* Cambridge: Harvard University Press, 2001.

Karnow, Stanley. *Vietnam: A History.* New York: Viking, 1983.

Kearns, Doris. *Lyndon Johnson and the American Dream.* New York: Harper, 1976.

Kellerman, Barbara. *The Political Presidency.* New York: Oxford University Press, 1984.

Kennan, George. "Polycentrism and Western Policy." *Foreign Affairs* 42 (January 1964): 171–83.

Kenworthy, E. W. "The Fulbright Idea of Foreign Policy." *New York Times Magazine,*
    May 10, 1959, 10–11, 74–78.

Keohane, Robert O. "Realism, Neorealism, and the Study of World Politics." In *Neo-
    realism and Its Critics,* edited by Robert O. Keohane. New York: Columbia Univer-
    sity Press, 1986.

Kimball, Warren F. *The Most Unsordid Act: Lend-Lease, 1939–1941.* Baltimore: Johns
    Hopkins University Press, 1969.

Kirk, Grayson. "World Perspectives, 1964." *Foreign Affairs* 43 (October 1964): 1–14.

Knock, Thomas J. "'Come Home America'; The Story of George McGovern." In *Vietnam
    and the American Political Tradition: The Politics of Dissent,* edited by Randall B.
    Woods, 82–120. Cambridge: Cambridge University Press, 2003.

Kolko, Gabriel. *Anatomy of a War: Vietnam, the United States, and the Modern Historical
    Experience.* New York: Pantheon, 1985.

Lane, Thomas. *The War for the World.* San Diego: Viewpoint Books, 1968.

Langguth, A. J. *Our Vietnam: The War, 1954–1975.* New York: Simon & Schuster, 2000.

"Legality of the United States Participation in the Viet Nam Conflict: A Symposium."
    Yale Law Journal 75 (1966): 1085–160.

Lepper, Mary Milling. *Foreign Policy Formulation: A Case Study of the Nuclear Test Ban Treaty
    of 1963.* Columbus, Ohio: Merrill, 1971.

Levering, Ralph B. *The Public and American Foreign Policy, 1918–1978.* New York: Morrow,
    for the Foreign Policy Association, 1978.

Lewis, Flora. "The Education of a Senator." *Atlantic Monthly,* December 1971, 55–64.

Logevall, Fredrik. *Choosing War: The Last Chance for Peace and the Escalation of the War in
    Vietnam.* Berkeley: University of California Press, 1999.

———. *The Origins of the Vietnam War.* Pearson/Longman: Harlow, England, 2001.

Longley, Kyle. "The Reluctant 'Volunteer': The Origins of Albert A. Gore's Opposition
    to the Vietnam War." In *Vietnam and the American Political Tradition: The Politics of
    Dissent,* edited by Randall B. Woods, 204–36. Cambridge: Cambridge University
    Press, 2003.

Lunch, William L. and Peter W. Sperglich. "American Political Opinion and the War in
    Vietnam." *Western Political Quarterly* 32 (1979): 121–44.

Mailer, Norman. *The Armies of the Night.* New York: New American Library, 1968.

Mann, Robert. *A Grand Illusion: America's Descent into Vietnam.* New York: Basic Books, 2001.

Matthews, Donald R. *U.S. Senators and Their World.* Chapel Hill: University of North
    Carolina Press, 1960.

Matusow, Allen J. *The Unraveling of America: A History of Liberalism in the 1960s.* New York:
    Harper, 1986.

McBirnie, William Steuart. *Who Really Rules America?* Glendale, Calif.: Center for
    American Research and Education, 1986.

McCormick, Thomas J. *America's Half-Century.* Baltimore: Johns Hopkins University
    Press, 1989.

McGhee, George C. "East-West Relations." Speech delivered before German Foreign Policy Society at the Redoute, Bad, Godesberg. Feb. 18, 1964.

McGirr, Lisa. *Suburban Warriors.* Princeton, N.J.: Princeton University Press, 2001.

McGovern, George. *Grassroots.* New York: Random House, 1977.

McKeever, Porter. *Adlai Stevenson: His Life and Legacy.* New York: Morrow, 1986.

McLuhan, Marshall. *Understanding Media: The Extensions of Man.* Rev. paperback ed. New York: McGraw-Hill, 1964.

McPherson, Harry. *A Political Education: A Washington Memoir.* Boston: Houghton Mifflin, 1988 [1972].

Mills, C. Wright. *The Power Elite.* New York: Oxford University Press, 1956.

Moise, Edwin. *Tonkin Gulf and the Escalation of the Vietnam War.* Chapel Hill: University of North Carolina Press, 1996

Murrin, John. "The Great Inversion, or Court Versus Country: A Comparison of the Revolution Settlements in England (1688–1721) and America (1776–1816)." In *Three British Revolutions,* edited by J. G. A. Pocock, 368–453. Princeton, N.J.: Princeton University Press, 1980.

Myers, David S. *Foreign Affairs and the 1964 Presidential Election in the United States.* Meerut, India: Sadhna Prakashan, 1972.

Namier, Lewis. "The Biography of Ordinary Men." In *Skyscrapers and Other Essays,* 44–53. Freeport, N.Y.: Books for Libraries, 1968 [1931].

Namier, Lewis, and John Brooke. *The History of the House Parliament: The House of Commons, 1754–1790.* 2 vols. London: London Parliament Trust of Her Majesty's Stationery Office, 1964.

Newfield, Jack. *Robert Kennedy: A Memoir.* New York: Dutton, 1969.

Oberdorfer, Don. "Noninterventionism, 1967 Style." *New York Times Magazine,* September 17, 1967, 29–31, 102–12.

———. "The Wobble on the Hill." *New York Times Magazine,* December 17, 1967, 30–31, 98–107.

O'Brien, Lawrence. *No Final Victories.* Garden City, N.Y.: Doubleday, 1974.

Oshinsky, David M. *A Conspiracy So Immense: The World of Joe McCarthy.* New York: Free Press, 1983.

Patterson, James T. *Grand Expectations: The United States, 1945–1974.* New York: Oxford University Press, 1996.

———. *Mr. Republican: A Biography of Robert A. Taft.* Boston: Houghton Mifflin, 1972.

Peirce, Neal R. *The Great Plains States.* New York: Norton, 1980.

———. *The Megastates of America.* New York: Norton, 1972.

Pentagon Papers. Vol. 3. New York Times ed. Toronto: Bantam, 1971; Gravel ed., Boston: Beacon, 1971.

Pepper, Claude, with Hays Gorev. *Pepper: Eyewitness to a Century.* San Diego: Harcourt, Brace, 1987.

Powell, Lee Riley. *J. William Fulbright and America's Lost Crusade.* Little Rock, Ark.: Rose, 1984.

Powers, Thomas. *Vietnam: The War at Home, Vietnam, and the American People, 1964–1968*. New York: Grossman, 1973.

Racic, Obrad. "NATO: Abandonment of the Legal Norms of the Constituent Treaty." *Jugoslovenska revija za medjunarodno pravo (Yugoslav Review of International Law)* 1–3 (1999): 116–51.

Raskin, Marcus. "JFK." In "AHR Forum: JFK and the Culture of Violence." *American Historical Review* 97 (1992): 487–99.

Reedy, George E. *The U.S. Senate: Paralysis or a Search for Consensus?* New York: Crown, 1986.

Reichard, Gary W. "Divisions and Dissent: Democrats and Foreign Policy, 1952–1956." *Political Science Quarterly* 93 (1978): 51–72. Reprinted in *To Advise and Consent: The United States Congress and Foreign Policy in the Twentieth Century*, edited by Joel H. Silbey, 1:273–94. Brooklyn: Carlson, 1991.

———. *Politics as Usual: The Age of Truman and Eisenhower*. Arlington Heights, Ill.: Davidson, 1988.

———. *The Reaffirmation of Republicanism: Eisenhower and the Eighty-third Congress*. Knoxville: University of Tennessee Press, 1975.

Reichley, James. "The American Squirearchy." *Harper's*, February 1966, 98–107.

Rivers, William L. *The Opinionmakers*. Boston: Beacon, 1965.

Robinson, Frank M., and Earl Kemp, eds. *The Truth about Vietnam*. San Diego: Greenleaf Classics, 1966.

Robinson, James A. *Congress in Foreign Policy: A Study in Legislative Influence and Initiative*. Homewood, Ill.: Dorsey, 1962.

Ross, Douglas. *Robert F. Kennedy: Apostle of Change*. New York: Trident, 1968.

Rothschild, John. "Cooing Down the War: The Senate's Lame Doves." *Washington Monthly*, August 1971, 6–19.

Rovere, Richard H. "Letter from Washington." *New Yorker*, October 6, 1962, 148–57.

———. "Notes on the Establishment in America." *American Scholar* 30 (1961): 489–495.

Safire, William. *Safire's Political Dictionary*. New York: Random House, 1978.

Schapsmeier, Edward L., and Frederick H. Schapsmeier. *Dirksen of Illinois*. Urbana: University of Illinois Press, 1985.

Scheer, Robert, and Warren Hinckle. "The Vietnam Lobby." *Ramparts*, July 1965, 16–24.

Schlafly, Phyllis. *A Choice, Not an Echo*. Alton, Ill.: Pere Marquette, 1964.

Schlesinger, Arthur M., Jr. *Robert Kennedy and His Times*. Boston: Houghton Mifflin, 1978.

Schmitz, David F. "Congress Must Draw the Line: Senator Frank Church and the Opposition to the Vietnam War and the Imperial Presidency." In *Vietnam and the American Political Tradition: The Politics of Dissent*, edited by Randall B. Woods, 121–48. Cambridge: Cambridge University Press, 2003.

Shannon, William V. *The Heir Apparent: Robert Kennedy and the Struggle for Power*. New York: Macmillan, 1967.

———. "The Making of President Robert Kennedy." *Harper's*, October 1966, 62–68.

Shapley, Deborah. *Promise and Power: The Life and Times of Robert McNamara.* Boston: Little, Brown, 1993.

Shesol, Jeff. *Mutual Contempt: Lyndon Johnson, Robert Kennedy, and the Feud That Defined a Decade.* New York: Norton, 1998.

Shoup, Lawrence H., and William Minter. *Imperial Brain Trust: The Council on Foreign Relations and United States Foreign Policy.* New York: Monthly Review, 1977.

Shulman, Jeffrey, and Teresa Rogers. *A Day for the Earth.* Frederick, Md.: Twenty-First Century, 1992.

Small, Melvin. *Johnson, Nixon, and the Doves.* New Brunswick, N.J.: Rutgers University Press, 1988.

Smith, A. Robert. *The Tiger in the Senate: The Biography of Wayne Morse.* Garden City, N.Y.: Doubleday, 1962.

Smoot, Dan. *The Invisible Government.* Dallas: The Dan Smoot Report, 1962.

Solberg, Carl. *Riding High: America in the Cold War.* New York: Mason and Lipscomb, 1973.

Spanier, John W. . *The Truman-MacArthur Controversy and the Korean War.* Cambridge, Mass.: Belknap, 1959.

Stebbins, Richard P. *The United States in World Affairs, 1967.* New York: Simon and Schuster, for the Council on Foreign Relations, 1968.

Steel, Ronald. *Walter Lippmann and the American Century.* New York: Vintage, 1980.

Stephanson, Anders. *Kennan and the Art of Foreign Policy.* Cambridge, Mass.: Harvard University Press, 1989.

Stern, Sol. "The Defense Intellectuals." *Ramparts,* February 1967, 31–37.

Stoler, Mark A. "What Did He Really Say? The 'Aiken Formula' for Vietnam Revisited." *Vermont History* 46 (1978): 100–108.

Stormer, John A. *None Dare Call It Treason.* Forissant, Mo.: Liberty Bell Press, 1964.

"Symposium on Neutrality Legislation." *American Law School Review* 8 (1938): 1085–1100.

Taylor, Glen. *The Way It Was with Me.* Secaucus, N.J.: Lyle Stuart, 1979.

Thomas, Evan. *Robert Kennedy: His Life.* New York: Simon & Schuster, 2000.

Turner, Kathleen J. *Lyndon Johnson's Dual War: Vietnam and the Press.* Chicago: University of Chicago Press, 1985.

Turner, William W. *Power on the Right.* Berkeley, Calif.: Ramparts, 1971.

Vandenberg, Arthur H., Jr., ed. *The Private Papers of Senator Vandenberg.* Boston: Houghton Mifflin, 1952.

van der Pijl, Kees. *The Making of an Atlantic Ruling Class.* London: Verso, 1984.

Wallace, Henry. *Century of the Common Man.* New York: Reynal and Hitchcock, 1943.

White, William S. *Citadel: The Story of the United States Senate.* New York: Harper, 1956.

Williams, William Appleman. *The Tragedy of American Diplomacy.* New York: Norton, 1972 [1959].

Willkie, Wendell. *One World.* New York: Simon and Schuster, 1943.

Wills, Garry. "Introduction." In *Scoundrel Time,* by Lillian Hellman, 3–34. Boston: Little, Brown, 1976.

————. *The Kennedy Imprisonment*. New York: Pocket Books, 1983.

Wiltz, John Edward. "The MacArthur Inquiry, 1951." In *Congress Investigates, 1792–1974*, edited by Arthur Schlesinger and Roger Bruns, 383–430. New York: Chelsea House, 1975.

————. "The Nye Munitions Committee, 1934." In *Congress Investigates, 1792–1974*, edited by Arthur Schlesinger and Roger Bruns, 247–84. New York: Chelsea House, 1975.

Windchy, Eugene C. *Tonkin Gulf.* Garden City, N.Y.: Doubleday, 1971.

Wittner, Lawrence S. *Rebels against War: The American Peace Movement, 1941–1960.* New York: Columbia University Press, 1969.

Woods, Randall Bennett. *Fulbright: A Biography.* Cambridge: Cambridge University Press, 1995.

Woods, Randall Bennett, ed. *Vietnam and the American Political Tradition: The Politics of Dissent.* Cambridge: Cambridge University Press, 2003.

Yoder, Jon A. "The United World Federalists: Liberals for Law and Order." In *Peace Movements in America*, edited by Charles Chatfield, 95–115. New York: Schocken, 1973.

Ziemke, Caroline F. "Richard Russell and the 'Lost Cause' in Vietnam, 1954–1968." *Georgia Historical Quarterly* 72 (1988): 30–77.

V. Unpublished scholarship

Downs, Michael Scott. "A Matter of Conscience: John C. Stennis and the Vietnam War." Ph.D. diss., Mississippi State University, 1989.

Flamm, Michael William. "'Law and Order': Street Crime, Civil Disorder, and the Crisis of Liberalism." Ph.D. diss., Columbia University, 1998.

Lewis, Jean P. "President Johnson Surveys the Congress." Paper, senior seminar in history, Georgetown University, 1990.

Mandel, Jerry E. "A Critical Analysis of the Form of Communication in Charles H. Percy's 1966 Senatorial Campaign." Ph.D. diss. (speech), Purdue University, 1968.

Morgan, Francesca Constance. "Unlikely Rebel: J. William Fulbright, His 1966 Hearings and Their Impact on American Politics." Undergraduate thesis, Harvard University, 1990.

Olsen, Gregory Allen. "Mike Mansfield's Ethos in the Evolution of United States Policy in Indochina." Ph.D. diss. (speech), University of Minnesota, 1988.

Scheidt, Anne-Marie. "Origins and Enactment of the War Powers Resolution, 1970–73." Ph.D. diss., State University of New York at Stony Brook, 1989.

Smiley, Sara Judith. "The Political Career of Thruston B. Morton: The Senate Years, 1956–1968." Ph.D. diss., University of Kentucky, 1975.

Stone, Gary Steven. "The Divided Center: Michael Harrington, American Social Democracy and the Vietnam War." M.A. thesis, Columbia University, 1991.

————. "The Senate and the Vietnam War." Ph.D. diss., Columbia University, 2000.

Zelman, Walter Arnold. "Senate Dissent and the Vietnam War, 1964–1968." Ph.D. diss., University of California–Los Angeles, 1971.

VI. Newspapers and Nonspecialized Periodicals

Atlantic Monthly.

Chicago Tribune.

Cleveland Plain Dealer.

Commentary.

Commonweal.

Dan Smoot Report.

Dissent.

Harper's.

I. F. Stone's Weekly.

Los Angeles Times.

Manchester Guardian.

Nation.

National Review.

New Republic

Newsweek.

New York Daily News.

New York Herald Tribune.

New York Post.

New York Times.

Philadelphia Inquirer.

Ramparts.

Reporter.

Saturday Review.

St. Louis Post-Dispatch.

Time.

U.S. News & World Report.

Wall Street Journal.

Washington Post.

VII. Transcribed Oral Histories

Dutton, Fred. Interviewed by Larry J. Hackman. Robert F. Kennedy Oral History Project. John F. Kennedy Library, November 18, 1969.

Edelman, Peter. Interviewed by Larry J. Hackman. Robert F. Kennedy Oral History Project. John F. Kennedy Library, July 15, 1969.

Holt, Pat. Interviewed by Donald A. Ritchie. *Pat Holt: Chief of Staff, Foreign Relations Committee, Oral History Interviews.* Washington, D.C.: Senate Historical Office, 1980.

Kennan, George. Interviewed by Louis Fischer (with appended correspondence between Kennedy and Kennan). John F. Kennedy Library, March 23, 1965.

Kraft, Joseph. Interviewed by Roberta Greene. Robert F. Kennedy Oral History Project. John F. Kennedy Library. March 7, 1970.

Marcy, Carl. Interviewed by Donald A. Ritchie. *Carl Marcy: Chief of Staff, Foreign Relations Committee, Oral History Interviews.* Washington, D.C.: Senate Historical Office, 1983.

McPherson, Harry. Interviewed by T. H. Baker. Lyndon Baines Johnson Library Oral History, September 19, 1968, interview 2.

Walinsky, Adam. Interviewed by Thomas F. Johnston. Robert F. Kennedy Oral History Project. John F. Kennedy Library, November 30, 1966. 2nd interview.

VIII. Interviews

Becker, Norma. Telephone interview, July 15, 1998.

Bingham, June. Telephone interview, June 30, 1997.

Braswell, Edward. Telephone interview, May 9, 1995.

Eller, Jerry. Telephone interview, 1995.

Jolovitz, Herbert. Telephone interview, April 11, 1995.

Lewis, Jean, Arlington, Va., September 10, 1995.

McGovern, George. Telephone interview, 1993.

McPherson, Harry, Washington, D.C., July 29, 1993.

Nelson, Gaylord. Washington, D.C., July 29, 1993.

Norwitch, Bernard. Telephone interview, May 10–11, 1995.

Reedy, George. Telephone interview, several dates 1995.

Ribicoff, Abraham. New York, N.Y., 1993.

Robnett, Harriet. Telephone interview, May 2, 1995.

Rostow, Walter W. Austin, Texas, 1993.

Schlesinger, Arthur M. New York, NY, 1995.

Schwartz, Harry K. Telephone interview. May 24, 1995.

Stempler, Jack. Telephone interview. September 27, 1994.

Sterne, Joseph R. L. Baltimore, Md., July 28, 1993.

IX. Miscellaneous

Congress and the Nation.

Congressional Quarterly Almanac.

Congressional Quarterly Weekly Report.

Council on Foreign Relations, *Annual Report* (1964).

Liberty Letter.

Neustadt, Richard E. Letter to author, July 29, 1994.

INDEX

Pell, Claiborne de Borda (cont.)
90, 103, 249n16, 250n23, 250n25, 252n51,
252n54, 252n64, 257n35, 258n52, 258n57;
at hearings (1968), 168–69, 271n28; influences on, 48, 139; and "peace feeler,"
64, 245n20; supports Mansfield amendment, 261n33; and Tet offensive, 270n2,
272n36, 273n62; withdrawal request by
South Vietnam, favors compliance if
made, 128
Pepper, Claude, 9, 231n2
Percy, Charles Harting, xiii, 132–34, 155,
202, 236n23, 263n52, 263n55, 268n64
Philippines, 5, 30, 53, 75
Prouty, Winston Lewis, 14, 202
pro-war demonstration, reviewed by Javits
and Robert Kennedy, 47
Proxmire, William, xii, 149, 202, 241n18,
247n6, 267n46
public opinion, 40, 164, 186, 233n25, 237n40,
262n39, 267n39, 269n3; effect on Johnson
of, 144, 160, 176; effect on senators of,
xx, 8, 47–48, 130, 138–39, 181, 240n13,
239n15; Gore favors "disciplining and
conditioning" of, 182; Johnson fails to
make amenable to withdrawal, xxix;
presidents' influence on, 13, 46; senators'
influence on, xx, 104, 126, 174, 176,
258n52

Randolph, Jennings. 150, 155, 202, 236n10,
246n34
refugees and escapees, hearings on, 178–80,
Fulbright attempts to prevent, 246n34;
Johnson concerned about, 179–89
Reischauer, Edwin Oldfather, 148
Reston, James Barrett, 8, 49, 134, 233n27,
242n36, 257n49
Rhodesia, xxii, 99, 156, 171
Ribicoff, Abraham Alexander, xiii, 155, 202
Ripon Society, 156
Robertson, A. Willis, 3, 46, 154, 202, 231n5,
239n4, 268n51
Roosevelt, Franklin Delano, xii–xiii, 42, 68

Root, Elihu, 73
Rostow, Walt Whitman, 179, 252n37
Rusk, Dean: anti-Communist regime, insists
on necessity of in South Vietnam, 79;
Communism, testifies is not monolithic
and should not be fought everywhere,
74, 100; Congo intervention, reassures
members of Congress on, 159; congressional relations, view of, 60, 78; credibility of U.S., testifies at stake in Vietnam,
94; Geneva Accords, testifies only provided for temporary demarcation line,
86; Laotian popular front government,
supported creation of, 123; Mansfield
resolution, opposes, 148; Members of
Congress for World Peace Through the
Rule of Law, addresses meeting of, 41;
necessity of intervention, testifies of,
101; pacifists, testifies of memory of at
Oxford in 1930s, 101; "peace feeler," tries
to mislead senators on, 245n20; war seen
as fight against foreign invasion rather
than a civil war, 92; witness at 1968 televised hearings, 166–75
Russell, Donald Stuart, 202
Russell, Richard Brevard, Jr., x, xii, 202, 209,
239n2, 239n23, 248n13; and Communist
infiltration of State Department, 267n46;
Congo intervention opposed by, 157–60,
178; and Dominican Republic invasion
dissension of Fulbright on, 70, 246n36;
domino theory rejected by, 129; Dutton
describes position of, 20; and Gulf of
Tonkin Resolution, 26–27, 29, 34, 267n48,
268n49; and Indochina, proposed intervention to lift siege at Dien Bien Phu, 6,
162, 269n79; Johnson advised by, 45–46,
60, 239n3, 250n26, 251–52n50; at meeting of leading senators on war (1965), 66;
resolution on national commitments,
144, 158, 160; withdrawal request by
South Vietnam, favors compliance with
if made, 129, 154